The Ministry of
WOMEN

The Ministry of
WOMEN

Gender and Authority in the Church

Kevin J.
CONNER

WHITAKER
HOUSE

Unless otherwise indicated, all Scripture quotations are taken from the King James Version of the Holy Bible. (A list of other Scripture versions used is included on a separate page.)

Unless otherwise indicated, dictionary definitions are taken from *Collins English Dictionary, Complete & Unabridged 2012 Digital Edition* © William Collins Sons & Co. Ltd. 1979, 1986 © HarperCollins Publishers 1998, 2000, 2003, 2005, 2006, 2007, 2009, 2012. Some definitions are taken from *The Cabinet Dictionary of the English Language* (London: William Collins, Sons, and Company). Some definition are taken from *Merriam-Webster's 11th Collegiate Dictionary*, electronic version, © 2004.

Some definitions of Hebrew and Greek words are taken from the electronic version of *Strong's Exhaustive Concordance of the Bible*, STRONG, (© 1980, 1986, and assigned to World Bible Publishers, Inc. Used by permission. All rights reserved.) or *Vine's Complete Expository Dictionary of Old and New Testament Words*, VINE, (© 1985 by Thomas Nelson, Inc., Publishers, Nashville, TN. All rights reserved.).

Boldface type, in the text as well as in the Scripture quotations, indicates the author's emphasis.

THE MINISTRY OF WOMEN:
Gender and Authority in the Church

Kevin J. Conner
KJC Ministries, Inc.
P.O. Box 300
Vermont, Victoria
Australia 3133

ISBN: 978-1-62911-678-5
Printed in the United States of America
© 2003, 2016 by Kevin J. Conner

Whitaker House
1030 Hunt Valley Circle
New Kensington, PA 15068
www.whitakerhouse.com

Library of Congress Cataloging-in-Publication Data (Pending)

1 2 3 4 5 6 7 8 9 10 11 **ᴜᴊ** 23 22 21 20 19 18 17 16

Other Scripture Versions Used

CONTENTS

Appendices

PREFACE TO THE NEW EDITION

T *he Ministry of Women* was first published in 1984, with several reprinted editions being made over the next eleven years or so. The author has been pleased with the good response to that smaller publication.

Over the years, however, it was felt that a more expanded and comprehensive text would be helpful. Controversy still continues in the various branches of the church over the role of women in church life. The issues of women being "silent" and not "usurping authority" over men still cause much debate. For those schools that do permit some form of ministry for women, the issues of "ordination" and women in leadership roles are points of diverse opinion. Is a woman able to function in any of the ascension-gift ministries listed in Ephesians 4:9–16? Can a woman be in any governmental position and role in the church, or are women to be in total subjection, submission, and obedience to men? Is leadership in the home and in the church to be totally male? These questions and others are addressed more fully in this expanded and enlarged edition of *The Ministry of Women*.

After much research, the writer himself has come to a fuller understanding and acceptance of the ministry of women in governmental roles. The writer, over the years, has come to hold a more neutral position (neither for nor against) regarding whether women should serve in an apostolic or eldership role.

In the school to which the writer belongs, men and women—if gifted—have been accepted in the role of prophet, evangelist, shepherd, or teacher. The question of apostleship and eldership has remained. After much research, the writer sees that *if* God calls, equips, and anoints either a man or a woman to ascension-gift ministries or governmental roles, then that is His prerogative. God is God!

Generally speaking, there are few men and women grasping and struggling to be in ascension-gift ministries or governmental roles in the church. It is just too much hard work and responsibility to inflict upon oneself unless the call of God is evident.

After much more study of the role, function, and ministry of women, the writer has concluded that there is really nothing a woman cannot do, any more or less than there is anything a man cannot do. The key is, again, the equipping of God. *If* God calls, equips, and anoints a man or a woman to do something, then that is His grace.

While there is greater emphasis in this expanded and updated edition of *The Ministry of Women* concerning a woman's role, it does involve both men and women in the redemptive community of God—the church. The purpose of redemption is to bring both men and women back to all that which was lost in creation, because of the fall.

Here "in Christ," men and women can be partners together in ministry. Here "in Christ," there is neither male nor female, but all are one in Him. Here "in Christ," gender distinctions, while still existing in the natural, are no longer barriers in the spiritual. The church is God's redeemed community, the functioning body of Christ, and all are redemptively equal, though each may be functionally different.

Sadly, for some believers, this issue will not be settled until Jesus returns. But our prayer is that all who read this book might be challenged in their thinking regarding this controversial area of church life. May men and women alike be encouraged to function together as partners in the body of Christ, as members of one another.

—*Kevin J. Conner*

INTRODUCTION: PRESENTING THE CONTROVERSIAL ISSUE

The subject of this text is one of great controversy. It has been so throughout church history and undoubtedly will continue to be until Christ comes again. The church has never been without controversy. The very fact that Jesus said, *"I will build my church; and the gates of hell shall not prevail against it"* (Matthew 16:18) confirms the church's openness to opposition and persecution.

Controversy comes from without and within. It has been truly said that controversy is never the enemy of truth; only prejudice is. Numerous are the heresies that have been hammered out on the anvil of truth.

One of the controversial issues pressing in upon the church in this generation is that which pertains to the proper roles, positions, and functions of men and women in the church. The issue, of course, especially concerns that of women functioning in the church, the redemptive community. It is not an issue that touches so much on the great redemptive truths of the Bible, but one that deals with what men and women may do in the redemptive community.

For centuries, the general philosophy has been that of a patriarchal society: Leadership is male, and this is so simply because the woman was the first sinner in the fall of mankind, as recorded in the book of Genesis.

In recent decades, this position has been challenged, giving rise to much debate, especially in the church as a whole, touching a number of the major denominations.

Several passages from the writings of the apostle Paul have been used as the "master passages" in Scripture to silence women in church life, or else to keep women in a subordinate role, in both the home and, more particularly, the church. Paul has been maligned over the inspired writings he recorded.

As will be seen, there are several schools of opinion that have arisen as to the proper roles of men and women in both the home and the church.

The pendulum, as always, seems to swing back and forth between the extremes. Some writers, men and women alike, break down any distinction between the roles of men and women, especially with regard to ministry in the church. Other writers would relegate women to the home, limiting their options of roles to wife, mother, and homemaker, often calling "submission" what is actually subjection or even suppression.

Any position regarding the role and function of men and women is up for evaluation in our present society. This is much more so in the Western world, in nations that have been strongly influenced by Christianity and its principles.

There are other nations where male dominance results in the total suppression of women. Viewed and treated as the servants and slaves of the men, women are confined to the home, the kitchen, or the nursery. Wives are seen as the slaves of their husband. It is only where the Judeo-Christian ethic has touched a nation that there has been some standard raised for the protection of womanhood, and for the family as a whole.

One of the great concerns, and fears, for many sincere believers—men and women alike—is the rise of militant feminism in secular society. In these days of "equal rights" and "women's liberation" movements, and various militant feminist movements, the church wonders whether that spirit is creeping into the church, as some demand "equal rights" for men and women in ministry. It is hoped that this is not so, though in some situations it may well be true. The true church, however, need not fear, as long as it stays within the boundaries of God's Word.

The church does, however, need to reevaluate the subject of men and women functioning as God intended them to within the redemptive community.

Sadly, it is a generation in which there is a reversal of roles as pertaining to men and women. Men are becoming more effeminate, while women are becoming more masculine. The "uni-sex" philosophy continues to pervade secular and religious society alike.

Many times, men decrease in masculinity as a reaction to having a dominant mother and/or a passive father. Global conflicts have drawn women into the workplace, into positions formerly filled by men, and have thus emptied the home. With the novel ability to become independent of a man's salary, women are free to fulfill their own career aspirations. Meanwhile, many men shirk their responsibility to be godly men, husbands, and fathers.

The prophet Isaiah, whose wife was a prophetess (see Isaiah 8:1–3), lamented this very condition in Israel's history when he said, *"Children are their oppressors, and women rule over them"* (Isaiah 3:12). The humanistic philosophy of "liberation" brings dissatisfaction to women as they try to be something they were not created to be. Frustration results when men fail to fulfill their manhood and women fail to fulfill their womanhood.

So, what is the biblical role of men and women, especially when it comes to church life? Does the Bible teach that leadership should be exclusively male? Are women to be subject and subordinate to men because of their role in initiating the fall of mankind? Are men superior to women? Are women to be confined to the home as wives, mothers, and homemakers? May women function in the church community in any role, including positions of leadership, governance, and rulership? Or are they limited in their options? Are those positions reserved exclusively for men?

As will be seen, there are some denominations that permit women to function in many areas but not in any leadership role. Perhaps the most controversial questions, as pertaining to women, are those concerning the ascension-gift ministries of Christ, listed in Ephesians 4:9–16. May a woman be involved in any of the fivefold ascension-gift ministries? Can a woman be an apostle, a prophet, an evangelist, a teacher, or a pastor? Or are these giftings strictly for men? And, finally, may a woman serve in the church as a deacon or an elder?

Many people argue, based on 1 Timothy 2, "Doesn't Paul clearly teach that women are to be silent in the church? Doesn't he teach that women are forbidden to teach in the church and take authority over men?"

There are thousands of godly men and women enrolled in Bible colleges and theological seminaries throughout the world. All of them are studying the Word of God, believing that there is a call of God on their life for a specific area of ministry. What is the purpose of it all, if women are *"to be in silence"* (1 Timothy 2:12) in the church? If women are not to preach or teach, as many interpret the Scriptures as saying, and only men can do such things, then what is the purpose of a woman studying the Word of God?

It is regrettable that some male expositors of Scripture deal with the subject in such a negative way. They evince a chauvinistic attitude toward women in ministry instead of considering what the Bible teaches on the subject as a whole. For centuries, the Christian church has been under male domination, which has affected theology and, in turn, the translation and interpretation of Scripture. As we will see, intrinsic to an individual's theology are certain beliefs about the roles of men and women, and this theology inevitably affects his or her translation and interpretation of Scripture.

This text seeks to present a balanced view of the role and function of both men and women, at home and in the church alike.

1

PRINCIPLES OF
INTERPRETING SCRIPTURE

There is no doubt that a person's theology (what he or she believes about God, man and woman, and so forth) affects his or her interpretation of Scripture. Theology affects hermeneutics—a fancy word for principles of Bible interpretation—and hermeneutics affects theology. Sound theology with sound hermeneutics makes for sound exegesis. But the end result of faulty theology and faulty hermeneutics is a faulty exegesis of Scripture.

When it comes to the field of hermeneutics, the context principle has been called "the FIRST principle of hermeneutics." There is an old adage that says, "A text out of context is a pretext." In *Interpreting the Scriptures*, the authors adapted this adage to say, "A text out of the context of the whole Bible is a pretext." This truth will be seen in the course of this chapter.

It should be kept in mind that the issue is not over the inspired Scriptures. True Bible-believing Christians do not dispute the fact that the Scriptures are God-breathed, inspired by the Holy Spirit of God.

Again, to quote *Interpreting the Scriptures*: "Generally speaking, Bible-believing Christians are united in accepting the facts of revelation and inspiration. However, the major divisions concern interpretation and application. The problem is not over *revelation* and *inspiration* so much as it is over *interpretation* and *application*."

How to interpret what was spoken to those who received the sacred writings by divine inspiration, what it meant to them, and how to apply the truths to the current generation—these are the major questions that concern preachers and teachers of the Bible. Different expositors come up with different interpretations of the same passages of Scripture. And out of interpretation comes application.

It is important, then, to have a proper interpretation of Scripture. Proper interpretation precedes proper application. The way we apply the Scriptures to our own generation must flow from our understanding of how the Scriptures were applied to the generation of the biblical writers.

Hermeneutics is a science and an art. The science is knowing the rules of interpretation; the art is applying those rules. The sixty-six books of the Bible were written for varying audiences: different cultures, different peoples, at different periods of human history. They must be interpreted in the context of the time and culture of when they were written. Expositors should not seize upon a passage written to address a local situation and presume to apply it to all nations, all churches, and all cultures for all times. Many parts of the Bible were written for a particular people group, providing instructions for a specific, temporary situation. Such biblical content was not intended for universal, timeless application—a fact that will become even clearer when we discuss some of Paul's writings concerning the behavior of men and women at home and in the church.

In the process of Scripture interpretation, there are four major gaps that have to be bridged in order to arrive at a proper exegesis. These gaps are as follows:

1. The Historical Gap

The interpreter needs to consider the historical setting of the biblical text. During what period of human history was the book written? What was the historical scenario of the people who received the writings? History is the background, the stage, the setting for the biblical writings.

2. The Geographical Gap

The interpreter needs to consider the geographic location of the people who received the biblical writings, due to the significant influence of location and all it entails.

3. The Cultural Gap

Culture encompasses how people live, providing the social context for the people who received the biblical writings. The interpreter needs to consider the customs of the people to whom the biblical authors were writing. He or she must consider if and how the writings treat cultural issues of the time and how they reflect aspects of the culture of both the authors and the audience.

4. The Linguistic Gap

The Scriptures were written primarily in Hebrew and Greek, and the English language often fails to express the exact meaning and intent of the original wording. Thus, the interpreter is wise to avail himself or herself of the linguistic tools available to help bridge the linguistic gap and provide an understanding of what the words meant to the authors and original recipients. Words must be understood in their grammatical context, and each verse or passage of Scripture must be interpreted according to the best use of the original language in which it was written. As was already noted, an individual's theology is so influential that it can even affect one's interpretation of Hebrew and Greek, hence the need for sound theology in bridging the linguistic gap.

Once the above four gaps have been bridged as much as possible, the interpreter must use the context principle—the first of all principles. By "context," we refer to the "whole-of-the-Bible" context. To use this principle, the interpreter must ask, "What does the whole Bible say on the given subject?"

To break down this process in greater detail, the Scriptures must be studied in terms of:

+ The verse context: What does the verse actually say?

+ The passage content: What does the rest of the passage say?

- The chapter context: What does the whole chapter say?

- The book context: What is the literary style of the book in which the passage is found?

- The Testament context: Is the verse in the Old Testament or the New Testament, and how is that significant?

- The Bible context: What does the Bible, as a whole, have to say on the subject in question? This is what is meant by "whole of the Bible" context!

The following are some additional principles to keep in mind when interpreting Scripture. No verse should be taken out of context. The meaning of each part of the verse, and of the whole verse, must be in agreement with the meaning of the overall passage. One cannot use one part of a verse to contradict what the rest of the passage is saying.

As much as possible, a verse should be interpreted in light of what it meant to the persons to whom it was originally written.

Again, any verse must be interpreted in light of the whole of Scripture—according to its "whole of the Bible" context. No single verse, passage, or book can be considered the whole of Scripture. The sixty-six books of the Bible make up the whole of Scripture.

The interpreter should always work from the clear to the obscure, and should never use an obscure verse or passage of Scripture to contradict any clear Scripture on the same subject. For example, 1 Corinthians 15:29 speaks of being *"baptized for the dead."* This obscure verse contradicts all the clear Scriptures on water baptism, and yet there is a group of people who use this Scripture to justify the practice of baptizing people in water on behalf of their deceased relatives. The clear Scriptures teach that water baptism should follow genuine repentance and faith, and that it is for living believers, not unrepentant dead people. The interpreter should move from the known to the unknown, not the other way around.

The interpreter should also seek to distinguish between biblical commands, biblical principles, and biblical customs. The following is an overview of their differences.

1. Biblical Commands

Biblical commands are those commands of God that are specific and meant for all times, all cultures, and all peoples of all nations—for example, the Ten Commandments, as listed in Exodus 20. Another example of biblical commands is found in Acts 15:29, when the apostles forbid the Gentiles to eat blood, practice idolatry, or engage in fornication. A positive biblical command is found in Matthew 28:18–20, where Jesus charges us to make disciples of all nations and to keep His commandments. Such instructions are clear commandments that are for all times, until He returns. The interpreter needs to discern whether a verse should be considered a biblical command for all times, cultures, and nations.

2. Biblical Principles

Biblical principles are those laws of God that are ascertained by an overall understanding of God's ways. In 1 Corinthians 9:9–10, the apostle Paul invokes a biblical principle to justify the practice of giving financial support to ministers of the gospel. He summarizes part of the law of Moses, which says, "Do not muzzle the ox that treads out the grain." Paul then asks: "Is it oxen that God is concerned about? Or does God say it altogether for our sakes?" He then answers: "Our sakes." This is a biblical principle, not a biblical command.

The same could be said about the habit of smoking. There is no specific biblical command that says, "You shall not smoke." However, the habit of smoking is discouraged in light of the biblical principle that our bodies are the temple of the Holy Spirit, and God does not want us to defile His temple. (See, for example, 1 Corinthians 6:19.) Smoking is a habit that defiles the body. There is no specific "chapter and verse" about smoking, but the biblical principle becomes a guideline to follow.

3. Biblical Customs

Then, expositors need to decide whether a verse reflects a biblical custom, by considering the customs contemporary to the writing of that verse. The following are examples of biblical customs that are not necessarily to be followed by all peoples in all times:

- The custom of washing the feet of one's guests as they arrived. (See John 13:14.) When Jesus told the apostles to do as He had done, was He establishing foot-washing as a command for all peoples and all times? Some people think so, and hold footwashing services. But in Western culture, most people wear shoes; sandals were the normal footwear of Jesus' day, meaning that the feet became dusty and needed routine washing. Thus, the custom of foot-washing is not counted as a command for all times and all peoples.

- Greeting one another with a "holy kiss." When Paul exhorted his readers to greet one another with a *"holy kiss"* (1 Corinthians 16:20), was he laying down a biblical command for all times and all peoples? No. The practice is still popular in some cultures, but not in the Western world, where it might even be considered offensive in some situations.

- The wearing of head veils, as mentioned by Paul in 1 Corinthians 11. Again, was Paul putting forth a command, or was he dealing with a custom of the Corinthian culture? Some nations and cultures require women to cover their heads, while others do not. This custom cannot be enforced universally.

- Slavery. In the books of Philemon and Ephesians, Paul seems to endorse the idea of masters having slaves. Yet slavery was abolished in the Western world in due time.

- Celibacy rather than marriage. (See 1 Corinthians 7:8, 27.) Paul's writings on this subject must be taken in their context. Elsewhere, Paul speaks highly of marriage, using it to illustrate the relationship between Christ and His church. He also says that to forbid marriage is a doctrine of demons. (See 1 Timothy 4:3.) Thus, in advocating celibacy, Paul was not laying down a commandment for all times, for all cultures, and for all peoples of all nations.

- Idiomatic expressions. Jesus uses such phrases as "the eye of a needle," "turning the other cheek," "going the extra mile," and "giving away your coat," all of which must be interpreted in the light of the times and customs of the culture of His day. (See Matthew 9:14;

5:39, 40–41.) Each had local and historical application for those times. Are these things binding today?

Biblical customs have to be considered when it comes to evaluating the proper role and function of men and women in the church. When Paul tells the women to keep silent in the church, and says that a woman is not to teach or to exercise authority over men, are these biblical commands, for all times, all races and cultures, or is Paul dealing with a cultural situation? These are the things that need careful consideration.

4. Biblical Context

Again, the interpreter and expositor of Scripture needs to consider cover each verse in context of the passage, the chapter, the book, the testament, and the whole of the Bible. What does the Bible, as a whole, have to say about the subject? What does the Bible, as a whole, teach about the role and function of men and women in church life?

In his prologue to the first complete English Bible, Myles Coverdale (1488–1569) provided a helpful set of instructions that echo the hermeneutics of this chapter:

> It shall greatly help thee to understand Scripture, if thou mark, not only what is spoken or written, but of whom, and unto whom, with what words, at what time, where, to what intent, with what circumstances, considering what goeth before and what followeth after.

By following Coverdale's admonition, one will bridge the historical, geographical, cultural, and linguistic gaps, using the context principle in all its concentric circles.

Definition of Key Terms

In the course of our study, words such as "role," "function," and "order" will be used quite frequently. These words, as used in this text, need to be clearly defined and understood.

Role: "the part played by a person in a particular social setting, influenced by his expectation of what is appropriate; usual or customary function: *what is his role in the organization?*" A role is any conspicuous action or duty performed by anyone. So, we speak of the "role" of men and women in the redeemed community.

Function: "the natural action or intended purpose of a person or thing in a specific role." We will seek to understand the proper "function" of men and women in the home and the church.

Order: "an established or customary method or state, esp of society." We are endeavoring to discover the order God designed for His followers—men and women—in the home and the church.

God created men and women with unique identities. Each person, male or female, is valuable to God—and He is *"no respecter of persons"* (Acts 10:34). Therefore, though there are two distinct genders, neither one is superior or inferior to the other; both are of equal value to God. Although they may be functionally different, men and women in Christ are redemptively equal.

In studying the Scriptures to understand the proper role, function, and order of men and women, the writer has endeavored to be the best interpreter of Scripture possible, and thereby to arrive at proper exegesis, by practicing sound hermeneutics grounded in sound theology.

Our exegetical approach will be after God's order in (1) creation and (2) redemption. What was God's order in creation? What was God's order for men and women under the Old Testament? Did Jesus' coming make any difference in the roles of men and women? Does redemption restore men and women to their original purpose at creation? What did the apostle Paul mean when he wrote, *"There is neither male nor female: for ye are all one in Christ Jesus"* (Galatians 3:28)? What about the Pauline passage that exhorts women to keep silent in the church? (See 1 Corinthians 14:34–35.) And again, what did Paul mean when he wrote, *"I suffer not a woman to teach, nor to usurp authority over the man, but to be in silence"* (1 Timothy 2:11)? What did God mean in Genesis 3:16 when He said the man would *"rule over"* the woman after the fall?

These are questions that need consideration, that need answers. And that is the purpose of this text. Each reader must draw his or her own conclusions based on an understanding that is reached by following the hermeneutical principles laid out in this chapter, which are the undergirding principles of Scripture exposition that the writer sincerely endeavored to use in this text.

2

IN THE BEGINNING—GOD

In commencing our study of the role, order, and function of men and women in the plan and purposes of God, what better place to begin than in the very nature and being of God as Father, Son, and Holy Spirit? The Bible opens simply and profoundly with the words, *"In the beginning God"* (Genesis 1:1).

In biblical revelation and through His own Self-disclosure, God has revealed certain qualities, attributes, and characteristics that are peculiarly and essentially His. God also made mankind—men and women—in His own image and after His own likeness. (See Genesis 1:26–28.) How can we understand that "image and likeness" of God in mankind if we do not understand God's revelation of Himself as in His Word? And just what is the "image and likeness" of God? As believers, we accept the biblical revelation of God. Without His Self-revelation, no one can know or understand the great and mighty God of the Bible.

The following list of attributes and qualities proves that God has really demonstrated, in His own nature and being, the attributes and qualities He desired to impart to the men and women He would create. Their manifestation in men and women is, of course, marred by the finite and fallen nature of mankind.

In the eternal Godhead, there is:

1. *Plurality of Divine Persons*

God has revealed Himself as Father, Son, and Holy Spirit. In the biblical revelation of God, there are three divine Beings.

2. *Equality of Divine Persons*

There is co-equality of the divine Persons. The Father, the Son, and the Holy Spirit are co-equal in majesty, glory, and power. There is none superior or inferior. Each Person is God, co-equal in glory and attributes to the others.

3. *Unity of Divine Persons*

These three divine Persons are in absolute unity of mind, will, and purpose. There is no discord in the eternal Godhead of Father, Son, and Holy Spirit.

4. *Priority of Divine Persons*

In the revelation of the Godhead, the Father is seen as "first among equals."

5. *Distinction of Function in the Divine Persons*

Father, Son, and Holy Spirit are distinguishable but indivisible. Each has a distinct role and function in the plan of creation and redemption.

6. *Order in the Divine Persons*

There is also divine order in the Godhead for the purposes of creation and redemption. The Father is revealed as the first Person, the Son is the central Person in the Godhead, and the Holy Spirit is revealed as the third Person in the Holy Trinity. (See Matthew 28:19.)

7. *Submission in the Divine Persons*

There is submission in the Godhead. The Holy Spirit submits to the Father and the Son. The Son submits to the Father. In the mystery of the Godhead, there is mutual submission in this divine order. It is inexplicable to the finite mind but is nevertheless true.

8. *Harmony Among the Divine Persons*

Because of these qualities, there is absolute and perfect harmony in the Godhead. Like the three notes in a musical chord, they differ in sound yet create a perfect, dulcet harmony. No discord can be seen or heard in the eternal Godhead.

9. *Perfect Holiness in the Divine Persons*

Father, Son, and Holy Spirit have a perfect hatred of sin, in all its hideous manifestation and expression. Holiness and righteousness are the attributes of the throne of God.

10. *Perfect Love in the Divine Persons*

Perfect love is the foundational character quality of the eternal Godhead. The Father loves the Son. The Son loves the Father. And both are bound to each other by Their love of the Holy Spirit. Holiness and love are the eternal character qualities in the divine Persons that make all three of Them function in perfect harmony.

11. *The Godhead Family in the Divine Persons*

The Father, the Son, and the Holy Spirit are portrayed in Scripture as the Godhead family, after which every human family takes it pattern. The original "pattern family" is that which is illustrated in the very nature and being of God. (See Ephesians 3:14–15 AMP.) How does Scripture reveal this family concept in the Godhead? It is revealed in the triune nature and being of God, as Father, Son, and Holy Spirit.

+ **The Father:** God has revealed Himself in many various ways, using many titles and names. He is referred to as Creator, King, Judge, Ruler, Lawgiver, and so forth. However, the dominant revelation of God in the Bible, especially in the New Testament, is that of God as Father. (See Isaiah 63:16; Deuteronomy 32:6; Psalm 103:13; Matthew 6:9; 2 Corinthians 6:17–18; Ephesians 3:14–15.) The prominent characteristics of Father God are love, concern, provision, authority, strength, and security.

+ **The Son:** Jesus, the eternal Son of God, becomes the "pattern Son" in the Godhead family. Both the Old Testament and the New Testament speak of His Sonship. (See Psalm 2:7, 12; Proverbs 30:1–4; Isaiah 7:14; 9:6–9; John 1:14; 3:16; Matthew 17:1–5.) The character qualities of the Son are seen in His total dependence, submission, and unquestioning obedience to the Father's will and Word. He is the beloved Son in whom the Father is well pleased.

+ **The Holy Spirit:** Although the Scriptures use masculine pronouns in relation to the Father, the Son, and the Holy Spirit, and although we do not ascribe femininity to the divine Persons, there are nonetheless obvious "mother qualities" in the Godhead family.

The Old Testament attributes maternal qualities and characteristics to the Godhead, especially in relation to the blessed Holy Spirit. *"In the beginning…the Spirit of God moved upon the…waters"* (Genesis 1:1–2). The Holy Spirit brooded as a mother dove upon the chaotic scene before the Word of order was spoken. In the New Testament, the Holy Spirit is seen descending as a dove upon the Lord Jesus at His baptism. (See Matthew 3:16.)

Speaking through the prophet Isaiah, the Lord says, *"As one whom his **mother** comforteth, so will I comfort you"* (Isaiah 66:13).

"God Almighty" is revealed as *El-Shaddai*, suggesting the maternal characteristics of God. *El* means "the strong one," and *Shaddai* is formed from the Hebrew word Shad, which means "the breast," invariably used for a woman's breast. (See Genesis 49:25; Job 3:12; Psalm 22:9; Song of Solomon 1:3; 4:5; Isaiah 28:9.) Thus, the almighty God is "the Strong and Breasted One." It is El Shaddai who calls Abraham to walk before Him and be perfect. (See Genesis 17:1.) Just as a baby draws life, comfort, nourishment, sustenance, and strength from the mother's breast, so the redeemed are to draw these things from the blessed Holy Spirit.

The fruit of the Spirit is listed in Galatians 5:22–23. Fruitfulness is a characteristic of the Holy Spirit. Believers also are *"born…of the Spirit"* (John 3:5), even as one is born of the mother in natural birth. (See John 3:1–5.) Some of the early church writings speak of "my Mother, the Holy Spirit" when speaking of being born of the Spirit.

The Holy Spirit is called *"Comforter"* (John 14:16, 26; 15:26; 16:7). He is like a mother in that He strengthens, nourishes, sustains, and comforts the people of God.

The concept of the family has its origins in the Godhead—a Trinity of Father, Son, and Holy Spirit that exhibits masculine and feminine qualities alike. These divine Beings serve as a model of the family structure of father, mother, and son/daughter.

12. The Tri-Unity of Divine Persons

God is revealed in the Bible as a triune Being—three divine Persons yet one God. Human minds may not be able to fathom the mystery of God in His triune nature and being. But this is how God has chosen to reveal Himself. Man accepts this Self-revelation, this Self-disclosure; or he stumbles along in the darkness of human reasoning.

God is one God, yet God is also triune—three in one, and one in three. This is the image and likeness of God, the God of the Holy Bible.

Again, God said, *"Let **us** make man in **our** image, after **our** likeness…. So God created man in **his** own image"* (Genesis 1:26–27) and in His own likeness. The qualities and characteristics seen in the Godhead must, at least, be part of the "image and likeness of God" in which men and women were created and made. In other words, as noted earlier, God has demonstrated and illustrated in His own eternal nature and being what He wanted to see demonstrated in the man and the woman He was about to create.

3

DIVINE ORDER IN CREATION

Two passages in Genesis—Genesis 1:26–28 and Genesis 2:18–25—provide an account of the creation of man and woman. This event preceded the entrance of sin into the world, showing the state of things *"in the beginning."*

There are some important things to notice as to the divine purpose and order as established in the creation of man and woman, and, as already seen, before the entrance of sin.

> *Then God said, "Let Us make man in Our image, according to Our likeness; let them have dominion…." So God created man in His own image; in the image of God He created him; male and female He created them. Then God blessed them, and God said to them, "Be fruitful and multiply; fill the earth and subdue it; have dominion…."*
>
> (Genesis 1:26–28 NKJV)

The term for *"God"* in this passage is *Elohim*, referring to Father, Son, and Holy Spirit. It is the Old Testament equivalent to the divine Persons in the eternal Godhead, seen more fully and clearly in the New Testament revelation. (See Matthew 28:19; 2 Corinthians 13:14.)

What, then, is the *"image of God"*? What is this *"likeness"* in which mankind, both male and female, was made? Let it be noted that both male and female—the man and the woman—were created in the image and like-ness of God. This "image and likeness" has been seen in the qualities and characteristics of the Godhead, as discussed in the previous chapter. The following are the corollaries we may draw about men and women, based on the qualities first exhibited by the Godhead.

In creating male and female in His image and likeness, God planned for:

1. Plurality of Being

There would be the man and the woman, and then the offspring born from their union.

2. Equality of Being

Men and women would be co-equal. In marriage and in family life, husbands and wives/fathers and mothers would be co-equal.

3. Unity of Being

Though two, the man and the woman would be one in heart, soul, and mind. They would also become one flesh in the union of marriage.

4. Priority of Being

The man was created before the woman, but this order in no way im-plies male superiority—just as, in the Godhead, the Father is "first among equals."

5. Distinction of Function of Being

The man would be the husband and father; the woman would be the wife and the mother. They would be of equal value but functionally different.

6. Order of Being

Again, there would be no superiority or inferiority but simply divine order. This was the divine arrangement in the creation of man and woman.

7. Submission of Being

There would be mutual submission between the man and the woman.

8. Harmony of Being

As in a musical chord, there would be harmony, not discord, between the man and the woman.

9. Holiness of Being

The man and the woman would live in the holiness of God. His righteousness would be seen in them. No sin would ultimately mar their marital bliss.

10. Perfect Love of Being

The man and the woman would show each other a selfless, self-giving love.

The above are the qualities of the image of God that He wanted to impart to His masterpiece of creation—mankind. With these Godlike qualities, the man and the woman would have an Edenic life. It would be paradise on earth, for them and for their offspring. Here would be the human family, the manifestation in creation of the Godhead family. This was the image and likeness of God in the man and the woman. This was God's will for them.

In the first creation account in Genesis, the emphasis is upon *"them"*:

*And God said, Let us make man in our image, after our likeness: let **them** have dominion over the fish of the sea, and over the fowl of the air, and over the cattle, and over all the earth, and over every creeping thing that creeps on the earth. So God created man in his own image, in the image of God created he him; male and female he created **them**. And God blessed **them**, and said to **them**, Be fruitful, and multiply, and replenish the earth, and subdue it: and have dominion over the fish of the sea, and over the fowl of the air, and over every living thing that moveth on the earth.*   (Genesis 1:26–28)

And again, "*This is the book of the generations of Adam. In the day that God created man, in the likeness of God made he him; male and female created he **them** and blessed **them**, and called **their name** Adam, in the day when **they** were created*" (Genesis 5:1–2).

In Genesis 2, we find further details on the creation of the woman:

> *And the* LORD *God said, "It is not good that man should be alone; I will make him a helper ["help meet"* KJV] *comparable to him."....And the* LORD *God caused a deep sleep to fall on Adam, and he slept; and He took one of his ribs, and closed up the flesh in its place. Then the rib which the* LORD *God had taken from man He made into a woman, and He brought her to the man. And Adam said: "This is now bone of my bones and flesh of my flesh."....Therefore shall a man leave his father and mother and be joined to his wife, and they shall become one flesh. And they were both naked, the man and his wife, and were not ashamed.* (Genesis 2:18, 21–25 NKJV)

From the above passages, we learn the following important truths:

1. Both man and woman were created in the image and likeness of God.

2. Both man and woman are partakers of the same name and nature. Both were called Adam ("Mr. and Mrs. Adam") before the fall. The male and the female equaled man, or Adam. The *"man"* in the image of God was "Ish" and "Ishshah." (See Genesis 1:27; 2:23; 5:2.) There was the masculine part of the man and the feminine part of the man made in God's image. The "woman" literally means "man-ess." It is more a generic term than a name. It is associated with Eve's relationship to Adam, which she was created to fill. That is, to be his counterpart, his wife.

3. Both man and woman were created to rule together and have dominion over the earth and all its creatures. There was no hierarchical arrangement before the fall. They were to reign as king and queen under God over creation. There was to be joint rulership.

4.   Both man and woman were blessed of God, to live in a harmonious marriage relationship—a partnership, side by side with each other.

5.   Both man and woman were of equal value as persons before God. Neither one was superior or inferior; neither was subordinate to the other. Before the fall, there was gender equality between male and female.

6.   Both male and female were sharers or partners together, sharing in joint rulership over all creatures under the Lord God, their Creator. Together, they would subdue the whole earth.

7.   Both male and female complemented and completed each other. The man was incomplete without the woman, and the woman was incomplete without the man. God said it was not good for the man to be alone. The woman was created to be a *"help meet,"* or *"helper,"* for the man. (See Genesis 2:18.) The Hebrew thought is that of a help; one who offers aid, support, and assistance. It is one who is *"suitable"* (NIV), one who is *"comparable"* (NKJV), one who is "fit" for him, one who is equal to him, corresponding completely to him. The relationship is one of partnership, of companionship. There is no sense of inferiority or subordination in these terms, for God Himself is our "Helper" in time of need. (See, for example, Genesis 49:25; Exodus18:4; 1 Samuel 7:12.) The same Hebrew word is used of God some nineteen times. It was not good for the man to be alone—on his own! The woman was to be the counterpart of the man. She was taken from the man and created as a woman by God Himself. Paul tells us that the woman is not without the man, and the man is not without the woman, in the Lord. (See 1 Corinthians 11:11.) They were created to complete each other, spiritually, emotionally, and physically, in a relationship of loving companionship and friendship.

8.   Both man and woman were equally responsible and accountable under God, to God, for their deeds.

9. Both man and woman were creationally equal but functionally different. The man would be the husband and father; the woman would be the wife and mother.

10. Both man and woman were called to be fruitful, to multiply, to replenish the earth. Neither one was capable of populating the earth without the help of the other. God intended for the man and the woman to reproduce themselves and fill the earth with a race of sinless beings. The woman is the womb-man, or the "man with the womb." (See Genesis 2:7–8, 18–25; Psalm 128:3.) Therefore, we have man and womb-man (wo-man), the feminine form of the same word for "man."

11. Both man and woman would share the duties of parenting and shoulder an equal responsibility for raising their offspring in the wisdom and knowledge of God.

12. Both man and woman would share leadership and authority in the home/in the family. Adam was to be Eve's covering and protection, not to rule over her.

13. Both man and woman walked in divine order, as joint-heirs of God's grace. Although the man was created first, and then the woman, this sequence in no way implies male superiority or female inferiority. Again, we see a demonstration of this principle in the Godhead: The Father is first among equals, the Son is second in Godhead order, and the Holy Spirit is the third Person. Creation order does not mean inequality or subordination.

14. Both man and woman manifested the glory of God in a unique way. Paul says that the woman is the glory of the man, and the man is the glory of God. (See 1 Corinthians 11:7.) The woman was made for the man, to complete him. (See 1 Corinthians 11:1–16.) A wife is a good thing provided by the Lord to be a wife, a mother, and a builder of the home. (See Proverbs 12:4; 14:1; 18:22; 19:14; 31:10–31.)

The above principles illustrate creation's order. This was God's arrangement for creation before the fall—His original plan, purpose, and intention for the man and the woman He created in His image and likeness.

Jack Hayford describes the creation order in this way:

It is impossible to adequately imagine or to project what the status of man-woman relationship was before the fall. But a powerful concept comes into view when Genesis 5:2 and 3:20 are placed side by side. The summary of 5:2 notes that at creation, man and woman were not only described as "one"—they were called, that is, named—one name. So total and complete was their partnership and mutuality that the matter of "position" was never in question. Their authority was mutual rather than equal. "Co-equal" may serve as a term, but the closest similarity to the original relationship would be that relationship apparent in the eternal godhead.

It is only the constant misquoting and misunderstanding of Genesis 2:18 that causes many to misconstrue "help meet" as a subordinate. The "help" was a completing partner; and the "meet" was a creature that is "appropriate" in design and potential as a completing partner.

It is after the fall that Eve is named, and thereby the woman comes to a separate identity from the man. In a very real way, the naming of Eve is a reflection of the tragic division sin placed between the two.

So complete was their union prior to this, one name served to identify them. Now the curse would be manifest in their different standing in terms of authority toward one another. And woman, inherently knowing that she was originally created to share a mutual place of authority with man, would, from generation to generation, labor against her appointed place under man's authority.

As we continue, we should keep in mind a reflection on creation order and God's original intention for the first man and woman. God has not forgotten His original purpose, and sin will not ultimately frustrate the purposes of God. Where there was failure in creation, no failure will be found in redemption!

In the varying schools of opinion over the role of men and women in the redemptive community, there are those who would take issue with the concept of the co-equality of man and woman in creation. Kevin Giles, in his excellent textbook *Created Woman*, notes six arguments used by those schools that invoke the Genesis account in sanctioning the subjection and subordination of woman by men in a hierarchical relationship. These arguments are noted here in outline form, with further comment. The arguments are as follows:

1. *Woman was created second.*

The argument is used that creation order makes man superior and women inferior, and therefore subordinate, to the man. The idea is that man was created first, thereby being placed in first position; the woman was created second and therefore must take second place. This argument is commonly used to justify the subordination of women. Yet female inferiority is nowhere implied in the Genesis 1:26–28 account.

If this line of reasoning were valid, then it would mean that the second Person in the Godhead—Jesus, the Son—was inferior to the first Person, who is Father God. Meanwhile, animals were created prior to mankind. Does that order mean that man is inferior to animals, and that he should be subservient to them? Along the same lines, John the Baptist came before Christ. Does John's precedence make Christ inferior to him? The answer to all this is evident. Man's being created first, and woman's being created after the man, is simply a fact of divine order in creation.

2. *Woman was created for Adam, as his helper.*

We have already discussed woman's designation as "help meet" or "helper." (See Genesis 2:18.) The woman was created to be man's partner, companion, complement, and completeness. She was designed as a help corresponding to him, equal and adequate to him. The same Hebrew word is used of God in identifying Him as our "Helper." This does not make God inferior to man. Thus, the role of woman as "helper" for man does not imply female inferiority.

3. *Woman derives her existence from man.*

Adam was made by a sovereign act of God, and the woman was "built" from Adam's rib. Because woman owes her origin to man, this point is used by some to justify the subordination of women to men. Yet Adam did not create Eve. Both man and woman owe their creation and existence to a sovereign act of God. Adam was asleep when God made the woman for him. (See Genesis 2:21–22.) Adam simply recognized Eve as bone of his bones and flesh of his flesh when God brought the woman to him. (See Genesis 2:23; 2 Samuel 19:12.)

Man and woman were equal as partners, made of the same stuff. Man was created from the dust of the earth. Does this make man lower than the dust? Not at all. Similarly, woman was created from man. Does this make the woman lower than man? Of course not. Man and woman, on their own, were incomplete without each other. Adam was complete only after Eve was created.

4. *Woman did not assign names to the animals.*

The fact that God brought the animals to Adam for naming (see Genesis 2:18–20) is a point often used to show the woman to be inferior and subject to the man. Adam had dominion over the animals. However, Genesis 1:28 tells us that dominion was given to the man *and* the woman. No animal proved a suitable partner for the man. Kevin Giles notes also that Adam did not name his wife. Instead, both were called by God under the name "Adam." (See Genesis 5:1–2.) Before the fall, they shared one and the same name, as is the case with most married couples today. After the fall, Adam named his wife as Eve (see Genesis 3:20), which was actually a name of faith, because Eve means "the mother of all living," or "the mother of the living one."

5. *Woman was not put in charge of the garden of Eden.*

This argument cites the fact that Adam alone was put in charge of the garden of Eden and given a direct command from God concerning the trees therein. (See Genesis 2:16–17.) Further reading, however, shows that God held both the man and the woman responsible for eating from the forbidden tree. Both of them disobeyed God's command. Both knew the command, regardless of how the woman had received it. (See Genesis 3:1–15.) Kevin Giles points out that the woman's mistake was listening to the serpent; the man's mistake was listening to his wife.

6. *Woman sinned first.*

This point is also used to justify the subordination of woman to man. But it was only after the fall that rulership over woman was given to the man. This reality will be dealt with more fully in chapter 5, "Order in Divine Judgment."

In conclusion: The six above points or arguments used to "prove" the subordination of woman to man *before the fall* are invalid, as a careful consideration of the earlier comments in this chapter should confirm. Man and woman were created as equals before God—co-heirs of divine grace; joint-rulers, as king and queen, over the creation of God on this earth. They demonstrated the divine order of the Godhead family as the original human family.

4

ORDER IN THE FALL

There are a number of passages of Scripture one must consider in order to gain a measure of understanding of what happened in the fall, or the entrance of sin into the human race.

The most detailed account is found in Genesis 3:1–7:

Now the serpent was more cunning than any beast of the field which the LORD God had made. And he said to the woman, "Has God indeed said, 'You shall not eat of every tree of the garden'?" And the woman said to the serpent, "We may eat the fruit of the trees of the garden; but of the fruit of the tree which is in the midst of the garden, God has said, 'You shall not eat it, nor shall you touch it, lest you die.'" Then the serpent said to the woman, "You will not surely die. For God knows that in the day you eat of it your eyes will be opened, and you will be like God, knowing good and evil." So when the woman saw that the tree was good for food, that it was pleasant to the eyes, and a tree desirable to make one wise, she took of its fruit and ate. She also gave to her husband with her, and he ate. Then the eyes of both of them were opened, and they knew that they were naked; and they sewed fig leaves together and made themselves coverings. (NKJV)

Along with this account, we will consider several passages from the New Testament, in order to obtain a fuller, clearer picture of that which took place in the entrance of sin and the fall of the original man and woman, who were made in the image of God.

The apostle Paul, in writing to the Corinthian believers, had this to say:

> *For I am jealous for you with godly jealousy. For I have betrothed you to one husband, that I may present you as a chaste virgin to Christ. But I fear, lest somehow, as the serpent deceived Eve by his craftiness, so your minds may be corrupted from the simplicity that is in Christ.*
>
> (2 Corinthians 11:2–3 NKJV)

And in his first epistle to Timothy, he said, "*For Adam was formed first, then Eve. And Adam was not deceived, but the woman being deceived, fell into transgression*" (1 Timothy 2:13–14 NKJV).

A careful reading of these three passages shows us precisely what took place in the garden with the temptation of the serpent in order to bring about the fall of the man and the woman, who were made in the image and likeness of God. Many expositors, in limiting their study to the Genesis account, miss out on the insights offered by the New Testament passages.

The Entrance of Sin into the World

1. Eve and Sin

It seems evident that the woman was away from her husband at the time of the serpent's temptation. The headship, covering, and protection of her husband, Adam, must have been absent; for it is difficult to imagine Adam standing there by her side, listening in as the serpent tempted his wife, and allowing her to partake of the forbidden fruit without stepping in to stop her. Would Adam have simply stood there and passively permitted her deception? That scenario is unthinkable for a "perfect" husband, as Adam was created to be.

Scripture records that Eve told her husband, "*The serpent beguiled me and I did eat*" (Genesis 3:13). This was Eve's own confession of how she was led into sin. No doubt God had given the original commandment to Adam, which he must have passed on to Eve. She knew the commandment, for she quoted it, albeit inaccurately, to the serpent. So, the woman was responsible, along with her husband, in the matter of obedience to the commandment of the Lord God.

"The serpent...said to the woman..." (Genesis 3:1). It may be asked, Why did the serpent target the woman and not the man, Adam? As Paul said, *"For Adam was first formed, then Eve. And Adam was not deceived, but the woman being deceived was in [fell into] the transgression"* (1 Timothy 2:13–14). Satan deceived the woman, not the man.

Paul expressed his concern for the Corinthians that, *"as the serpent beguiled [deceived] Eve..., so [their] minds should be corrupted from the simplicity that is in Christ"* (2 Corinthians 11:3). Eve recognized and admitted to her husband that she had been deceived by the serpent, Satan himself.

Thus, the woman became the first sinner. The serpent deceived the female of the species by his subtlety. Eve was the first to partake of the fruit of the forbidden tree. Then, she gave to her husband, Adam, to eat. And eat he did, thereby deliberately disobeying the commandment he had received. (See Genesis 2:16–17.)

In the fall, the woman assumed a position of leadership over the man— her headship and husband. She ate first of the fruit, then gave some of it to her husband. In creation's order, man was made first, then the woman. In the fall, this divine order was reversed: The woman sinned first, and then the man. Eve was the first to sin—the original sinner. Adam confessed to God, *"The woman...gave me of the tree, and I did eat"* (Genesis 3:12). There was a reversal of the roles that were divinely established in creation. The woman sinned by taking from the tree of the knowledge of good and evil, and the man sinned in taking the fruit of the tree from the woman, his wife.

Thus, the man, who was to be the first in order, was taking orders from the woman. The order of creation was reversed. The woman was deceived first. Adam and Eve alike violated their proper positions, thereby instituting a role reversal.

Eve was deceived by *"doctrines of devils"* (1 Timothy 4:1–2), so to speak. She needed to have "a covering on her head because of the angels" (see 1 Corinthians 11:10). The husband is the covering; thus, the woman honors her head when she honors her husband. (See 1 Corinthians 11:1–16.) It was the fallen angel, Satan, who deceived the woman. She was away from, or out from under, her covering, her headship. As already noted, it is hard to conceive that Adam would have stood silently by and watched, without intervening, while his wife was deceived by the devil.

It would appear, then, that the serpent thought the woman would be more easily led astray, onto the path of sin and disobedience. Thus, in a sense way, the woman usurped the man's authority. In the same vein, the man subordinated himself to the woman, possibly out of love for her, by obeying her (and disobeying God) and partaking of the forbidden fruit. As a result, sin corrupted the loving headship of the man and the mutual submission of this original marriage. Both man and woman became guilty rebels before God.

2. *Adam and Sin*

As if to balance out the heavy weight laid on the first woman as the first sinner, the Scriptures provide other passages that lay great weight and blame on the first man, Adam.

When Eve sinned, she did so because she was deceived by the serpent. But when Adam sinned, he was not deceived. He sinned willfully, knowingly, deliberately. Who, then, was the "greater sinner"—Eve or Adam? The one who was deceived, or the one who sinned deliberately? As grave as Eve's sin was, the greater blame and condemnation are laid on Adam, the man, for he rebelled knowingly against the commandment of God.

Paul's writings on the matter lay the blame on the man, Adam. Adam was the "seed-bearer" of the human race. When Adam sinned, he brought sin and death on the whole of the unborn human race. Note what Paul says concerning this rebellious act of Adam:

+   *"In Adam all die"* (1 Corinthians 15:22).

+ *"Adam was not deceived"* (1 Timothy 2:14).

+ *"By one **man** sin entered the world, and death by sin...passed upon all men, in whom all have sinned"* (Romans 5:12).

+ When Adam sinned, we all sinned, for we were all *"in Adam"* (1 Corinthians 15:22).

In Romans 5:12, Paul places the emphasis on the *"one man"*—Adam. He does not argue that Eve was the greater sinner of the pair, that Eve was guiltier than Adam. No, he identifies Adam as the greater offender because he was not deceived; he sinned intelligently, not by way of deception.

Note the emphasis on the *"one man"* in Romans 5:12–21. At least eight times in this passage, the word *"one"* is used, always pointing to the one man. It does not say, "By one woman sin entered the world" but *"by one man."*

+ *"By one man sin entered into the world"* (Romans 5:12).

+ *"Death reigned from Adam* [because of Adam's transgression]" (Romans 5:14).

+ *"Through the offence of one many be dead"* (Romans 5:15).

+ *"By one that sinned"* (Romans 5:16).

+ *"The judgment was by one to condemnation"* (Romans 5:16).

+ *"By one man's offence death reigned by one* [in other words, by one offense, death reigned by one man]" (Romans 5:17).

+ *"By the offence of one judgment came upon all men to condemnation"* (Romans 5:18).

+ *"For as by one man's disobedience many were made sinners"* (Romans 5:19).

Consider, too, the following Scriptures from the Old Testament:

+ *"If I covered my transgressions as Adam* [mankind]..." (Job 31:33).

+ *"But like Adam they have transgressed the covenant..."* (Hosea 6:7 NASB).

When God came into the garden for His evening fellowship after the fall, He called, "Adam, where are you?" And it was Adam who replied, *"I heard Your voice in the garden, and I was afraid because I was naked; and I had myself..."* (Genesis 3:9–11 NKJV).

Thus, sin and death are attributed to the man, Adam. The unborn generations of the human race were in his loins as his unborn seed. The greater blame is on him, for he was not deceived, as Eve was. There is no room for male pride in the willful transgression of God's commandment, with the corresponding penalty. Adam sinned willfully, knowingly, deliberately, and rebelliously! Rebellion has been defined as willful resistance against established authority. Adam's initial sin was absolute disobedience to the divine command, in the full light of the death penalty. Adam obeyed his wife's word but disobeyed God's Word. He sinned with his eyes wide open.

In creation's order, it was man and then woman, the male and the female.

In the order of the fall, it was woman and then man, the female and the male.

There are the hard, cold facts in the account of the fall. It is God's inspired account of the entrance of sin into the human race through the original man and woman, the parents of the whole human race.

In Summary

1. Both the man and the woman disobeyed the Word, the will, and the commandment of God.

2. Both the man and the woman sinned, even though the woman was the first to sin.

3. Both the man and the woman became sinners through disobedience to the Word of God.

4. Both the man and the woman discovered their nakedness once the "glory of God" that had been their covering had fallen off them.

5. Both the man and the woman hid from the presence of God as He walked in the garden in the cool of the evening.

6. Both the man and the woman fashioned fig leaf coverings to make themselves presentable to God, once they had become aware of their nakedness.

7. Both the man and the woman were responsible for their sinful disobedience. God confronted each of them individually, as well as corporately. God held Adam responsible for what he and Eve had done together. Eve ate from the tree; Adam ate what Eve gave to him. Both sinned in eating, and both were charged as having eaten from the tree.

8. Both the man and the woman came under the death penalty, bringing sin, sickness, disease, and the curse on the unborn human race.

9. Both the man and the woman came under divine judgment and made themselves subject to the curses of the earth.

10. Both the man and the woman put themselves in need of redemption, as sin brought them both down to the dust of death.

11. Both the man and the woman, made in the image and likeness of God, caused their image to become marred by sin; the image of God in mankind is now marred in spirit, soul, and body.

12. Both the man and the woman forfeited access to the tree of eternal life.

13. Both the man and the woman were driven out of God's earthly paradise.

14. Both the man and the woman needed to wait for a Redeemer to come and open the way back to the paradise of God and the Tree of Eternal Life.

15. Both the man and the woman were totally lost, apart from the saving grace of God.

Such is the scene today! Men and women need God's saving grace, or they are eternally lost. In this fallen world, there is no ground for the "guilt and blame" game that goes on in the "battle of the sexes."

The order of creation—man and then woman—was disrupted by the order of the fall, which came by way of woman and then man.

5

ORDER IN DIVINE JUDGMENT

The entrance of sin into the world, via the original pair, completely altered the blissful paradise of Eden. God had proclaimed to Adam that the death penalty would be imposed on him and his wife if they violated His commandment. *"The wages of sin is death"* (Romans 6:23). The holy, righteous nature of God demands that He punish sin.

We consider now the order of divine judgment placed on the tempter and the guilty pair. This order has definite design as it pertains to man and woman, husband and wife. God had in mind the redemption of mankind, but before that could occur, judgment against sin had to be carried out. The purpose of redemption would be to bring mankind back to God's order in creation before the entrance of sin, but this, through redemption, would be on a higher level of relationship broken by the fall.

Judgment has to do with a judicial sentence being executed against violated divine law. Sin must be judged before redemption is possible.

Notice the order in God's declared judgment.

1. *Judgment on the Serpent*

So the LORD God said to the serpent: "Because you have done this, you are cursed more than all cattle, and more than every beast of the field;

*on your belly you shall go, and you shall eat dust all the days of your life.
And I will put enmity between you and the woman, and between your
seed and her Seed; he shall bruise your head, and you shall bruise His
heel."*   (Genesis 3:14–15 NKJV; see also Isaiah 65:25)

+ The serpent, or Satan (see Revelation 12:9; 2 Corinthians 12:2–3),
  was cursed with an irrevocable, eternal curse. The first creature
  to be cursed of the Lord God was the tempter himself. Satan, the
  fallen angel, brought about the fall of man. There is absolutely no
  redemption for this fallen angel or for the other angels who fell
  with him. He is the originator of sin, both in heaven, among the
  angelic beings, and on earth, with the man and the woman, who
  were made in the image of God.

+ The serpent would eat dust all the days of its existence. Perhaps
  there is some symbolic significance to the word "*dust*," for man was
  made from the "*dust of the earth.*" Satan feeds on mankind's fallen
  nature.

+ There would be enmity—that is, conflict, antagonism, and warfare—between the serpent and the woman. This goes beyond
  women (or men) being fearful of snakes! The devil has a particular
  hatred of women, as proven through history. It all started when
  the woman exposed the serpent as the one who had deceived her.
  (See Genesis 3:13.) Ultimately, woman is a type, or symbol, of the
  church, the bride of Christ, which Satan hates with a perfect hatred. (See Ephesians 5:23–32.)

+ This enmity would be between "*your* [Satan's] *seed*" and "*her Seed.*"
  There would be two seed lines: the "serpent seed" and the "woman
  seed," with a battle line drawn between them. History has indeed
  proven this to be so. There is the godly line and the ungodly line;
  those who are of the devil, and those who are of God. There are the
  true and the false, the wheat and the tares (see, for example, Matthew 13:30), the seed of the woman (those who put their faith in
  God) and the seed of the serpent (the faithless).

+ The Seed of the woman would bruise the serpent's head, and the
  seed of the serpent would bruise the heel of the Seed of the woman.

A male Child would be born of a virgin woman that would crush the serpent's head, dealing the deadly blow of divine judgment. The language here is generally recognized as an enigmatic revelation of the virgin birth of Christ Jesus. Though Christ would become the "bruised heel" on Calvary by the serpent (Satan), yet He would bring about the "bruised head" of the serpent. (See Romans 16:20.) The ultimate picture is seen in Revelation 12, where the male Child causes the casting out of *"that old Serpent, called the devil, and Satan…into the to earth"* (verse 9), and eventually to the Lake of Fire. The bruise of the head would be the deadly wound from which any recovery would be impossible. The bruised heel would be recovered, but not the bruised (crushed) head! The serpent brought about the fall of the woman, but God will use the woman to judge the serpent at the appointed time.

♦ There is no doubt that Eve believed the Lord's promise of a Seed that would crush the head of the serpent, the one who had deceived her. When she gave birth to her first son, Cain, she thought he was that seed. When Adam named his wife "Eve," it was a name of faith. "Eve" means "the mother of all living," or "the mother of the Living One."

The seed of the woman, therefore, would be the good seed, the godly line, the children of the kingdom of light. The seed of the serpent would be the evil seed, the ungodly line, the children of the kingdom of darkness. (See 1 John 3:7–10; John 8:41–43.) The godly seed line continued through Abraham, Isaac, and Jacob unto the Lord Jesus Christ and the church. (See Genesis 22:16–18; 26:4–5; 28:14; 1 Chronicles 17:11–12; Galatians 3: 16, 29.)

Jack Hayford notes that the original female had three names:

> **Man, or Adam:** the same word in Hebrew. (See Genesis 5:1; 1:27.)
>
> **Woman:** more a generic designation than a name, associated with Eve's relationship to Adam, which she was created to fill. Literally means "man-ess." (See Genesis 2:23.)

Eve: meaning "life," "life-giving," or "mother of all who have life." A name expressive of the prophetic life bound up within her. Adam named her Eve *after* they both had sinned. Previously, they were together as "man"; after the fall, her new name represented their tragic division. (See Genesis 3:20.)

But "the seed of the woman" would bruise and crush forever "the seed of the serpent." This was the prophetic word of the Lord God spoken to that old serpent, Satan, the devil, the deceiver of mankind, and the archenemy of God in creation and redemption.

The next divine judgment was spoken to the woman.

2. Judgment on the Woman

To the woman He said: "I will greatly multiply your sorrow and your conception; in pain you shall bring forth children; your desire shall be for your husband, and he shall rule over you."

(Genesis 3:16 NKJV; see also 2 Corinthians 11:2;
1 Timothy 2:13–15; Ephesians 5:22)

It is important to see that while the serpent (Satan) was cursed with an irrevocable curse, God did *not* curse the man and the woman made in His image! They were affected by the curse on the earth and by sin, but God did not personally curse them. He did not curse His own image. It is evil to say that all women are under the curse of God because of Eve's sin. Both men and women are affected by the curse of sin and death. But the first man to receive the curse of God was Cain—liar, murderer, and rejecter of the blood of the lamb. Notice, then, the divine judgment on the woman, the original sinner in Eden's paradise.

- There would be multiplied sorrow on the woman. History has proven how much sorrow and grief have fallen on the women, in numerous ways.

- There would be amplified pain in the bringing forth of children. None but the woman can know the sorrows and difficulties of pregnancy, childbirth, and motherhood but mothers. *The Amplified Version* speaks of *"grief and…suffering in pregnancy and the pangs of childbearing; with spasms of distress"* (Genesis 3:16 AMPC). History provides ample examples of this grief.

✦ There would be *"desire"* for the husband, and the husband would *"rule"* over his wife. There would be male dominance in the family. The man would rule the woman, and this because the woman had brought about the fall of the man. Before the fall, man and woman ruled together. But with the entrance of sin on the scene, the roles were changed, and man was given rulership over the woman.

The third part of this judgment on the woman needs some careful consideration. Understanding and interpreting this clause has been a great point of difference and controversy among expositors. This clause has been the grounds for male dominance, and for women being made subject to men, both in the home and in the redeemed community at large. The verse has been taken by many men to mean that *all* men are to rule over *all* women. This is simply not so. God speaks particularly to the husband/wife marriage relationship, as seen in 1 Timothy 2:13–15. It is a situational remark, not a general rule for male rulership or the dominance of men over women.

There are two words that need to be understood clearly in order for us to arrive at a proper understanding and interpretation of this final clause of divine judgment on the woman—Eve—and, as a result, on all women of the human race. But let us first note some other translations of Genesis 3:16:

*"Yet your **desire** will be for your husband, and he will **rule** over you."*

(NASB)

*"Your **desire** will be for your husband, and he will **rule** over you."*

(NIV)

*"Yet even so, you shall **welcome** your husband's affections, and he shall be your **master**."* (TLB)

*"Your **desire** shall be for [toward] your husband, and he shall **rule** over you."*

(NKJV)

*"Yet your **desire** and craving shall be for your husband, and he will* **rule** *over you."*   (AMP)

♦   **"Desire"** (Hebrew, *teshuwqah*): "in the original sense of stretching out after, a longing" and translated "desire." The word is used three times in the Old Testament. It is spoken of Adam (see Genesis 3:16), of Cain (see Genesis 4:7), and of the bride (see Song of Solomon 7:10).

Katharine C. Bushnell defines the word shuq in its simplest form as "to run…to run repeatedly…to run back and forth." cause to run over, to control, to dominate," or "a turning." The woman will "turn to, run back and forth [from], and turn frequently" to her husband.[1]

Bushnell translates the verse in this way: "You are continually turning to your husband, and he shall rule over you." As Eve turned from God and turned to her husband, giving him the fruit of the forbidden tree in the fall, so she would continue to turn to him. She would endeavor to control him, to dominate him; but he would rule over her. Adam may have felt that Eve had overruled him in her eating of the fruit, and now, the reaction would be for him to rule over her from then on.

Jack Hayford posits the following:

> The fact is that man—even redeemed men in the church—are slow to outgrow the reactionary posture he has been forced to take because of the results "the fall of man" have worked in woman.
>
> In Genesis 3:16, as those facets of the sin-curse bearing on woman-kind are being enunciated by God, she is told, *"Thy desire shall be to thy husband and he shall rule over thee."*
>
> The Hebrew word *teshuwqah*, translated "desire," is essentially descriptive of a fallen trait. In essence, "You shall desire to have your husband's place of authority. You shall want his

---

1. Katharine C. Bushnell, *God's Word to Women*, 57. https://godswordtowomen.files. wordpress.com/2010/10/gods_word_to_women1.pdf#page=134&zoom=auto,-142,823.

place of leadership over you, but it shall not be. He shall be your authority."

God is not even commenting on whether or not a woman is as good as or as potentially capable as a man. He is simply declaring that, under the present conditions to which flesh has come, she shall be wider his authority. He prophesies that this shall not be easy for her. 'Thy desire shall be unto thy husband... to take away his rule over you, to assert yourself...." (But this would not be so.)[2]

- **"Rule"** (Hebrew, *mashal*): "to have authority, dominion, power, to reign" (Refer Strong's 4910). It is the same word as used in Genesis 1:18. The sun would "rule the day" and the moon would "rule the night." Compare STRONG 4475, Genesis 1:16, 18, and STRONG 4910, Genesis 3:16. Both Hebrew words mean "dominion, govern, reign, have power, and to rule."

The same word is spoken to Eve as also to Cain. God said to Cain, "Sin is crouching at the door; it desires to have you, but you must master it." (See Genesis 4:7.) In Genesis 3:16 and Genesis 4:7, the same two Hebrew words are used.

The judgment on the woman was this. Before the fall, the man and the woman ruled together, had dominion together, reigned together over creation. Now, the man would rule over the woman, the husband would rule over, reign over and have dominion over his wife. And this, because the wife had dominion over the husband in the fall.

Human history has shown the tragic results and application of male rulership over the woman. Most non-Christian nations, cultures and religions evidence this cruel and tyrannical domination of woman. Such cultures are cruel, oppressive, domineering, and depressive in their subjection and subordination of women to men. Women in these cultures are the slaves of the man, his whims, passions, and power. It is only in nations that have been influenced by the Judeo-Christian ethic that women have found relief from oppressive male dominance.

2. Hayford, *On the Question of a Woman's Place in Church Leadership*.

Adam and Eve both disobeyed God's command. Sin damaged God's creation and dramatically affected the world, especially in the realm of human relationships. Sin brought about "gender wars" and the "battle of the sexes" entered the human race with the original man and woman. Mindsets like male chauvinism and secular feminism are a result of the fall. The fall brought about division and dominance, which resulted in a broken, fractured relationship. Hierarchy was established and partnership in marriage was ruined. As already noted, before sin, man and woman ruled together. After sin, the man would rule over the woman. This rule was a result of the fall. The image of God was "male and female," not "male over female" or vice versa. The entrance of sin changed the course of human history. It affected the stature and role of both man and woman. Sin disrupted God's order of creation.

A careful reading of 1 Timothy 2:11–14 implies that Eve usurped Adam's authority. In talking with the serpent, she was deceived into eating the forbidden fruit. It would seem that Eve disobeyed the command that the Lord gave to Adam—and to her, as well, through Adam's lips.

> *Let the woman learn in silence with all subjection* [submission]. *But I suffer not* [do not permit] *a woman to teach or to have* [or to usurp] *authority over a man, but to be in silence. For Adam was formed first, then Eve. And Adam was not deceived, but the woman being deceived, was* [fell] *in transgression.* (1 Timothy 2:11–14 NKJV)

This passage is not speaking of all men and all women. It has to do with Adam and Eve, with a husband/wife relationship, and with marital situations. Paul was speaking of Eve's usurping authority over Adam by eating the forbidden fruit, and then giving him the forbidden fruit to eat. Adam's sin was plain rebellion against God's law. There was no deception, just rebellion in his submission to his wife's offer of forbidden fruit.

It is evident there was more judgment on the woman because of her initiative in the fall. So now, instead of the man and the woman sharing dominion through joint-rulership, man was given rulership, or headship, while woman was placed under subjection. The man would rule the woman—the husband would rule the wife—and the wife would submit to her husband.

The fall of man positioned husbands over their wives. Hierarchical rule, with the subordination of women to men, was a result of the fall.

It is absolutely important to note that when God told Eve, *"Your desire shall be for your husband, and he shall rule over you"* (Genesis 3:16 NKJV), this was not a command of God to the man. It was simply a prophetic statement foretelling what would happen. It was a statement of a future fact, just as when Jesus told Peter he would deny Him three times. (See Matthew 26:34; Mark 14:30; Luke 22:34.) Jesus did not command Peter to deny Him; He simply foretold, prophetically, that he would do so.

Again, God did not command Adam to rule Eve. He simply told her what would happen. It was a prophecy of what would be. It was not His perfect will. Let me state that a different way: Man's rule over his wife was not God's original intention. It came about as a result of the fall.

In the beginning, before the entrance of sin into the world, woman was not ruled by man. Adam did not rule over his wife. They ruled together, as joint-heirs over creation. In the beginning, God did not subordinate woman to man, Eve to Adam. This rule was not a result of God's ordinance but a result of sin. This rule is of a fallen order, grounded in the fall. It was never God's will, God's purpose, or God's command. Sin changed the family order, placing man as head of the woman, resulting in a "chain of command" that is still in effect today. (See Ephesians 5:23.) When redemption's plan is completed, this order will expire.

Human history and the tragic breakdown of the marriage relationship is evidence of this rule, this dominance of husband over wife, man over woman. Subjection, regretfully, has become suppression of the woman. The wife, or the woman, is subdued under the guise of submission. All this is the result of the fall and the declared judgment of God of what would happen as a result of sin. Redemption's plan would bring the man and the woman back to God's original plan in due time.

(**Note:** The reader will note that much has been written on the matter of the rule of man over the woman. This has been necessary because of the misunderstanding and misinterpretation of this statement of God. It has been taken *as a command of God* that man should rule and dominate the woman, that woman is subordinated to man. But it is simply *a statement of*

God of what would happen after the fall. It was never God's perfect will. It was—and is—a result of the fall and the entrance of sin. It is a fact of human life!)

3. Judgment on the Man

> *Then the* LORD *God took the man and put him in the garden of Eden to tend and keep it. And the* LORD *God commanded the man, saying, "Of every tree of the garden you may freely eat; but of the tree of the knowledge of good and evil you shall not eat, for in the day that you eat of it you shall surely die."…Then to Adam He said, "Because you have heeded the voice of your wife, and have eaten from the tree of which I commanded you, saying, 'You shall not eat of it': Cursed is the ground for your sake; in toil you shall eat of it all the days of your life. Both thorns and thistles it shall bring forth for you, and you shall eat the herb of the field. In the sweat of your face you shall eat bread till you return to the ground, for out of it you were taken; for dust you are, and to dust you shall return."* (Genesis 2:15–17; 3:17–19 NKJV)

The divine judgment on Adam is seen in the above passages. Because of man's willful disobedience of God's command and simultaneous obedience of his wife, Eve, God pronounces judgment on man and also on the earth. Adam was the chief offender because he was not deceived, as was his wife. It was "Adam's transgression"—*"Sin is the transgression of the law"* (1 John 3:4)—that brought judgment on the whole human race. Eve sinned by deception; Adam sinned by transgression.

+ The earth would come under a curse. Thorns and thistles would affect the produce of the earth. Keep in mind that God did not curse Adam or Eve, the man and the woman made in His image and likeness. Cain received the curse of God when he rejected God's plan of redemption in blood atonement. This is what ultimately brings people under a curse. However, Adam and Eve, and all mankind, were affected by the curse on the earth and on all creation because of sin.

+ Man would eat of the fruit of the field in sorrow all the days of his life.

- Work, which had been pleasurable before the fall, would now be in sweat and toil; all would be hard labor.

- The earth would be cursed with thorns and thistles, and would turn against the man through whom it fell. Creation rises and falls with the man and woman with which it fell. Although not spelled out specifically in these verses, the whole of the animal creation "fell" with the man, becoming wild, carnivorous, and fearful of the man under whose rulership and dominion it was placed.

- Death would return the man and the woman back to the dust of the earth from where man was taken. (See Ecclesiastes 2:23; 3:20; Job 21:26.) "Dust you are, and to dust you shall return" (see Genesis 3:19) was the word of the Lord to Adam.

- Sin and death would pass on to all of Adam's race, as yet unborn and in his loins. (See Romans 5:12–21.) *In Adam all die* (1 Corinthians 15:22). The curse of sin is death, and all mankind come under that curse until sin is dealt with by the Lord God in His Son, Jesus Christ.

The history of mankind has certainly attested to the divine judgment on woman, man, and the earth.

This is the order of divine judgment: first on the serpent (Satan), then on the woman, and then on man and the earth. The whole of creation groans for redemption's plan.

6

ORDER IN REDEMPTION

The order in redemption is actually a "new creation order." The "old creation order" was "in Adam," while the "new creation order" is "in Christ." (See 1 Corinthians 15:22; 2 Corinthians 5:17.) This does not, in the present, annul the old order but rather transcends it into a higher order. It is from creation to redemption.

At the risk of some repetition, we note God's promise of redemption, and the order in redemption. This order would be a virgin woman and her Seed, Christ Jesus. This Seed would bring redemption to fallen men and women.

In the midst of these judgments on the serpent, the woman, the man, and the earth, God promised that redemption would come by way of "the Seed of the woman." In Genesis 3:15, God is speaking to the serpent, Satan himself. He promises that *"I will put enmity between you and the woman, between your seed and her Seed; He shall bruise your head, and you shall bruise His heel."* This promise is a prophecy.

A careful consideration of these words, and the implications here, shows that in spite of the judgment pronounced on the woman, God actually gives the promise of redemption that would come through the woman!

The serpent deceived the woman, but the seed of the woman would crush the serpent's head. Even though sin and death entered by the woman, God would bring redemption from sin and death through the woman.

The promise is not given to Adam, the seed-bearer of the unborn human race. All the seed in Adam's loins were affected by his sin and would be born in sin, shaped in iniquity. All would need redemption, both men and women. It, therefore, was not "the seed of the man" but "the seed of *the woman!*"

The truth of the virgin birth of Christ is implicit in these words. It is the gospel of redemption set forth in an enigmatic prophecy and promise. Woman, in the natural course of life, cannot conceive seed of herself. There has to be the implantation of the seed of the man. But the promise here is beyond that which is in the natural. It is super-natural. It would have to be of God Himself as no man could fulfill that promise.

God would use a woman for the bringing of His only begotten Son, the Savior of the world. He would not use a man, but the seed of the woman. The Savior, however, would be a Man. A Man would be born of a woman to redeem both the man and the woman back to God and His image from which both fell.

To repeat the truth once again: Eve evidences her faith in this prophetic promise when she said, "*I have gotten a man from the* LORD" (Genesis 4:1) after the birth of Cain. Eve thought Cain was that promised seed. Such was not the case, as the Genesis account reveals. Cain, though born of Adam and his wife, was spiritually "the seed of the serpent"—a murderer, a liar and a blood-of-the-Lamb rejecter. (See Genesis 4.) Adam also evidenced his faith in the prophetic word when he named his wife "Eve"—"the mother of all living, the mother of the living one." He did not name her "the mother of all dying!" This was the evidence of the faith of both the woman and the man, Adam and Eve.

The promised seed line would continue through Abraham, Isaac, Jacob, Judah, David and finally the Virgin Mary, of whom, Christ after the flesh was born. (See Isaiah 7:14; 9:6–9; Matthew 1:1–17, 18–21; Luke 3:30–33; Galatians 4:4.)

Human history has shown—and still shows—that there is a satanic hatred and enmity against the woman. Undoubtedly the woman incurred Satan's enmity when she exposed the serpent as the deceiver. Also, when God promised that the seed of the woman would crush the serpent's head. All this would incur satanic hatred.

In New Testament times, Paul teaches us that the man is a type of the Man, Christ Jesus; the woman is a type of the church, and the child is a type of the seed of the woman that would crush the serpent's head. In other words, this is the ultimate cause of satanic attack on the human family; man, woman and child, or, father, mother and offspring. Satan hates the man. Satan hates the woman. Satan hates children. Satan hates all mankind. Man was made a little lower than the angels. Satan is a fallen angel and brought about the fall of man. God will use mankind to bruise the serpent's head. Hence the enmity, the warfare, the conflict and Satanic hatred.

Paul, in the Pastoral Epistles, refers back to these important chapters of Genesis. Fuller details will be considered in the appropriate time. A brief outline, however, needs to be given here as it relates to this present chapter. Note the "orders" that Paul speaks of in 1 Timothy 2:13–15.

1. Order in Creation—*1 Timothy 2:13 with Genesis 1:26– 28; 2:18–25*

"For Adam was first formed, then Eve." Here Paul refers back to Genesis, to the beginning, to the creation of the man and the woman in divine order, the order of creation. Man was formed first, and then the woman, Eve.

2. Order in the Fall—*1 Timothy 2:14 with Genesis 3:1–13*

"And Adam was not deceived, but the woman being deceived was in [fell into] *the transgression."* Here Paul takes us back to Genesis once again, to the beginning. The woman sinned first. The woman fell first because of being deceived. But Adam fell voluntarily, deliberately, of his own rebelliousness. Eve and Adam were the original sinners, but Adam brought the seed of sin on the whole human race, as yet unborn in his loins.

3. Order in Redemption—*1 Timothy 2:15 with Genesis 3:15*

We note several translations on this somewhat difficult verse. There is no doubt that Paul again has the Genesis account in mind and the penalty laid on the woman in the divine Word.

> *Notwithstanding, she [the woman] shall be saved in childbearing, if they continue in faith and charity and holiness, with sobriety.*
>
> (1 Timothy 2:15)

> *But women will be saved [kept safe] through childbearing—if they continue in faith, love and holiness with propriety.* (NIV)

Most of the translations follow similar wording.

The problem with these similar translations imply that salvation for a woman would come through bearing children, in faith, love and holiness. This, however, makes salvation or redemption through works — bearing of children. This is contrary to Scripture. There is, no doubt, a promise to women that the Lord will be with them in the bearing of children, especially believing women, women of God. But redemption is not made available because of bearing children, few or many. What then is this difficult verse saying beyond a surface reading of the words?

The Amplified Bible seems to translate this verse more clearly and certainly more in harmony with the total biblical revelation.

> *Nevertheless [the sentence put upon women of pain in motherhood does not hinder their souls' salvation, and] they will be saved [eternally] if they continue in faith and love and holiness, with self-control, [saved indeed] through the Childbearing or by the birth of the divine Child.* (1 Timothy 2:15)

This is far more in keeping with the theology of Scripture on redemption being available for both men and women through the Lord Jesus Christ, the divine Child, not through women having children, few or more. Salvation and redemption is not available through works, through bearing children, though some religious orders would teach this. All children are born sinful. Only the Christ Child is the sinless Son of God by reason of the virgin birth through Mary. This is not to do away with the Lord's grace being with the woman in natural childbirth, but the truth is certainly deeper than the surface reading. Salvation is not made available through a woman, or any woman having many children. Salvation is not available through any man, only through the Man, Christ Jesus.

Paul is saying that the woman (the Virgin Mary) will bring forth the Man, Christ Jesus, the Savior, who will die to make redemption available for both man and woman. He will bring both men and women back to God's original order. It will be out of the old creation order, "in Adam" and into the new creation order, "in Christ." (See 1 Corinthians 15:22.)

As already noted, fuller consideration will be given to this Pauline passage in due time. It is, however, noteworthy that it is in the context of the Timothy passage, as outlined here, that Paul says a woman was not to teach or usurp authority over the man. The implication should be evident to any serious student of the Word.

The commandment had been given to Adam. He, no doubt, would have passed the word to his wife, as she knew of the commandment as she referred to it in the conversation with the serpent. The woman took and ate of the forbidden tree, and then gave to her husband. What she said in conversation to her husband, Adam, is not recorded. But, in this matter "she seized the authority" over God's Word as given to Adam, gave to her husband, and he willingly, deliberately, knowingly and rebelliously violated God's commandment and ate of the fruit of the tree. He was not deceived.

The chief point? Though sin and death came by the woman, and then through the man, redemption would come by a woman and the Savior, the Man Christ Jesus. Blessing is secured through Christ's birth by a human mother, a woman. There is salvation for the woman, even though she was made subject to man's authority because of the fall. Though the woman would experience suffering in childbirth (see

Genesis 3:16), a Child born of a woman would crush the serpent's head (see Genesis 3:15).

Paul, softening the seeming severity on the woman in the reasons as given in 1 Timothy 2:13, 14, brings in the first prophecy of redemption from Genesis 3:15 with 1 Timothy 2:15, showing that redemption will come through the woman.

Jesus Christ will bring us back to God's original order which will be the Man (Christ) first, then the woman (the church), which is the new-creation order. (See Ephesians 5:23–33.) However, even though Christ has made redemption possible by the work of Calvary, and even though both men and women can be restored to that from which they fell in Adam, there will still be a divine order.

In the order of redemption, Christ (the Man) is first, then the woman; the church is next in place and order. This will be so throughout eternity. Christ is the Head of the church, and the church is His body. This is divine order. Redemption brings order back to the home, the marriage, as it was originally seen in Adam and his bride. Redemption brings order in the church between men and women in the redeemed community. The natural and the spiritual blend together in divine order, as Paul shows in Ephesians 5:23–33. Natural and spiritual relationships between husband and wife (as between Adam and Eve), and between Christ and His bride (the church), are woven together in the divine revelation as given to Paul.

In Conclusion

As the passages from Genesis and 1 Timothy are considered, God, in the midst of His pronounced judgments, exalts the woman to be the channel of redemption for all mankind. Redemption would make possible restoration of covenantal relationship that was broken through sin. The ultimate result of this will be the consummation of all things when Christ returns to earth a second time.

Every man since Adam owes his birth to a woman. Why then despise the womb (and the woman) who brought them to birth with much suffering and travail? The same is true of every man and every woman. All owe their conception and birth to a man and a woman, to a father and a mother. Men and women in the redeemed community owe their salvation to the Man Christ Jesus, who was born of a woman, the Virgin Mary! Male pride, chauvinism, and hierarchical attitudes should be subdued and humbled at the power of these redemptive truths. The promise of the Lord God, the channel of the Virgin Mary, and the birth of the Christ Child become the fulfillment of redemption, as seen in Genesis 3:15.

7

ORDER IN THE ISRAELITE HOME

From Adam and Eve were born two sons named Cain and Abel. These two sons begin the ungodly and godly lines from Adam to Noah. With the development of human families and the human race, human wickedness increased. The great wickedness caused the judgment of God to fall on the human race in the form of a flood. God wiped out mankind from a wicked earth and preserved to Himself the family of Noah.

Sometime after the flood, God chose a man by the name of Abraham. From him would come a chosen seed line, the chosen nation of Israel. In the period of the Patriarchs, God had chosen families to continue the godly seed line. Such families are seen to be men and women of faith, seen in:

+ Abraham and Sarah

+ Isaac and Rebekah

+ Jacob and Rachel and Leah

+ Joseph and Asenath

Hebrews 11 speaks of these as men and women who *"by faith"* followed the Lord. From Adam through to Moses there was a period of some 2,500 years.

Under the Law, from Moses through to Malachi—a period of some 1,500 years—the chosen nation of Israel was prominent in the ongoing purposes of God in redemption. In the chosen nation, there were many examples of godly men and women, as well as ungodly ones.

In the chosen nation, God laid down laws for the honor, sanctity, safety, security, and protection of the family. In the Israelite home, men and women were primarily homemakers. Men were called to be godly husbands and fathers; women were called to be godly wives and mothers. And both men and women were called to teach and train their children in the laws of the Lord, in His statutes and judgments. Israel was called to be a holy nation in the midst of the corrupt Gentile nations. Fathers, mothers, sons, and daughters were to be examples of families taught, trained, and living in divine truths.

In the Gentile nations, the woman received little honor. She was viewed as the slave, victim, and chattel of the man. In the chosen nation of Israel, God gave a number of laws for the honor and protection of the women.

The Ten Commandments call for honoring God as well as the family. The commandments condemned adultery. The civil laws condemned rape, fornication, harlotry, incest, sodomy, and adulterous relationships. Most of these acts were punishable by death. (See Exodus 20; Deuteronomy 21:10–14; 22:13, 28; Numbers 5:11–31.)

These laws were given to safeguard the home and family. They were especially given to protect the woman from evil misrule and from the misinterpretation and misapplication of the Word of God in Genesis 3:16. These laws would safeguard the woman's right and preserve her freedom as an individual.

Younger women were not permitted to make vows without the protection of a husband or father. (See Numbers 30.) The ideal woman, with her godly husband, is described in Proverbs 31:10–31. The book of Proverbs also provides many warnings against adultery.

The following summary covers some of the biblical statutes concerning fathers, mothers, and children.

+ Children were to fear and reverence their father and mother. (See Leviticus 19:3.)

- Anyone who cursed his or her father and mother would die. (See Leviticus 20:9; Exodus 21:17; Matthew 15:14.)

- There was to be moral purity in the home. (See Leviticus 18:7; 20:19.)

- Children were to honor their father and mother. This commandment was the only one with a promise of long life attached to it. (See Exodus 20:12; Deuteronomy 5:16; Matthew 15:4; Mark 7:10; Ephesians 6:2.)

- The death penalty was placed on any who killed his or her mother and father. (See Exodus 21:15.)

- Any rebellious and stubborn children who did not obey their father and mother were to be stoned to death. (See Deuteronomy 21:18–19.)

- Children were to hear the instructions of their father and mother. (See Proverbs 1:8; 6:20; 10:l; 15:20; 19:26; 20:20; 23:22–25; 28:24; 30:11, 17.) Wise sons and daughters made for glad fathers and mothers.

- Fathers were to teach their children the laws of the Lord. (See Deuteronomy 6:7–9; 11:19–20.)

Homes in Israel were primarily to be places of godliness, integrity, and honor. The family was the basic unit of society, the foundation of the chosen nation of Israel. As went the family, so went the nation.

In Israel, the woman, as a wife and mother, exercised great influence—sometimes more influence than the father, who would have spent most of his waking hours away from the home, working in the field. Under the divine laws, the Israelite women had great liberty, were charged with noble tasks, and occupied a social standing that commanded far more respect than did those women who lived in Gentile nations.

Godly women had great influence in the nation; ungodly women seemed to lead the way in idolatry and immorality. (See Jeremiah 7:8; Ezekiel 8:14; Exodus 22:18.) The man was to honor his wife, and the wife was to honor her husband as well as her father.

With all the dignity and protection given to women in Israel, however, there were things that God permitted, even though those things were never part of His perfect will. God permitted bigamy, polygamy, and concubinage. Men were permitted to have many women, but women were not permitted to have many men; a woman who did so was counted as a harlot, or a prostitute. This was not so of the man. Adulterers, whether male or female, were to be stoned to death. (See Leviticus 20:10; Deuteronomy 22:22; Numbers 5:11–31.)

Again, it was never God's perfect will for a man to have multiple wives. Such a situation was permitted because of the sinful nature—because of man's weakness and inability to restrain his own unlawful passions. God's ideal was monogamy, a marriage of one man to one woman, as characterized the original marriage—that of Adam and Eve. And the new covenant reinstituted the original plan for monogamous marriages.

So, God's order in the Israelite home was a godly father and a godly mother, and children being brought up in the nurture and admonition of the Lord. Parents were to instruct their children in the laws, the statutes, and the judgments of God. The children were to honor their father and mother and to live in obedience to God's holy laws, by which they would be blessed with long life. This was the ideal of God for family life in Israel, a nation chosen to be an example to the Gentile nations.

8

MINISTRY IN OLD TESTAMENT TIMES

Israel is referred to as *"the church in the wilderness"* (Acts 7:38). As seen in the previous chapter, the primary role and function of most men and women in Old Testament times was that of being homebuilders and homemakers.

However, God, for His own purposes, singled out certain men and women for spiritual, political, or social leadership in the chosen nation of Israel. As always, there were good and evil leaders alike. The nation of Israel rose and fell accordingly. A study of the Old Testament ministries reveals five particular leadership callings:

1. **Elders:** the male leaders of the tribes of the nation. Later on, the elders ruled over the synagogues.

2. **Judges:** the deliverers or saviors of the various tribes or of the nation under the various periods of servitude experienced in the book of Judges.

3. **Priests:** the mediatorial ministers, serving the people in the sacrificial order of redemption in the tabernacle, or the temple services.

4. **Kings:** the national or political leaders in Israel. When the nation divided, there were kings of various dynasties over the house of Israel but one continuous dynasty of the house of David reigning over the house of Judah.

5. **Prophets:** the spiritual leaders, more particularly. They became, as it were, the voice of God to kings, priests, judges, and elders. The prophets actually held the highest spiritual office in the land. While the priests represented the people to God, the prophets represented God to the people.

As noted, there were good leaders and evil leaders in each of these roles. The leadership was primarily male; elders were male, and priests were male. In the patriarchal era, the father and husband, as head of the household, was also the priest of the family, exhibited in such examples as Adam, Noah, Enoch, Abraham, Isaac, Jacob, and Job. In due time, Moses and Aaron, and the whole of the Levitical tribe, were chosen to be the priestly tribe to the other twelve tribes of Israel.

Kings were male, though queens could reign if there were no male heir to the throne. Judah had only one queen, but she was a wicked usurper, the wicked Queen Athaliah. (See 2 Kings 22.) When the daughters of Zelophehad came before Moses, Eleazar the high priest, and the princes of the congregation, they were able to receive their inheritances according to the law of the Lord. If there had been no male heirs, then the inheritance could have been passed on to the daughters. Therefore, if there had been no male heirs to the throne, the throne could have passed to a daughter. (See Numbers 26:33; 27:1–11; Joshua 15:6–19; 17:3, 4; Job 42:14.)

However, even though leadership was predominantly male, God, by His own will and according to His own purposes, did choose women to be prophets, and even one woman was chosen to be a judge. Other women were called and blessed with various spiritual services and became leaders in the nation, accepted as such, even in a male-dominated society.

The following are the spiritual services, ministries, and functions that were available to both men and women, even though they were predominantly performed by men.

1. The Prophetic Ministry

Both men and women were called by God to be prophets of the Lord to His people. Such were to have the prophetic word of the Lord and to be the mouthpiece of God to the nation. Of the various callings in

Old Testament times, prophet was considered the highest. To be the mouthpiece of the mind of God—no calling could be greater. (See Jeremiah 1:9; 15:19.) The office and ministry of prophet was considered a higher calling than that of judges, kings, elders, and priests in Israel.

A. Male Prophets

There is no debate or question as to whether God calls men to be prophets. The biblical examples are many: Moses, Aaron, Samuel, Shemaiah, Iddo, Ahijah, Azariah, Hanani, Jehu, Jehazaiah, Eleazar, Joel, Isaiah, Micah, Nahum, Zephaniah, Elijah, Elisha, Micaiah, Jonah, Amos, Hosea, Zephaniah, Habakkuk, Jeremiah, Daniel, and Ezekiel. These men were seen as prophets of vision and divine utterance, as seers of the miraculous, each in his own measure of giftedness and calling.

B. Female Prophets

The Bible includes some women who were also called of God to the prophetic office. These prophetesses were recognized and accepted in Israel by the evident anointing of God upon their lives and ministry. As such, they were the mouthpieces of God who spoke the Word of the Lord. We will now consider in greater detail several of these women called to the prophetic ministry.

1.) Miriam

Miriam was an influential prophetess in the nation of Israel. The Hebrew word *nebiah* means "a female preacher." She was also a gifted worship leader who sang the song of the Lord and led the women of Israel with timbrels and dancing before the Lord. (See Psalm 68:25; Exodus 15:20–21; Numbers 12:1–10.)

God actually classed Miriam with her brothers Moses and Aaron, both prophets, and declared through the prophet Micah, *"For I brought you up out of the land of Egypt, and redeemed you out of the house of bondage; and I sent before you Moses, Aaron, and Miriam"* (Micah 6:4 NKJV).

2.) Huldah

Huldah was also called a prophetess. Huldah was married to a man named Shallum, and they lived at the college in Jerusalem. She was the *"keeper of the wardrobe"* (2 Kings 22:14; 2 Chronicles 34:22). (See 2 Kings 22:12–20; 2 Chronicles 34:22.) In these passages, we have the account of King Josiah sending the High Priest, the scribe, and several other individuals to inquire of the Lord via Huldah the prophetess. Here, we see leading men from the royal court recognizing the Word of the Lord in the mouth of this female prophet and accepting the message she delivered from God. *"She said unto them, Thus saith the LORD God of Israel, Tell the man that sent you to me, Thus saith the LORD…"* (2 Kings 22:15). There was no male prejudice against Huldah's message, in spite of her being a woman, a female prophet.

3.) Isaiah's Wife

The wife of Isaiah is called a prophetess, and she shared her husband's ministry. (See Isaiah 8:1–3.)

4.) Noadiah, Jezebel, and Other False Female Prophets

In the post-exilic period, Nehemiah had to deal with a false prophetess by the name of Noadiah. (See Nehemiah 6:14.) Jeremiah and Ezekiel, who were true prophets of the Lord, also had to minister in the face of false prophets and false prophetesses. (See Ezekiel 13:17–24; Jeremiah 14.) And in Revelation, the church at Thyatira is reproved for abiding a woman named Jezebel who was a teacher and a prophetess spreading false doctrine that involved idolatry and immorality. The *"angel of the church"* (Revelation 3:1) was rebuked for allowing this false prophetess to minister evil, corrupt doctrine. It was not because she was a woman or a prophetess, but because of the corrupting doctrines she taught.

5.) *Anna*

Anna the prophetess was an elderly widow who served in the temple at Jerusalem. We are told that she *"departed not from the temple, but served God with fastings and prayers night and day"* (Luke 2:37). When Joseph and Mary brought the child Jesus to the temple, Anna entered that very instant and gave thanks to the Lord, then spoke of Him to all who were looking for redemption in Israel. (See Luke 2:38.) She was actually the first woman to publicly proclaim Jesus to the people at the time of His circumcision and naming in the temple. Thus, here was an instance of public speaking by a prophetess, and that before men and women. The Jews accepted Anna as a prophetess. What a great woman of God.

Again, the highest calling God ever gave to an individual in the Old Testament was that of a prophet or prophetess—those upon whom He placed the prophetic mantle. To be His mouthpiece and His voice to the people of God was a great and noble calling indeed. Prophets and prophetesses were the channels through whom God spoke to His people.

Although Israel was a male-dominated society, the leaders of the people recognized female prophets and accepted the word of the Lord in their mouths. They did not reject the testimony of such women due to male chauvinism.

God blessed these women under the old covenant, and used them to foreshadow the new covenant, when the Holy Spirit would be poured out on *"all flesh,"* whether men or women, as foretold by the prophet Joel. (See Joel 2:28–32.)

For those who do not accept women's participation in church ministry or leadership, one must wonder how they explain the existence of prophetesses under the old covenant. It also seems ironic to accept that the new covenant is greater than the old covenant (see, for example, Hebrews 8:6), and then to say that the new covenant forbids women from being prophetesses. If, under the old covenant, female prophets were called of God to be spiritual leaders and to ministered to men and women alike, then there is no obvious reason why the calling of prophet should be limited to men only under the new covenant. On the contrary, under the new covenant, one would expect that many more women, along with men, would be called to minister in the prophetic office.

While there were more male prophets than female prophets in the Old Testament, it does not alter the fact that God calls both men and women to this ministry, according to His will, as spiritual leaders to their nation.

Also, it is not a genuine reason to reject female prophets because of false female prophets being around in Israel's history, leading the people astray. These were many false male prophets, against whom the true prophets Jeremiah, Ezekiel, Nehemiah, and Elijah had to contend. True prophets of God have always had to contend with false prophets. Whatever may be said of false prophetesses may also be said of false prophets!

2. The Role of Judge

God, according to His own will and purpose, called certain individuals to be judges in Israel. There were some twelve male judges and one female judge in early Israel. These judges were called to be deliverers, judges, and saviors of a people who had long been in servitude to their surrounding nations. There were good judges, and there were bad judges.

A. Male Judges

Othniel, Ehud, Shamgar, Gideon, Tola, Jair, Jephthath, Ibzan, Elon, Abdon, Samson, and Samuel were the old-covenant judges. Some of these men were good judges, and some were bad judges. The judges were national leaders, many times seen as military leaders against the nations that oppressed the people of God.

B. Female Judge

While the judges were predominantly male, God did choose at least one female judge. God is God, and He can do as He wills. A judge was clearly a position of leadership in the nation. Deborah was chosen in the period of the judges, when Israel was without a king—the period before the monarchy came into being. (See Judges 4–5.) The same Hebrew word *shaphat* is used of her and the male judges in Israel, from the various tribes.

Deborah is spoken of as a judge, a prophetess, and a mother in Israel. (See Judges 4:4; 5:7–15.) She was also a song leader. (See Judges 5:1–3.) Deborah ruled forty years as a judge in Israel. She had authority as a prophetess, a revealer of God's will to Israel. She was also the military head of ten thousand men when Barak refused to go to battle without her lead. The wife of a man named Lapidoth, Deborah had a heart toward the governors of Israel, who offered themselves willingly among the people. A curse fell on some of the inhabitants because they failed to come to the help of the Lord under Deborah's leadership; the reason for this refusal was likely due, at least in some cases, to the fact of Deborah's being a woman. Blessing came on another woman, Jael, who was used to smite the head of Sisera, the enemy of the people of God. Deborah also sang with Barak the song of the Lord, the second song recorded in Scripture. No other judge besides Deborah was called a prophet, as well, until Samuel, the last of the judges and the beginning of the prophets.

Thousands of men and women recognized the call of God on Deborah's life and responded to her leadership. No fault of hers is recorded in the Bible. One wonders how those who reject women in church leadership would have responded if they had lived in Deborah's time.

As a mother in Israel, Deborah was honored. God's command is to honor both father and mother. (See Exodus 20:12; Deuteronomy 5:16; Proverbs 1:8; Romans 13:8–9.) This precept is applicable to both the natural and the spiritual realms. Just as natural fathers and mothers are to be honored (see Proverbs 6:20; 23:22; 30:17; Exodus 21:17; Ezekiel 22:7; Deuteronomy 27:16), so are spiritual fathers and mothers. God provided both the father and the mother image in Israel, naturally and spiritually.

Spiritual fathers are seen in such men as Moses, Aaron, Joshua, Gideon, David, Elijah, and Elisha. Spiritual mothers are seen in women like Miriam, Deborah, Huldah, Anna, and others. What a great honor! In Israel, God instituted parental authority, state authority, and spiritual authority in the various ministries He anointed.

3. The Worship of God

The people of God are called to be worshippers of God. A redeemed people are a worshipping people. This worship involves singing songs and playing musical instruments. A careful study of the Word of God shows that every revival and awakening in Israel, led by godly kings, involved a restoration of the type of worship found in the tabernacle of David, as seen in the following accounts:

+ The establishment of David's tabernacle—1 Chronicles 15–16

+ The dedication of Solomon's temple—2 Chronicles 3–5

+ Godly King Jehoshaphat—2 Chronicles 20

+ Godly King Hezekiah—2 Chronicles 29–30

+ Godly King Josiah—2 Chronicles 35:1–19

+ The restoration from Babylon—Ezra 2:65; 3:1–13; Nehemiah 12:27–47

+ The prophetic word of Amos—Amos 9:11–13

In the restoration from Babylon, there were *"singing men and singing women"* (Ezra 2:65; Nehemiah 7:67). Men and women were involved in rebuilding the walls of Jerusalem after the Babylonian captivity ended. (See Nehemiah 3:12.) The temple chambers were set aside for the singers. (See Ezekiel 40:44.) God accepted the worship of both men and women in the Old Testament. Women played a great part in the ministry of worship, in both the tabernacle of David and the temple of Solomon, as well as in earlier time periods.

+ The song of Moses is recorded in Exodus 15.

+ In the *"church in the wilderness"* (Acts 7:38), Miriam the prophetess sang along with her brother Moses; she was also the leader of worship and dance with the women playing tambourines. (See Exodus 15:20; Micah 6:4.)

+ The notable prayer-song of Hannah is recorded in 1 Samuel 1:28; 2:1–11. Her song of prayer and praise provides the first specific use of the term *"anointed"* (or "the Messiah") in Old Testament era. This was a revelation given by God through the mouth of a godly woman, a woman blessed of God. (See 1 Samuel 2:20.)

+ Heman the singer had daughters, as well as sons, who sang the songs of the Lord in the tabernacle of David. (See 1 Chronicles 25:5, 6; 6:33.)

+ There were certain psalms that were designed "for women's voices." The superscript on Psalm 46 speaks of *alamoth*, which means "a lass, damsel, veiled or private. A virgin." It is suggested to be a choir of singing maidens, or song of the virgins. Psalm 68:25 speaks of the damsels playing their timbrels along with the singers and players on instruments. This psalm is prophetic, finding its fulfillment in the 144,000 virgins singing a new song and playing upon their harps in Mount Zion, according to the order of the tabernacle of David. (See Revelation 14:1–4.) Other writers suggest that the "treble voices" could be referring to either young men or young women as the musicians played their psalteries.

+ Singers and musicians went before the ark of God. Men and women rejoiced and danced before the Lord. (See Psalm 68:25; 87:7.)

+ Several notable prophetic songs were sung in the temple at the time of the births of John the Baptist and the Messiah Jesus.

  › The song of Elizabeth—Luke 1:41–45

  › The song of Mary–Luke 1:46–55

  › The words of Anna the prophetess—Luke 2:36–38

What does all this prove to us? That women were nowhere commanded to be *"in silence,"* even under the Old Testament. Men and women were called of God for special ministry as it pleased Him.

4. *Service in the Tabernacle of Moses*

Both men and women were involved in the service of the tabernacle of Moses. Men such as Bezaleel and Aholiab were anointed and skilled of God to build the tabernacle. Women provided their mirrors or looking glasses for the making of the brazen laver. (See Exodus 36:1–2; 38:8.)

In Exodus 38:8, we are told of *"the women assembling, which assembled at the door of the tabernacle of the congregation."* Another version renders this phrase "assembled by troops" (asv, Margin). And 1 Samuel 2:22 mentions *"the women who served at the entrance of the tent of meeting"* (niv). The word *"assemble"* means "to be in the host, or to serve it" and is also translated "perform" or "wait upon." These were "serving women."

5. *The Nazarite Vow*

The Nazarite vow was an option for women as well as for men. The Nazarites made a voluntary vow to the Lord for a period of time. They were consecrated and separated to the Lord for sacred purposes. (See Numbers 6:1–27.) This separation to the Lord included total abstinence from wine, strong drink, and any fruit products of the vine tree.

6. *Feasts of the Lord*

Though it was compulsory for men to attend the three annual festival occasions of Passover, Pentecost, and the Feast of Tabernacles (see Deuteronomy 16:16), women and their children, manservants and maidservants, and widows and orphans were also welcome to attend these feasts. (See Deuteronomy 16:9–12, 13–15.) The Passover feast was celebrated in the home; the feasts of Pentecost and Tabernacles were public occasions of rejoicing before the Lord for His continued blessing. All these events were fulfilled in the Lord Jesus Christ—the Passover Lamb—as well as in the Upper Room, where men and women were filled with the Holy Spirit on the day of Pentecost. (See Acts 2:1–4.)

Other Observations of Women in the Old and New Testaments

There are numerous instances of women being used of God as examples of faith. The Old and New Testaments make note of many godly women. There were, as always, evil women, just as there were both godly and evil men.

The following is a brief survey of a number of women in the Bible, with special emphasis on those women who were God-fearing women of faith.

+ Sarah, the mother of faith, even as Abraham is the father of all who believe. (See Genesis 12–23, especially Genesis 17:15–16; Hebrews 11:11.) On one occasion, God actually instructed Abraham to obey his wife. (See Genesis 21:2.) It is interesting to note that Adam obeyed his wife, Eve, for the worse, while Abraham obeyed his wife, Sarah, for the Lord's best.

+ Rebekah, the bride of Isaac. The Lord spoke to her about the destiny of her twin sons before they were even born. (See Genesis 24:15–20; 25:21–23.) She relayed the Word of God to her husband, Jacob.

+ The daughters of Job were beautiful, and each one received an inheritance from her father after he was healed by the Lord. (See Job 42.)

+ Tamar was counted more righteous than her father-in-law, Judah, and she is included in the genealogy of the Messiah. (See Genesis 38:26; Matthew 1:3.)

+ The harlot Rahab was saved by faith. Her name is also listed in the Messiah's genealogy. (See Joshua 2:12–21; Hebrews 11:31; Matthew 1:5.)

+ An angel of the Lord revealed God's will concerning the birth of Samson, first of all, to Samson's mother (Manoah's wife), then later to Manoah. (See Judges 13:2–7.)

+ God used a certain woman to drop a millstone on the head of the wicked usurper Abimelech, bringing victory to Israel. (See Judges 9:52–54.)

+ Ruth, a Gentile and a Moabitess, came into the faith of Israel; her name is also found in the genealogy of the Messiah. (See Ruth 1–4; Matthew 1:5.)

+ Hannah, the wife of Elkanah, was a godly woman of prayer. When her son, Samuel, was born, she sang a prophetic song of the Lord and was the first person to speak of "the Anointed," or the Messiah, in old-covenant times. (See 1 Samuel 1–2.) God bypassed the old prophet Eli and spoke to this woman of God about the birth of her son, who would become the first in a long line of prophets.

+ Abigail gave King David a word of wisdom about her foolish husband, Nabal. David was humble enough to receive it, and thereby saved himself from bloodshed that he have would regretted. God struck wicked Nabal, and he died soon after the word of wisdom was given. (See 1 Samuel 25.)

+ Certain women had faith for the resurrection of their children. (See 2 Kings 4:18–37; Hebrews 11:35.)

+ Widows were honored of God, who established many laws to protect widows and orphans. (See Exodus 22:22; Deuteronomy 14:28; 16:11; 24:17; Jeremiah 49:11.)

+ God blessed and used widows to minister hospitality to the prophets of God, namely, Elijah and Elisha. The widow of Zarephath and the Shunammite woman are examples. (See 1 Kings 17; 2 Kings 4; Luke 4:25–26.)

+ A wise woman saved a city from attack by Joab by delivering the head of Sheba the son of Bichri. (See 2 Samuel 20:15–22.)

+ It was a little girl's testimony that persuaded Captain Naaman to go to the prophet of God in Israel and seek healing from the true God who could heal his leprosy. (See 2 Kings 5.)

+ It was a wise woman of Tekoa who intervened on behalf of Absalom. (See 2 Samuel 14:2–19.)

+ The Queen of Sheba came all the way to Jerusalem to see and learn from the wise King Solomon. (See 1 Kings 10:1–13; Matthew 12:42; Luke 11:31.)

+ Queen Athaliah was a wicked mother who usurped the authority of the throne by killing off the royal seed. (See 2 Kings 8:26; 2 Chronicles 22:1–12.)

+ Esther was a godly queen who saved her own nation from destruction by obedience to the counsel of Mordecai and risking her life before her husband. (See Esther 4:11.)

+ The Ethiopian eunuch served under Candace, the Queen of Ethiopia. He came to Christ after his visit to Jerusalem and under the ministry of the evangelist Philip. (See Acts 8:27–40.)

+ Wisdom is personified as the figure of a woman. (See Proverbs 1:20; 7:4; 9:1–6.)

+ The virtuous woman of Proverbs 31, and her wonderful qualities, are praised by her husband and her children. (See Proverbs 31:10–31.)

+ Women "published the good news" and divided the spoils of the battle fought and won. (See Psalm 68:11.) Various commentators believe that these women were evangelists who spread the good news of Christ's victory over the enemy.

+ God spoke of His nation Israel as a "woman," thus including both men and women under this figure. (See Jeremiah 3:1–20.) The church is spoken of as the "bride of Christ," and this figure also includes both men and women. (See, for example, Ephesians 5:23–32.)

+ Hebrew feminine nouns are often used in the Old Testament to refer to male or female persons, or groups of people that include both men and women. (See Isaiah 12:6; 40:9 NKJV; ASV; Psalm 68:11 NASB.)

+ Isaiah 40:9 speaks of a woman who brings *good tidings* to Zion. This woman certainly brought "good tidings" to Jerusalem, to all people—men and women—who would hear her.

In Conclusion

Many women are mentioned in the Old and New Testament—godly women of faith and excellent character, such as Eve, Rahab, Ruth, Naomi, Miriam, Esther, Sarah, and Rebekah; and ungodly women like Jezebel, Michal, the wife of Lot, and Queen Vashti. There were women who were harlots, who destroyed the lives of men as well as themselves. (For a fuller, more enriched study of the notable female personalities mentioned in Scripture, the reader is encouraged to consult Herbert Lockyer's excellent book *All the Women of the Bible.*) Yet there is not a single command in the Old Testament telling women to be silent or to refrain from speaking unless men were present. In the light of the context of the Old Testament (the old covenant), such commands are not to be found.

9

OLD TESTAMENT PROPHECIES OF NEW TESTAMENT TIMES

There is no doubt that, with the coming of the Lord Jesus Christ, a new dispensation, a new arrangement of God, was ushered in. Not only did Christ become the Savior of mankind—men and women—but the Holy Spirit came and raised the status of men and women "in Christ" to a level not seen under the old covenant. The new covenant made possible the restoration of all that man and woman had lost in the fall.

Jesus Himself spoke much about the coming of the Holy Spirit and His ministry in the church—the people of God, the new community—as well as His operations in the world, including His power to convict sinners.

The Holy Spirit would come in fulfillment of not only the promise of Jesus but also many Old Testament prophecies, especially the prophecy of Joel given several hundreds of years before Christ came. It was a prophecy that concerned *"these last days"* (Hebrews 1:2), and it is found in Joel 2:28–32. The Old Testament times are spoken of as "the former days," while this new dispensation is spoken of as *"these last days."*

We will note in full the prophecy of Joel, and then Peter's quotation of that prophecy on the day of Pentecost. It should be remembered that the early church had no "New Testament." The New Testament, as we know it, was still in the process of being written; and its authors continually referenced the Old Testament Scriptures for an explanation of all that God was doing in their midst.

The Old Testament	The New Testament
The prophet Joel— Joel 2:28–32	The apostle Peter— Acts 2:14–21
And it shall come to pass afterward that I will pour out My Spirit on all flesh; your sons and your **daughters** *shall prophesy, your old men shall dream dreams, your young men shall see visions. And also on My* **menservants** *and on My* **maidservants** *I will pour out My Spirit in those days. And I will show wonders in the heavens and in the earth: blood and fire and pillars of smoke. The sun shall be turned into darkness, and the moon into blood, before the coming of the great and awesome day of the* LORD. *And it shall come to pass that whoever calls on the name of the* LORD *shall be saved. For in Mount Zion and in Jerusalem there shall be deliverance, as the* LORD *has said, among the remnant whom the* LORD *calls.* (NKJV)	*But Peter, standing up with the eleven, raised his voice and said to them, "Men of Judea and all who dwell in Jerusalem, let this be known to you, and heed my words. For these are not drunk, as you suppose, since it is only the third hour of the day. But this is what was spoken by the prophet Joel: 'And it shall come to pass in the last days, says God, that I will pour out of My Spirit on all flesh; your* **sons** *and your* **daughters** *shall prophesy, your young men shall see visions, your old men shall dream dreams. And on My* **menservants** *and on My* **maidservants** *I will pour out My Spirit in those days; and they shall prophesy. I will show wonders in heaven above and signs in the earth beneath: blood and fire and vapor of smoke. The sun shall be turned into darkness, and the moon into blood, before the coming of the great and awesome day of the Lord. And it shall come to pass that whoever calls on the name of the Lord shall be saved.'"* (NKJV)

In the *"last days,"* beginning with the first coming of Christ and closing with His second coming, God promised to pour out His Spirit on *"all flesh."* Before the cross, the Holy Spirit was available only to chosen vessels of the chosen nation, Israel. After the cross, the Holy Spirit was made available to all people of all nations.

Before the cross, the Holy Spirit came upon the select few—mostly men, with a few women. After the cross, the Holy Spirit came upon many people, both men and women, without distinction. The Spirit was poured out on all flesh. Not only this, but the Spirit was made available to Jews and Gentiles alike—to the chosen nation, and then to all nations without distinction.

Before the cross, the seal of the Abrahamic covenant was circumcision, an option exclusive to males. After the cross, the seal of the new covenant, which became the circumcision of the heart, was available to both males and females. It is of the heart, of the spirit, and not of the flesh. Under the old covenant, only males were chosen to be priests. Under the new covenant, all believers, men and women, are *"kings and priests unto God and his Father"* (Revelation 1:6; see also Revelation 5:9–10). All this is because of the Spirit.

The Holy Spirit confirmed all that Jesus said about Him. He confirmed the prophecy of Joel made several hundred years prior to Christ's birth. The Holy Spirit was made available to sons and daughters, to servants and handmaidens. That is, the Holy Spirit came upon men and women, regardless of nationality, social status, and other distinctions. The Holy Spirit is now available for *all* men and women who are "in Christ."

The tragedy is that various schools of opinion would place restrictions on what the Holy Spirit can do in and through men and women, especially women.

The prophecy of Joel is clear and not enigmatic. The Holy Spirit is equally available to men and to women, and He can use men and women in any areas of ministry, as He wills, without any man-made restrictions.

It is a new day, a new dispensation, a new era, a new covenant. The work of the Holy Spirit under the old covenant was vastly different from His work under the new covenant. This is true for both men and women, and even more for women who are "in Christ." It is inconsistent to teach that the new covenant is better than the old covenant (see Hebrews 7:22; 8:6) while misusing the writings of Paul to prohibit women from participating in Spiritfilled functions and ministry.

10

THE ORAL LAW—THE TALMUD

A careful study of the Old Testament Scriptures shows that the family was highly honored. The family unit of father, mother, and children is set forth as God's ideal. And in Israel, the calling by God of men and women alike to divine service was recognized, accepted, and honored.

Over the years, however—especially as a result of the Babylonian captivity and the formation of the Talmudic writings—there developed a distinctly negative attitude toward women that is not found in the Scriptures. This attitude stemmed from the impression that because the first woman, Eve, ushered sin and death into the world, all women are forever guilty before God, and the whole human race, for Eve's crime.

When the Lord Jesus was on earth, the Jews frequently complained that He did not conform to their religious traditions. These traditions— the comments and decrees of their elders from the time of Ezra onward— were called the spoken or oral law.

The Jews, generally speaking, still regard the oral law as authoritative—often of equal authority as the Old Testament Scriptures. During the second century after Christ, the oral law was compiled into a book— the Talmud—consisting of fourteen large folio volumes written in Hebrew and Aramaic.

Even after Pentecost, many of the believing Jews continued to see the oral law as binding on them. These Jews would become the Judaizers who opposed Paul and caused him such trouble in the young churches he established, as may be seen in his epistles to the Galatians and the Corinthians. Some of the views and "laws" of the Talmud, taught by these legalistic Judaizers, brought confusion into the churches regarding the proper roles of men and women in the new covenant community.

The following are sample quotations from the apocryphal book of Ecclesiasticus, also known as The Wisdom of Ben Sirach:

+ *"All wickedness is but little to the wickedness of a woman: let the portion of a sinner fall upon her"* (Ecclesiasticus [Sira] 25:19).

+ *"Of the woman came the beginning of sin, and through her we all die"* (Ecclesiasticus [Sira] 25:24).

+ *"If she go not as thou wouldest have her, cut her off from thy flesh, and give her a bill of divorce, and let her go"* (Ecclesiasticus [Sira] 25:26). (This verse helps us to understand how easy it was for Jewish men to divorce a woman for any and every cause. [See Matthew 19:3.])

+ *"The whoredom of a woman may be known in her haughty looks and eyelids"* (Ecclesiasticus [Sira] 26:9).

+ *"A shameless woman shall be counted as a dog..."* (Ecclesiasticus [Sira] 26:25).

+ *"For from garments cometh a moth, and from women wickedness"* (Ecclesiasticus [Sira] 42:13).

Such Scriptures reveal a negative attitude toward women. The tragedy is that, after the Greek version of the Old Testament was completed in Alexandria (285 BC), these uninspired apocryphal writings were also translated and incorporated into that version. The Scriptures in Hebrew were set aside, and this Greek version, along with the Apocrypha, became the accepted version of God's Word. The apocryphal writings were counted as of equal authority as the inspired writings.

Many of the early church fathers quoted the Apocrypha as authoritative and were influenced by its writings, even though not one book of the Apocrypha is ever quoted in the New Testament.

But the evil seeds of negative words and attitudes toward women because of the first woman's sin had been sown into the minds of Jewry.

John A. Anderson, in *Women's Warfare & Ministry*, exposes this changed attitude toward women as evidenced in the Jewish Talmud. He cites two notable women from Old Testament times, Deborah and Huldah, who were called to be prophetesses in Israel.

Writes Anderson: "Pride does not become women. Two women were proud and they both had unlovely names. One was BEE (Deborah), and one CAT (Huldah). Of Deborah it is written 'And she sent and called Barak and went not herself.' And of Huldah it is said, 'Say unto the man that sent you unto me.' And she did not say, 'Unto the king.'"[3]

The oral law provides the following rules concerning women:

- "Women may bequeath on death to their children, their brothers and husbands but cannot inherit from them"—Baba Bathra.

- "One must not accept bailments from women, from slaves or children"—Baba Bathra.

- "A woman should not read in the Torah (Law) for the honour of the Synagogue"—Megilla.

- "Rather have the roll of the Law burned than have it taught to women"—Rabbi Eliezer.

- "The testimony of one hundred women is not equal to that of one man."

- "The witness-oath applied to men and not to women" (Oaths). Thus the evidence of women cannot be taken under oath.

- "A man's corpse may be laid in the street over which to hold an oration, but not a woman's. The greatest man in the city may accompany a man's corpse, but he is not to be troubled over a woman's corpse"—Ebel Rabbathie.

- "It is a shame for a woman to let her voice be heard among men"—Megilla.

---

3. John A. Anderson, *Women's Warfare & Ministry* (Chief Jewish Rabbi. Braemar, Aberdeenshire, UK), 12–13.

The Talmud records that Rabbi Eliezer reproved a lady for asking a question about the law while in the synagogue. In the synagogue, women were denied recognition. A congregation consisted of at least ten men—no matter how many women were present, only the men counted. Under the oral law, the woman was dishonored in life and in death. Contempt was heaped upon her, and she was basically considered a non-person. Meanwhile, in the home, Jewish mothers were honored.

Other quotations are noted here also:

+ "A hundred women are not better than two men."

+ "When a boy comes into the world, peace comes into the world; when a girl comes, nothing comes"—Babylonian Talmud.

+ "A woman is a pitcher full of filth with its mouth full of blood, yet all run after her"—Babylonian Talmud (Shabboth 152A).

+ "Let the words of the Law be burned rather than they should be delivered to a woman"—Rabbi Eleazer, Talmud. Rabbinical prohibitions even ruled out a mother's teaching the Torah to her own children. (Timothy, having a Greek father and a Jewish mother and grandmother, however, had been blessed from a child to have been given knowledge of the Scriptures. [See 2 Timothy 1:5; 3:15.])

+ "The wise men have commanded that no man should teach his daughter the Law for this reason: that the majority of them have not got a mind fitted for study, but pervert the words of the Law on account of the poverty of their minds"—The Talmud.

+ "Men come to learn, and women come to hear"—Jewish Law.

+ "Whoever teaches his daughter the Torah is like one who teaches her lasciviousness."

Women were not privileged to receive an education in the ancient pagan world. The Greeks did not educate their women. Jewish rabbis expressly forbade women direct access to God's Law. They taught that women's minds were incapable of learning.

Socrates used to say every day that there were three blessings for which he was grateful to Fortune: "First, that I was born a human being and not one of the brutes; next, that I was born a man and not a woman; thirdly, a Greek and not a barbarian."

The Jewish version of this statement, obviously influenced by the Greco-Roman worldview, was captured by the rabbi who said, "Every day you should say, Blessed are You, O God, that I am not a brute creature (a dog), nor a Gentile, nor a woman" (Talmud tractate Menanoth, 43b. Epstein Translation).

Another, similar version recited in the liturgical Morning Prayer of devout Jewish males during the time of Christ and of Paul went like this:

"Blessed be He who did not make me a Gentile;

Blessed is He who did not make me a woman;

Blessed be He who did not make me an uneducated man (or a slave)"—Tosefta.

William Barclay writes that women had no part in the synagogue services. They were sequestered in a section of the synagogue where they could not be seen and where they could not participate in the worship.

Strict rabbis would not talk to a woman in public, not even their wives, daughters, or sisters. Some Pharisees even closed their eyes when they saw a woman approaching.

It was into this kind of Jewish world and culture that Jesus came! It was the Babylonian Talmudic traditions of the elders that Christ and His apostles had to overthrow. First, the apostles themselves had to be delivered from acceptance of and adherence to these traditions. The church fathers evidenced a bias against women because of their acceptance of the Talmudic and apocryphal writings as authoritative. Many cruel and heartless things were done and said concerning women, in large part because society had been infected by the evil attitudes of the Talmudic writings.

Understanding this backdrop provides us with greater insights and understanding of Christ's ministry of grace and kindness to women. No wonder women loved Jesus and were drawn to Him! He was the Savior of all—both men and women. Understanding this setting also throws additional light on the writings of Paul in his epistles to the churches concerning the roles of men and women in the new covenant community, as will be seen more fully in later chapters.

But let us now proceed to our next chapter, "Then Jesus Came."

11

THEN JESUS CAME

When Jesus came as "the seed of the woman" to "bruise the serpent's head" (see Genesis 3:15), He came to redeem men and women back to God and through redemption restore both back to Edenic glory and more. He came as the Emancipator of mankind. He was the greatest Friend of men and women.

But Jesus came to a male-dominated Jewish culture. Judaism was basically a man's religion that devalued and suppressed women. The teachings of the Talmud, the Apocrypha, and the traditions of the elders prevailed over the authority of the inspired Scriptures.

Jesus came to change all that. Sin had marred or destroyed the male-female partnership of the Edenic covenant, and He came to redeem and restore men and women back to God, to reconcile their relationship with God and with one another, as God originally intended. Jesus came to make access to God available for all.

Jesus treated men and women as having equal value before God, and He sought to bring all people back to God's highest level, God's original purpose, and to lift man from his fallen state. His coming ushered in a new day of grace. This is evidenced in the biblical record of what Jesus said, did, and was. The four Gospels illustrate Christ's efforts to emancipate women from the bondages of tradition and of Talmudic law and to bring them into the liberty of the gospel of Christ. Jesus came to establish the kingdom of God, which meant cutting right across Jewish culture, including the religious and social taboos that were contrary to God's holy Word.

Jesus was not a male chauvinist, nor was He a secular feminist. Again, He saw men and women as having equal value in the sight of His Father God, and He respected and treated both accordingly. Men were not treated as superior, nor were women treated as inferior.

A study of the Gospels shows Jesus cutting right across the traditions of the elders and the Talmudic laws—and angering the religious leaders in the process. When the Pharisees and scribes asked Jesus, *"Why walk not thy disciples according to the tradition of the elders…?"* (Mark 7:5; see also Matthew 15:2), Jesus told them that they laid aside the commandments of God in order to keep their own traditions, the traditions of men, which made of no effect the Word of God. (See Mark 7:6–13.)

Christian tradition makes much of the twelve male apostles in the Gospels, because they were *"the twelve apostles of the Lamb"* (Revelation 21:14). The Gospels are most often viewed as the ministry of Christ and the twelve. However, a major underlying theme running through the four Gospels is that of Christ's ministry to women. This chapter will note, in particular, the ministry of Jesus to women in the four Gospels, and the ways in which Jesus elevated women in value, to prepare men and women alike for their roles and functions in the redeemed community—the new-covenant church! The redemption Christ enacted forever changed the roles of men and women.

The Gospels pay particular attention to, and place particular emphasis on, women. Surely, this fact points to, and is meant to prepare us for, the new-covenant times, when men and women would be partners together in the redemptive community—the church!

Jesus and Women in the Gospel of Matthew

We will begin our discussion by considering the gospel of Matthew, where the emphasis on women contradicts many of the traditions and biases of the Jews' religion. Surely, this is so because the account was written under the inspiration of the Holy Spirit, to reveal God's purposes for women in the redemptive process.

✦   Hebrew genealogies predominantly mention the names of the first-born males—no females. Yet the genealogy of Jesus, as laid out in Matthew, mentions five women by name. (See Matthew 1:1–16.) And what a significant list of names in the genealogy of the incarnate Messiah! There is:

> ›   Tamar—Matthew 1:3. Tamar conceived by her father-in-law, Judah, and continued Judah's line after the deaths of his sons Er and Onan. (See Genesis 46:12.) It was not a good beginning.

> ›   Rahab—Matthew 1:5. Rahab was the heroine of the battle of Jericho, yet she was a harlot, and a Gentile—a Canaanite. But she came into grace through faith, and entered into the line of the Messiah. (See Joshua 2:1–21; 6:17–25; Hebrews 11:30–31.)

> ›   Ruth—Matthew 1:5. Ruth was a Moabite, of Lot's line, and certainly not nobility. Yet she became the mother of Obed by Boaz, and grandmother of King David. She came into the chosen race by grace.

> ›   Bathsheba (the wife of Uriah)—Matthew 1:6. Through an adulterous relationship with David, she conceived Solomon. Grace brought her into the line of Messiah.

> ›   Mary—Matthew 1:16. Mary, a pure virgin, became the mother of Jesus through a miraculous conception by the power of the Holy Spirit. (See Matthew 1:20–21.) God gave to her, a woman, the highest, most esteemed role ever: that of bringing forth the Savior of all mankind.

The Messiah's genealogy included Hebrew and Gentile women. What redemptive grace is seen in Matthew's mention of these women by name. Had the account been edited by the dictates of male-dominated Judaism, such would not have been the case. But Matthew was guided by the Holy Spirit, not the prevailing spirit of the times.

✦   Jesus told parables featuring men *and* women, including:

> The parable of a man sowing a mustard seed—Matthew 13:31–32

> The parable of the two sons—Matthew 21:28–32

> The parable of the two men in the field—Matthew 24:40

> The parable of the woman and the leavened meal—Matthew 13:33

> The parable of the two women grinding at the mill—Matthew 24:41

> The parable of the wise and foolish virgins—Matthew 25:1–13

o When the woman with an issue of blood touched Jesus, not only was she instantly healed, but Jesus commended her for her faith. (See Matthew 9:20–22; Mark 5:34.) It would have been against the law for a woman with ceremonial defilement and uncleanness to touch a man, and more so a rabbi. The Jews feared defilement. No Pharisee or scribe would have dared to let that woman touch him. And yet, as she touched the hem of Jesus' garment, healing virtue flowed from Him to her.

o Jesus raised the daughter of the ruler Jairus from the dead. (See Matthew 9:18–19, 23–26.) According to the law, touching a dead bone or a dead body made one ceremonially defiled—unclean—for several days. In this case, however, the clean One cleansed the unclean. The Undefiled never became defiled. (See Hebrews 7:26.) Because Jesus was the perfectly clean, sinless One, anything unclean that He touched became clean.

o In fielding questions about adultery, Jesus addressed the real issue—adultery of the heart, the mind, more than the actual deed or act. (See Matthew 5:28–32.) Jewish Law permitted a man to divorce his wife "for any cause," yet Jesus reproved this practice and He called it sin.

o Jesus honored John the Baptist, then declared that the least in the kingdom—women, according to the Jews—was greater than John. (See Matthew 11:11.)

o Jesus spoke highly of the queen of Sheba, a Gentile queen who came from a far country to hear the wisdom of Solomon and see the glory of his kingdom. Yet the Jews rejected the wisdom of the One *"greater than Solomon"* (Matthew 12:42) and the message of the kingdom of God.

o Jesus tested the faith of a Gentile woman by taking the traditional Jewish stance toward Gentile women. She was a Canaanite, yet she had the faith to overcome racial, gender, and social barriers in order to see her demon-possessed daughter delivered by Jesus. Jesus commended her faith, and her daughter was immediately healed. (See Matthew 15:22–28; Mark 7:25–30.) This event pointed to the entrance of the Gentiles by faith in Christ, into the kingdom of God.

o Jesus honored the institute of marriage. He confirmed that marriage was to be indissoluble in nature, because the union of one wife and one husband was God's original pattern. (See Matthew 19:3–11.) Jesus did not endorse polygamy, even though the practice was permitted under the law of Moses. Jesus condemned divorce "for every cause" but one. (See Deuteronomy 24:1–3; Mark 10:2–12.) Jesus condemned fornication and adultery, as did the Law, to protect the sanctity of marriage and women. (See Matthew 5:27–32; John 8:1–11.) By doing this, Jesus countered the male mentality that allowed for a husband to divorce his wife for almost any reason. Jesus spoke of men's hardness of heart as He sought to bring men and women alike back to God's original purposes in Eden.

o   In the house of Simon the leper in Bethany, Jesus allowed a notorious woman to anoint His head with precious ointment. She let her hair down in front of Him, and He allowed her to touch Him. The disciples reacted harshly against this woman, but Jesus commended her for her loving act and for her insight concerning His coming death and burial. He declared that her act of faith would be preached in all the world for a memorial of her. (See Matthew 26:6–13; Luke 7:36–50.)

o   Matthew is the only gospel writer who recorded the account of Pilate's wife approaching her husband after her God-given dream, and seeking the release of Jesus. (See Matthew 27:19.) If Pilate had listened to his wife, he might have prevented the eternal injustice seen in the crucifixion of the Christ of God, related in detail in the nineteenth chapter of John's gospel.

o   Women followed Jesus to Calvary's cross when the men had forsaken Him. The daughters of Jerusalem wept on the route to Calvary, as Jesus comforted them with His words. (See Matthew 27:55–56; Mark 15:40–41; Luke 23:49–55.)

o   When most of the apostles had fled or left for other reasons, it was a group of women, including Mary Magdalene; Mary, the mother of James and Joses; and the mother of Zebedee's children, who remained at the cross and witnessed Christ's death. (See Matthew 27:55–56.)

o   Women were also last at the tomb and saw how the body of Jesus was laid and how He was buried. Mary Magdalene and another Mary sat over against the tomb until it was sealed. (See Matthew 27:57–61.)

o Women were the first witnesses of the resurrected Christ. They were the first witnesses of the empty tomb. The angel of the Lord told the women that Jesus was risen, invited them to come and see where the Lord had lain, and then ordered them to go and tell the disciples (male and female) that Christ was indeed risen. (See Matthew 28:1–8.)

o Jesus personally appeared to Mary Magdalene in the garden near His tomb. (See Matthew 28; John 20:11–18.) She told the disciples she had seen the Lord and relayed the words He had spoken to her. Perhaps because a woman—Eve—sinned in the garden of Eden, Jesus appears to another woman—Mary—at the garden tomb, revealing Himself as the risen Christ!

o Women were the first to be greeted by the resurrected Christ Himself, to touch His nail-pierced feet and to worship Him. (See Matthew 28:9–10.) Jesus appeared personally to the women before He showed Himself to any of the male apostles, and those women were sent to tell the apostles. (See Matthew 28:7; Luke 24:1–10, 22.)

o The other three Gospels show that the male disciples did not believe the witness and testimony of the women. Jesus reproved them for their unbelief. (See, for example, Mark 16:9–14.) The Talmud did not acknowledge as legitimate the witness or testimony of a hundred women over against one man, but these women were authentic witnesses of the risen Christ.

It is significant that women were witnesses to some of the most important events of Christ's ministry here on earth: His death, His burial, and His resurrection. Women were the first to report the news of His resurrection to the disciples—to the men! But because of a culturally and religiously ingrained prejudice against women, the men doubted their testimony. The testimony of women was not accepted in Jewish courts of law. Jesus defied that law by instructing the women to witness and testify of His resurrection—whether or not the men believed it! He confirmed their testimony subsequently by numerous appearances to the men and the women. Every gospel confirms that women were the first witnesses of the risen Christ—not the men! (See Matthew 28:1–10; Mark 16:1–8; Luke 24:1–12; John 20:1–18.)

What manifest grace! He who was *"the seed of the woman"* came to re-deem both men and women, to reconcile them to the Father. He humbled Himself to be born of a woman to emancipate both men and women from the kingdom of Satan.

Jesus and Women in the Gospel of Mark

Some of the following examples are also seen in the gospel of Matthew and have already been presented, but there are nuances of detail that make them worth mentioning again.

+ Jesus healed the mother of Simon's wife when she was sick with a fever. He took her by the hand, and immediately the fever left her. She rose and served Him. (See Mark 1:29–31.) Jesus had no fear of defilement by touching her. Again, this attitude was opposite that of the rabbis of His time. To touch any woman besides one's wife, regardless of the circumstances, was highly improper, especially for a Jewish rabbi. It was also improper for a woman to serve a meal to a Jewish rabbi. Jesus defied all these man-made traditions. (See also Matthew 8:14–15; Luke 4:38–39.)

+ Jesus raised the concept of family above the natural definition of the term. When the disciples told Him that His mother and broth-ers desired to see Him, Jesus replied, "Who is my mother, or my brethren?...For whosoever shall do the will of God, the same is my brother, and my sister, and mother" (Mark 3:33, 35; see also Mat-thew 12:46–50; Luke 8:19–21.) In so doing, He taught that only those who do the will of God are truly His brothers and sisters— His family. It did not matter whether they were male or female; the deciding factor was whether they were doing the will of God. This is basically a repudiation of the natural and temporal by that which is spiritual and eternal. "First the natural, afterward the spiritual" is the principle Jesus was teaching here. (See 1 Corinthians 15:46.)

+ Jesus raised the daughter of Jarius from the dead. He took her by the hand, and resurrection life entered into her. (See Mark 5:22–23, 35–43.) He who was the Resurrection and the Life did not fear any defilement from touching a dead body. The daughter was twelve, considered to be of marriageable age. The Pharisees and scribes avoided contact with the dead as much as possible.

+ Jesus allowed the woman with an issue of blood to touch the hem of His garment, and she was instantly healed of a disease that would have excluded her from all religious rituals, as she was unclean, a defiled person. (See Mark 5:25–34.) It was an act of public humiliation for Jesus to expose her before the crowd when He perceived that virtue had gone from Him, but Jesus cut across Jewish prejudices by commending her for her bold faith and by calling her "daughter." (See also Matthew 9:20–22; Luke 8:43–48.)

+ Jesus ministered to the Syrophoenician woman—a Gentile. (See Mark 7:24–30.) Jesus tested her by His following Jewish tradition. He speaks of the Gentile dogs who eat the crumbs from their master's table. The woman stood the test, and her faith was rewarded with the instantaneous healing of her daughter. As a Gentile woman, she scaled cultural, social, and gender barriers to faith in Christ. This foreshadowed the coming into faith of the Gentiles in the book of Acts and the reception of the gospel by the Gentile world. (See also Matthew 15:22–28.)

+ Jesus honored widows. Sitting over against the temple treasury, He commended a widow who threw in a mite, in contrast to the rich men who did not even miss what they could well afford to give. In Jesus' day, the religious leaders generally exploited widows. Jesus told the disciples that this widow had given all her living. (See Mark 12:41–44; Luke 20:21:1–4.)

+ Under the old covenant, only kings, prophets, and priests were anointed—and always by other men, never by women. Yet Jesus allowed women to anoint His head and His feet. (See Mark 14:3–9;

see also Matthew 26:6–13; Luke 7:36–50; John 12:1–8.) No priest, Pharisee, or scribe would have permitted such an act, certainly not by a woman. The Pharisees and even the apostles were quite indignant about the kind of women who presumed to anoint Jesus and touch Him in such a manner. One woman wept tears on His feet and then wiped His feet with her hair—her "glory." (See 1 Corinthians 11:15.)

* Mark's gospel confirms what the other gospels say about the women who witnessed the death, burial, and resurrection of the Lord Jesus. (See Mark 15:40–16:8.) Women were last at the cross and the tomb, and first at the resurrection. They were the first witnesses who gave the message of the resurrected Christ to the disciples—to men. (See also Matthew 27:57–28:10; Luke 23:50–54; John 20:1–2, 11–18.) The stone was rolled away to let the men in to see the empty grave clothes, not to let Jesus out of the tomb. (See Mark 16:4; see also Matthew 28:16–17; Luke 24:10–12, 13–35; John 20:2–10.)

* Prior to His ascension, Jesus commissioned men and women alike to take the gospel into all the world. (See Mark 16:15.) Men and women were to preach the gospel to every creature, with signs following the preaching of the Word. (See also Matthew 28:19–20; Acts 1:8.)

The gospel of Mark simply confirms all that Matthew recorded. Jesus respected women. He honored them. He commanded them to be His witnesses, and gave to women the great honor of witnessing His death, burial, and resurrection!

Jesus and Women in the Gospel of Luke

The book of Luke has been called "the gospel of womanhood" because of its emphasis on women and their relationship to Jesus.

In his *Guide to the Gospels*, W. Graham Scroggie writes:

[A] characteristic of Luke's Record is his portraits of womanhood. Study the incomparable accounts of Elisabeth, and the Virgin (i-ii), of Anna (ii), of Martha and Mary (x), and his references to Mary called Magdalene, to Joanna, to Susanna (vii. 2, 13). There are also his graphic pictures of the widow of Nain, of the woman who was a sinner, of the woman who was "bowed together," and of the women who ministered to Jesus of their substance (vii, xiii, viii).

In addition to these Luke introduces an interrupting woman (xi. 27), a woman sweeping in a house (xv. 8ff.), a persistent widow (xviii. 1 ff), women who "bewailed and lamented" Jesus (xxiii. 27), women who witnessed the crucifixion (xxiii. 49) and women in the resurrection story (xxiv).

The word "woman" occurs in Matthew 30 times, in Mark, 19 times, in John, 19 times, but in Luke, 43 times; and it is worthy of note that the gospels have no record of any woman who actually opposed Jesus Himself during His ministry.

Not without reason has this been called "the Gospel of womanhood become Christian, or on its way to Christ." It is impressive that these notices of women are given in the Gospel for the Gentiles, for among them especially woman was degraded, and all of them who came into contact with the Saviour could have said, "Christ first taught us that we were women." The Rabbis in their liturgy thanked God that they were not born women, but Christ has enfranchised them socially and spiritually, and has given them a place of great honour in history.

For a good illustration of the prominence given to women in this Gospel,...compare chap. xi. 31, 32 with Matt. xii. 41, 42, and note that in the latter passage the "men" are mentioned first, but in Luke, "the queen." Note, also, that Matthew says, "The men of Nineveh shall rise in judgment with this generation" (xii. 41), but Luke says, "a queen of the south shall rise up in the judgment with the men of this generation" (xi. 31). Every woman, and especially women in the East, should thank God for this Gospel.[4]

---

4. W. Graham Scroggie, *A Guide to the Gospels* (Grand Rapids, MI: Kregel Publications, 1995), 374–375.

Luke authored both his gospel and the Acts of the Apostles, so the same theme continues in the latter book, as will be seen in due time. In outline form, we note further details on what Scroggie has so excellently written.

1. The Annunciation to Mary of the Christ Child is given in Luke 1:26–38. The angel Gabriel appeared to the Virgin Mary, announcing the birth of the Messiah through her. The greatest honor of bringing forth the Messiah, the Savior of the world, was given to a virgin woman—not to a man. A woman was the first to hear of the divine incarnation. The birth would be a miraculous birth. As were the births of Ishmael (see Genesis 16:7–12), Isaac (see Genesis 17:1–21), and Samson (see Judges 13:2–21), so would be the birth of Jesus. There was a divine or angelic appearance, a sense of fear, a message giving the name and mission of the child, and a corresponding sign.

2. Mary, Joseph's wife, accepted in total faith the word of the angel and the responsibility of being the mother of Messiah, the incarnate Christ. The prophecies of "the daughter of Zion" (see, for example, Isaiah 37:22) could well apply to Mary in her response to Gabriel's prophetic word of the mystery of the incarnation.

3. Where did Luke obtain this information? Undoubtedly from Mary and Elizabeth themselves—their own personal testimony and experience. (See Luke 1:1–4.) He took them at their word, as no men were around when the divine visitations took place.

4. The Song of Mary ("The Magnificat") is found in Luke 1:46–55. Mary, the virgin, acknowledged her need of salvation when she sang, *"My soul doth magnify the Lord, and my spirit hath rejoiced in God my Savior"* (Luke 1:46–47). It was a prophetic song, as was the utterance of Elizabeth in Luke 1:42–45. The spirit of prophecy was upon them both. At the glorious announcement of the birth of John the Baptist, Messiah's forerunner, and then of the birth of Messiah by the Virgin Mary, the Spirit came on these women.

5. Anna the prophetess spoke of redemption in Jerusalem. (See Luke 2:36–38.) The temple priests recognized and accepted her as a prophetess and allowed her to minister accordingly.

6. Luke 2:1–40 records the birth of Jesus by the Virgin Mary. Jesus was born of Mary in fulfillment of the prophetic word concerning the seed of the woman. (See Genesis 3:15.) What exaltation of womanhood is seen here, that the very Son of God Himself was born of a virgin woman! (See Matthew 1:18–25.)

7. Jesus, as a young boy of twelve, realized that He must be about His Father's business. He told His earthly parents, Joseph and Mary, the truth of this. Even though Mary did not fully understand the statement, she kept Jesus' words in her heart. (See Luke 2:41–52.)

8. Jesus had earthly kin, including a mother, brothers and sisters, a cousin, and an aunt. (See Mark 6:3; Luke 1:36; John 19:25.) He recognized these natural relationships but also realized that the spiritual superseded the natural, as was seen when He said that those who did the will of God were His true mother, brothers, and sisters.

9. Jesus ministered to the widow of Nain by raising her only son from the dead. He was not concerned about becoming defiled by touching the dead, for He was the Resurrection and the Life. Like the prophets Elijah and Elisha, who also raised the dead, so did the Lord Jesus. Jesus did not concern Himself with the laws of uncleanness. He ministered to a brokenhearted widow and brought the joy of her existence back to life. (See Mark 1:29–31; Luke 7:11–17.) Jesus devoted time and energy to widows in need. He mentioned the widow of Zarephath and how the prophet Elijah was sent to her. (See Luke 4:24–26.)

10. Jesus ministered forgiveness to a woman and commended her great faith. She was a sinful woman, and defiled according to the law. Yet Jesus ignored the taboos of His time and let a woman touch Him. He accepted her devotion. (See Luke 7:36–50; John 8:17.) Because she had been forgiven much, she loved much. She

knew firsthand faith and peace and sins forgiven through her encounter with Jesus. The Pharisees would never have associated with the likes of her, let alone allow a woman to touch them. Her act was totally improper, especially for a rabbi, but Jesus was the Savior of the world—the Savior of men and women.

11. Jesus allowed women to accompany Him on His ministry tours. They ministered to Him of their substance as He went from town to town. They traveled along with the male apostles. Joanna is mentioned by name; she was the wife of Chuza, Herod's steward. (See Matthew 27:55–56; Luke 8:1–3; 23:49–24:11; John 19:25–27.) It meant that these women heard Jesus' words, absorbed His preaching and teaching, and witnessed His ministry of healing and miracles.

12. By contrast, according to the dictates of Judaism, women were allowed to hear the Word of God in the synagogue but could not be the disciple of a rabbi (unless that rabbi was their husband). But Jesus taught women from the Word of God. Women traveled on His ministry team, along with the twelve.

13. Here again in Luke's gospel, Jesus confirmed that only those who do the will of God are, in spiritual reality, the family of God. (See Luke 8:19–21; 11:27–28.) Obedience to the will of God is what matters.

14. Luke also records the account of Jesus raising Jarius' daughter from the dead. (See Luke 8:41–42, 49–56.) Uncleanness and death never defiled Jesus. He was the Resurrection and the Life.

15. Luke also includes an account of the woman with the issue of blood touching Jesus and receiving miraculous healing. (See Luke 8:43–48.) Jesus did not become ceremonially unclean or defiled by that woman's touch, as a Pharisee or scribe would have become. He who was clean made the unclean clean! Sin, uncleanness, and ceremonial defilement could not touch the sinless Son of God. He was "holy, harmless, undefiled, separate from sinners," yet He was also the Friend of sinners. (See Hebrews 7:26; Matthew 11:19.)

16. Jesus did not silence the woman in the crowd who lifted up her voice in blessing upon Him. (See Luke 11:27–28.)The scribes and Pharisees would have commanded her to be quiet.

17. Jesus spoke of the Queen of the South, the Queen of Sheba, who came to ask Solomon many hard questions. She would rise up with the men in judgment because she responded to the wisdom of King Solomon, while the generation of Jesus rejected His wisdom as the King of Kings. (See Luke 11:31.)

18. The woman crippled by Satan with a spirit of infirmity for eighteen years was loosed from this condition by Jesus as He laid hands on her. (See Luke 13:11–13.) She was a believer, a daughter of Abraham by faith. She glorified God, and Jesus did not silence her. This healing took place on the Sabbath day, much to the indignation of the ruler of the synagogue. Jesus reproved him for his attitude, saying, *"Thou hypocrite, doth not each one of you on the sabbath loose his ox or his ass from the stall, and lead him away to watering? And ought not this woman, being a daughter of Abraham, whom Satan hath bound, lo, these eighteen years, be loosed from this bond on the sabbath day?"* (Luke 13:15–16). The ruler should have rejoiced at the wonderful miracle of the healing of this woman.

19. Luke alone provides for us the wonderful account of Mary and Martha. (See Luke 10:38–42.) Mary and Martha were both disciples of Jesus. On this occasion, Mary is sitting at the feet of the Master, being taught the Word of God. While the rabbis of that time counted women as being incapable of receiving truth, Jesus taught some of the most profound divine truths to women. Women were not supposed to learn, let alone teach. Only male disciples sat at the feet of their teachers. Yet Jesus commended Mary for taking this position as a female disciple. The religious leaders of Christ's day saw women as slaves and servants for men, fit only to be homemakers, housekeepers, and mothers. Jesus defied this way of thinking and showed men and women to be of equal value and learning abilities.

20. Jesus told a parable of a woman finding her lost coin and rejoicing to illustrate the Father's joy in finding lost sinners. (See Luke 15:8–10.)

21. Jesus told His disciples to *"remember Lot's wife"* (Luke 17:32) as an example of "looking back" once a person becomes His disciple. He also spoke in the same context of women grinding at the mill: *"Two women shall be grinding together; the one shall be taken, and the other left"* (Luke 17:35).

22. Jesus told the parable of the widow and her pleas with the unjust judge to avenge her enemy. (See Luke 18:1–8.) He used this story to teach the truth that God hears the prayers of His people when they are persistent in making requests, for He is a just Judge.

23. In answering questions about the life to come, Jesus said that the woman who had seven husbands in this life and age would not be joined to her husbands in the resurrection age. There would be no marriage or death in the age to come. (See Luke 20:27–40.)

24. Jesus commended the widow who had cast all her life's savings into the temple treasury, and this in contrast to the rich men who would not even miss what they gave. (See Luke 21:1–4.) In the temple, there was the court of the women, the court of the Gentiles, and the court of the Priests and Jews. Jesus came to break down these dividing walls that existed between men and women, Jews and Gentiles. Jesus reproved strongly those Jews who exploited widows for their own gain and profit. (See Luke 20:46–47.)

25. Women grieved for Jesus on the way to Calvary. He comforted them and told them not to weep for Him but for the calamities that would soon come on the Jewish nation. He did not silence them. (See Mark 15:40–41; Luke 23:27–31.)

26. Luke confirms the significance of the presence of women at the death, burial, and resurrection of Jesus in that he mentions them by name. The male apostles had fled for their lives, fearing for their own safety. The women remained, and became true eyewitnesses of the last events pertaining to Christ's earthly life. They

witnessed His death (see Luke 23:46–49), His burial in the tomb (see Luke 23:50–56), and His resurrection (see Luke 24:1–11, 22–24). They were sent to witness to the eleven apostles, who did not believe their testimony because of male prejudice.

27. Luke confirms in Acts the same truth concerning the Lord's blessing on both men and women. There were men and women praying together in the upper room, and God promised to pour out His Spirit on men and women. Men and women together believed in the Lord. (See Acts 1:14; 2:18; 5:14.)

Jesus and Women in the Gospel of John

The gospel of John gives a measure of special attention to women, in accounts that are peculiar to John's gospel alone. We will note the most prominent instances.

* In John 2:1–11, we have the first recorded miracle of Jesus. He is at a wedding, and the hosts run out of wine. When Mary, the mother of Jesus, seeks to take command of the situation—and of Jesus—Jesus gently reproves her by saying, "*Woman, what have I to do with thee? mine hour is not yet come!*" (John 2:4). On the surface, His comment does not seem to honor His mother, as the Ten Commandments instruct all to do. (See, for example, Exodus 20:12.) But Mary needed to realize that she was the mother of Jesus according to His humanity, not according to His deity.

* As Jesus hung on the cross, He turned over the responsibility of caring for His earthly mother to the beloved apostle, John. (See John 19:25–27.) The only commandment ever given by Mary, the mother of Jesus, was, "*Whatsoever he saith unto you, do it*" (John 2:5).

* In John 4:4–42, we have the account of Jesus talking with and revealing His identity to the woman of Samaria. The details are remarkable. Jesus destroys national, gender, social, and religious barriers to reach this woman with the message of His salvation. In considering this exchange, it is important to note the following:

> Jesus came to the woman. He had to pass through Samaria, not only geographically but also spiritually, in the Father's will, to meet a needy person.

> The Jews traditionally had no dealings with the Samaritans, so there were national and racial barriers to bridge.

> Jesus, a Man, was talking to a woman alone. He bridged the gender barrier.

> This woman was full of ill repute, a public sinner. She had had five husbands, and the man she was living with then was not her husband. Therefore, she was technically unclean.

> This woman was a Gentile, a Samaritan.

> A rabbi would not have been seen speaking to a woman such as this in public, let alone without others present. Jesus bridged the cultural gap.

> Jesus taught this woman the greatest, most notable passage on worship that is found in all of Scripture. The word "worship" is used some ten times in this passage. This "theology of worship" was not given to a male, or even to the apostles. From where did John obtain this account? Surely, it must have come from the woman herself! This is the richest teaching on worship in the whole Bible, and it was delivered to a woman.

> This woman received a revelation of (1) who Jesus was, (2) what the Father is looking for in the realm of worship, and (3) the marks of a true worshipper.

> Jesus confirmed the marriage relationship of a husband and wife, as God originally intended.

> The woman believed and received Jesus as the promised Messiah. She came to true faith, then went to "the men" of the city and told them all that had happened at the well. The result? The men of the city believed this woman and went to see Jesus for themselves. Many Samaritans came

to faith in Christ, not only because of the woman's witness and testimony but also because they then went and heard Him for themselves. Jesus stayed in Samaria for two days, sharing the good news of the gospel. He certainly did not impose any silence on this woman when it came to her evangelistic witness.

> The disciples were amazed that Jesus would talk to this kind of woman. Did they get the message—that Jesus came to redeem men *and women* back to the Father? This woman was undoubtedly the "firstfruits" of the gospel for that city. Her conversion surely prepared the way for Philip some years later, when he went and evangelized in the city of Samaria, and the church was established there. (See Acts 8.)

♦ In John 8:1–11, we have John's account of Jesus' dealings with a woman caught in the act of adultery. The Pharisees would have had the woman stoned to death, according to the Law of Moses. (See Leviticus 20:10.) Jesus, however, invoked the very law the Pharisees professed to uphold in order to convict their consciences and cause them to drop their suit. Their hypocrisy is seen in the fact that the law of Moses—which they professed to be upholding—demanded that both the man and the woman found in adultery be stoned to death. Why did they not bring the man? Where was the man, if the woman had been caught *"in the very act"* (John 2:4)? Once the Pharisees had left, Jesus ministered grace and truth to the woman. He did not accuse or condemn her. By the law, she was already condemned. But in grace, He forgave her; in truth, He told her to *"go, and sin no more"* (John 2:11). In this wisdom, Jesus upheld the Law of Moses while also ministering *"grace **and** truth"* (John 1:17) to a needy woman.

♦ John 11:1–45 tells of the resurrection of Lazarus by Him who is *"the resurrection, and the life"* (John 11:25). Through this event, Martha and Mary, Lazarus' sisters, came to full faith in Jesus as the Son of the Living God, and confessed their faith. Many are the lessons that may be learned from these two sisters, these women of faith. They were true disciples of Christ Jesus. He was their Friend.

♦ John also records the anointing of Jesus by Mary, as do the other gospels. Jesus broke all the taboos about women touching men, let alone anointing a rabbi with ointment. (See John 12:1–8.)

♦ Jesus spoke about a *"woman…in travail"* (John 16:21) rejoicing after her male child is born. There is no doubt about the enigmatic truth in this saying. It is possible that He was alluding to "the woman" (Eve) and "the seed of the woman" that would be born to crush the serpent's head. (See Genesis 3:15; John 16:21–24; Revelation 12:1–4.) But it would be the woman who would bring forth the Savior of the world—of all mankind.

♦ In John 19:25–28, Jesus showed His compassion on widows when He made provisions for His own mother, Mary, to be cared for by John. And this Jesus did while hanging on the cross, suffering the agonies of crucifixion, in the hour of His death.

♦ The final reference to women in John's gospel relates to Mary Magdalene. (See John 20:1–2, 11–18.) This passage describes Mary's discovery of the empty tomb after Christ's resurrection, her encounter with two angels in the tomb, and her meeting Jesus. At first, she thought He was a gardener, and asked whether He had taken Jesus' body away. But Jesus, as the great Shepherd of the sheep, called her by name: "Mary" (John 20:16). Immediately, she recognized Him as her risen Lord. Jesus then told her to go and tell the brethren that she had seen the Lord. (See John 20:17–18.) Mary was the first to see the risen Christ, and she was chosen to give the supreme witness of His resurrection, and that to men.

One cannot consider the four Gospels and their record of the earthly life of Jesus without noticing that He had a special ministry to women. In concluding this chapter, let me reemphasize several points.

Of all the events recorded in the Gospels, several of the most theologically significant events were witnessed by women in particular. Thus, women are qualified to be *witnesses of the Christ* and to testify of Him. Their testimony stands in any court. At the risk of being repetitious, I have noted again here the most crucial events in the life of Christ, of which women were the major witnesses.

1. The Virgin Birth

The account of the virgin birth of Jesus is built first upon Mary's account of the visit of the angel Gabriel to her, also called the annunciation. Mary alone knew what had happened when she was overshadowed by the Holy Spirit. No man was around. Luke provides these details from Mary in his gospel. Other details must have been given by Joseph, to Matthew, of the angel's assuring word to him of the virgin birth of the Christ Child. (See Matthew 1:18–25.)

2. The Life and Ministry of Christ

There were numerous women who observed the life and ministry of Christ and were touched by the same. What is seen in the four Gospels is the account of just a few of these major events in the life and ministry of Christ, during which He interacted with both men and women. The specific testimonies of women are irrefutable. They "saw and heard" and were therefore qualified to be witnesses and to speak of what they had seen and heard. (See 1 John 1:1–3.)

3. The Crucifixion—His Death

The apostles fled once Jesus was arrested in the garden of Gethsemane. Peter followed "afar off" and wept bitterly after his denial of the Lord. John lingered near the cross until Jesus told him to take care of His mother, Mary. It was the women who saw the final events of the crucifixion, and they must have given testimony to the ones who were chosen and inspired to write the Gospels.

Many women beheld the Lord's death afar off. (See Matthew 27:55; Mark 15:40–41; Luke 23:27–31.) Luke speaks of a *"great company of... women"* (Luke 23:27), who included:

+ Mary Magdalene

+ Mary, the mother of James and Joses

+ The mother of Zebedee's children

- Salome
- Mary, the mother of Jesus (See John 19:25–27.)
- Jesus' mother's sister, Mary, the wife of Cleophas

These women were the last ones present at the cross. So much of the testimony of the Gospels must have come from them and been passed on to the male disciples who wrote it down.

4. His Burial in the Tomb

Two women named Mary were still around when Jesus' body was buried in the tomb. We are told about the Mary who sat over against the tomb. They saw where and how His body was placed in Joseph's tomb. (See Luke 23:55–56.) Women were the last also at the tomb.

5. His Resurrection

Again, women were the first ones at the empty tomb. Mary Magdalene and the other Mary had brought spices to anoint Jesus' body. When they arrived, they found an angel sitting on the stone door in his brightness. These women were the first to receive the declaration that *"he is risen"* (Matthew 28:6). The angel invited them to see where Jesus' body had been laid. Then he instructed them to go and tell the rest of the disciples that Jesus had risen and would see them in Galilee. The women ran to do so, filled with fear and joy. As they were on their way, Jesus appeared to them. They fell at His feet and worshipped Him. He confirmed the angel's words, charging them to inform the disciples of His resurrection and to tell them He would meet them all in Galilee. (See Matthew 28:1–10.)

Mark provides other details. He tells of the *"young man"* (Mark 16:5) in the tomb who spoke of the resurrected Jesus of Nazareth. He told the two women named Mary to go and inform the disciples *and Peter* that Jesus had risen and would meet them in Galilee. (See Mark 16:1–8.)

On that same resurrection day, Jesus Himself appeared first to Mary Magdalene, who had been delivered from seven demonic spirits. She told the disciples, as they were in mourning, that Jesus was alive. But, being that she was a woman, they did not believe her. (See Mark 16:9–11; John 20:1, 11–18.)

Luke names Mary Magdalene, Joanna, Mary the mother of James, and other women with them who told the eleven of Jesus' resurrection. But the eleven counted the words of the women as *"idle tales"* (and did not believe them. (See Luke 24:1–11, 22–24.) The men probably thought the women had dreamed or hallucinated Christ's resurrection due to wishful thinking.

Peter and John went to the tomb to see for themselves, and they found everything to be just as the women had said. (See John 20:1–10.) In the mouth of two or three witnesses, the resurrection story was confirmed. (See Deuteronomy 19:15; John 8:17; Matthew 18:16.) True Bible witnesses must have "seen" and "heard" before they could "witness with the mouth."

What a challenge to male thinking these testimonies must have been. A woman alone knew the truth of the virgin birth of Christ as the answer to Genesis 3:15. Women were the witnesses to the final events of Christ's death, burial, and resurrection. They were also the first witnesses of the resurrected Christ. Last at the cross and first at the tomb—this is the testimony of the women.

These five events were the most crucial events in the earthly life of Jesus, and the Lord Jesus Christ allowed women to be witnesses of them, and to share their testimony with men.

With all that is written in this chapter, there is nothing of women "keeping silence" or being kept from speaking with authority in the presence of men. Christ Himself endorsed these occasions of testimony, and He Himself gave the women the word to proclaim the good news!

Women, therefore, were chief witnesses of Christ's...

1. Incarnation

2. Crucifixion

3. Burial

4. Resurrection

Women were last at the cross, first at the tomb, and the first witnesses of the resurrection of the Christ of God. As such, they were truly qualified to witness and testify of all that they had seen and heard!

In Conclusion

Even a cursory consideration of Jesus' earthly life provides great insight into His attitude toward men and women.

Jesus broke with the traditions of the elders. He undercut the Babylonian Talmudic laws. He rejected Apocryphal teachings. Jesus broke with the taboos and bondages of legalistic Judaism and Phariseeism.

He honored men and women equally. He blessed widows. He taught women as His disciples and accepted the ministrations of women. He talked freely with women, as well as with men. He healed women, regardless of ceremonial uncleanness or the risk of defilement. He let them touch Him, wash His feet, dry Him with their hair, and anoint Him with precious ointment. What would have defiled the religious leaders never defiled Jesus.

And then, women—not the male apostles—witnessed the most important events of Jesus' death, burial, and resurrection. He specifically instructed women to go and tell His male disciples about His resurrection. Jesus never told women to be silent in the presence of men or in His own presence. Women ministered to Him, learned of Him, and testified about Him.

Jesus was always kind and gentle, gracious and forgiving, courteous to, and respectful of women. He honored women and treated them as having equal value with men. He did not discriminate between men and women, as both were made in the image of God. He loved men and women. He came to redeem both sexes back to God, back to relationship with God and with each other, as God originally intended. Through His redemption, He established the new covenant that would restore men and women to the glory of the Edenic covenant—and more!

True Christianity brings the greatest honor, respect, and freedom to women, and this above all other nations and cultures.

The Muslim world degrades women. A Muslim man may divorce his wife with a verbal declaration. The wife is then left to fend for herself, often through prostitution, or risk starvation. A woman involved in adultery is likely to have her hands or feet cut off, or even to be stoned to death. Not so the man.

The Hindu religion degrades women also. Hindus worship the male organs, a total perversion in this system of Satan.

In many parts of Africa, the women are to bear children and be the slaves of the men.

In the Western world, influenced by the Judeo-Christian ethic, women have had the greatest honor, as a whole, in society. However, with the cultural explosion and the rise of humanistic philosophy, feminism, and the women's liberation movement, the great blessings of the family, marriage, and home are being undermined. *"If the foundations be destroyed, what can the righteous do?"* (Psalm 11:3). Male and female humanists spread their philosophies that work like leaven in the educational systems, and all this under the guise of "liberty."

Only the laws of God revealed under the Judeo-Christian ethic can truly protect the family and preserve the institution of marriage and uphold the honor and dignity of men and women. Militant secular feminism and humanism expose their own evils of gender prejudice.

The Lord Jesus came to be the Savior and Redeemer of the world, of mankind, both men and women. He is also the Emancipator of woman and Reverser of the effect of judgment brought about by the fall. A woman—Eve—brought about the fall of men and women. But it was also a woman—Mary—who brought about the birth of the Savior of all mankind, men and women.

12

FOUR POSITION SCHOOLS

In our studies thus far, we have considered the revelation of God and His divine qualities in His eternal being, and then His purpose in creating man and woman. We have seen how the entrance of sin through the fall of man interrupted God's purpose. The roles of men and women in family and in ministry in Israel's history have also been discussed, as were the changes in attitudes toward women that came about because of the Talmudic laws, the traditions of the elders, and the uninspired apocryphal books. It was into this scene that Jesus came to redeem and restore men and women back to God's original purpose, through the new covenant.

Our studies have spanned the old covenant era—the time between the creation of the first Adam to the incarnation of the last Adam, the Lord Jesus Christ. We now progress to a discussion of the role and function of men and women in the new covenant era.

One of the issues that has remained throughout the centuries of church history, and continues today, is that which pertains to the proper roles and functions of men and women in the areas of public ministry and church leadership.

This issue springs largely from two passages from the Pauline letters: 1 Corinthians 14:34–35 and 1 Timothy 2:11–15.

Let your women keep silent in the churches, for they are not permitted to speak; but they are to be submissive, as the law also says. And if they want to learn something, let them ask their own husbands at home; for it is shameful for women to speak in church.

(1 Corinthians 14:34–35 NKJV)

Let a woman learn in silence with all submission. And I do not permit a woman to teach or to have authority over a man, but to be in silence. For Adam was formed first, then Eve. And Adam was not deceived, but the woman being deceived, fell into transgression. Nevertheless she will be saved in childbearing if they continue in faith, love, and holiness, with self-control.

(1 Timothy 2:11–15 NKJV)

Many people ask, "Doesn't Paul teach that women should be silent in the church? Doesn't Paul teach that women are forbidden to teach men or usurp authority over men, and that women are to learn in silence?"

Four major schools of thought and opinion that have arisen out of the interpretation of these Pauline passages. As seen in chapter 1, a person's theology affects his or her hermeneutics, and a person's hermeneutics affects his or her theology. Hermeneutics and theology together affect a person's translation and interpretation of the Hebrew and Greek Scriptures.

As a reminder, it is not so much a matter of inspiration and revelation but a matter of interpretation and application. How are the Pauline passages to be interpreted? What did Paul's writings really mean to the people he was addressing? How are these Pauline passages to be applied in our generation, to situations today?

More specifically, we will consider the following questions:

+ What are the proper roles and functions of men and women relative to home life and church life? Can a woman preach and teach?

- ✦ Can a woman speak before men in church life?

- ✦ Should a woman occupy a leadership role in the church?

- ✦ Should a woman occupy a governmental position in the church?

- ✦ Is a woman to be totally and absolutely *"silent"* in church life?

- ✦ Is the New Testament church to be a male-dominated society, with women in a subordinate role to male rule, both in the home and at church?

These are questions seeking answers in our generation, as they have over many generations.

Following, in brief, is an overview of the four schools of interpretation that have arisen out of the understanding of these Scripture passages.

School One	School Two	School Three	School Four
Denominations that believe, teach and practice:	Denominations that believe, teach and practice:	Denominations that believe, teach and practice:	Denominations that believe, teach and practice:
The role, place, position, and function of women are each restricted to the home as a wife, a mother, and a housekeeper.	The role and function of women is primarily in the home as a wife, a mother and a housekeeper.	The role and function of women includes the home as wife, and mother but also includes church life.	The role of both men and women is in creation and redemption orders. Creation order is home life, and redemption order is church life.

School One	School Two	School Three	School Four
In Church life, silence in its full meaning is imposed on all women. Women have no function in church life. This is based on the Pauline passages in 1 Corinthians and Timothy. Leadership is male.	For church life, women may function in prayer, music, choir, teaching children, and social and spiritual helps. However, no woman is permitted in any position of leadership.	Women have a role in music, choir, prayer, Sunday school teaching of children, spiritual and social work and teaching other women. Women may function in the gifts of the Spirit. Women may go to the mission field for spiritual and social work.	Men and women, as called and equipped by God may function in any area of church life according to the measure of grace and gift given. Men and women are redemptively equal according to Gal. 3:28.
Women are totally restricted in church life.	Women restricted from leadership positions in church life.	Women may function in some leadership roll, but not in ascension-gift ministries or eldership	Men and women may function in any area of church life and leadership position as gifted of God.

As seen here, these are the four positions held by various denominations in the Christian church. These have been columnized above in brief, as an in-depth look is not the purpose of this study. The purpose of this book is to provide scriptural support of the fourth school in its position on the proper role and function of men and women in the redeemed community—the church.

It is to be recognized that the issue of the roles of men and women, and especially the latter, in the church will not be finally resolved until Jesus comes. Every denomination and local congregation needs to decide its own position on the matter.

The following proposition sets forth the position of this text:

"In Christ" there is neither male nor female. All are one in Christ, and Christ is in all. (See Galatians 3:28.) That is to say, men and women are redemptively equal. National, racial, social, cultural, ritual, and gender distinctions are no longer to be viewed as barriers to a person's role and function in the church, the body of Christ.

Therefore, men and women alike are called and equipped of God to function in the body of Christ according to their particular spiritual gifting, whether it be leadership, one of the ascension-gift ministries, deaconship, eldership, or another type of grace-gift. Men and women may function based on their Christlike character qualities, their spiritual maturity, the measure of grace-gifts given them, and the anointing of the Holy Spirit upon them. Both men and women are called to function together in divine order, in love and harmony, as members of the body of Christ, under Christ's headship.

13

PAUL ON CREATION
AND REDEMPTION

Paul's writings on the roles of men and women in his epistles to the Corinthians and to Timothy have caused him to become the most maligned, misunderstood, and misinterpreted apostle of the New Testament. Paul cannot be rightly understood apart from an understanding of Pauline theology.

There is no doubt that Paul presents a dichotomy of theology when it comes to his position on the roles of men and women. He presents what may be called a "creation order" and also a "redemption order." On a number of occasions, Paul blends the creation and redemptive orders together. Creation and redemption are interwoven in the Pauline tapestry of revelation.

How is this seen? Several important "man/woman" passages illustrate this interweaving of the creation and redemption orders. The following chart helps focus this truth more sharply.

A. The Old Creation and the New Creation

The Old-Creation Order	The New-Creation Order
Creation	Redemption
1. In this order, there are male and female, husbands and wives, fathers and mothers, and children.	1. In this order, there is the redemptive community. In Christ, there is neither Jew nor Greek.
2. In this home order, there is the natural house.	2. In Christ, there is neither bond nor free.
3. If a man knows not how to rule his own house…. (See 1 Timothy 3:5.)	3. In Christ, there is neither male nor female.
4. It is first the natural house (1 Timothy 3:1–16), then the spiritual house (1 Corinthians 15:46).	4. In Christ, there is neither circumcision nor uncircumcision.
	5. In Christ there is neither Barbarian nor Scythian.
	6. All are one in Christ, and Christ is all in all.
	7. This is the spiritual house of the living God—the church (Galatians 3:28; Colossians 3:11; 1 Timothy 3:1–16).

B. The Marriage Relationship

Another example of the creation/redemption orders is seen in Ephesians 5:23–33. Here, Paul weaves together the creation/redemption motif. Understanding these interwoven distinctions will help us to understand more clearly and fully the roles of men and women in the redemptive community—the church.

In this passage, Paul weaves together first the natural marriage relationship of a husband and wife, and then the spiritual marriage of Christ and His church. (See 1 Corinthians 15:46.)

Creation Order—The Natural Marriage of a Man and Woman	Redemption Order—The Spiritual Marriage of Christ and His Church
1. Wives, submit to your own husbands.	1. As to the Lord.
2. The husband is the head of the wife.	2. Even as Christ is the head of the church and He is the Savior of the body.
3. Let the wives be subject to their own husbands in everything.	3. As the church is subject to Christ.
4. Husbands, love your wives.	4. Even as Christ also loved the church and gave Himself for it, that He might sanctify it with the washing of water by the Word, that He might present it to Himself a glorious church, not having spot or wrinkle, or any such thing, but that it should be holy and without blemish.
5. So ought men to love their wives as their own bodies. He that loves his wife loves himself. For no man ever hated his own flesh, but nourishes and cherishes it.	5. Even as the Lord the church, for we are members of His body and of His flesh and of His bones.
6. For this cause shall a man leave his father and mother, and shall be joined to his wife and they two shall become one.	6. This is a great mystery, but I speak concerning the Christ and the church.
7. Nevertheless, let every one of you in particular so love his wife as himself, and the wife see that she reverence her husband.	

C. *The Creation of Man and Woman*

Who can fail to see the interweaving of the creation story of Adam and Eve from Genesis 1–2 with the redemption story, of Christ and the church, in 1 Corinthians 11:3–16?

In creation, it is Adam and his bride, Eve. In redemption, it is Christ and His bride, the church. Creation made way for redemption. This is the picture of Scripture revelation.

The Creation Order	The Redemptive Order
1. The Head of every man is Christ, and the head of the woman is the man.	1. And the Head of Christ is God.
2. Man is the image and glory of God, and the woman is the glory of the man.	
3. The man is not of the woman, but the woman is of the man.	
4. Neither was the man created for the woman, but the woman for the man.	
5. Nevertheless, neither is the man without the woman, neither the woman without the man	5. In the Lord.
6. For as the woman is of the man, even so is the man also by the woman.	6. But all things are of God.

Here, again, Paul weaves the creation of man, then the woman from the man from the Genesis story. Adam was created first, then the woman, Eve, taken from Adam's side. Yet every man and woman since the original couple owes his or her conception and birth to a man (a father) and a woman (a mother), so that neither would exist without the other. This reality brings man and woman to the same level, demanding humility on both sides. An understanding of 1 Corinthians 11:3–16 leaves no room for male superiority or female inferiority. Every person, whether man or woman, stands before God as equal with everyone else, owing his or her existence to both sexes and, ultimately, to God the Creator Himself.

D. Creation and the Fall of Adam and Eve

Once again, Paul weaves together the creation/redemption motif, in contrast and in context. The passage of 1 Timothy 2:11–15, outlined here, will be considered more fully in the appropriate place. For now, it is sufficient to note that chapters 1 through 3 of Genesis are woven together in the context of these verses.

There is the creation of man, Adam (see Genesis 1), then the creation of the woman, Eve (see Genesis 2), and then the fall—first of the woman, deceived by the serpent, and then of the man, by willful rebellion (see Genesis 3). But there is also the promise of redemption that would come through the woman, seen in the birth of "Seed of the woman," or the Christ-Child. (See Genesis 3:15; 1 Timothy 2:15 AMP.) The great doctrines of creation, the fall and entrance of sin, and redemption are woven together in this most significant passage of Pauline theology.

The Creation Order	The Redemption Order
1. Let the woman learn in silence with all subjection.	
2. I do not permit a woman to teach nor usurp authority over the man, but to be in silence.	
3. For Adam was first formed, then Eve.	
4. And Adam was not deceived, but the woman being deceived was in (fell into) the transgression.	
5. If they continue in faith, charity, and holiness with sobriety.	5. Notwithstanding, she shall be saved in the bearing of the Christ Child. (AMP)

A careful consideration of these passages above confirms the truth that Paul authored a theological dichotomy—the blending and union of the creation and redemption orders.

1. The Creation Order

In the creation order, Paul deals with man and woman, husband and wife, father and mother, and the children in the Christian home. He asserts that the Christian house is to be a household of faith where the members manifest Christlike character qualities and live in loving harmony. In the redemption order, these roles are unchanged. The creation-order roles of male and female remain. Jesus Himself also confirms this order of creation, male and female, equal as persons but functionally different. Men and women are of equal value as persons in the sight of God. There is no male superiority/female inferiority, counter to what was taught by the Jewish rabbis. Men and women are equal as persons, and are to be partners together. There is to be unity in the bond of marriage, as God ordained. (See Genesis 1:27; 2:18–25; Matthew 19:3–9; Mark 10:2–9; Ephesians 5:23–33; Colossians 2:18–21; 1 Corinthians 7; 11:1–16.)

In his Word to husbands and wives in 1 Peter 3:1–7, Peter confirms Paul's creation order. Home order is the order of creation. Man and woman, husband and wife, are called to be sharers and partners together. They are *"heirs together of the grace of life"* (1 Peter 3:7). Together, they share the responsibility of bringing up children in the nurture and admonition of the Lord. The husband is to be the head of the home and the primary provider for his family, but this does not imply male superiority or female inferiority. Male and female are equal as persons before God, though they are functionally different. And each one is incomplete without the other. There is to be loving care and mutual submission in God's order and divine arrangement, as in the creation account. There is a shared leadership responsibility in the family as husband and wife use their complementary giftings to fulfill their God-given roles. God's order, before the fall, was man and woman/ husband and wife, and then the family.

2. The Redemption Order

Paul also holds to the redemptive order, which first appears in the book of Genesis, where creation and redemption were woven together by God Himself. In the midst of God's pronounced judgments on (a) the serpent, Satan (see Genesis 3:14–15), (b) the man, Adam (see Genesis 3:17–19), (c) the earth (see Genesis 17), and (d) the woman, Eve (see Genesis 3:16), God gave the wonderful promise of redemption.

Redemption would come through "the Seed of the woman." (See Genesis 3:15.) Thus, even though sin and death entered the world via the woman, God would bring redemption through her, as well. However, her Seed would be a Man, born of a woman, to redeem fallen men and women back to God and to restore them to the image of God that was marred by the entrance of sin. God would use a woman to bring forth His only begotten Son, the Savior of the world. God would not use "the seed of a man," even though the Savior would be a Man. He would use "the Seed of the woman"!

Both men and women owe their redemption to the Man born of a virgin woman, Mary—of whom was born the Man Christ Jesus! The Lord Jesus came to earth to bring men and women back to God's original purpose and order in creation, through His redeeming grace. It is through redemption that men and women are restored to God's image and become new creations, of a higher order than the original creation—Adam and Eve.

The new covenant of redemption restores to mankind all that was lost in the Edenic covenant of creation. Every truth in Scripture has, as it were, two "railway lines" on which it must run. Both lines have to be kept in proper position and tension. So, the truths of creation and redemption run parallel throughout the Word of God, from Genesis to Revelation. Both must be kept in proper position and tension; otherwise, disaster occurs. Expositors should not use the creation order of Genesis chapters 1 through 3 to suppress redemption's order, which is above and beyond that of creation. (See Galatians 3:28; Colossians 3:11.)

The redemptive order is "in Christ" (2 Corinthians 5:17), as we will discuss in greater depth in the next chapter.

14

MEN AND WOMEN "IN CHRIST"

Probably the pinnacle of Pauline theology concerning creation and redemption is summed up in the text of 1 Corinthians 15:21–22:

For since by man came death [creation], *by Man also came the resurrection of the dead* [redemption]. *For as in Adam all die* [creation], *even so in Christ shall all be made alive* [redemption].   (NKJV)

From the divine viewpoint, all mankind is classified according to one of two representative men. All are either "in Adam" or "in Christ." Naturally speaking, we are all "in Adam," having inherited sin, sickness, disease, the curse, and death from the first created man. Once a person, male or female, accepts Christ and His work on the cross, he or she is spiritually placed "in Christ," thereby inheriting such divine blessings as righteousness, health, and everlasting life. This is an important truth for us to lay hold of if we are to understand the proper roles of men and women in the Christian church.

From the writings of Paul, we can ascertain what it means to be "in Adam" versus "in Christ." The columns set out here will sharpen our focus on this truth.

	"In Adam" 1 Corinthians 15:22	"In Christ" 1 Corinthians 15:22
1	The First Adam	The Last Adam
2	The First Man	The Second Man
3	Created Son of God Luke 3:38	Incarnate Son of God— Luke 3:22
4	By one man's	By one Man's
5	Disobedience	Obedience
6	Sin entered the world	Righteousness entered the world
7	Death by sin	Life by righteousness
8	Living soul— 1 Corinthians 15:47	Quickening spirit— 1 Corinthians 15:45
9	Of the earth, earthy— 1 Corinthians 15:47–48	Lord from heaven, heavenly
10	Many made sinners	Many made righteous
11	Condemnation	Justification—Romans 5:12–21
12	The Old Creation	New creation—Galatians 6:15; 2 Corinthians 5:17
13	Old man—Ephesians 4:22; Colossians 3:9	New man—Ephesians 4:24; Colossians 3:10
14	Jews and Gentiles	Neither Jew nor Gentile— Galatians 3:28
15	Bond (slaves) and free	Neither bond nor free
16	Male and female— Genesis 1:27	Neither male nor female
17	Barbarian and Scythian— Colossians 3:11	Neither Barbarian nor Scythian
18	Circumcision and uncircumcised—Galatians 6:15	Neither is there any circumcision nor uncircumcision
19	Fallen state	New-creation state
20	The curse	The blessing

21	Damnation through transgression—1 Timothy 2:13–14	Restoration through redemption—1 Timothy 2:15 (AMP)
22	Joint rulership and dominion now forfeited through sin	Joint rulership and dominion restored in Christ
23	Man rules over the woman	Man and woman partner together
24	Man is head of the woman	Christ is Head over man and woman
25	Woman subordinated—hierarchical	Mutual submission—co-equality
26	Fallen creation's point of view	Redemption's point of view
27	Old-creation order—realistic	New-creation order—idealistic
28	First the natural—1 Corinthians 15:46	Afterward the spiritual

A major key to men and women functioning effectively in the church—the redemptive community—is to see both genders as no longer being "in Adam" but "in Christ." Is a man "in Christ"? Is a woman "in Christ"? Then he or she is a new creation in Christ.

+ "*If anyone is in Christ, he is a new creation*" (2 Corinthians 5:17 NKJV).

+ "*For in Christ Jesus neither circumcision availeth any thing, nor uncircumcision, but a new creature*" (Galatians 6:15).

+ "*For ye are all one in Christ Jesus*" (Galatians 3:28).

+ "*But Christ is all, and in all*" (Colossians 3:11).

The definitive statements of Paul regarding the redemptive order are found in Galatians 3:28 and Colossians 3:11, printed here in their entirety.

There is neither Jew nor Greek, there is neither bond nor free, there is neither male nor female: for ye are all one in Christ Jesus.

(Galatians 3:28)

Where there is neither Greek nor Jew, circumcision nor uncircumcision, Barbarian, Scythian, bond nor free: but Christ is all, and in all.

(Colossians 3:11)

In Christ...

1. **There is neither Jew nor Greek.** In Christ, national and ethnic barriers cease to exist. There is no ground for racism.

2. **There is neither bond nor free.** Social distinctions, such as class and socioeconomic status, cease to exist in Christ. Such are no longer barriers in Christ.

3. **There is neither male nor female.** In Christ, gender distinctions do not cease to exist, but gender barriers do. Men and women are redemptively equal—of identical value and worth before God.

4. **There is neither circumcision nor uncircumcision.** Ritual barriers cease to exist. Under the old covenant, the process of circumcision was for males alone. Under the new covenant, baptism took the place of circumcision, so that the key process is available to males and females alike. The rite of circumcision was removed from Christianity, as Paul clearly taught. (See Galatians 6:12–13; 2:1–14.)

5. **There is neither Barbarian nor Scythian.** Racial, tribal, and other such barriers cease to exist in Christ. Cultural distinctions are not to hinder relationship and fellowship in Christ, since all believers belong to a new culture—the culture of the kingdom of God.

6. **All are one in Christ.** Christ is all and is in all. Regardless of gender, race, color, culture, status, and other distinctions, are all one "in Christ." Christ is all, or everything; and He is in all, so that all believers must be seen as being "in Christ"!

Remember the prayer of the Jewish man: "I thank God that I am not (1) a Gentile, (2) a slave, or (3) a woman." When church life is conducted "in Christ," barriers between men and women are not of a national, social, ritualistic, intellectual, or sexual nature but rather on the plane of spirituality.

There is no doubt that Paul was speaking from a spiritual viewpoint when he presented the redemption order. Yet when he spoke of the creation order, he referred to the natural sphere.

In the natural sphere...

1. **There is Jew and Greek.** (See Romans 1:16; 1 Corinthians 10:32.) In the verse from 1 Corinthians, Paul says not to give offense to the Jew, to the Greek, or to the church of God—the three ethnic divisions of the human race in his day.

2. **There is bond and free.** (See Ephesians 6:5–9.) Paul addresses masters and slaves and offers guidelines regarding how both groups, as believers, are to behave toward each other.

3. **There is male and female.** (See Ephesians 5:23–6:4.) As already seen, Paul speaks often of the relationships between man and woman, husband and wife, father and mother, and parents and children. (See, for example, Colossians 3:20; Exodus 20:12; (see also Ephesians 6:1–3.) Sexual distinctions are not dissolved in the natural, or physical, realm. A man is still a man, and a woman is still a woman.

4. **There is circumcision and uncircumcision.** At various points in his writings, Paul refers to Jews and Gentiles, to the circumcised and the uncircumcised. (See Ephesians 2:11; Galatians 6:15; Philippians 3:1–3.)

In the natural or physical realm, the four above categories of distinctions do exist; and, for most people, they still act as barriers. But in the spiritual sphere, these barriers dissolve. All believers, whether male or female, are one "in Christ" and should be seen "in Christ." That is the real issue. "In Adam," there is male and female, as all people have descended from him. But "in Christ," there is neither male nor female, as all are born again and are new creations.

In the Home: Paul speaks of the man (whether husband/father or son/brother) and the woman (whether wife/mother or daughter/sister). (See Colossians 3:18–19; Ephesians 5:21–33; 1 Corinthians 7:2.) He also speaks of grandmothers (see 1 Timothy 1:5), the unmarried (see

1 Corinthians 7:23), widows (see 1 Corinthians 7:39), and sisters (see Philemon 2). So, in the creation order, these distinctions are valid.

In the Church: In the spiritual house of God, there is neither male nor female, neither bond nor free, neither circumcision nor uncircumcision, and so forth. All believers are members one of another, called to function in the body of Christ—the church, the community of God's redeemed.

Thus, we have the order of creation and the order of redemption. All believers are "new creatures"—new creations. The "old creation" is male and female; the "new creation" is neither male nor female.

The realm of Adam sphere belongs to creation; the realm of Christ belongs to redemption. The first is the natural order, after the flesh; the second is the spiritual order, after the Spirit. In church life, spiritual order, while not nullifying the natural order, supersedes social barriers, even as the new creation supersedes the old creation.

The question is, Do we see one another—man and woman—according to the lens of "in Adam" or the lens of "in Christ"? Jew and Greek, slave and free, circumcision and uncircumcision, male and female, Barbarian and Scythian—all are one in Christ. All, as persons, are redemptively equal. In Christ, there is equality and unity, since we are members one of another, and of the one body of Christ. But the parallel lines of Pauline theology that are the "old creation" order and the "new creation" order must be kept in position and held in tension to avoid disaster in the church.

If these things are biblically so—and they are—then the Lord may call, equip, and anoint men and women alike with talents, grace-gifts, ministry gifts, and leadership abilities as He wills. What man can say to the Lord that He may not do this? Is there a chapter and verse that maintains that these giftings are available exclusively to men and not to women? Are there to be untold millions of non-functioning members in the body of Christ just because they happen to have been born female? The truth is, all believers are redemptively equal as persons, whether male or female, though they may be functionally different according to the measure of the gracegifts God has given them.

At the cross of Christ, the middle walls of partition have been broken down between Jews and Gentiles, men and women, bond and free, circumcised and uncircumcised, Barbarian and Scythian. One can look at men and women through the lens of creation, "in Adam," or through the lens of redemption, "in Christ." Both sides of the cross offer a different point of view—either the Adamic covenant or the new covenant.

In the temple courts, there was the court of the women, the court of the Gentiles, the court of the Jews, the court of the priests, and so on. No one dared to enter another's court, on pain of death. But Jesus broke down these walls at Calvary. And yet, the further away from Calvary people walk, the higher these old walls are rebuilt.

If a woman is not seen as being of equal value to a man, then this is another form of Judaism corrupted by Talmudic laws. If a woman is considered mentally inferior to a man, or to be suffering under the curse of Eve, it is an instance of Phariseeism. Such prejudice and bias in men's attitudes toward women are indeed examples of legalism at its worst.

Man and woman were both made in the image of God. Therefore, both male and female must be seen "in Christ" as new creatures being restored and conformed to the image of God, from which both fell. Unless this truth is laid hold of, men will continue to misuse the Scriptures to suppress women under the guise of submission and thereby rob them of the role and function they were intended to fill within the many-membered body of Christ.

It is significant that God's Word depicts the church using both masculine and feminine pictures and pronouns. In speaking of the apostolic ministries, Paul invokes the image of "*father*" (1 Thessalonians 2:11) and that of "*mother*" (1 Thessalonians 2:7 NKJV). Two figures of the church are used to show that both men and women—the male and the female—should be seen as one, and those are the body of Christ (male) and the bride of Christ (female).

1. The Body of Christ (Male)

The church is called the body of Christ, of which Christ is the Head, and men and women are the members, or other body parts. According to this picture, both men and women are included in the masculine pronoun. The church is "*one new man*" (Ephesians 2:15) and is to come to *"a perfect man"* (Ephesians 4:13). (See also 1 Corinthians 12; Romans 12.)

2.   *The Bride of Christ (Female)*

The church is also depicted as the bride of Christ, as well as the wife of the Lamb. (See, for example, Ephesians 5:23–33; Revelation 19:1–7; 2 Corinthians 1:2–3.) This feminine image encompasses men and women alike.

Both of the above pictures of the church—one masculine, one feminine—encompass male and female believers alike. Both are used in a spiritual sense, and they cannot be used one against the other. In the redemptive community, there is neither male nor female. All true believers are "the body" (masculine) and also "the bride" (feminine).

How, then, should believers view one another? Men and women need to be seen as "in Christ," where gender distinctions are not what prevents someone from fulfilling a particular role in church life. It is the order of the new creation that must prevail, for…

+ Both men and women are saved by grace. (See Ephesians 2:8–9; 1 Peter 1:18–19.)

+ Both men and women are indwelled by the Spirit of God. (See Romans 8:9.)

+ Both men and women are counted as temples of the Holy Spirit. (See 1 Corinthians 6:19–20.)

+ Men and women have the same standing in God. (See Romans 5:1–2.)

+ Men and women are of equal value as persons. (See 1 Corinthians 11:11–12.)

+ Men and women are interdependent, for each is of the other.

+ Both men and women become new creatures once they are reconciled to God. (See 2 Corinthians 5:11–21.)

+ Both men and women may be baptized in the Holy Spirit. (See 1 Corinthians 12:11; Acts 2:1–21.)

+ Both men and women have access to God through Christ. (See 1 Corinthians 11:4–5, 13.)

+ Men and women are redemptively equal before God.

+ Both men and women may be baptized into Christ. (See Galatians 3:27–28.)

+ Both men and women are priests unto God under the new covenant. (See Revelation 1:6; 5:9–10; 1 Peter 2:5–9.)

+ Both men and women are "in the Lord." (See 1 Corinthians 11:1–16.)

Therefore, both men and women are to function in the church accordingly as God gives grace and gifts to them. (See 1 Corinthians 12; Romans 12:1–8.)

Let's take a look at the implications of the above truths, in light of what Jesus Christ did for us on the cross.

+ Before the cross, there were sacred places, such as the temple; now, the church is God's temple.

+ Before the cross, there were sacred people, such as the priests and elders; now, all Christians are the sacred people.

+ Before the cross, there were sacred offices, such as the ministering priests; now, all believers, whether male or female, are called to be kings and priests unto God and His Christ.

+ Before the cross, there was a "sacred gender," the male, considered to be predominantly called of God; now, all believers, whether male or female, are called by God to function in the body of Christ as it pleases Him.

+ Before the cross, there were sacred religions, such as Judaism; but now, true Christianity is a relationship with God through Christ.

+ Before the cross, there were sacred headships, such as the high priest in Israel; now, the Lord Jesus Christ is the great High Priest after the order of Melchizedek. (See Psalm 110:4.)

+ This is what it means to be "in Christ"!

15

ORDER IN THE CHRISTIAN HOME

It has already been seen that Paul deals with the theological dichotomy of creation and redemption. Creation order deals more specifically with order in the home, while redemption order deals more specifically with order in the church. However, they are as two sides of the same coin. In this brief chapter, we will look in greater depth at the order in the Christian home.

Paul deals with creation's order in the Christian home, offering teaching and instruction for the husband/father, the wife/mother, and the children. (See Ephesians 5:23–34; Colossians 3:18–21; 1 Peter 3:1–7; 1 Corinthians 7; 11:1–16).

The work of redemption is to restore the man and the woman to the proper divine order. And if order is to be found anywhere, it should be found in the Christian home. The relationship between every Christian married couple should illustrate and typify the relationship between Christ and His bride, the church.

In his writings, Paul makes it very clear that the husband/father is the head of the home—the covering, the protective lover, the provider. He is just as explicit that the wife is to submit with love, honor, and reverence to her husband's headship. She is under the protection of his love and covering. Though the husband and wife are co-equal as persons, yet there is divine order, as seen in the original creation of the first man and woman, Adam and Eve. (See 1 Corinthians 11:3, 7; Ephesians 5:22, 25, 28, 33; Genesis 1:17–28.)

The husband is to love his wife as Christ loves the church. The wife is to submit herself to her husband and reverence him just as the church is to submit to Christ. Peter confirms this very truth in 1 Peter 3:8.

The basic calling of God on the woman is to be a daughter, a wife, a mother, and a homemaker. The basic calling of God on the man is to be a son, a husband, a father, and a homebuilder/provider.

Together, the husband and wife make a team. They are partners in marriage. (See Genesis 2:18–25; 1 Corinthians 11:1–10; Ephesians 5:23–33; 1 Peter 3:1–8; Proverbs 12:4; 14:1; 31:10–31; Titus 2:4, 5; 1 Timothy 5:14.)

The greatest ministry a married woman can have is to her husband and children, sharing responsibility with her husband in establishing a household of faith. And the greatest ministry a man can have is to establish, with his wife, an exemplary Christian home. To see one's family coming to faith in Christ and receiving eternal life—what greater honor could there be for a husband and wife? Surely, this "ministry" supersedes all others.

Humanistic philosophy seeks to destroy the first basic institution God ordained—the family—by depicting the homemaker wife as a slave. And *"if the foundations be destroyed, what can the righteous do?"* (Psalm 11:3).

Blessed is the man who has a prudent wife who can guide the house, love her husband, love her children, and be the glory of her husband. (See Proverbs 19:14; 18:22.)

In the home, there is the natural house. Here, the wife is subject to the husband as the husband is subject to Christ. She exercises authority because she is under the authority of her husband; she does not usurp his authority. The man is the covering, the protection, and the head of the house because he himself is under the covering, protection, and headship of Christ. (See 1 Corinthians 11:1–3.) He exercises authority because he himself is under authority. For how can a man exercise headship over his wife if he himself is not under the headship of Christ? God is the Head of Christ, who is the Head of the man. And the man—the husband—is the head of his wife. Together, husband and wife exercise headship over their children until those children grow old enough to leave the home in order to establish their own homes.

The Christian home should be an illustration and demonstration of divine order. For, once again, how can a man or a woman exercise ministry in the house of the Lord, the church, if his or her own house is out of divine order? Beyond the natural house and the home order, God may have placed a spiritual calling on either the man or the woman relative to the church, His spiritual house, or the house of God. But just as it is in the natural, so it is in the spiritual. There must be divine order for both the man and the woman.

Paul links both "houses" together in dealing with the qualifications of elders and deacons in 1 Timothy 3:1–16. He asks, How can a man rule in the house of the living God (the church) if he cannot rule in his own house (the family)? One is dependent on the other. If the church is out of order, it is generally because the homes of those who lead the church are out of order. Get the homes in order, and the church will be in order. Jesus is Lord of the home, and He is also Lord and Head of the church.

16

PAUL ON WOMEN "KEEPING SILENCE"

Before launching into a discussion of what the Bible teaches on the place, role, and function of men and women in the church, the redemptive community, we must consider the so-called "problem Scriptures" of Paul's writings.

It is worth noting that those who would "silence" women in the church and prohibit their participation in public ministry and church leadership often invoke Paul's writings to defend their position. We believe that Paul's writings on this subject have been greatly misunderstood, misinterpreted, and misused by those who desire to keep even godly women from functioning in the body of Christ. In some cases, there does not appear to be honest exegesis of the Pauline passages quoted, and they have been used to rob women of their rightful ministries in the church.

Numerous local churches throughout the world consist of more believing women than believing men. With the imposition of "silence" of women in church life, that means that over one half of the Christian community is rendered mute. Paul's words have indeed been distorted and misused to disengage untold thousands of believing women from their rightful role and function within the body of Christ.

There are two primary passages of Paul's writings used to justify the suppression of women in church life: 1 Corinthians 14:33–35 and

1 Timothy 2:8–15. As will be seen, these passages were written to treat local situations in several local churches of Paul's day, and they should not be viewed as universal commands or timeless laws, as they are by those who use them to silence women and limit their participation in public church life, according to their God-given giftings.

In this chapter, we will deal first with a passage in Paul's first epistle to the Corinthians. Under the guise of submission to authority, this is one of the chief passages used and abused to suppress the role and function of women. It is a great tragedy that Paul has been branded a male chauvinist because of this passage and another in, written to Timothy at Ephesus.

We will begin by considering several different translations of 1 Corinthians 14:33–35. The mention of *"the law"* in each version refers to Genesis 3:16:

> *For God is not the author of confusion, but of peace, as in all churches of the saints. Let your women keep silence in the churches: for it is not permitted unto them to speak; but they are commanded to be under obedience as also saith the law. And if they will learn any thing, let them ask their husbands at home: for it is a shame for women to speak in the church.*   (1 Corinthians 14:33–35)

> *For God is not the author of confusion but of peace, as in all the churches of the saints. Let your women keep silent in the churches, for they are not permitted to speak; but they are to be submissive, as the law also says. And if they want to learn something, let them ask their own husbands at home; for it is shameful for women to speak in church.*   (1 Corinthians 14:33–35 NKJV)

> *...for God is not a God of confusion but of peace, as in all the churches of the saints. The women are to keep silent in the churches; for they are not permitted to speak, but are to subject themselves, just as the Law also says. If they desire to learn anything, let them ask their own husbands at home; for it is improper for a woman to speak in church.*   (1 Corinthians 14:33–35 NASB)

For God is not a God of disorder but of peace. As in all the congrega-
tions of the saints, women should remain silent in the churches. They
are not allowed to speak, but must be in submission, as the Law says.
If they want to inquire about something, they should ask their own
husbands at home; for it is disgraceful for a woman to speak in the
church.　　　　　　　　　　　(1 Corinthians 14:33–35 NIV84)

For He [Who is the source of their prophesying] is not a God of confu-
sion and disorder but of peace and order. As [is the practice] in all the
churches of the saints (God's people), the women should keep quiet in
the churches, for they are not authorized to speak, but should take a
secondary and subordinate place, just as the Law also says. But if there
is anything they want to learn, they should ask their own husbands
at home, for it is disgraceful for a woman to talk in church [for her to
usurp and exercise authority over men in the church].
　　　　　　　　　　　　　　(1 Corinthians 14:33–35 AMP)

Biblical Hermeneutics

In order to come to a clearer and fuller understanding of this Pauline passage, the expositor needs to follow proper hermeneutical principles. As discussed earlier, expositors should not interpret any passage of Scripture in the light of their own bias and personal mind-set about the proper role and function of women in the church. As mentioned previously, there is no doubt that a person's theology (what he or she thinks about God and mankind, including women) will affect how he or she interprets and understands the Scriptures. Theology affects hermeneutics, and hermeneutics affects theology. The end result of faulty theology and faulty hermeneutics is a faulty exegesis.

In the process of interpreting Scripture, the expositor must bridge any historical, geographical, cultural, and linguistic gaps before he or she can ascertain more accurately the writer's intention.

Remember what was said by Myles Coverdale: "It shall greatly help thee to understand Scripture, if thou mark, not only what is spoken or written, but of whom, and unto whom, with what words, at what time, where, to what intent, with what circumstances, considering what goeth before and what followeth after."

So, in studying the controversial Pauline passages from 1 Corinthians and 1 Timothy, one needs to consider such questions as the following: Who was Paul writing to? What were the circumstances? What words did Paul use? What was his purpose in writing? What was the historical and cultural setting for the epistle? Was Paul responding to questions addressed personally to him? Or was he dealing in general with local problems of his day? Were his words meant to apply to all times, or were they addressed specifically to the local setting and culture of his time? These questions, and others, must be kept in mind as one interprets the "problem Scriptures" of Paul.

Context of Paul's First Epistle to the Corinthians

The Corinthian church was founded by Paul, as described in Acts 18:1–17. The city of Corinth, a seaport, was infamous for its sensuality. There was the temple of Corinth, where some of the temple prostitutes were converted from their heathenish culture and ways to Christ at the church. Chloe's household had taken reports to Paul, along with a number of questions that needed answers. Paul's first epistle was penned as a response to these questions and to address many problems in the newfound church. Each chapter of 1 Corinthians seems to deal with a specific problem, question, or disorder in the church at Corinth.

It was not until about ad 90 that Paul's letters were collected and put together. The cause for this first letter is set out in 1 Corinthians 1:10–11; 7:1; 16:17. It may have been sent by Timothy. (See 1 Corinthians 4:17; 16:10, 11.) It is an epistle of reproof, the epistle of New Testament church order. It was written about ad 53–57, during Paul's stay at Ephesus, on his third missionary journey. (See Acts 19.)

Throughout this epistle, Paul painted a picture of men and women "in Christ," in proper order and relationship, both in the home and in the church. A brief overview will set the groundwork for a proper exposition and understanding of 1 Corinthians 14 and its comments on the "silence of women" in church life. Here, in brief, are the various problems dealt with in 1 Corinthians.

1. The problem of divisions and contentions—1 Corinthians 1:10–11; 16:17–18

2. It would seem that Stephanas, Fortunatus, and Achaicus had reported to Paul some of the difficulties in Corinth. Timothy was sent by Paul, probably with this epistle, to the church. (See 1 Corinthians 4:17, plus postscript.) But it was the house of Chloe—probably a house church—that brought the major report to Paul. Paul responded to the report of this woman, along with the brothers, and wrote accordingly.

3. The problem of worldly wisdom and human philosophy—1 Corinthians 1–2

4. The problem of carnality and personalities—1 Corinthians 3–4

5. The problem of vanity and pride—1 Corinthians 3–4

6. The problem of incestuous relationships—1 Corinthians 5

7. The problem of immorality in the church—1 Corinthians 6:1–20

8. Paul warned that fornicators, idolaters, adulterers, homosexuals, the effeminate, and others living in sin would not enter the kingdom of God.

9. The problem of church discipline—1 Corinthians 6

10. The problem of lawsuits among believers—1 Corinthians 6

11. The problem of married and unmarried—1 Corinthians 7

This chapter deals with a host of questions concerning marriage and marital status.

+ Verses 1–6: Each woman is to have her own husband and each man his own wife. There is equality between husband and wife; there is neither superiority nor inferiority. There must be mutual respect and care for each other.

+ Verses 7–9: Some have the gift of celibacy, but not all. It is better to marry than to burn with lust.

+ Verses 10–11: If one is married, he or she is not to divorce his or her spouse, even as the Lord Jesus also said. This piece of instruction confirms the order of creation—that there is no male superiority or female inferiority. Both sexes are equal as persons before God. (See also Matthew 5:32; 19:3–9; Mark 10:2–12; Luke 16:18.)

+ Verses 12–16: Believers and unbelievers should remain together, as it is possible they will come to salvation and faith in Christ. Both are equal as persons to the Lord.

+ Verses 25–35: Celibacy is recommended, as the time is short.

+ Verses 36–38: Commands are given concerning engaged couples.

+ Verses 39–40, 10–11: Paul deals with widows and marriage in the Lord.

Nowhere in this chapter is the idea of male domination presented, but rather the equality of persons, whether men or women, before the Lord.

1. The problem of meats offered to idols—1 Corinthians 8

2. The problem of itinerant ministers and support—1 Corinthians 9

3. Here, Paul says that an itinerant minister can "lead about a sister, [or] a wife" (1 Corinthians 9:5) the same as any of the apostles can do. This principle applies just as much today as it did back then.

4. The problem of idolatry and immorality—1 Corinthians 10

5. The problem of "headship" and "covering" in the married state—1 Corinthians 11

The culture and custom of Paul's day demanded that a woman wear a veil, or a head covering, even though long hair was given to the woman for a covering and her glory. (See 1 Corinthians 11:10, 13–16.) Some had come from synagogue life to church life. But the wearing of a veil was not a law or a command of God given for all times. It was optional, not mandatory. There is no command in the Old Testament that a woman must be veiled. Again, wearing a veil was simply the custom and culture of Paul's time. The wearing of head coverings by women varied within the Greek, Roman, and Jewish cultures.

At this point, it seems appropriate to further investigate this matter of the veiling, or covering, of men and women, seeing as the "veil" and "silence" of women are interrelated issues. Did Paul "veil" women? Did he silence them?

Paul's first epistle to the Corinthian believers is a single, cohesive letter. Verses 3–16 of chapter 11 and verses 29–40 of chapter 14 could have been written only minutes apart. In 1 Corinthians 11, Paul wrote about men and women and "covering," as well as men and women "praying and prophesying." Then, in 1 Corinthians 14, he wrote about "women keeping silence in the churches." Did Paul change his mind over the course of writing a few chapters of the same epistle? Was he writing under the inspiration of the Spirit, or not? Did he, by the time he got to 1 Corinthians 14, forget what he had written in 1 Corinthians 11? Did Paul tell women to be veiled when praying and prophesying in 1 Corinthians 11, only to tell them to be silent—i.e., to neither pray nor prophesy—in 1 Corinthians 14? These questions may sound ridiculous, but it is necessary to ask them, considering some scholars' interpretation of the Pauline writings.

In 1 Corinthians 11:2, Paul instructs the Corinthians to "*keep the ordinances*," or to maintain the traditions prevalent at that time. Certain "traditions" or "customs" were in vogue in Corinth as noted here concerning men and women being "covered."

Ernest Gentile, in some notes, had this to say on these verses: "In verse 4 Paul speaks about a man 'having his head covered.' The words may be literally translated, 'having something hanging down from his head.' Actually, this part of Paul's teaching was more shocking to the Jews of that day than the teaching of women's veils is to us. A Jew accustomed to the ways of the synagogue would not find Paul's teaching strange.

Referring to the tallith, a four-cornered shawl having fringes consisting of eight threads, each knotted five times, and worn over the head in prayer. It was placed upon the worshipper's head at his entrance into the synagogue. The Romans, like the Jews, prayed with the head veiled....The Greeks remained bareheaded during prayer or sacrifice, as indeed they did in their ordinary outdoor life. The Grecian usage, which had become prevalent in the Grecian churches, seems to have commended itself to Paul as more becoming the superior position of the man.[5]

In verse 6, Paul speaks about the woman being "shorn" or "shaven," which means "[having] the hair cut close, or to be entirely shaved as with a razor."[6] Paul was concerned about the testimony of women in the church. If in her new liberty in Christ, the women would "cast off the veil" (Conybeare's Translation), it would have the same effect on her acceptability as if she were to adopt the socially repugnant sign of the courtesan— having close-cropped hair or a shaven head. "In a woman this was, at that time, a sign of disgrace indicating that she was an adulteress."[7]

Lamsa's translation from the Aramaic says it clearly: "For if a woman does not cover her head, let her also cut off her hair; but if it be a shame for a woman to be shorn or shaven, let her cover her head."[8]

In verse 10, when Paul speaks of the woman having "power on her head," Phillips' translation says, *"For this reason a woman ought to bear on her head an outward sign of man's authority...."*

The covering of the head by a woman in church grew out of the Jewish social culture. It was a custom too ingrained in the social life of Christians in Palestine and Syria to be lightly dismissed by the Christian women in Asia Minor and Greece. Even as it was, Paul's liberation of men to go bareheaded in religious gatherings challenged the Judaizers' tradition.

"...in the East it would be difficult for men to worship at places where women were unveiled during preaching or prayers. The men would be looking at the women instead of worshipping. This is because men do not see women's faces on other occasions. Thus, to see the face or arms of a woman is unusual."[9]

---

5. Marvin R. Vincent, *Word Studies in the New Testament*, Vol. III (New York, NY: Charles Scribner's Sons, 1903), 246.
6. Ibid.
7. A. M. Stibbs, E. F. Kevan, and F. Davidson, *The New Bible Commentary* (Grand Rapids, MI: Wm. B. Eerdmans Publishing Company, 1953), 983.
8. George M. Lamsa, *New Testament Commentary: Acts to Revelation* (Nashville, TN: Holman Bible Publishers, 2007).
9. Lamsa, *New Testament Commentary*, 272.

In summarizing the basic contents of 1 Corinthians 11:1–16, one has to consider the social customs of Paul's times. Paul attempted to instruct a new Christian church in reasonable behavior that would best convey the message of Christ to that generation in that society.

"The social customs which provide the background for his thought are, of course, different from ours, but the factors involved are the same; namely, modesty, propriety and orderliness."[10]

If a man or woman is to be used by God in some charismatic manifestation, the effectiveness of his or her ministry could be compromised by his or her outward appearance. Paul respected the customs and laws of the land. Some of these customs still prevail in certain nations today. In our time, Christian men and women should dress moderately, appropriately, and wisely, so as to give the proper impression from a Christian viewpoint in our social environment. Men need to look like men, and women need to look like women, especially as they claim to be Christian and operate in the gifts and manifestations of the Spirit in church life. (End of notes adapted from Ernest Gentile.)

In verses 7–12, Paul refers back to the creation order as spelled out in Genesis 1:26–27; 2:18–25. Both the male and female were created in the image of God, being equal as persons, though different in function. Each one is incomplete without the other. Though different, both are equal and complementary. Man is the image and glory of God. The woman is the glory of the man. The two became one flesh, and they are interdependent. The woman was made from man, for man, and after the man; yet all men owe their existence and natural birth to a woman—their mother. Unity, equality, and diversity are seen in the male and female, both of which are shadows of Christ and His church. (See Ephesians 4:15–16; 5:23–33.)

Right in the middle of his words concerning men and women, Paul speaks about *men* praying and prophesying and *women* praying and prophesying. These verses are so overlooked by those schools who invoke 1 Corinthians 14:33–35 to "silence" women in the church. Here, it is clear that *men and women may pray and prophesy.* This truth needs to be considered in a proper exegesis of 1 Corinthians 14:33–35.

---

10. Stibbs, Kevan, and Davidson, *New Bible Commentary.*

Paul discourages men from having to wear a covering on the head. He encourages women to follow custom and social culture by wearing something on the head. However, he is not laying it down as a law, as he finalizes this passage by saying, *"If a woman has long hair, it is a glory to her: for her hair is given her for a covering* [literally, a veil]. *But if any man seem to be contentious, we have no such custom, neither the churches of God"* (1 Corinthians 14:15–16). There is no commandment in all of Scripture that says men and women must wear a covering veil, a scarf, or a hat in the presence of the Lord or in the presence of one another.

We resume the outline of problems in the church at Corinth addressed by Paul in his first epistle to the Corinthians:

1. The problem of heresies in the church—1 Corinthians 11

2. The problem of disorder at the Lord's table—1 Corinthians 11:17–34

3. The problem of disorder concerning the gifts of the Spirit—1 Corinthians 12

4. The problem of a lack of divine love—1 Corinthians 13

5. The problem of disorder over tongues, interpretation, and prophecy—1 Corinthians 14

6. The problem of women disrupting church services by asking questions of their husbands, thereby disturbing public gatherings—1 Corinthians 14:36–40

7. The problem of debate over the doctrine of bodily resurrection—1 Corinthians 15

8. Final commands concerning division—1 Corinthians 16

The Problem of Women and Silence

It is at the close of 1 Corinthians 14 that Paul deals with the issue of women in church life and church order. It is evident that the wives were being talkative, disrupting the services with their vocalized questions. Paul exhorts them to be silent in the church service and to ask their questions of their husbands at home. In so doing, Paul was not giving a commandment for all women of all ages and all churches for all times. He was dealing with the local situation at Corinth and the women who were disturbing the gatherings. The principle of order and peace in the church is applicable for all times, but it is not a commandment silencing women from any or all ministry in public meetings. Men and women alike may pray and prophesy, according to 1 Corinthians 11:5.

But this brings us to a consideration of these verses phrase-by-phrase as we bridge the cultural gap between the Corinthian believers and us.

1. *"God is not the author of confusion, but of peace, as in all the churches…"* (1 Corinthians 14:33).

It is clear that there has been some confusion in the gatherings at Corinth.

Various translations show that God is not the author of confusion, tumult, or unquietness. He is the God of peace, and He desires His peace and order to prevail in all the churches.

2. *"Let your women keep silence in the churches"* (1 Corinthians 14:34).

Reading on to include verse 35, we see that Paul was referring specifically to wives, not to women in general: *"And if they will learn any thing, let them ask their husbands at home."* The *Revised Standard Version* translates verse 34 as *"Let the women,"* not *"Let your women."* Even so, Paul was not making a general statement to silence all women for all times in the churches. Refer again to 1 Corinthians 11:5, where Paul provides instructions on how women were to pray and prophesy. And this statement came only a few chapters earlier than the verse under current consideration!

The Greek word for *"women"* here is *gune* (STRONG 1135), meaning "a woman, specifically a wife." Again, Paul is speaking of the wives who were asking questions, and he directs them to inquire of their husbands—not in the church but at home.

The Greek word for *"silence"* in verse 34 is *sigao*, from *sige* (STRONG 4601–4602), and it means "to be silent," "to hiss, or hush, silence." The same Greek word is used in Acts 15:12, 13; 21:40; 12:17; Romans

16:25; 1 Corinthians 14:28, 30, 34; Revelation 8:1; and Luke 9:36; 20:26.

If a person speaks in tongues, and there is no interpreter in the church, then that person is to *"keep silence"* (1 Corinthians 14:28). If the prophets have something revealed to them, then the first is to *"keep silent"* (1 Corinthians 14:30 NKJV) and let the others speak. And if a woman wants to ask questions of her husband, she should wait to do so at home, and *"keep silent"* (1 Corinthians 14:34 NKJV) in the church. It is not a mandate to silence the woman in the church any more than it is to silence the person speaking in tongues or the speaking prophet.

There are Old Testament Scriptures commanding silence in the presence of the Lord. (See Zephaniah 1:7 NKJV; Jeremiah 8:14; Zechariah 2:13.) Such verses exhort the inhabitants of the earth to be quiet in the presence of the Lord and His majesty. They are not commanding timeless or eternal silence.

To be silent means "to be mute, not even to utter a sound." So, was Paul talking about total, absolute silence? Absolutely not! How many congregations or denominations require strict and absolute silence of women in their church gatherings? Does women "keeping silence" mean that they cannot sing in the congregation, in a choir, or as a soloist, in praise and worship to the Lord? Can women pray or teach in Sunday school, or what? Can a woman read the Scriptures aloud in a public meeting? The answer to such questions is evident.

3. *"For it is not permitted unto them to speak;…for it is a shame for women to speak in the church"* (1 Corinthians 14:34–35).

Questions may be asked here. Who did not permit women to speak? Where was it not permitted, "chapter and verse"? From Genesis to Malachi, there is absolutely nothing in the whole of the Old Testament that says women are not permitted to speak. No "law" can be found anywhere in the Bible forbidding women to speak in public.

It has already been seen how women did speak in Old Testament times, even as prophetesses for God Himself. Miriam (see Exodus 15:20),

Deborah (see Judges 4–5), the daughters of Zelophehad (see Numbers 27:1–7), Huldah (see 2 Kings 22), women who prophesied in song (see 1 Chronicles 25), women who prophesied out of their own heart (see Ezekiel 13:17), and Anna (see Luke 2:36–38)—all these women were permitted to speak in public before men and women alike, and there is no mention of their speaking from behind a veil or other head covering with muffled voice.

Jesus also allowed women to speak in public places. (See Luke 8:47; 13:13.) Peter used Joel's prophecy to speak of men and women prophesying under the Spirit's inspiration. (See Acts 2:16–18.) Philip had four daughters who prophesied. (See Acts 21:9.)

So, where is it written that women "are not permitted to speak"? The mandatory silence of women was imposed by the Judaizers who incorporated synagogue "laws" regarding women into church life. It is not commanded in the Bible.

German lexicographer Schleusner, in his *Greek-Latin Lexicon*, says that the expression "as also says the law" refers to the oral law of the Jews. Here are his words: "The oral laws of the Jews or Jewish traditions… In the Old Testament no precept concerning this matter exists…." He goes on to say that it was "forbidden by Jewish traditions for women to speak in the synagogue."

It has already been seen that the Talmud, unlike the Old Testament, did command women to be silent, as the following quotations remind us:

+ "Out of respect to the congregation, a woman should not herself read in the Law."

+ "It is a shame for a woman to let her voice be heard among men."

+ "The voice of a woman is filthy nakedness."

+ "Let the words of the Law be burned rather than committed to women."

Surely, it should be evident that Paul was quoting the Jewish legalists who wanted to silence the women in the Christian churches, as had been done in the Jewish synagogues. It was Jewish law, not biblical law, that silenced women; and most of the related "laws" arose out of the misuse and abuse of Genesis 3:16, which speaks of the husband ruling over the wife, or men ruling over women.

We now turn our attention to the word *"speak"* in the verses under consideration.

The Greeks used several different words to express speech, each of which is translated by the same English word, *speak*:

+ *Legein*—"to deliver an ordered discourse"
+ *Eipien*—"to speak in ordinary conversation"
+ *Lalein*—"to chatter, babble, prattle, gabble, or talk in an undertone"

It is the word *laleo*, meaning "to talk, utter words," that is used in 1 Corinthians 14:34–35. In *Liddell & Scott's Lexicon*, the following meanings are given: "to chatter, babble; of birds, to twitter, chirp; strictly, to make an inarticulate sound, opposed to articulate speech; but also generally, to talk, say." Other related words mean "to bicker, argue, strive or cause confusion in the church; to whisper to each other."

So, Paul was not forbidding all spoken discourse by men or women, only certain kinds, such as questionings, dogmatic dissertations and disputations, or arguments that would cause a commotion. Talkativeness, chattering, whispering in undertones—these activities usually prompted a disturbance for both the speaker and the listeners.

Paul was correcting the Corinthians for allowing disorder in their services. He was saying, "Let the wives be quiet; they are not permitted to babble or to talk in an undertone in the church, for in so doing, they are disturbing both speaker and hearers."

In those days, it was customary for the men to sit on the opposite side of the church from the women—a practice that is observed still today by some denominations and sects. Thus, to ask a question of her husband regarding something she did not understand, a woman would have had to call out across the room, thereby disrupting the meeting. The women in the church at Corinth had very recently been converted from heathendom. They were hungry for the gospel and anxious to learn, having little to no education. Thus, they disturbed the meetings with their eager questions. Paul told them to be quiet and to ask their questions of their husbands at home. He was not talking about women praying or prophesying, singing or speaking. Of course, these women would have needed believing husbands if they hoped to fulfill this injunction of Paul. Even in the synagogues, women were untaught, segregated from the men, and expected to remain silent. This was not so in the church, hence the disturbances.

Halley's Bible Handbook says: "It was customary in Greek and Eastern cities for women to cover their heads in public, except those of immoral character. Corinth was full of temple prostitutes. Some of the Christian women, taking advantage of their newly found liberty in Christ, were laying aside their veils in church meetings, which thus horrified those of more modest type. They are here told not to defy public opinion as to what was considered proper in feminine decorum."[11] Lamsa comments that in the East, "During the services, they (the women) stand or sit by themselves, in a portion of the church reserved for them."

Many contemporary denominations that enforce "silence" in their churches permit women to sing, either with the congregation or as soloists; to pray aloud at prayer meetings; to teach Sunday school; and even to serve as overseas missionaries! What a contradiction this is to these denominations' interpretation of Paul's writings, both in 1 Corinthians and 1 Timothy.

The New English Bible translates 1 Corinthians 14:34 this way: "*Women should not address the meeting.*" *The Amplified Bible* says, "*The women...are not authorized to speak, but should take a secondary and subordinate place*" in the churches. Both these translations are not compatible with Paul's teachings here or elsewhere, and reveal the prejudice of the translators.

Paul was simply saying that the wives were not to disturb the gatherings by asking questions, speaking in ignorance, and chattering among themselves. He was not enforcing absolute silence of women in the churches. The women/wives were not to be boisterous, headstrong, or domineering; but neither were the men/husbands!

11. Henry H. Halley, *Halley's Bible Handbook with the New International Version* (Grand Rapids, MI: Zondervan, 2000), 596–597.

4. "But they are commanded to be under obedience as also saith the Law" (1 Corinthians 14:34).

This verse does not say that the law commands silence but rather *being "under obedience."* In speaking of obedience, Paul may have been alluding to Genesis 3:16, which pronounced the rule of the husband over the wife. However, there is not one verse, from Genesis to Malachi, where the Law of Moses commands women to be silent. The simple fact that God assigned ministries to women in the Old Testament further refutes this idea.

The phrase *"as also saith the law"* (1 Corinthians 14:34) has been the cause of much controversy. The following are two different interpretations of this phrase.

a.   Some expositors believe that Paul was merely echoing the vocabulary used by the Judaizers in their questions, and quoting some of their law, as recorded in the Talmud. These Judaizers were using this "law" to silence women and prohibit them from speaking in the Christian church, as in the synagogues. It is possible, therefore, that Paul was quoting what the Judaizers at Corinth had been saying to justify their efforts to silence the women completely. If this is so, Paul was reproving the Judaizers in saying that the Word of God came *unto* them, and not *from* them, and that he himself was giving the commandments of the Lord. (See 1 Corinthians 14:36–40.) It should be remembered that Jewish law did command the silence of women. According to the Talmud, it was a shame for a woman to let her voice be heard among men. In this case, it would have been appropriate to invoke the Talmud to stop the women from chattering among themselves during the services and from calling out questions to their husbands on the other side of the building.

b.   Some expositors follow this second view, which does not violate the whole context of Scripture concerning the role of women in the home or the church.

Women—specifically married women—are to be under obedience to their own husbands. Paul's epistles instruct wives to obey their husbands. (See Ephesians 5:23–32; Colossians 3:18–20; 1 Peter 3:1–8.) Some authorities, as noted above, believe that Genesis 3:16, and Adam's rule over his wife, is "the law" being referred to in 1 Corinthians 14:34.

In the light of the Corinthian problem, it is scripturally correct to say that the wives who were disturbing the services by *asking questions*, or *chattering*, needed to come under obedience to their husbands, and not embarrass them but rather ask them their questions at home.

Jews and Gentiles did not worship together until they came to realize that the cross had broken down the dividing walls. They did not worship together as one until they saw that they were "in Christ," where there is neither Jew nor Greek, male nor female, but all are one. (See Ephesians 2:12–19; Galatians 3:26–29.) The Judaizers tried to bring the Gentiles under the bondage of the Law, as well as the Talmudic laws, and Paul continually spoke against such legalism. In the Jewish synagogues, the pulpit was located in the middle of the floor, and the men would gather around it, while the women were generally assembled in the balcony. While the word was being ministered, it was permissible for a man to stop and ask the speaker a question. But Paul was telling the women not to yell down to their husbands but to wait until they were home, as they were creating noise and confusion in the services. The ones who were learning were to keep quiet, not the ones who were teaching. Thus, again, Paul was dealing with wives, not with women's ministry!

In the words of Ernest Gentile:

> Under obedience as wives to husbands, as also says the Law. Talkative wives embarrass their husbands and it is poor behaviour in public church gatherings. A good place to show proper husband-wife relationships is in public gatherings indeed. Therefore, talkative wives should not disrupt public meetings and embarrass their husbands, or the church, or the angels (let alone talkative men).[12]

---

12. Ernest Gentile, *What Does the Bible Teach about the Role of Women in Church Leadership?* (San Jose, CA: Publisher, Year).

According to Jewish tradition, men came to the synagogues to teach and to learn; women came to hear. Men would read a lesson from the Scriptures—something women were not permitted to do. Women could not teach in the schools, either, not even if their pupils were the youngest of children. But two women, Lois and Eunice—probably because of a Greek husband and father—did teach Timothy the Scriptures. (See 2 Timothy 1:5; 3:15–17.)

John Anderson had this to say:

> A friend wrote the Chief Rabbi of England asking if the two verses, 1 Corinthians 14:34–35, are taken from the Jewish Talmud. The Rabbi replied that the passages are not literally reproduced from the Talmud but that there are close parallels. The Chief Rabbi thus confirms my statement that these verses are taken from the Talmud, even though there was no confirmation necessary. The English translation of the Talmud, with its fourteen volumes, were placed on a table in the library of Aberdeen University for me to examine, and I visited them daily until I found that these two verses were taken from the Talmud.[13]

5. *"And if they will learn anything, let them ask their husbands at home"* (1 Corinthians 14:35).

It is evident in this verse that Paul is specifically addressing the problem of the wives *asking questions* during the course of the services. It is for this reason that Paul tells the women—the wives—to stop chattering and disturbing the gatherings by calling out questions to their husbands. If they are seeking answers, Paul says, they had best ask their husbands at home. Thus, Paul's injunction that women are to be silent should be interpreted in light of its context.

Paul was not forbidding women to speak. He was not commanding total silence. He was commanding the silence of women who were

13. John Anderson, *Women's Warfare & Ministry* (Braemar, Aberdeenshire, UK: Publisher, Year).

chattering, disturbing the meetings by calling out questions to their husbands.

Katharine C. Bushnell writes:

> As to asking questions of their husbands at home, some of these Corinthian women would be widows, some perhaps divorced on account of their Christian faith, some with Jewish husbands, and some with heathen husbands, some not married at all. And so would it be in the church throughout all subsequent ages of its history. Paul is represented as sending all these to their "husbands." If Paul did so foolish a thing, he drove some back to heathenism for spiritual help; others back to Judaism for spiritual help; many others he deprived of all opportunity to get their questions answered, since they had no husbands. In fact, a majority of the Christian women would have been left in ignorance of important spiritual truths, by such a ruling.[14]

So, the comments on the asking of questions were meant for the Christian wives of Christian men present at the meeting, for they implied that the women in question had believing husbands. The believing wives of unbelieving husbands would need to inquire of other believing men or women. As noted, if this was not the case, then some women would be sent back to heathenism, or to Judaism, for spiritual help; in some cases, they would receive no help at all, since many women were without a husband.

Peter, who did not contradict Paul on this matter, exhorted believing wives to be godly women so that their unbelieving husbands may be won to the Lord—not by the wives' preaching the Word to their husbands but by example, because of their Christian lifestyle. (See 1 Peter 3:1–8.)

The Christian women in Corinth were eager to learn spiritual truths. The frustration of failing to understand because of an inability to read clearly led them to call out to their husbands, sitting elsewhere in the

---

14. Katharine C. Bushnell, *God's Word to Women* (North Collins, NY: Publisher, 1923), 81–82.

gathering, for answers and clarification. Paul admonished the women to be quiet and to wait until they got home, where they could then inquire of their believing husbands.

The key concept in 1 Corinthians 14 is edification. Everything done in the assembly was supposed to edify—to build up—the members of the body of Christ. Disturbances, chattering, mutterings in undertones, and questions called out to husbands certainly would not have edified those gathered at the church in Corinth. The services needed structure and order for praying, prophesying, and public speaking.

Quotable Quotes

To further support the position set forth in this chapter, the following quotations from reputable commentaries on the passage under consideration have been supplied.

1. Matthew Henry

> Seeing there were women who had spiritual gifts of this sort in that age of the church,...and might be under this impulse in the assembly, must they altogether suppress it? Or why should they have this gift, if it must never be publicly exercised? For these reasons, some think that the general prohibitions are only to be understood in common cases; but that upon extraordinary occasions, when women were under divine afflatus, and known to be so, they might have liberty of speech.[15]

Many of the greatest commentators have felt that these prohibitions against women publicly witnessing for Christ were out of harmony with the rest of Scripture. The reason is now obvious. The prohibitions are those of the Judaizers, based upon the oral law, which had its birth in apostate Israel. As a travesty of God's holy law, it may well be regarded as a counterfeit Bible, inspired by the archenemy, and Paul quotes it in order to refute it.

---

15. Matthew Henry, *An Exposition of the Old and New Testament, Vol. 3* (London: Joseph Ogle Robinson, 1828), 1059.

2. Catherine Booth

[First] Corinthians xiv 34, 35 is the only one in the whole book of God which even by a false translation can be made prohibitory of female speaking in the Church; how comes it then, that by this one isolated passage, which, according to our best Greek authorities, is wrongly rendered and wrongly applied, woman's lips have been sealed for centuries, and the "testimony of Jesus, which is the spirit of prophecy," silenced, when bestowed on her? How is it that this solitary text has been allowed to stand unexamined and unexplained, nay, that learned commentators who have known its true meaning as perfectly as either Robinson, Bloomfield, Greenfield, Scott, Parkhurst, or Locke have upheld the delusion, and have enforced it as a Divine precept binding on all female disciples through all time? Surely there must have been some unfaithfulness, "craftiness," and "handling of the word of life deceitfully" somewhere. Surely the love of caste and unscriptural jealousy for a separated priesthood has had something to do with this anomaly. By this course divines and commentators have involved themselves in all sorts of inconsistencies and contradictions; and worse, they have nullified some of the most precious promises of God's word. They have set the most explicit predictions of prophecy at variance with apostolic injunctions, and the most immediate and wonderful operations of the Holy Spirit in direct opposition "to (supposed) positive, explicit, and universal rules."[16]

3. James L. Beall

In those days, custom dictated that men and women be separated in public services. This was true in the Jewish synagogues and Greek gatherings as well. Women were usually confined to a side room or a screened-off balcony where

---

16. Catherine Booth, *Female Ministry; or, Woman's Right to Preach the Gospel* (London: Morgan & Chase, 1870), 19.

they could barely hear what was being said. Consequently, attention would soon lag and they were on their way talking and chattering. In some buildings, the men and women were separated by an aisle. Since most of the women were not as well educated as their husbands, they lacked understanding in some things. Evidently, when a question would arise, the women would disrupt the service by demanding an immediate on-the-spot explanation. Paul corrected this situation by telling them not to disrupt the service, but ask their questions at home with their husbands. The apostle was dealing with a situation peculiar to that day, not ours. In many areas, the church services were conducted in homes because of the lack of public buildings. Would women such as Priscilla, Chloe, and Phoebe, who were called "ministers" to the church, be expected to practice total silence in their own home? It does not seem likely, does it?[17]

In India today, some places still separate the men and the women. In Cairo, Egypt, this writer was in a church service where men and women were actually separated by a wooden stained wall built up to the middle of the pulpit. In China, a missionary told of the separation in the church gatherings of men and women and the like disturbance that Paul spoke of having to be handled.

4. *Catherine Booth*

And, first, we will select the most prominent and explicit passages of the New Testament referring to the subject, beginning with 1 Corinthians xi. 1–15: "Every man praying or prophesying, having his head covered, dishonoureth his head. But every women that prayeth or prophesieth with her head uncovered, dishonoureth her head: for that is all one as if she were shaven," etc. "The character," says a talented writer, "of the prophesying here referred to by the apostle is defined 1 Corinthians xiv. 3, 4, and 31st verses. The reader

17. James L. Beall, *The Female of the Species* (Detroit, MI: Bethesda Missionary Temple, 1977).

will see that it was directed to the "edification, exhortation, and comfort of believers;" and the result anticipated was the conviction of unbelievers and unlearned persons. Such were the public services of women which the apostle allowed, and such was the ministry of females predicted by the prophet Joel, and described as a leading feature of the gospel dispensation. Women who speak in assemblies for worship, under the influence of the Holy Spirit, assume thereby no personal authority over others; they simply deliver the messages of the gospel, which imply obedience, subjection, and responsibility, rather than authority and power."[18]

5. *Dr. Adam Clarke, on 1 Corinthians 11 and the matter of men and women prophesying during church gatherings*

Whatever may be the meaning of praying and prophesying, in respect to the man, they have precisely the same meaning in respect to the woman. So that some women, at least, as well as some men, might speak to others to edification, and exhortation, and comfort. And this kind of prophesying, or teaching, was predicted by Joel, ii. 28, and referred to by Peter, Acts ii. 17. And had there not been such gifts bestowed on women, the prophecy could not have had its fulfilment. The only difference marked by the apostle was, the man had his head uncovered, because he was the representative of Christ: the woman has hers covered, because she was placed by the order of God, in a state of subjection to the man; and because it was a custom, both among the Greeks and Romans, and among the Jews an express law, that no woman should be seen abroad without a vail. This was, and is, a common custom through all the East; and none but public prostitutes go without vails. And, if a woman should appear in public without a vail, she would dishonour her head, her husband. And she must appear like to those women who

---

18. Booth, *Female Ministry*, 5.

had their hair shorn off as the punishment of whoredom, or adultery.[19]

In Summary

In concluding this chapter, then, it is not an honest treatment of Pauline thought to use 1 Corinthians 14:34–35 to silence all women in all churches for all times, or to exclude them from public ministry.

Paul is not arguing for the perpetual silencing and subordination of women. Paul does not twist the Scriptures, but some schools today have twisted Paul's statements to suppress women and to subjugate them to men, desiring to bind and silence women forever. But Paul is not giving a timeless restriction. He is simply dealing with a local situation of disorder in the Corinthian church. The principle, of course, is applicable in all generations that women (and men) should behave decently and in order in church gatherings, and not chatter among themselves, talk in a disruptive manner, or domineer by asking questions that would be best answered at home, depending on the inquirers' marital status.

First Corinthians 14:34–35 cannot be used to contradict 1 Corinthians 11:4–5. In the latter passage, men and women alike may pray and prophesy. Prophecy can include words of edification, exhortation, comfort, and even preaching and teaching. Paul did not forget what he had written in 1 Corinthians 11 when he penned 1 Corinthians 14. He did not contradict himself in these passages. He did not prohibit women praying or prophesying, only from chattering, babbling, and asking questions out of place. Paul would not contradict the prophet Joel concerning men and women prophesying, nor would he contradict the apostle Peter when he quoted Joel's prophecy at Pentecost.

If the context of 1 Corinthians 14 is spread to 1 Corinthians 14:26–40, then the idea of silencing women for all times from any type of public ministry becomes all the more ludicrous.

In 1 Corinthians 14:26, Paul asks, *"How is it then, brethren? when ye come together, every one of you hath a psalm, hath a doctrine, hath a tongue,*

---

19 Adam Clarke, *The Holy Bible Containing the Old and New Testaments, Vol. 6* (New York, NY: A. Paul, 1832), 226.

hath a revelation, hath an interpretation. Let all things be done unto edifying." Does this phrase *"every one of you"* ·strictly refer to the *"brethren,"* or to men only?

And again, in 1 Corinthians 14:31, Paul writes, *"Ye may all prophesy one by one, that all may learn, and all may be comforted."* Three times, Paul uses the word *"all."* Does this word refer only to the men and not the women, when there may have been more women than men in the church? All may prophesy, all may learn, all may be comforted—does he mean all the men but not the women?

When one considers the eleventh and fourteenth chapters of 1 Corinthians together, one sees that Paul is simply saying men and women may pray and prophesy in public gatherings, but the women (the wives) must not disrupt the services by asking questions of their husbands, or by chattering among themselves. Women, as well as men, need to learn together in a meek, quiet spirit and maintain church order, as God is not the author of confusion, in the churches or elsewhere. (See 1 Corinthians 14:33.)

17

PAUL ON WOMEN
USURPING AUTHORITY

Without doubt, the weightier argument for the silence, subordination, and subjugation of women, and their exclusion from public ministry, is 1 Timothy 2:8–15.

As a reminder, proper hermeneutics require that the expositor bridge the historical, cultural, and linguistic gaps between the biblical writer and the writer's generation, and the expositor's own generation. This will be done with as reasonable brevity as appropriate in the exegesis of this passage.

Several different translations of the Pauline passage under consideration are quoted here.

I desire therefore that the men pray everywhere, lifting up holy hands, without wrath and doubting; in like manner also, that the women adorn themselves in modest apparel, with propriety and moderation, not with braided hair or gold or pearls or costly clothing, but, which is proper for women professing godliness, with good works. Let a woman learn in silence with all submission. And I do not permit a woman to teach or to have authority over a man, but to be in silence. For Adam was formed first, then Eve. And Adam was not deceived, but the wom-

an being deceived, fell into transgression. Nevertheless she will be saved in childbearing, if they continue in faith, love, and holiness, with self-control. (1 Timothy 2:8–15 NKJV)

Therefore I want the men in every place to pray, lifting up holy hands, without wrath and dissension. Likewise, I want women to adorn themselves with proper clothing, modestly and discreetly, not with braided hair and gold or pearls or costly garments, but rather by means of good works, as is proper for women making a claim to godliness. A woman must quietly receive instruction with entire submissiveness. But I do not allow a woman to teach or exercise authority over a man, but to remain quiet. For it was Adam who was first created, and then Eve. And it was not Adam who was deceived, but the woman being deceived, fell into transgression. But women will be preserved through the bearing of children if they continue in faith and love and sanctity with self-restraint. (1 Timothy 2:8–15 NASB)

I want men everywhere to lift up holy hands in prayer, without anger or disputing. I also want women to dress modestly, with decency and propriety, not with braided hair or gold or pearls or expensive clothes, but with good deeds, appropriate for women who profess to worship God. A woman should learn in quietness and full submission. I do not permit a woman to teach or to have authority over a man; she must be silent. For Adam was formed first, then Eve. And Adam was not the one deceived; it was the woman who was deceived and became a sinner. But women will be saved through childbearing—if they continue in faith, love and holiness with propriety. (1 Timothy 2:8–15 NIV84)

I will therefore that men pray every where, lifting up holy hands, without wrath and doubting. In like manner also, that women adorn themselves in modest apparel, with shamefacedness and sobriety; not with broided hair, or gold, or pearls, or costly array; but (which becometh women professing godliness) with good works. Let the woman learn in silence with all subjection. But I suffer not a woman to teach, nor to usurp authority over the man, but to be in silence. For Adam was first formed, then Eve. And Adam was not deceived, but the woman being deceived was in the transgression. Notwithstanding she shall be saved in childbearing, if they continue in faith and charity and holiness with sobriety.   (1 Timothy 2:8–15 KJV)

A. Bridging the Gaps

Before seeking to bridge the linguistic gap by studying the language of Paul in this passage from 1 Timothy, it will be helpful to bridge the historical and cultural gaps of the epistle.

1. The Church at Ephesus

The epistle was written to Timothy, Paul's son in the faith, who was the senior leader of the church at Ephesus. (See 1 Timothy 1:1–3; postscript in several translations.)

The church at Ephesus had a great foundation laid, especially by the apostle Paul, the writer of the Pastoral Epistles—1 and 2 Timothy, and Titus. A brief outline is here supplied of the founding of the church. (For the full details, the reader is encouraged to read Acts 18:23–28; 19–20.)

+   Apollos spent some time at Ephesus. An eloquent man mighty in the Scriptures and fervent in spirit, he taught diligently the things of the Lord. However, he knew only the baptism of John. In time, Aquila and Priscilla came to Ephesus, took Apollos aside, and taught him *"the way of God more perfectly"* (Acts 18:26). Apollos was indeed a teachable teacher. He then moved on to Corinth for some ministry. (See 1 Corinthians 3:1–7, 21–23.)

+   Paul then came to Ephesus, having passed through there on a previous occasion. Paul found certain of John's disciples there, and noticed a lack of the Holy Spirit's presence and power. After baptizing these disciples into the name of the Lord Jesus Christ, Paul laid hands on them, and they received the Spirit, with the evidence of speaking with tongues and prophesying.

+   Paul ministered in the Jewish synagogue for some three months and then moved into the school of Tyrannus. He ministered in

Ephesus for some two years. Ephesus became a great church, from which the gospel sounded out in all Asia. The seven churches in Asia seem to have all been founded out of this place. (See Revelation 1:10–12.)

+ Special miracles were done through Paul. The church was founded on the principles of the doctrine of Christ. (See Hebrews 6:1–2.) The name of the Lord was magnified in the city, and many who were involved in witchcraft burned their magic books and artifacts. In spite of the opposition from the tradesmen of the city, who made silver shrines of the goddess Diana, the Lord added members to the church.

+ Undoubtedly, Paul's ministry in Ephesus included the conversion to Christ of those from the cult of Diana. Paul had lectured in the Greek secular school of Tyrannus for two years after his time in the synagogue. Certain Greek women responded to the gospel in Athens (see Acts 17:34), and it is safe to assume the same would have been true here; in other words, men were not the only ones responding.

+ In Acts 20:13–38 is given Paul's profound farewell speech to the elders of Ephesus. He warned them, exhorted them, and challenged them to feed the flock of God as genuine overseers of the church of God, purchased with God's own blood. He also warned them of the danger of elders rising from within and drawing disciples after themselves, and then the danger of grievous or ferocious "wolves" coming from without to destroy the flock of God. He finally commended them to the grace of God, amid tears and prayers for them all as they bid him farewell at the ship that would take him away.

+ The pinnacle of Pauline truth concerning the church is found in his epistle to the Ephesians, where Paul presents the *"great mystery"* (Ephesians 5:32) of the marriage of Christ and His church. (See Ephesians 5:22–34.) The contrast is to that of the cult of Diana and the doctrines of demons floating around the city that forbade marriage, among other things. (See 1 Timothy 4:3.) But in John's letter to the same church some years later, he laments the Ephesian believers' having left their first love, and calls them back to true repentance. (See Revelation 2:1–7.)

✦   The epistles of Timothy were written to Timothy, the "angelos" of the church at Ephesus (see 2 Timothy 4:22 postscript), to address the troubles that had arisen in the church over the eight to ten years since its foundation, and Paul's farewell message to the elders.

It is evident that certain men and women had become false teachers, and Paul encourages Timothy to deal with them accordingly. (See 1 Timothy 1:1–4; 2 Timothy 2:17; 4:14–15.) Paul mentions three specific men in the church—Hymenaeus, Alexander, and Philetus—as troublemakers who need to be dealt with in order to keep the church healthy. These men were probably were some of the *"grievous wolves"* (Acts 20:29), or "elders from within" that would destroy the flock of God.

Thus was the setting of Paul's epistles, and the strong exhortations, charges, warnings, and rebukes that Paul gave to Timothy in order to cleanse the church of both internal problems and external pressures. The church situation, as a whole, needs to be considered when it comes to the exegesis of 1 Timothy 2:8–15.

2. The City of Ephesus

The historical background and culture of the city of Ephesus provide an interesting background to aid in our understanding of the epistles to Timothy. From various Bible encyclopedias may be gleaned the following information, as adapted for our purposes here.

Legend has it that Ephesus was founded by the Amazons between the thirteenth and twelfth centuries BC. The city was the fourth largest in the Roman Empire, and it lay on the western coast of modern Turkey, in ancient Asia Minor.

Ephesus maintained one of the strongest goddess worship centers in history. It was the worship of the "Great Mother," or "Maternal Principle," who allegedly gave birth to both humans and the gods. In pre-Hellenistic times, a famous shrine was built to the "Mother Goddess," and tradition held that the original image had been brought by Amazons—women warriors—from the land of the Taurians on the Black Sea. "This idol was first placed in an oak tree but was later removed to a sanctuary, about which the rest of the habitation grew."[20]

Acts 19–20 speaks of the power of the cult of Diana (Roman name), or Artemis (Greek name). The silver shrines to the goddess Diana generated much revenue for the city of Ephesus. "Great is Diana of the Ephesians" was the cry, and many people believed that the original goddess had fallen from heaven. (See Acts 19:24, 27–28, 34–35.) When Paul preached that there was only one true God, Creator of heaven and earth, and the Ephesians came to faith in Christ, the businessmen of the city caused a riot. Believers burned their silver shrines, their magic books, and other witchcraft paraphernalia. (See Acts 19:18–20.) Countless pilgrims made their way into the city for worship festivals each year, and much wealth was poured into the treasuries of Ephesus, which became an enormous banking and finance center for all Asia Minor.

In the magnificent temple to Diana, there were over one hundred pillars, each one a gift of a king. This whole mammoth city, as well as much of the ancient world, worshipped Diana. Meanwhile, the relative value of a woman was almost nil, as far as her being recognized by the society of that day. Girls did not go off to school to be taught by the rabbis in the synagogue, as the boys did, but rather stayed home and became chattel. The Babylonian Talmud records that "to teach doctrine to a woman is to eat swine's flesh." In many cases, when a woman gave birth and the child was discovered to be a daughter, the mother was advised to let her child die from exposure and neglect. The most prominent position a woman could obtain was to be a temple prostitute, considered able to control the souls of men. Because the business of temple prostitution was connected with the trade guilds, the woman who controlled the worship through sensuality and the spirit of divination held a significant place of power over the men who, on other planes, treated her as dirt. Therefore, she was able to arise to a place of significance and worth, albeit through the misuse of her body. Subsequently, in the Christian church, a similar situation prevailed.

20. Richard Clark Kroeger and Catherine Clark Kroeger, *I Suffer Not a Woman: Rethinking 1 Timothy 2:11–15 in Light of Ancient Evidence* (Grand Rapids, MI: Baker Academic [a division of Baker Publishing Group], 1992), 31.

The women were the gaudiest, loudest, noisiest, most aggressive show-pieces one could imagine. In short, they ran the show. This was the artificial and incorrect expression of a desire for fulfillment and worth in all areas of life, and it was this situation Paul was addressing, as will become clearer in the exegesis of 1 Timothy 2:8–15.

Various commentaries show that by the middle of the third century BC, Ephesus was inhabited by Jews, composing a population of 75,000 persons. As such, they were able to contend successfully for civil rights. There is evidence of Ephesian Jews being involved in magic, as they absorbed much of the culture of their surroundings.

Certain elements of Judaism, especially certain biblical stories, were adopted by the larger society. However, many of these elements became distorted and perverted. A kind of Jewish Gnosticism developed accordingly—an awful mixture of truth and error—as a syncretistic religion that held power over the Ephesians.

Lanny Hubbard of City Bible Temple in Portland, Oregon, in his paper "The Ordination of Women," provides from his research the following background for the 1 Timothy passage:

> Paul wrote the epistle to Timothy who was the bishop of the church in the city of Ephesus. This city was the largest, most influential city in all of Asia Minor. Paul saw that a strong church in this location was crucial to the gospel penetrating the whole region. This is why he personally spent two years there getting everything off to a good start.
>
> The book of Acts records the events of his ministry there. It was highlighted by great demonstrations of power, but also by great resistance from some of the local people. The city was affected by several things that greatly influenced the society as well as the new church. First, there was the presence of many cultic beliefs and practices. This gave rise to many false teachings that affected the way that people thought, and these often came into direct conflict with the teachings of the church. The nature of these false teachings not only adulterated the truth of the gospel message,

but they allured people back from Christianity to their old pagan ways. The result is that some were abandoning their faith in Jesus Christ to go back to their old sinful lifestyle.

The second thing that affected the society was the worship of Diana. Not only did the religion tie in with the economic stability of the region, but also it greatly affected the thinking of the people. Following are some of the elements in the beliefs of Diana that would run into direct conflict with those of Christianity.

1. Diana was believed to be the creator of life. She was a fertility figure that was responsible for the creation of mankind. Therefore, all men owed their existence to her and came out of her. This places a female as the origin for men.

2. She was believed to be the source of all wisdom and knowledge. Woman was seen as the wiser of the genders. This could also be added to a gnostic belief of that time that placed Eve as the hero (the "illuminator" of mankind) of the Eden narrative. According to their teaching, Adam was deceived and ate the forbidden fruit. It was not the fault of the woman. Interestingly, Eve and the serpent were seen as the wise ones in the story.

    Adam, they said, was Eve's son rather than her husband, a belief that reflected the gnostic doctrine that a female deity could bring forth children without male involvement. Eve taught the new revelation to Adam, and being the mother of us all, was the progenitor of the human race.

3. The presence of a female deity as the leading god of a region demonstrates the place of that gender in that society. The fact that the leading god was female showed a very high social status for females in that culture. It shows that women greatly influenced commerce, as well as the thinking of the society. The epistle to the Ephesians records that there was a group of very wealthy women in the church. Their wealth was seen in the elaborate clothing that they wore to the services. What we can learn is that the city had in it some very wealthy

businesswomen. They were allowed to function independently of any man. They had no dependency for a man as was common in a patriarchal culture. Therefore, in their thinking, no man had authority over them simply because he was a male.

This produced a social condition called matrilineal. A matrilineal society is one in which the wealth and authority rests in the hands of women. Women determined who would receive the family inheritance, not the father. Men would reside in positions of authority only as women of influence allowed it. It was not a matriarchy, where a woman had to be in the highest position of authority; it was simply that a man could not be in power without the women's approval.

This created a role reversal in the home. Husbands had no authority over the wives. Diana never married and she had a hatred for the males who pursued her, sometimes killing any who tried. She stayed a perpetual virgin. The thought of children and the confining responsibilities of married life did not appeal to her at all. She was seen as a roaming huntress, independent and going wherever she wanted to. She was not bound down by domestic life. In fact she was disappointed when a young virgin girl decided to marry and become a wife. They had to first offer a sacrifice to her before they got married in order to appease her. The result was a whole degrading view of marriage, and child rearing. Note: there is a lot of material in 1 Timothy about marriage, child rearing, and domestic life. This may explain why Paul had to refer so much to it.

4. All these together produced in the women a strong sense of freedom and independence from men. This attitude would come into the church. It would affect the families in the church. Conflicts between husbands and wives would go back to the basic elements of what Diana stood for. Is it any wonder Paul has to write in the epistle to the Ephesians "wives submit yourselves to your husbands."[21]

---

21. Lanny Hubbard, *The Ordination of Women* (Elders Retreat. Portland, OR: City Bible Church, 2000).

B. *The Epistle to Timothy*

We continue to note, with some additions, Lanny Hubbard's excellent comments:

To the church at Ephesus, with this cultural background, Paul wrote the passage we are now considering. In 1 Timothy 1:7 and 2 Timothy 4:3, Paul points to the presence of false teachers in Ephesus. These false teachers were bringing dangerous teachings into the church. Paul did not necessarily mention them by name, but he did speak about their character, to make them easy to identify.

The following are the character traits he mentioned:

1. They are proud—1 Timothy 6:4

2. They know nothing—1 Timothy 1:7; 6:4

3. They become obsessed with disputes—1 Timothy 6:4

4. They have corrupt minds—1 Timothy 6:5

5. They are destitute of the truth—1 Timothy 6:5

6. They suppose godliness is a means for gain—1 Timothy 6:5

7. They are deceptive—1 Timothy 4:1–3; Titus 1:10–13

8. They are immoral—1 Timothy 1:19, 20; 2:16, 19; Titus 1:15–16

Also, 2 Timothy 4:3–4 says that the time will come when men will not endure sound doctrine but will give way to the seductive lies of false teachers who traveled through the area. These individuals were going around teaching the following, from which we have many clues as to the problems that Timothy was facing in the new church at Ephesus:

1. Other doctrines (too many to name!)—1 Timothy 1:3

2. Myths and fables (endless genealogies; questions that cannot be answered)—1 Timothy 1:4; 4:4, 7; Titus 1:14

3. Jewish Law (Mosaic rituals and legalism of the law that are powerless to save)—1 Timothy 1:7; Titus 1:10, 14; 3:9

4. Genealogies—1 Timothy 1:4; Titus 3:9

5. That which is contrary to sound doctrine—1 Timothy 1:10

6. Doctrines of devils—1 Timothy 4:1

7. That marriage is forbidden—1 Timothy 4:3

8. That certain foods are to be abstained from—1 Timothy 4:3

9. Old wives' fables—1 Timothy 4:7

10. Idleness, gossip, and wandering—1 Timothy 5:11–15

11. Vain babblings—1 Timothy 6:20

12. Argumentation—1 Timothy 6:4, 20

13. Things falsely called knowledge (Gnosticism)—1 Timothy 6:20

14. Rebellion against civil leaders—1 Timothy 2:1–3

15. Reverence of other mediators besides Christ—1 Timothy 2:5

16. Association of wealth with godliness—1 Timothy 2:9; 6:5–10, 17–19

17. Female superiority (domineering women seizing authority over men in the home and/or the church)—1 Timothy 2:11–13

18. That Adam was deceived, not Eve (Gnostic teaching)—1 Timothy 2:14

19. A position that was anti-marriage, anti-creation, and anti-childbearing—1 Timothy 2:15; 5:14; 4:3, 4

20. Controversial words—1 Timothy 2:14

21. Profane and vain babblings that lead to ungodliness, and spiritual gangrene caused by the word of Hymenaeus and Philetus, who said the resurrection was past, and overthrew the faith of some believers—2 Timothy 2:16–18

22. A form of godliness but no real power—2 Timothy 3:5

23. Resistance of the truth—2 Timothy 3:6–7

24. Deceit and self-deception—2 Timothy 3:13

25. Unwholesome doctrine, fables, and unsound teachings—2 Timothy 4:1–4

The book of Titus is also considered to be one of the Pastoral Epistles. It was addressed to Titus, who had to handle similar problems in Crete, as seen in Titus 1:9–16:

> For there are many unruly and vain talkers and deceivers, specially they of the circumcision: whose mouths must be stopped, who subvert whole houses, teaching things which they ought not, for filthy lucre's sake. One of themselves, even a prophet of their own, said, the Cretians are alway liars, evil beasts, slow bellies. This witness is true. Wherefore rebuke them sharply, that they may be sound in the faith; not giving heed to Jewish fables, and commandments of men, that turn from the truth. Unto the pure all things are pure: but unto them that are defiled and unbelieving is nothing pure; but even their mind and conscience is defiled. They profess that they know God; but in works they deny him, being abominable, and disobedient, and unto every good work reprobate.

After telling Titus that the mouths of such must be stopped, as they were subverting whole houses (probably house churches), Paul told him that, after two or three admonitions, he was to reject from the fellowship those who had proven themselves to be heretics; for they are subverted, guilty, and self-condemned. (See Titus 3:9–11.)

In contrast to this extended list, Paul admonished Timothy about what ought to be taught in the church at Ephesus, as in all churches:

1. Words of faith—1 Timothy 4:6

2. Good or sound doctrine—1 Timothy 4:6

3. Godliness of lifestyle—1 Timothy 4:7, 8, 12; 6:3

4. Salvation—1 Timothy 4:10

5. The uniqueness of Christ as Mediator between man and God— 1 Timothy 2:5

6. The sacrifice of Christ—1 Timothy 2:6

7. The incarnation of Christ, God manifest in the flesh—1 Timothy 3:16

8.   The ascension and glorification of Christ—1 Timothy 3:16

It is significant that the word "*doctrine*" is used some seventeen times in the Pastoral Epistles, more than in any other book of the New Testament. This fact points to Paul's main concern, and shows what it was that Timothy and Titus both had to contend with. They needed to teach sound, wholesome doctrine to counter the false teachings of leaders in Ephesus and Crete, whether those leaders were men or women.

To ensure that the truth was taught in the churches, Paul devoted much of 1 Timothy to leadership. Only through the placement of good leaders in the church can error be prevented from coming in and polluting what God had started. Paul therefore listed the qualifications necessary for those who would hold these positions of authority.

Many of the comments made in these sections refer specifically to the male gender, but there are also sections dedicated to wives, and others for deacons, that apply to women. It is also interesting to note that many of the things Paul says to men, he also says specifically to women. Note the things that are specifically spoken to both genders in 1 Timothy:

Character Quality	To Men	To Women
Sober, temperate nature	3:2	3:11
Blamelessness	3:2; 6:14	5:7
Sober-mindedness	3:2	2:15
Honorableness	3:2	2:9
Faithfulness in marriage	3:2, 12	5:9
Not given to wine	3:3	3:11

The consistency in Paul's treatment of the two genders is found in his usage of the word "likewise," literally, "in the same way." This word is used in 2 Timothy 2:9 and 3:11 and in Titus 2:3, all verses that address women. Women were to have the same moral character as the men. There was no double standard set up that would distinguish the two.

C. *Passage and Textual Study—1 Timothy 2:1–10*

Having bridged the historical and cultural gaps relative to the church and city of Ephesus, we are now in a better position to make a careful study of 1 Timothy 2, especially the controversial passage of verses 11–15. We still need to bridge the linguistic gap between ourselves and the letter's original audience. What did the words mean to their intended hearers? They should mean the same to us, if we understand what they initially meant in their original social and cultural context. The context of the passage is viewed more fully here before verses 11–15 are expounded linguistically.

1. *1 Timothy 1:19–20*

Lanny Hubbard has this to say: "The context of the passage under consideration goes back to 1 Timothy 1:19–20. Here, Paul is reminding Timothy of the dangers in the false teaching that was going around the Ephesian area. The result of their teaching was that it had led some to reject their faith in Jesus Christ. The example given of two people who fell prey to this were Hymenaeus and Alexander. They were guilty of blasphemy, or speaking out against God. This confrontational and antagonistic lifestyle becomes the basis for what immediately follows."

2. *1 Timothy 2:1–7*

First Timothy 2:1 begins, *"I exhort therefore…."* This means that what is about to be said is connected to what has just been stated. The saints at Ephesus are called to pray for their political leaders. By supporting them, instead of resisting them, it would eventually pay off because the leaders would do a better job resulting in a peaceful and quiet life for the citizens. Paul states that the intended goal for his advice is so that the saints could live lives without disturbance or conflict. They could demonstrate godliness and reverence in all they did. This not only provides them with a more enjoyable life. but it is also pleasing in the sight of God. Verse 4 adds to this the point that God desires men everywhere to be saved. This desire, however, can be affected by how God's people live their lives in front of their societies. The conduct of the saints can either attract the unsaved to the Lord or they can keep them from Him. The demeanor of the Christian is an important witness to the unsaved that Christianity has something significant to offer them.

3. 1 Timothy 2:8–10

In verse 8, Paul then focuses on the specific responsibilities of both men and women that will pave the way for the fulfillment of God's desire— that people come to salvation. To the men, he says, *"Pray."* This sounds simple enough, but he adds that they are to pray *instead of* getting angry or doubting. The implication is that the men may have had a tendency to argue among themselves. The result of these conflicts was to generate doubt rather than faith among themselves and even among others. The goal of the prayer Paul exhorts in verse 1 is to enable the people to live quiet, peaceful lives in all godliness. This entire passage is calling for prayer that will promote a peaceful life of faith for the saints.

Verse 9 starts with the words *"In like manner also."* Thus, the advice that follows in the next verse is linked with what was just said. If the advice given to men was to pray so that they could live peaceful lives, it means the following advice to the women has to do with the same subject. Women are encouraged to dress modestly, in a fitting manner for women who profess godliness. (See 1 Timothy 2:9–10.) This is because those who came to the gathering of the church wearing extremely expensive or suggestive clothing were likely to cause a disturbance among the men by distracting them from the things of God. They were also likely to create an atmosphere of competitiveness among the women that would bring unrest to the whole group. Thus, they were to demonstrate their faith not in their shows of wealth but by their godly character.

Again, in verse 1, Paul encourages the men to *"pray every where, lifting up holy hands, without wrath and doubting."* Then, *"in like manner also"* (verse 2), Paul encourages the women—implying that the women may also "pray" and "lift up holy hands." It is not consistent to say the men can pray and not the women. However, the women are to dress modestly and behave soberly, as godly women. Chrysostom, Calvin, and many later commentators have argued that these verses were penned in order to direct men *and* women on how to lead prayers when the church was assembled. Men are to pray without anger or argument. Women are to pray in modest dress. So, Paul's desire that men should pray everywhere, with uplifted hands and a right attitude, extends to women as well. Women are to pray everywhere, with holy hands lifted, dressed in modest apparel.

"Lifting up holy hands" was a customary posture during public prayer, as an expression of a helpless appeal to God and a surrender to His will. The prayers were to be made *"without wrath and doubting,"* as only God's grace could restrain man's wrath and only faith in God could dissolve doubts.

In contrast to the women of the city of Ephesus who dressed in gaudy, extravagant garments to flaunt their wealth, Paul encourages the women of the church at Ephesus to *"adorn themselves in modest apparel."* They are to evidence *"shamefacedness"* (that is, reverence, not shame over being a woman!) and *"sobriety"* (self-restraint). They should *"not [have] broided [braided] hair, or gold, or pearls, or costly array; but (which becometh women professing godliness) good works"* (1 Timothy 2:9–10). The word for *"apparel"* in verse 9 is the Greek *katastole* (STRONG 2689), or a loose garment that reached the feet and was worn with a girdle or belt.

That Paul desires men *and* women to pray everywhere, lifting holy hands to God, should be kept in mind when one considers Paul's subsequent comments on women being silent. In 1 Timothy 2:11–12, he is simply confirming 1 Corinthians 11:4–5 and its implication that men *and* women may pray and prophesy.

In 1 Timothy 2:10, Paul speaks of women professing godliness by their good deeds. One woman who followed this injunction was Dorcas, who was *"full of good works and almsdeeds which she did"* (Acts 9:36). The Greek word for *"professing"* in 1 Timothy 2:10 is *epaggellomai* (STRONG 1861), coming from STRONG 1909 and the base of STRONG 32. It means "to announce upon (reflexively), i.e. (by implication) to engage to do something, to assert something respecting oneself," and it is translated "profess, (make) promise." The component parts of this word are STRONG 1909, *epi*, meaning "superimposition (of time, place, order, etc.), as a relation of distribution...i.e. over, upon...direction...

towards, upon," and STRONG 32, *aggelos*, meaning "to bring tidings...a messenger; especially an "angel"; by implication, a pastor." It is translated "angel, messenger."

The Greek word *epaggellomai* is used some fifteen times. In thirteen of those references, it has to do with something promised; in 1 Timothy 2:10; 6:21, it has to do with something professed. Something is promised to somebody often publicly.

Professor Ramsay (*The Expositor*, 1909) says of this very word in 6:21 that it "regularly implies that the person mentioned came before the public, with promises, in order to gain supporters; it is applied to candidates for municipal favor and votes in the Greek cities, who publicly announced what they intended to do for the general benefit, if they gained public support."

By implication, then, these *"women professing godliness"* were female preachers or teachers seeking to gain support for the cause of Christ in the church at Ephesus. And it would appear that some of these women were employing the wrong methods of seeking to gain support. It should be remembered that the Ephesian church was not meeting in some great cathedral. More likely, the church met in private homes, or house churches. It is difficult to imagine the hostess of a house church being "veiled" and "silenced," with men exclusively overseeing the gathering.

To summarize, we see from 1 Timothy 2:8–10 that Paul believed men *and* women could pray. They could pray everywhere. They could pray with uplifted, holy hands. The men were to pray with a good attitude, in peace and faith. The women were to pray with a good attitude, while dressed in modest apparel. And the women professing godliness, speaking publicly, and making promises were to demonstrate their godliness in their good works. This is groundwork for the next passage we will consider: 1 Timothy 2:11–15.

4. *1 Timothy 2:11–15*

Probably no other Scripture has been used more than this one to limit women's ministry in church life. With regard to the topic of our study, this passage is the most crucial, because it addresses not only a woman speaking in public but also a woman occupying a position of authority among or over men. The context—verse, passage, chapter, and book— needs to be kept in mind as we bridge the historical, cultural, and linguistic gaps in order to come to a biblical interpretation of what Paul meant, what his words meant to Timothy and the other hearers, and what his words should mean to us today.

Katharine C. Bushnell translates and punctuates the passage (verses 8–15) this way:

> Verse 8. I desire that the men pray everywhere lifting up holy hands, without wrath and doubting, and the women likewise [or "in like manner"].
>
> Verse 9. [I desire women] to array themselves in a befitted catastola, with reverence and restraint, not with braids, or gold, or pearls, or costly garments.
>
> Verse 10. But as becomes women proclaiming godliness, with good deeds.
>
> Verse 11. Let a woman learn, quietly, in all subjection [to God].
>
> Verse 12. Now I permit a woman neither to teach nor exercise authority over a man, but let her be in quietness.
>
> Verse 13. For Adam was first formed, then Eve.
>
> Verse 14. And Adam was not deceived [when he sinned]; but the woman, having [first] been thoroughly deceived, became [involved] in the transgression [of Adam],
>
> Verse 15. And she will be saved by the Child-bearing [i.e., the bearing of Jesus Christ], if they abide in faith, and love and sanctification with self-restraint.

Our exegesis is based on the King James Version of Scripture, with other translations being used, as appropriate, as light is thrown on the passage.

a. **"Let the woman learn" (verse 11).**

Paul's emphasis here is on women learning. In Jewish tradition, women did not always have the privilege of learning. Women were in bondage to the teachings of Judaism and traditions of the Talmud and the Mishna, which had been exalted to a place of authority equal to, and even higher than, the Scriptures. As has already been seen, the Talmud demeaned women in many ways, with such precepts as "Let the law be burned rather than committed to a woman," and "He that teaches his daughter the Law, is as though he taught her to sin."

The men became self-centered and self-fulfilled, resulting in a male-dominated society in which women were not permitted to become learned in the Scriptures. The result was the general illiteracy and ignorance of women—Jewish women, and even more so, Gentile women.

As we touched on earlier, Jesus Christ came to earth to break down these walls of separation and to destroy these instances of bondage. The gospels show how Jesus allowed women to learn from Him. He was addressing men and women alike when He said, "Come unto me,…take my yoke upon you, and learn of me" (Matthew 11:28–29). As already noted, His attitude toward women was in absolute contrast to that of the scribes and Pharisees.

Paul echoed Christ's attitude toward women by acknowledging that the women in the church could learn. His position was that they need no longer be kept under the bondage of illiteracy and ignorance of divine things.

Also, as previously discussed, the Ephesians worshipped the goddess Diana (also called Artemis) and were greatly influenced by the teachings of Gnosticism. The women needed to learn the truth of God's Word so they would not be influenced and deceived by the false teachers moving through society, or by those who wove their way in the believers' homes, the house churches. Paul wanted the women to learn. He did not believe women were incapable of learning the Word of God and things pertaining to the gospel. They were to learn so as not to be deceived, as Eve was. (See 1 Timothy 2:14.) They needed to learn first, before they could teach!

b. **"Let the woman learn in silence...[and] be in silence" (verses 11–12).**

A surface reading of these two verses, with their repetition of the word "silence," would point to total or absolute silence. Yet the Greek word used in both instances is hesuchia (STRONG 2271), meaning "stillness, quietness." *Thayer's Greek Lexicon* translates it as follows: "quietness: descriptive of the life of one who stays at home doing his own work, and does not officiously meddle with the affairs of others; silence." It implies a still or peaceable state, brought about, for example, by keeping one's seat and not disturbing the environment. *Strong's Exhaustive Concordance* renders it this way: "stillness, i.e. desistance from bustle or language." It does not mean absolute silence, in contrast to Acts 21:40; 1 Corinthians 14:28; and Revelation 8:1, where the Greek word used is *sigé* (STRONG 4602), meaning "to hiss...or hush; silence."

The Greek word *hesuchia* does not refer to women being uncommunicative, mute, or speechless, but rather means they are restful, at peace, tranquil. The same Greek root is translated as *"peaceable"* in 1 Timothy 2:2, *"quiet"* in 1 Peter 3:4, and *"quietness"* in 2 Thessalonians 3:12.

Timothy, as Paul's companion and son in the faith, knew of the women who traveled with Paul. He knew of Paul's writings to the Corinthian church (see 1 Corinthians 4:14–17), and what Paul taught in all the churches. He knew that Paul had told women to be silent in the church gatherings, meaning they should not chatter, babble, or ask questions of their husbands out of place in the services. (See 1 Corinthians 14:34–35.) He knew that women could pray and prophesy in proper order in the services. (See 1 Corinthians 11:4–5.) Timothy knew, then, that Paul was not speaking of total, absolute silence in 1 Timothy 2:11–12.

Paul penned 1 Corinthians 11:4–5; 14:34–35 while he was at Ephesus, about AD 53–57. Timothy would have known that Paul wrote his epistle to the Ephesians during his first imprisonment in Rome, somewhere about AD 57–62. Now, Timothy receives his own epistle, some ten years after Paul's release from prison. When he first reads it, he understands Paul to mean the following:

> › Women may pray and prophesy. (See 1 Corinthians 11:4–5.) Thus, Paul does not demand absolute silence of them.

> › Men and women may pray in the church, provided they pray with decorum and the right attitude. (See 1 Timothy 2:8–10.)

> › Sons and daughters are to prophesy. (See Acts 2:17.)

> › Older women are to teach the younger women. (See Titus 2:3–5.) Again, the *"silence"* commanded in 1 Timothy 2:11–12 cannot and does not mean absolute silence!

Timothy was aware that Paul had been at Philip's house, where Philip's four daughters prophesied. (See Acts 21:9.) He also knew of Paul's love for Aquila and his wife, Priscilla, who were teachers together. (See Acts 18:24–26; Romans 16:3; 2 Timothy 4:19.) He certainly knew of Phoebe, the deaconess of Cenchrea. (See Romans 16:1–2.) The epistle of 1 Timothy itself has enough comments to make clear Paul's thoughts on women, even woman presbyters. Timothy would also have known of Paul's word to Titus about old women teaching younger women. (See again Titus 2:3–5.) Paul would not have contradicted himself. Thus, Timothy would have understood that Paul was not commanding the absolute silence of women.

Most churches and denominations today, generally speaking, do not take Paul at his literal word. Otherwise, women would not be permitted to sing hymns and spiritual songs, even though all people are commanded to do so in Colossians 3:16 and Ephesians 5:19. Nor would they be allowed to pray in a mixed congregation of men and women, let alone in exclusively women's meetings. Nor could they teach Sunday school classes, instruct the children and youth, and so forth.

Paul is simply saying that the woman is to learn in quietness and stillness. She is to be peaceful, restful and tranquil in her spirit and attitude, not disturbing in her life or language. Paul is not calling for muteness or dumbness, nor is he barring women from all forms of communication. He is saying that women, like men, are to be quiet, peaceful, restful in spirit, not striving out of a spirit of discord. In 1 Corinthians and 1 Timothy alike, Paul affirms that women may pray and/or prophesy, and learn, as well—as long as they do so with a meek and quiet spirit (which the men are also expected to keep).

c. **"Let the woman learn...with all subjection" (verse 11).**

The Greek word for *"subjection"* here is *hupotassó* (STRONG 5293), coming from *hypó*, "under," and *tasso*, "to arrange." In the context of the New Testament, it speaks of the marriage relationship. (See, for example, Titus 2:5.) Paul is saying that the woman is to learn in a spirit of quietness and submissiveness. It means that she should not assert her rights but should yield to the preference of others, especially that of her husband. The word *"woman"* is in the singular; Paul does not say "women," plural. A careful, fuller study of verses 13–14 confirms that Paul is dealing with a husband/wife situation rather than a church situation, just as for Adam/Eve, the first husband/wife situation to which Paul refers. Yet this nuance is often overlooked by expositors.

When Paul wrote his epistles, Christian women were being liberated from the bondage of Jewish tradition and law, and the only example they had in the Ephesian culture was that of the pagan priestesses who controlled everything in the temple of Diana in a wild, unrestrained manner.

The *"subjection"* Paul speaks of here does not mean submission to the men but *submission in the church.* He is saying that the women must not be like the false teachers, whether men or women, with whom Paul was dealing through Timothy.

He says, further, that...

> Women are to be in subjection to the proper church order. (See 1 Timothy 2:11.)

> Children are to be in subjection, as well. (See 1 Timothy 3:4.)

> Wives are to be in subjection to their own husbands. (See 1 Peter 3:1, 5.)

> All believers are to submit (be subject) to one another. (See Ephesians 5:21.)

Paul is saying, "Let the women learn, but let them learn in a quiet and peaceful spirit, and with willing submission, or a proper attitude."

d. *"But I suffer not a woman to teach"* (verse 12).

The Greek word for *"teach"* here is *didaskó* (STRONG 1321). The related Greek words have to do with the instructor (himself or herself) or the instruction (the substance of what is taught). Thus, the term, as used in this verse, involves both the teacher and the teaching, or doctrine.

So, what is Paul saying here? Is he laying down a law for all times, for all cultures, for all Christians, for all nations, that no woman is allowed to teach in any manner? Are women to be in absolute silence in church life, universally? Or is Paul speaking of a local situation with which Timothy needs to deal, or is already dealing?

It would appear that Paul is making a double prohibition here. He does not permit a woman to (1) teach, and/or (2) to usurp authority over a man. The word *"suffer,"* in this case, means "permit" or "allow." So, Paul is saying he does not permit, allow, put up with, or tolerate a woman teaching or usurping authority over the man.

The familiar word "teach" is used many times throughout the New Testament. This verse, in particular, links the term "teach" with the matter of a woman having authority over a man. Therefore, we can see that Paul was not referring to any type of teaching, but only that which is connected with authority. The two thoughts belong together and should not be separated into two distinct ideas.

In no way can Paul be made to say that he forbids all women in all places for all times to teach. In his pastoral epistle to Titus, Paul says that the older women are to be *"teachers of good things"* (Titus 2:3) as they *"teach the young women"* (Titus 2:4), and then he lists eight things that the older women are to teach the younger women.

A "teacher of good [things]" is STRONG 2567, *kalodidaskolos*. This Greek word is made up of *kalos*, meaning "beautiful, chief, good, valuable, virtuous," and *didaskolos*, meaning "an instructor" but generally translated as a specific type of instructor, such as a doctor, a master, or a teacher. So, Paul is saying that a woman can be a teacher of good things; and an older woman is to teach good things to younger women. A woman may teach what has been laid in apostolic doctrine. Neither a man nor a woman should originate "new doctrine," but both may teach what is already laid down in *"the apostles' doctrine"* (Acts 2:42). There is no new teaching or doctrine to be added to what is already laid down in the Word. How can a woman be silent and yet teach younger women?

Again, there is no honest way to say that Paul is forbidding all women, everywhere, for all times, to teach. To do so is to put words in his mouth that he neither spoke nor wrote, as well as to contradict his other writings. Paul acknowledged Priscilla and Aquila as teachers of the Word of God and as his companions in the gospel. Both of them—the husband, Aquila, and the wife, Priscilla—were teachers.

If Paul's words are taken literally, as intending to silence all women, universally, then untold thousands of women who teach their children the Scriptures, as did Timothy's own mother and grandmother (see 2 Timothy 1:5; 3:14–15), or teach other children—boys and girls, young people, youth/adults—should stop their teaching. Thus, over half the members of the body of Christ worldwide should be totally silent. What a ridiculous concept!

Paul is dealing with a local situation. He is not saying, "I suffer not a woman to teach," as proven by Titus 2:3–5. He is saying, "I suffer not a woman to teach in an authoritative or domineering manner over the man." This is the kind of teaching Paul is forbidding. The same Greek word is used in 1 Timothy 2:11 and Titus 3:4. Women may teach, just not in a manner that usurps authority over men.

The role of teacher was a ministry of great esteem. Jesus was the "Master Teacher." He was the Rabbi. (See, for example, John 3:1–5.) He was the Establisher of all true doctrine for the church. As the Master Teacher, He passed this doctrine on to the apostles, who in turn passed it on to the church and to various ministries the Lord had gifted. (See Acts 2:42.) Since that time, it has been a rule that all teachers, whether men and women, must teach according to the Word of God, not originating any contrary or unsound doctrine. That is the theme of the Pastoral Epistles.

In 1 Timothy 2:13–14, there is the implication that Eve seized authority over her husband, Adam, and "taught" him something she had received from the tree of knowledge of good and evil. That is the implication in the whole of this passage, as will be developed more fully later on.

A negative example of a woman usurping authority over a man is found in Revelation 2:20, where the Lord says to the angel of the church at Thyatira, through the apostle John, "*Notwithstanding I have a few things against thee, because thou sufferest that woman Jezebel, which calleth herself a prophetess, to teach and to seduce my servants to commit fornication, and to eat things sacrificed unto idols.*" Some commentaries suggest that the *"Jezebel"* of the church at Thyatira (which means "ruled by a woman") was the wife of the *"angel,"* or *angelos*—the minister of the church. Whether or not this was so, the issue here is that a woman was suffered (permitted) to teach false doctrine, immorality, and idolatry, thereby seducing the people of God by erroneous teaching that was contrary to the apostles' doctrine.

Note that the words *"woman"* and *"she"* in 1 Timothy 2:11–13 are singular, as is the word *"man"* in 1 Timothy 2:12. This fact seems to point to a particular woman who was usurping authority over "the man," her husband, either at home or in the church. The plural pronoun *"they,"* in reference to women, is not used until verse 15 of 1 Timothy 2. And in verses 13–14, Paul does refer to one man, Adam, and one woman, Eve, who were the original married pair, the first man and the first woman.

Paul cannot be made to say that he was forever subjecting all women to all men through all ages. The wife is subject to her own husband, not to any other man, whoever he might be, in the setting of the home or the church. The teaching that "man is the ruler, and woman the ruled" at all times and in all situations is contrary to the whole tenor and revelation of the Bible. Man is not superior because he is a man. A woman is not inferior because she happens to have been born a woman. All are co-equal "in Christ"; no one is superior or inferior.

In summary, Paul is saying that the woman should learn in a meek, quiet spirit and attitude, and in proper order, whether at home or in church. The woman must not teach in an authoritative manner over the man, whether he is her husband or the ruler in the church. That is what Paul, in principle, has said so far.

e. *"But I suffer not a woman…to usurp authority over the man"* (verse 12).

The Greek word for *"man"* is *anér* (STRONG 435). Some expositors say that Paul uses it here to speak expressly of "the husband." This word makes 59 appearances throughout the Pauline epistles, 34 of which the King James Version translates it as *"husband."* Of the remaining 25 occurrences, 18 are cases where the text is clearly speaking of a husband. Therefore, it seems reasonable to translate it in the same way in this case, so that 1 Timothy 2:12 may be understood as saying, "The woman is not to usurp authority over her husband."

The context of verses 13–15 speak of Adam and Eve, the first husband and the first wife, and points to the event of Eve usurping authority over her husband, Adam, in the fall. Thus, the woman—a wife—must not usurp authority over the man—her husband—but be in subjection to him.

This is also the word of the Lord through Paul in his other epistles. (See, for example, Ephesians 5:22–33.)

Unfortunately, some translators have shown their bias on this matter. Consider the wording of 1 Timothy 2:12 in *The Living Bible*: *"I never let women teach men."* And *The Amplified Bible* renders the latter part of this verse as follows: *"[The woman] is to…keep silence [in religious assemblies]."*

As a reminder, the words *"woman"* and *"man"* are singular, not plural. In context, Paul is speaking of Adam (the man) and Eve (the woman), whose relationship makes the statement applicable to married couples. The verse should not be forced to fit all church-life situations, though the same principle would often apply. Further proof that Paul was referring to the husband/wife relationship is verse 15, where the wife's being saved through childbirth is mentioned, *"if they* [the wives] *continue"* a Christian lifestyle.

The issue here is that which pertains to "authority." Paul writes that he does not permit a woman *"to usurp authority over the man"* (1 Timothy 2:12). That is, he does not permit a wife to usurp authority over her husband.

The word *"usurp"* in this verse has become a matter of great debate. The Greek word, *authenteó* (STRONG 831), is used only once in the entire New Testament. There are two prominent aspects taught by commentators on this word, which are noted here.

1.) Seizing the authority

Linguistically the phrase *"usurp authority"* is "to act on one's own authority; to exercise authority; to have mastery or be dominating; to be an autocrat." It is to be dictatorial.

Various translations render this phrase as follows:

o   *"exercise authority over"* (NASB)

o   *"have authority over"* (ROTHERHAM)

- o "to rule over" (Alford)
- o "to claim authority" (Conybeare's translation)
- o *"to domineer over"* (BERKELEY)
- o *"dictate to"* (MOFFATT)
- o "issue commands" (Knox)
- o *"lord it over"* (TLB)
- o *"practice...domineering over a husband"* (williams new testament)
- o "to exercise authority on one's account,...to usurp authority" (*Vine's Complete Expository Dictionary of Old and New Testament Words*)
- o "to have full power and authority over" (*Liddell & Scott's Greek-English Lexicon*)
- o "to hold sovereign authority; assume authority; act on one's own authority; presume; play the despot; act arbitrarily" (Lampe)
- o "to have authority; domineer over someone" (Bayer)

Most other translations simply say, for example, "take authority over the man," or "to take or assume and hold in possession by force or without" authority over the man. To usurp authority is to arrogate, to seize control, to seize authority over—in this case, by a wife over her husband. As illustrated by Jezebel, as mentioned in Revelation 2:20, it is a forcible seizure of power over the man, the husband. It is self-willed arbitrary behavior of the woman spoken of here. Paul is dealing with a very strong kind of authority being exercised.

Speaking on this passage, Jack Hayford comments:

> In this spirit, the woman is not to "usurp authority," i.e., not to be domineering (authentew). This verb occurs this one time in the entire New Testament. The intent of instruction here is against an

overbearing, demeaning control of her spouse. If the idea intended had to do with authority in the divine structure of the church, other terms more consistent with New Testament usage would have been employed.

Ernest Gentile says:

> It appears, therefore, that our paragraph under consideration is basically talking of the proper husband/wife relationship and their respective testimony to the world. The men are unashamedly to take the leadership in prayer and the women are to dress moderately and maintain a demeanor that is modest and serious. Women have the need and the right to learn (at that time women were not given educational and vocational opportunities like men), and they will do so if they maintain a contented, peaceable spirit, free of strife and discord, as they listen to the instructions and explanations of their husbands. Paul forbids the wives to dominate their husbands.

2.) *The Originator of Man*

Don Rousu in adds some further thought to the matter of "usurping authority." He writes of his radical shift regarding the role of women in ministry, and how this major passage in Timothy has been used to silence women in church life. He comments on the fact that valuable evidence has accumulated on the original Greek use of the word *authentein*. He believes that translators have missed the original use of this word. We note some of his thoughts: "Research shows that the meaning of 'authentein' changed dramatically over a period of 1,100 years. When we first find it in classical literature of the 6th century BC, the word usually meant 'to initiate or to be responsible for a murder.'"

Two Texts on Women (Ben Wiebe, *Horizons in Biblical Theology*, June 94) comments on the word *authentein*. In classical use, the word refers to the violent act of murder or suicide. In the Hellenistic period this use of the word widens to include the performance of a criminal act, concerned with personal initiative or aggressive action (*Josephus*). Philo, in a single reference, uses the word to refer to the act of suicide. The word continues to be used to refer to actions of power against others. In these occurrences of the word close in time to the New Testament, there is one essential element: *authentein* signifies action against or the perpetration of a crime against another. The word included a substantially negative element (i.e., to act aggressively against another, to instigate forceful action or to dominate others)."

Don Rousu continues:

> Jumping ahead to 200 or 300 AD this word usually meant "to claim ownership of property" either rightfully or wrongfully through fraud. During the same period it could also mean "to usurp power." However around the time the New Testament was written, the most common meaning of authentein was "to be, or claim to be the author or the originator of something." To underscore the point with a pun, this appears to be the authentic translation of authentein, the crucial verb of 1 Timothy 1:12.
>
> Not only have the translators overlooked the prevailing meaning of the word "authentein" at the time the New Testament was written, but they also seem to have missed the cultural context in which Paul wrote his letter to Timothy.
>
> I believe Paul is saying, "I am not allowing (present tense for that situation) a woman to teach or to proclaim herself the originator of man (authen-

tein).".…Paul goes on to say "she must be in agreement," meaning agreement with the Scriptures and with sound teaching in the Church.

He continues in this vein saying, "Adam was formed first, then Eve." This statement militates against the doctrine of Eve as progenitor. He also says, "Adam was not deceived, but the woman was! And sinned!" This statement directly contradicts the notion that Eve was the "illuminator," and carrier of new revelation.

> I submit that this translation is possibly the most legitimate because it fits the social context, is true to the Greek, speaks to the troubled situation, and lines up perfectly with all of Paul's other teachings and practices concerning women.

As has already been seen on the history and culture of Ephesus, Gnosticism taught that Eve was the first virgin, the one who had no husband, and was the originator of life. She was the "illuminator," full of all wisdom, and Adam was actually given life when he saw her co-likeness lying flat upon the earth. She "commanded" him to live, and when Adam saw her, he said, "You will be called 'the mother of the living,' because you are the one who has given me life."

This Gnostic belief is a heresy, of course. The Bible clearly teaches that Adam was created first, then Eve. The idea that *authentein* may mean "originator" instead of *"usurp authority"* seems to fit in light of the rest of the verse: *"For Adam was formed first...."*

This passage could very well have been written to attack the Gnostic teaching that Eve was the creator of man. A further blow is dealt when Paul says in 1 Timothy 2:14 that it was Eve who was deceived. The "Eve" of Gnosticism could not have been deceived, because she was considered to be the "all-wise illuminator." This would be an endeavor to deal with the prevailing mother-goddess heresy and the Gnosticism emerging in the time of Timothy and Titus. Paul was correcting either "a woman" or "a wife" who was teaching some kind of heresy.

All translators and commentators recognize that the meaning of words can and does change over the centuries. But, putting together the various meanings of this word *authentein*, it would seem that a certain woman (specifically, a wife) was seizing authority and teaching the false doctrine that woman is the originator of man, hence Paul's refutation of the Ephesian goddess Diana and the Gnostic heresy in the verses that follow, as he emphasizes that. Adam was formed first, then Eve. Adam was not deceived, Eve was.

It is also worth pointing out that when Paul speaks of *"authority"* in 1 Timothy 2:12, he does not use the Greek words *exousia* or *kyrieuo*, which he does employ in certain other discussions of authority. Here, as we have noted, he uses the word *authentein*, which speaks of a specific kind of authority.

Following is a list of definitions of *authentein* compiled from various Greek lexicons.

1. "to have rule over, dominion"—*Analytical Lexicon of the Greek New Testament*

2. "to act on one's own authority, autocrat. It comes from autos—oneself, and entea—to arm or take weapons. It is a person who takes arms into his own hands and exercised the power to kill another"—*Linguistic Key to the Greek New Testament*

3. "murder, absolute mastery, acting on one's own authority. It comes from autos—oneself—and entea—to arm or take weapons. It is a person who takes arms into his own hands and exercises the power to kill another. The passage deals with wives and husbands. She is not to do something that would cause her to try to master her husband. She should avoid any activity that would in

any way affect her marriage relationship"—*Word Study Dictionary*

4. "to hold sovereign authority. To assume one's own authority or act arbitrarily. To presume on one's own authority. The related word authentia means independence or on one's own initiative. It carries the idea of license, arbitrary, unauthorized, high handed, or tyranny. It is one who plays the despot"—*Patristic Greek Lexicon*

5. "to domineer over someone"—*Bauer's Greek-English Lexicon*

6. "to exercise authority on one's own account or usurp authority"—*Vine's*

Lanny Hubbard provides the following insights:

> There is a difference between this word and others traditionally used by Paul for authority. Though the definitions provided seem to vary to a degree, there is a common aspect shared among most of them. This word has the idea of self-initiating. This person forces themselves into a controlling position over others. They are not responding to a legitimate appointment to a position, but are violently taking the position under their own personal directive. This is tyranny and revolution.
>
> The verse then connects the act of teaching to this quality. It is not mere teaching but teaching that promotes oneself, or tears down another. In this passage, it is directed to the wives and their relationship to their husbands. The silence that is next mentioned represents a peaceful lifestyle not disturbed with this activity. When we consider back to some of the characteristics of Diana worship, such a negative look of men and marriage, it

is easy to see where these ideas could have originated.

Rick Johnston offers the following comments on the word *usurp*:

> The correct dictionary definition of "usurp" is "to take possession of, by use, to seize and hold in possession" (Webster's). This literal definition is probably closest to the original Greek idea although it does not employ the full idea of this type of authority indicated in the Greek. In most discussions of the issue, the idea of usurp is to throw off or pre-empt the authority of a man. This is not, as we will see, the idea presented in the text. It is interesting to note that the word used in this particular passage for authority is a word used only once in the entire New Testament. It is not one of five other words for authority used in the New Testament, used to express all other aspects of authority, but it is here used only once to express a certain type of situation which was readily understood in New Testament times.
>
> The Greek word authentein means "one who acts upon the basis of his own authority, one who does a thing himself." In classical usage, "one who with his own hand kills either himself or others." It is the word from which the English word "autocrat" comes which means to self-govern. It is a self-styled authoritarian exercise by a woman in the church at Ephesus.
>
> This is the word used to express the idea of 'absolute power or sway like that of an autocrat or despot', 'playing the master' is the idea connected with its sister term in the literary usage of the word. The concept of a certain type of au-

thority here is evident. An authority that is taken or grasped by one from nowhere (not having a source) and exercised in a despotic manner. Thus an artificial authority is created. For any authority exercised not having been received of another is an artificial, contrived or pseudo authority. To a situation in the church common to their understanding, Paul speaks very plainly. A woman is not to, on the basis of her own authority (an artificial authority, not a delegated authority), rise up and begin to teach the congregation and thereby not recognize the headship and leadership already established in the congregation. This was the situation in the pagan temple where the women conducted the whole religious ceremony from the worship to the teaching through the power of immorality and the spirit of divination. This same pattern was prevalent in the true church at Ephesus, the city where this type of worship was propagated.

Hopefully, enough of an argument has been made on the issue of "usurping authority"—an act that should not be committed at all, by men or women.

Paul is not saying that a woman can neither exercise nor "have" authority. He is saying a woman must not seize authority. A wife must not be arrogant, bossy, or domineering over her husband. A woman should not be a self-appointed, self-styled leader. She must not teach doctrine that is contrary to the apostles' doctrine. And whatever is said of the woman also applies to the man. Men and women may exercise authority, but neither one should usurp a position of authority or seize authority by force. This is what Lucifer (Satan) tried to do—his original sin—which resulted in his fall before the throne of God. (See Isaiah 14:12–14.)

We have already mentioned Jezebel, the wife of Ahab, as an example of a woman who "seized authority"; she brought about the murder of Naboth, in order to secure possession of his vineyard. (See 1 Kings 21; Revelation 2:20.) Wicked Queen Athaliah is another example of a wife who usurped a man's authority: she seized the throne of Judah after killing all the royal seed. (See 2 Kings 11.) These are examples of the type of authority Paul is dealing with here. The authority in the church must not be self-styled and authoritarian but must be under the authority of Christ, the Head of the church. Godly women must not be characterized by the qualities of the goddess Diana, as in the pagan temple of Ephesus!

Paul is saying, in short:

o Women are to learn in a quiet and peaceful spirit and attitude.

o Women are not to teach that which is contrary to the apostles' doctrine.

o Women/wives must not usurp or seize authority over the men/husbands, but each wife is to be in subjection to her husband. The husband is the head of the wife, as Adam was of Even. And both are under the headship of Christ.

o Women are not forbidden to teach; in another passage, Paul talks of the importance of older women teaching the younger women. He also acknowledged a female teachers, Priscilla, and her husband, Aquila, who were teachers together and ministerial companions of his at Ephesus.

o A wife must not be domineering over her husband. A woman may exercise authority as she acts under authority, but both she and her husband should be under the authority of Christ. (See 1 Corinthians 11:3.) God is the Head of Christ; Christ is the Head of the church and of man; and man is the head of the woman.

o   Woman was not the originator of man. Adam was formed first, then Eve.

o   Woman is not the illuminator of man. Adam was not deceived; Eve was.

On the basis of Kroeger and Kroeger's understanding of *authentein*, the translation of 1 Timothy 2:12 may read, "I do not permit a woman to teach or declare herself the originator of man. But she is to be in (peaceful) conformity (with the Scriptures as a respectful student)...."

Bushnell translates it: "I suffer not a woman to teach or to control a man."[22]

And Williams translates it: "I do not permit a married woman to practice teaching or domineering over a husband; she must keep quiet."

Jack Hayford translates it: "Women need to learn—to be teachable—and to receive in a quiet and submissive spirit those things being taught. Further, I refuse to give place to a woman who practices a bossy and domineering way toward her husband. She is to be quiet."

f.   *"For Adam was first formed, then Eve"* (1 Timothy 2:13).

With regard to this statement, it is needful to keep in mind some of the teachings of the cult of Diana and the various groups of Gnostics around Ephesus.

As Don Rousu reminds us:

> Timothy was in Ephesus. Ephesus was the world centre of paganism governed spiritually by the female deity Artemis whom the Romans called Diana. The cult of Artemis taught the

22. Bushnell, *God's Word to Women*, 121.

superiority of the female and advocated female domination of the male. It espoused a doctrine of feminine procreation, teaching that this goddess was able to bring forth offspring without male involvement. The cult was characterized by sexual perversion, fertility rites, endless myths, and elaborate genealogies traced through female rather than male bloodlines. Magic, and all manner of demonic activity flourished.

Also present in Ephesus was a contingent of Jewish gnostics who represented the first century's equivalent of the New Age movement. The Greek word for "gnostic"·is "gnosis" meaning "knowledge." Gnostics acknowledged spirit guides and combined the teachings of Artemis with the teachings of the Old Testament. An example of their distortion of Scripture is evident in their version of the Old Testament story of Adam and Eve.

In the most prevalent gnostic version of the story, Eve was the "illuminator" of mankind because she was the first to receive "true knowledge" from the serpent, whom gnostics saw as the "saviour" and revealer of truth. Gnostics believed that Eve taught this new revelation to Adam, and being the mother of all, was the progenitor of the human race. Adam, they said, was Eve's son rather than her husband. This belief reflected the gnostic doctrine that a female deity could bring forth children without male involvement.

...

These gnostic teachings infiltrated the Church, and in writing to Timothy, Paul encouraged him to confront the people from peddling their false teachings in the Church and to admonish others to turn away from myths and endless genealogies. He told him to oppose those who speak falsely of the living God, warn people about the doctrines of demons, avoid stupid, senseless controversies, and have nothing to do with old wives' tales such as the corrupted story of Adam and Eve. He urged Timothy to use the Scriptures as an antidote "for sound teaching, reproof, correction, and training in righteousness."[23]

George Byron Koch makes the following comments on 1 Timothy 2:13.

> Remember that present in the city of Ephesus were two similar heresies which were likely infecting the church:
>
> One of them was that the goddess Diana was the fertile creator of mankind. All men were birthed from Diana, as were all women. She was the author of all of them. This is what the surrounding culture believed, and this surely influenced the church just as the strong beliefs of our present culture—about sex, for example—affect the beliefs of many church members and teachers.
>
> A second, similar heresy came from the Gnostics, prevalent in Ephesus, and throughout Asia Minor: Eve was the <u>mother</u> of Adam, and the author of mankind!
>
> There's much more to this Gnostic teaching than is useful to consider here, but the basic theology was this: Eve was the goddess, and Eve created, with the help of the serpent, Adam. In fact, the God of the Bible is portrayed in these texts

---

23. Rousu, "Truth about Women in Public Ministry."

as an insecure minor deity who tries to prevent the wonderful work Eve and the serpent are doing in creating new gods—the humans. This heresy takes the very sin of Adam and Eve, and turns it into an act to be praised, led by Eve as mother/author of mankind and the serpent as her lover!

Realizing that this is a heresy Paul will want to combat vigorously, let me read you another translation of the Greek into English, which is as legitimate a translation as the common one, but simply makes more sense in context: "I do not permit a woman to teach that she is the author of man. She must be in conformity (that is, with scripture and orthodox teaching). For Adam was formed first, and then Eve."

This is very Pauline. Paul explains an error, and then he corrects it. I believe this is what Paul is doing here. This heresy, among many others, was being taught: that woman was the author of man. In effect, what Paul is saying is "this is not what Scripture tells us. This may be what the cult of Diana believes, and what the Gnostics believe, and it is a heresy taught in this church, but it is not what scripture tells us. And if a woman is to teach, she must not teach that woman is the author of man—because scripture teaches that Adam was formed first, and then Eve."[24]

In light of these comments, the statement "Adam was first formed, then Eve" makes more sense to our minds. Paul gives two arguments to refute the false teachings in Ephesus, both of the cult of Diana and of the Gnostics. One of Paul's arguments refers back to the creation order (see chapter 4); the other invokes the order of the fall (see chapter 5).

24. George Byron Koch, "Shall a Woman Keep Silent? Part 2," Tape #112 (June 2, 1996). Church of the Resurrection, Chicago, Illinois.

> Adam was first formed, then Eve—verse 13 (creation's order).

> Adam was not deceived; Eve was—verse 14 (transgression's order). Eve sinned first, then Adam followed.

In the first argument, Paul is referring back to God's order in creation. (See Genesis 1:26–28; 2; 1 Corinthians 11:9.) Adam was created first, and then Eve was created out of Adam.

What Paul is *not* saying, contrary to the belief of some expositors, is that because woman was created second, she is inferior to man and is therefore to take second place as an inferior being. Paul is not advocating the permanent, universal subordination of woman to man. In chapter 4, we saw that Adam was not superior to Eve, nor was Eve inferior to Adam. Both were made in the image of God. (See Genesis 1:26–28.) They were co-equal as persons before God. This truth is demonstrated in the co-equality of the Persons in the Godhead, with Father, Son, and Holy Spirit being co-equal as divine Persons, but in divine order. There is no superiority or inferiority in the Godhead. It is simply divine order. Under the new covenant, men and women are redemptively equal, of identical value and worth before God. (See Galatians 3:28.) Both Adam and Eve were sinners. Both needed salvation. And both needed to be redeemed through Christ alone.

Even great theologians like Martin Luther and John Calvin taught that the female sex is "inferior to the male sex" and should be subordinated to man. Adam Clarke also taught that "God designed [the man] that he should have the pre-eminence. The structure of woman's body plainly proves that she was never designed for those exertions required in public life. In this the chief part of the natural inferiority of woman is to be sought."[25]

Paul sets the creation order aright, refuting the Gnostics and the cult of Diana, who claimed that Eve was the originator of man, that woman was created first, and that man is of the woman and is therefore dependent upon, and inferior to, her. So, the creation

---

25. Adam Clarke, *Commentary on the Bible* (1831), sacredtexts.com.

order was Adam first, then Eve. Both were co-equal as persons in the sight of God. There was no superiority or inferiority but co-equality, yet they were functionally different, being male and female. The first man/husband and first woman/wife were the joint-rulers of creation. Both were created in divine order. That is the point Paul reestablishes here.

g. **"And Adam was not deceived, but the woman being deceived was in the transgression" (verse 14).**

Here, in 1 Timothy 2:14, divine order is reversed. As we discussed in chapter 5 of this text, the woman, Eve, was deceived first. She fell into transgression, for sin is the transgression of God's law. (See 1 John 3:4.) She gave to her husband, and he ate of the forbidden fruit with her. (See Genesis 3:1–6.) Adam was not deceived, for he had been given the original command not to eat of the forbidden tree in Eden. (See Genesis 2:16–17.)

In the creation order, it was Adam, then Eve. In the fall, the order was reversed: It was Eve, then Adam. In the passage under consideration, it was in the fall that the woman "seized authority over the man"—Eve took the authority over her husband, Adam. She first took of the forbidden fruit, and then, by implication, she "taught" her husband what she had experienced.

In his second epistle to the Corinthians, Paul says, *"But I fear, lest by any means, as the serpent beguiled* [deceived] *Eve by his subtilty* [craftiness], *so your minds should be corrupted from the simplicity that is in Christ"* (2 Corinthians 11:3). In the preceding verse, Paul tells the Corinthian believers that he had "betrothed" them to one husband—Christ—and wanted to present them to Him, the Bridegroom, *"as a chaste virgin"* (2 Corinthians 11:2). It is after making this statement that Paul mentions the first virgin, Eve, and refers to the way she was beguiled away from her husband, Adam. Thus, he is saying that wives must not domineer their husbands or teach that which is contrary to the divine Word. The woman must not follow Eve's footsteps in defying her husband and being *"turned aside after Satan"* (1 Timothy 5:15).

This is the picture we get from Paul's epistles to the Corinthians and to Timothy.

Katharine Bushnell comments:

> In verse 13, the Apostle declares that Adam, having been first formed, and hence being older than Eve, was "not deceived." Paul is not here comparing the quality of Eve's sin to Adam's sin: if that were the case the illustration would be out of place for application to Christian workers....Paul does not argue that a wilful sinner, like Adam, is of more value than a deceived person.[26]

> Earlier, Bushnell quotes Bishop Ellicott, who "declares the sense of this verse to be; 'He [Adam] sinned, quite aware of the magnitude of the sin he was committing. Eve, on the other hand, was completely, thoroughly deceived.' The word means more than 'deceived,' as translated. It means 'thoroughly deceived,' in Eve's case...."[27]

Glenda Malmin writes:

> Paul gives further reasoning for this limitation in verses 13 and 14 of 1 Timothy 2. He says, *"For Adam was first formed, then Eve. And Adam was not deceived, but the woman being deceived was in the transgression."* Paul is addressing the issue here by reason of divine order. He is saying that the chronological order of creation proves that Eve was not intended to direct Adam. If God had intended for woman to have ruled over man, this was a time in history when He could have evidenced it. Paul goes on to explain his reasoning by the fall. It was Eve who was deceived in the

26. Bushnell, *God's Word to Women*, 134–135.
27. Bushnell, *God's Word to Women*, 134.

matter of doctrine. By assuming leadership over the man, via her powers of persuasion, she ate the deception first and then gave it to man. So we see that the fall was not only caused by disobedience to God's command to not eat, but also by violating the divinely appointed functional relationship between the sexes. Woman assumed the headship role, and man (with full knowledge of what he was doing) submitted himself to her leadership and ate. It is important to note here, that both man and woman violated their divinely ordered positions at this time. Romans 5:19 says, *"For as by one man's disobedience many were made sinners, so by the obedience of one shall many be made righteous."* Again, I would like to point out that through Jesus Christ both man and woman are redeemed to their proper roles—equal value with distinct order.[28]

How Paul's words here have been misinterpreted and misapplied. Various schools invoke this Pauline phrase to say that women are more open to deception, more easily deceived, than men, and they point to cults founded by women in order to make their point. Yet Christian Science (Mary Baker Eddy), Spiritualism (the Fox sisters), witches (see 1 Samuel 28), theosophy, and Seventh-day Adventism (Ellen G. White) prove nothing more than the fact that many false and mixed religions and cults have also been founded by men. There have been more cults started by men than by women, as church history has proven. Both men and women are prone to failure and open to deception apart from the grace of God.

Some extremely cruel and unkind statements have been said of women because of Eve's transgression, which Paul does not echo in 1 Timothy or any other of his epistles. Eve is held responsible for the sin of the whole world. "Eve is to be blamed for all evil and

---

28. Glenda Malmin, *Woman, You Are Called and Anointed* (Portland, OR: City Christian Publishing, 2000).

death and that she and all her sex are more prone to sin and error than men."[29] Aristotle called them "mentally, morally, and spiritually inferior to men."[30] "Women are more open to deception and false doctrine than man, therefore women need to be continually subordinated to men." These and other unkind statements summarize the opinion that has been held historically by many men, even godly men, and all because of a misinterpretation of Paul's writings, and of Scripture as a whole.

Irenaeus said, "Having become disobedient, she [Eve] was made the cause of death, both to herself and to the entire human race."[31]

Tertullian was most outspoken in addressing women when he said, "Do you not know that you are an Eve? God's verdict on the sex still holds good, and the sex's guilt must still hold also. *You are the devil's gateway*, you are an avenue to the forbidden tree. You are the first deserter from the law divine."[32]

Chrysostom [said] women are to be subject because they are "captivated by appetite." Her sex is "weak and fickle...collectively." "She taught once and ruined all." Commenting on 1 Cor. 14:34–35 he describes women in comparison to men as "some sort of weaker being and easily carried away and light minded." Luther says it was Eve who went "astray"; she "brought on transgression." This shows that "Adam is approved as superior to Eve" because "there was greater wisdom in Adam." Calvin concludes that because the woman "seduced the man from God's commandment, it is fitting that she should be deprived of all her freedom and placed under a yoke." To women he says, is to be imputed "the ruin of the whole human race." The Puritan, Matthew Poole, believed this verse was penned by the apostle, "to keep the woman humble, in low opinion of herself, and the lower order wherein God hath fixed her."[33]

29. Kevin Giles, "A Critique of the 'Novel' Contemporary Interpretation of 1 Timothy 2:9-15 Given in the Book, *Women in the Church*, Part I," *The Evangelical Quarterly*, 12.
30. Glenn S. Sunshine, *Why You Think the Way You Do: The Story of Western Worldviews from Rome to Home* (Grand Rapids, MI: Zondervan, 2009), 43.
31. Bushnell, *God's Word to Women*, 43.
32. Bushnell, *God's Word to Women*, 43.
33. Giles, "Critique," 162–163.

Undoubtedly, Eve was thoroughly deceived, as she admitted to the Lord God. Some women at Ephesus were being deceived by false teachers and false teachings, whether of the Judaistic Gnostics or the cult of Diana. Some of these women (or one particular woman, at least) had seized authority and taught false doctrine in a domineering manner. But to say that women are more susceptible than men to believe deceptive doctrines simply is not so.

A study of the use of the word "deceive" and its various forms in the New Testament shows that all Spirit-filled believers, whether men or women, are warned about deception. Men and women alike need a love of the truth to preserve them from deception. (See 2 Thessalonians 2:1–12.) Various cults in Christendom prove this to be so. Millions of Christian women have to learn to "trust male teachers" and pray that they be not deceived! No woman can help having been born a female, any more than a man can help having been born a male. In 1 Timothy 2:15, Paul echoes the truth that salvation comes through the *"seed of the woman,"* not the "seed of Adam."

In chapter 5, we discussed the matter of the entrance of sin into the world. Who was the greater sinner, Adam or Eve? The man or the woman? Let's weigh the facts.

> › Eve was thoroughly deceived. She fell into transgression by deception. (See 1 Timothy 2:13–14; 2 Corinthians 11:2–4.) She confessed her transgression to the Lord God, much to the chagrin of the serpent, Satan. (See Genesis 3:1–6.) She disobeyed God through deception, having been tricked into transgressing God's law and Word.

> › Adam sinned deliberately, knowingly. He was not deceived but sinned with his eyes wide open to the consequences. It was a deliberate act of disobedience to take the forbidden fruit from his wife, Eve, and to eat of it. Then, when the Lord confronted him about his willful act of disobedience, Adam tried to deflect the blame for his sin on to God Himself. He said, "The woman *You* gave me, she

gave me to eat." (See Genesis 3:12.) In other words, it was God's fault, because He was the One who gave the woman to Adam. Adam's sin was plain rebellion.

If the first woman, Eve, was open to deception, then the first man, Adam, was open to willful rebellion and disobedience! Paul did not write "by one woman sin entered the world" but *"by one **man** [Adam] sin entered into the world, and death by sin; and so death passed upon all men"* (Romans 5:12). It was "in Adam" that all sinned, and "in Adam" all die. (See 1 Corinthians 15:21–22.) Who was the greater sinner—the man or the woman? All the unborn generations were in Adam's loins when he sinned. There is no ground for pride or egotism on the part of either the man or the woman. All people are under sin and in need of redemption by the Son of God, who was born of a woman.

In Summary

The picture gained from 1 Timothy 2:11–15 must be viewed in conjunction with Genesis 1–3 in order for proper exegesis to occur.

> God created Adam first, before Eve—Genesis 1:26–28

> Next, God created Eve out of Adam—Genesis 2. This is creation order.

> Eve was the first sinner. She was thoroughly deceived by the serpent—Genesis 3. This is the order seen in the fall.

> Eve gave to her husband, Adam, who was not deceived but sinned willfully, knowingly, and deliberately.

> Eve "seized authority" over her husband, Adam, in taking of the forbidden fruit. She should have gone to Adam the moment the serpent, Satan, began to engage her in conversation. Instead, she listened to the serpent and accepted his false teaching (doctrine) about mankind being as gods, knowing good and evil.

> So, in Ephesus, a woman (or several women) who had not learned the truth of sound doctrine had seized author-

ity and were teaching their husband(s), in a domineering manner, false doctrine.

> Paul asserts that a woman is not to teach in this manner. A woman must submit to her husband in a meek, quiet spirit and attitude, and learn the Word so that she might avoid being deceived, as Eve was.

> A woman (a wife) may exercise authority but must not seize authority, usurping the position of her husband or a ruler in the church.

h. ***"Notwithstanding she shall be saved in childbearing, if they continue in faith and charity and holiness with sobriety" (verse 15).***

On the surface, this verse seems difficult to interpret. However, its interpretation is possible, in the light of the whole of biblical revelation and an understanding of Pauline theology.

After what Paul has said about Adam being formed first and then Eve, and that Adam was not deceived, but Eve was, Paul finishes this passage on a more positive note by saying that although the woman brought about the fall of man, yet there is salvation available for the woman, and this includes salvation for the man.

The student should consider again how closely this passage in 1 Timothy relates to the passage from Genesis, as this brief summary shows.

1. Adam was created first (creation's order)—Genesis 1; 1 Timothy 2:13

2. Eve came from Adam (creation's order)—Genesis 2; 1 Timothy 2:13

3. Eve was deceived; Adam transgressed (sin's order)— Genesis 3; 1 Timothy 2:14

4. Redemption would become available through the seed of the woman (redemption's order)—Genesis 3:15; 1 Timothy 2:15

Various interpretations of 1 Timothy 2:15 have arisen, some of them totally contradictory to the context of the whole of the Bible. But we need to consider the several views given in order to arrive at what we believe to be the scriptural view.

H. A. Kent, in his *Pastoral Epistles*, presents four interpretive views of this verse.[34] They are here noted in brief, with additional comments.

1.) *Physical Salvation Through Childbirth*

Women will be saved in the bearing of children if they abide in the faith. This is the view of theologians who are thoroughly set in a patriarchal culture, not the mind of God as revealed in Scripture.

Chrysostom read Paul to be saying that although women must continue to accept the consequences for Eve's sin, there is a word of encouragement for them. "Be not cast down, because your sex has incurred blame…the whole sex shall be saved, notwithstanding, by childbearing."

Luther argued that Eve's "penalty remains" for all women. "The pain and tribulation of childbearing continue"; "These penalties will continue until judgment." Then, addressing women directly, he says, "You will be saved if you subject yourselves and bear children with pain." Women's salvation, he adds, is not apart from faith; yet it is "for bearing children." In writing specifically on marriage, he is even more forthright. He says that if women "bear themselves weary—or ultimately bear themselves out—that does not matter. Let them bear themselves out. This is the purpose for which they exist."

Calvin believed these words were added for the consolation of women. In case it should "reduce women to despair to hear the whole ruin of the human race imputed to them…Paul reminds them that although they must suffer temporal punishment, the hope of salvation remains for them.'

---

34. See Homer A. Kent, *The Pastoral Epistles* (Chicago, IL: Moody Press, 1982), 115–120.

Thus, the teaching is that women's special domain is to bear children. This is how they will work out their salvation. What physical labor on the land was to Adam, so childbearing would be to Eve. (See Genesis 3:16.) Many Bible translations say that women will be saved through having children, meaning saved physically.

However, this view is rejected because many women, godly as well as ungodly, have died in childbirth. They were not "saved" (Greek, *sozo*) in the physical sense, as the term is often used to indicate in the Bible. (See, for example, Mark 5:23; Luke 8:36.) No woman comes to salvation or gains entrance to heaven by bearing few or many children. If that were the case, then what of the widows, the old maids, the barren wives, and the immoral women? If this were so, then it would indicate that salvation is by works—in the bearing of sinful offspring. And if this were true, then women would be trying to have as many children as possible, in order to merit salvation. This idea is contrary to all Scripture. Salvation comes by grace, through faith. It is not of works. (See Ephesians 2:5–8.)

2.) *Spiritual Salvation Through Childbirth*

Whereas the previous view holds that a woman is saved physically through bearing children, this view holds that women are saved spiritually if they bear children. The matter is that many women are never spiritually saved, regardless of how many children they may bear. The truth noted above is also applicable here: Salvation comes only by total faith in Christ.

3.) *Spiritual Salvation in the Home*

This view holds that a woman is saved spiritually as long as she fulfills her role in the home as a godly wife and mother. Its weakness is that many women are good wives and mothers and have good homes, but they never come to salvation through faith in Christ alone.

4.) *Spiritual Salvation Through the Incarnation of Christ*

This view holds that salvation came through the Christ-Child, through the incarnation of the Messiah, as was promised to Eve, the first woman and the first sinner, in Genesis 3:15. This view is in harmony with Scripture revelation and is the soundest view of them all. In the midst of judgment on the woman is the promise of mercy to and through that same woman and her Seed. The order is: (1) creation, (2) the fall, and then (3) redemption!

o It is Eve who is under discussion here, and that which took place in the fall.

o It is the Seed of the woman who is to bruise the head of the serpent, the one who brought about the fall of the woman.

o The "child-bearing" mentioned refers not to the birth of just any child but the birth of the Christ-Child.

o Eve was saved by faith in the coming "Seed"—Christ.

o Thus, all women—and all men, as well—could be saved through the birth of the ChristChild, and the redemption He would provide to bring mankind back to God, thereby restoring the divine order.

o In the context of the whole Bible, this view is the most sound and the most harmonious with the Scriptures of the virgin-born Son of God. (See Genesis 3:15; Isaiah 7:14; 9:6–9; Matthew 1:18–21; Luke 1–2; Galatians 4:4.)

The *Amplified Bible* translates 1 Timothy 2:15 this way:

Nevertheless [the sentence put upon women of pain in motherhood does not hinder their souls' salvation, and] they will be saved [eternally] if they continue in faith and love and holiness with self-control, [saved indeed] **through the Childbearing** or **by the birth of the divine Child**.

And the *Centenary Translation* renders it as follows: "*Notwithstanding she will be saved by the Child-bearing.*"

Some translations do recognize that the Greek text reads "through **the Childbearing**," pointing to someone else besides the act of bearing children. That "Someone" is indeed the Christ-Child, the Messiah.

The early church fathers interpreted the verse this way. Ignatius, Irenaeus, Justin, and Tertullian all saw that, despite the responsibility women bear for the fall, they will be saved through *"the Childbearing"*—that is, the birth of the Messiah by the second Eve, Mary.

Katharine C. Bushnell's quotations from Professor James Orr are insightful here:

> One's mind turns first to that oldest of all evangelical promises, that the seed of the woman would bruise the head of the serpent....The 'seed' who should destroy him is described emphatically as the woman's seed....It remains significant that this peculiar phrase should be chosen to designate the future deliverer. I cannot believe the choice to be of accident. The promise of Abraham was that in his seed the families of the earth would be blessed; there the male is emphasized, but here it is the woman—the woman distinctively. There is, perhaps, as good scholars have thought, an allusion to this promise in 1 Timothy 2:15, where, with allusion to Adam and Eve, it is said 'But she shall be saved through her (or the) childbearing' (RV).
>
> ...
>
> By general consent the narratives in Matthew 1 and 2 and Luke 1 and 2 are independent; that is,

they are not derived one from the other, yet they both affirm, in detailed story, that Jesus, conceived of the Holy Spirit, was born of a pure virgin, Mary of Nazareth, espoused to Joseph, whose wife she afterwards became....Matthew's narrative is all told from Joseph's point of view, and Luke's is all told from Mary's. The signs of this are unmistakable. Matthew tells about Joseph's difficulties and action, and says little or nothing about Mary's thought and feelings. Luke tells much about Mary—even her inmost thoughts—but says next to nothing directly about Joseph. The narratives are not...contradictory, but are independent and complementary....Both together are needed to give the whole story.

...

It is sometimes argued that a virgin birth is no aid to the explanation of Christ's sinlessness.... The birth of Jesus was not, as in ordinary births, the creation of a new personality. It was a divine Person—already existing entering on this new mode of existence.

...

The belief in the virgin birth of Christ is of the highest value for the right apprehension of Christ's unique and sinless personality."[35]

So, although the woman was deceived by the serpent, yet it is through the woman the Savior would be born, who would crush the serpent's head. It would not be the "seed of man" but the "Seed of woman," a Seed no man could bring forth. God miraculously brought forth this Seed through a woman, the Virgin Mary. Every believer, man or woman, owes his or her

---

35 James Orr, *The Fundamentals*, Vol. 1, quoted in Bushnell, *God's Word to Women*, 189–190.

salvation to the "Seed of the woman"—Jesus Christ. There is no room for boasting by any member of the male species. A woman sinned, and another woman brought forth the Savior.

Both Adam and Eve sinned. Both needed redemption. Both could be redeemed only through the virgin-born Redeemer, Christ Jesus. God sent forth His Son (deity), born of a woman (humanity), under the Law to redeem us from the Law. (See Galatians 4:4.) Jesus had a divine Father and a human mother. The highest honor is given to the woman, not to the man. An unbiased understanding of this glorious truth will balance out any seeming harshness attributed to Paul's words in 1 Timothy on Adam and Eve in creation and the fall, and their need for redemption.

It is worth noting the heresies Paul deals with in 1 Timothy 2 as he exhorts his son in the faith, Timothy, in sound doctrine, confirming the Genesis account.

The City of Ephesus	The Church of Ephesus
False Doctrine in Ephesus	Sound Doctrine in the Church
1. Eve was created before Adam.	1. Adam was first formed, then Eve.
2. Woman is the originator of man.	2. Eve was taken out of Adam.
3. Eve was the illuminator of Adam.	3. Adam was not deceived.
4. Adam was deceived, not Eve.	4. Eve was deceived.
5. Child-bearing is evil.	5. Child-bearing is blessed of God, as the Seed of the woman will crush the serpent's head.
(See 2 Corinthians 11:3; Genesis 3:1–6.)	(See 1 Corinthians 15:21–22; Romans 5:12–14.)

i.   *"…if they continue in faith and charity and holiness with sobriety"* **(verse 15).**

Paul concludes this passage by encouraging the women of the church at Ephesus to continue in a life of holiness. They were not to follow the ways and whims of the cult of Diana or the female socialites of Ephesus. They were to continue in:

> Faith—that is, trust and reliance on God through Christ, not in themselves.

> Charity—that is, pure love toward God and Christ, the divine kind of love. (See 1 Corinthians 13.)

> Holiness—that is, a lifestyle of sanctification, set apart to God for His holy use, and not as the women in Ephesus who participated in the immoral cult of Diana.

> Sobriety—that is, self-restraint and self-control over all sinful impulses and desires, as women of God.

E. Divine Order for Men and Women in Home and Church Life

One of the remarkable things about the Pastoral Epistles is the numerous references to both men and women. The Pastoral Epistles concern divine order in both home and church life, for men and for women. Because some schools have used an incorrect interpretation of Paul's writings in 1 Corinthians and 1 Timothy to silence women and exclude them from public ministry, it will be helpful for us to see how Paul instructs both men and women in Christian behavior, whether in regard to life at home or in the church. He addresses the following categories: men and women, elders and wives, deacons and wives, older and younger widows, children, and the unmarried.

Instructions for the Men of the Church

♦ Avoid the teachings of Hymenaeus, Alexander, and Philetus, who opposed Paul and embraced false doctrine—1 Timothy 1:19–20; 2 Timothy 2:17

- Men should pray in a proper attitude—1 Timothy 2:1–10

- An elder ("*bishop*" KJV) must be the husband of one wife—1 Timothy 3:2

- A deacon must be of good character, and must be the husband of one wife—1 Timothy 3:12

- Marriage and certain meats are forbidden only by "doctrines of devils"—1 Timothy 4: 1–4; see also Genesis 1:26–28; 2:18–25; 9:1–4

- Timothy must reject old wives' fables—1 Timothy 4:7

- Elders who sin must be rebuked before all, that others may fear—1 Timothy 5:17–20

- Slaves are to serve their masters as if serving Christ—1 Timothy 6:1–2

- Certain teachers creep into houses and deceive others with false teachings—2 Timothy 3:6

- Timothy is to greet Priscilla and Aquila, as well as the household of Onesiphorus—2 Timothy 4:19

Instructions for the Women of the Church

- Women should pray dressed in modest attire—1 Timothy 2:8–9

- Deacons' wives must exhibit good character and constant faithfulness—1 Timothy 3:8–13

- Older women are to be treated as mothers, younger women as sisters, in all purity—1 Timothy 5:2

- Women who are true widows indeed may be cared for by the church, if they qualify—1 Timothy 5:3–10, 16

- Younger widows should marry, bear children, and keep their houses in order; they should not wander from house to house as busybodies and as gossipers—1 Timothy 5:3–15

- A woman must learn in a meek and quiet spirit and attitude—1 Timothy 2:11

+ A woman is not to seize authority in order to teach that which is contrary to the apostles' doctrine—1 Timothy 2:12

+ A wife is not to domineer her husband—1 Timothy 2:13–14

+ Women will be saved in childbearing, ultimately through the birth of the Christ-Child—1 Timothy 2:15

+ Women are to continue in faith, love, holiness, and sobriety—1 Timothy 2:15

A serious consideration of all the above references to men and women in 1 and 2 Timothy reveals that there men and women who were out of order. In Acts 20:29, Paul warned the believers about false teachers, grievous wolves, and deceiving elders who twisted the truth. They also twisted Paul's language, as Peter explained in his second epistle. (See 2 Peter 3:15–16.)

There was a certain woman, or perhaps various women, out of order; they seized authority over their husbands and taught false doctrine, possibly that of the cult of Diana, or perverted and distorted Jewish Gnosticism. Paul encourages and challenges Timothy to guide the church back into divine order. Thus, his Pastoral Epistles deal with proper order as it relates to men and women, both at home and in the church.

In either sphere, there is no grounds for male chauvinism or militant feminism. Men and women are to function at home and in the church according to God's established order. Expositors cannot use 1 Timothy 2 against 1 Corinthians 11, Ephesians 5, or Galatians 3:28. Paul's teachings on the roles of men and women "in Christ" have to be held in proper tension. What was written to Timothy pertained specifically to the church at Ephesus and could not be considered a mandate for all the churches in Asia. Paul is not laying down a law for all times and all churches in all nations. Rather, he is encouraging Timothy to stop those men (elders) and women (female teachers) who were disrupting the services, teaching false doctrine, and acting in a domineering, authoritarian way in the church at Ephesus. It was a local, not universal, situation. The principle that apples in all situations, anywhere and everywhere, is that men and women are to flow together in a meek and quiet spirit, evidencing Christian character, submission, and obedience to divine authority. Men and women are to maintain their distinct roles in the home and in the church as they walk "in Christ" and evidence the Christian lifestyle in the midst of a heathen society.

In Summary

From all that we have seen in 1 Timothy, along with certain passages from Genesis, we note Paul's emphasis on divinely established order.

Order in the Creation	Order in the Fall of Mankind	Order in Redemption	Order in Home and Church
Genesis 1–2	Genesis 3	Genesis 3:15	1 Timothy 2
Adam was first formed.	Woman fell first.	Promise of the Seed of the Woman to crush the serpent's head.	Man and woman.
Then Eve.	Man fell next.		Husband and wife.
Husband and wife.	Wife/husband.	Woman brings forth the Christ-child.	Christ and church.
Order of Creation.	Usurped authority over the man and reversed divine order in the Fall.	His Father is God.	Believing women continue in faith, love, holiness, with sobriety.
		His mother is Mary.	Wife subject to her husband—not to usurp authothity
		The Messiah seed.	Learn in quietness.
		Cross of redemption.	

18

PAUL ON HEADSHIP AND COVERING VEILS

Having considered two of the Pauline passages on the "silence of women" and "women usurping authority" (1 Corinthians 14:34–35; 1 Timothy 2:11–15), we now turn to one other passage requiring some comment. It is 1 Corinthians 11:1–16, which deals with the matter of "headship" and "covering veils" as pertaining to men and women.[36]

Imitate me, just as I also imitate Christ. Now I praise you, brethren, that you remember me in all things and keep the traditions just as I delivered them to you. But I want you to know that the head of every man is Christ, the head of woman is man, and the head of Christ is God. Every man praying or prophesying, having his head covered, dishonors his head. But every woman who prays or prophesies with her head uncovered dishonors her head, for that is one and the same as if her head were shaved. For if a woman is not covered, let her also be shorn. But if it is shameful for a woman to be shorn or shaved, let her be covered. For a man indeed ought not to cover his head, since he is the image and glory of God; but woman is the glory of man. For man is not from woman, but woman from man. Nor was man created for

36. For a more thorough study of 1 Corinthians 11:1–16, please refer to Kevin J. Conner, *Headship, Covering (Hats) & Hair* (Victoria, Australia: Acacia Press, 1995).

the woman, but woman for the man. For this reason the woman ought to have a symbol of authority on her head, because of the angels. Nevertheless, neither is man independent of woman, nor woman independent of man, in the Lord. For as woman came from man, even so man also comes through woman; but all things are from God. Judge among yourselves. Is it proper for a woman to pray to God with her head uncovered? Does not even nature itself teach you that if a man has long hair, it is a dishonor to him? But if a woman has long hair, it is a glory to her; for her hair is given to her for a covering. But if anyone seems to be contentious, we have no such custom, nor do the churches of God.

(1 Corinthians 11:1–16 NKJV)

Debates and questions that have arisen over this passage and others related to it raise the issue of "headship," "authority," and "covering veil," especially as these subjects relate to women in either the home or the church.

Some schools of thought interpret this passage as meaning that if the man is the head of the woman, then the woman must be in subjection to the man. Male headship necessitates female subordination, or the woman being under the man's authority, her submission being symbolized by a covering veil on her head. Without such a veil, the woman is seen as exhibiting insubordination, or even rebellion, against authority.

This is one of the positions that we will address in this chapter, as we discuss certain key words employed by Paul.

A. *The Divine Order of Headship—1 Corinthians 11:1–3*

The first key word we will consider, "*head*," is used some eleven times in this passage. The particular verses are as follows:

+ "*The **head** of every man is Christ*" (verse 3).

+ "*The **head** of the woman is man*" (verse 3).

+ "*The **head** of Christ is God*" (verse 3).

+ "*Every man praying or prophesying, having his **head** covered, dishonors his **head***" (verse 4).

+ *"Every woman who prays or prophesies with her* **head** *uncovered dishonors her* **head***, for that is one and the same as if her* **head** *were shaved"* (1 Corinthians 11:5).

+ *"For a man indeed ought not to cover his* **head***..."* (verse 7).

+ *"...the woman ought to have a symbol of authority on her* **head***"* (verse 10).

+ *"Is it proper for a woman to pray to God with her* **head** *uncovered?"* (verse 13).

A cursory glance at the above references shows that the word *"head"* is used in both the natural and the spiritual sense, or the symbolic sense. Note the order of headship in these verses, as arranged here:

GOD is the Head of Christ

↓

CHRIST is the Head of the man

↓

MAN is the head of the woman

↓

WOMAN

↓

CHILDREN (if applicable)

It is evident that the word *"head"* is used in spiritual/symbolic sense, not a physical sense, in verse 3. In verses 4 and 5, it is used in both a spiritual and a physical sense. And in verses 7 and 10, the word is used in an actual, physical sense. There is interplay in Paul's use of the word. None can deny the fact that Paul is laying out an order of headship here, an order that relates to the divine and human orders alike.

Creation reveals the eternal power and attributes of the Godhead—Father, Son, and Holy Spirit—mentioned specifically in such Scriptures as Acts 17:29, Romans 1:20, and Colossians 2:9: *"In him* [Jesus Christ] *dwelleth all the fullness of the Godhead bodily"* (Colossians 2:9). The Godhead is a picture of divine order that is echoed in 1 Corinthians 11:3, where Paul sets forth an order of headship for the Corinthians to follow.

Because Christ is under headship, He can exercise headship. Because Christ Himself is under authority, He can exercise authority. He is, in His Manhood, perfectly submitted to the Father, totally obedient to the Father's will. In the finality of redemption's plan, *"the Son Himself will also be subject to Him who put all things under Him, that **God** may be all in all"* (1 Corinthians 15:27–28 NKJV). The whole divine order has to do with relationship: there is wonderful, loving, and perfect relationship in and between the divine Persons in the blessed Godhead. As previously mentioned, God has illustrated and demonstrated, in His own nature and being, an order that He wants to see replicated in the Christian family and in the family of God, which is the church.

As already discussed, the divine order is as follows: God is the Head of Christ. Christ is the Head of man. The man is the head of woman. Christ is also the Head of the church. The Son is subject to the Father, and the Holy Spirit is subject to the Father and the Son. God has demonstrated in His own nature and being the order that He desires His creatures to follow.

The question is, What does the word *head* mean? Does it mean "authority"? "Rule"? "Control"? "Mastery"? Does it speak of a hierarchical form of authority, or government? Does it speak of a chain of command? Is man to be the authority over woman? Are women to be subject to men, whether in the home or in the church? Is the husband to be the head over the wife? These are the questions requiring answers.

In response, two major theories are submitted for consideration here.

The Natural/Physical Sense

Strong's Greek Concordance simply defines the Greek word *kephalé* (STRONG 2776) as probably coming from the primary *kapto* (in the sense of seizing); the head (as the part most readily taken hold of), literally or figuratively; translated "head." (See 1 Corinthians 11:3, 4, 5, 7, 10.) The word *kephalé* is used some fifty times in the New Testament to refer to the corresponding body part of a person or animal; seven times, it is used in a metaphorical sense.

Strong's Hebrew Concordance defines the Hebrew word *rosh* (STRONG 7218) from an unused root apparently meaning "to shake" the head (as most easily shaken), whether literally or figuratively; in many applications, it speaks of place, time, and rank. (See Genesis 3:15; 40:20; Deuteronomy 28:13.)

The *American Dictionary of the English Language* provides a great variety of uses of the word, with the following primary definitions of the noun and verb forms[37]:

+ **Head (noun):** The uppermost part of the human body.... This part of the human body contains the organs of hearing, seeing, tasting and smelling; it contains also the brain, which is supposed to be the seat of the intellectual powers, and of sensation. Hence the *head* is the chief or most important part, and is used for the whole person, in the phrase, let the evil fall on my *head*

+ **Head (noun, positional [figurative]):** A chief; a principal person; a leader; a commander; one who has the first rank or place, and to whom others are subordinate; as the *head* of an army; the *head* of a sect or party

+ **Head (verb):** To originate; to spring; to have its source, as a river.

Vine's Expository Dictionary:

Kephalé (STRONG 2776), besides its natural significance, is used:

a. Figuratively in Romans 12:20, to speak of heaping coals of fire on a "head," and *"Your blood be upon your own heads"* (Acts 18:6).

b. Metaphorically, to refer to the authority and direction of God in relation to Christ; of Christ in relation to believing men; of the husband in relation to the wife (see 1 Corinthians 11:3); of Christ's relation to the church (see Ephesians 1:22; 4:15; 5:23; Colossians 1:19; 2:19); and of Christ's relation to principalities and powers (see Colossians 2:10).

---

37. *American Dictionary of the English Language*, Noah Webster, ed., 1828 (online), http://webstersdictionary1828.com/Dictionary/head.

c. Symbolically, of the imperial rulers of the Roman powers, as seen in the apocalyptic visions of the "seven heads." (See Revelation 13:1, 3; 17:3, 7, 9.)

To summarize the definitions of the word *head*:

+ *Head*, in the positional and figurative sense, means a chief; a principal person; a leader; a commander; one who has first rank or place and to whom others are subordinate. God is the Head of Christ. Christ is under the Father's authority. The Father is the first Person in the relationship of the members of the Godhead. There will come a time when the Son will give all authority that was given to Him back to the Father, for the accomplishment of God's eternal purposes. (See 1 Corinthians 11:3; 15:23–28.)

+ Christ is the Head of the church. (See Ephesians 1:22; 5:23.)

+ Christ is also the Head over all principalities and powers. (See Colossians 2:10; 1 Peter 3:22.) Christ exercises authority (headship) because He is under authority (headship). He is the Chief, the Captain of our salvation, the Leader, the Commander of the armies of God. In all things He has the preeminence. (See Colossians 1:18.) He is the Authority in and over His body, the church.

+ In a symbolic sense, *head* means, source, supply; spring; originator. Christ is the Head of the rivers of the Holy Spirit, the Source from whence all the Spirit's operations flow. He is the Baptizer in the Spirit, and the fullness flows from Him who received the Spirit without measure. (See John 1:30–33; 3:33–34; 7:37–39.)

Much of what has been written in recent years limits the meaning of the word *head* to "source, supply, and origin," perhaps as an overreaction to authoritarianism or the hierarchical control of woman by man. Because of an overemphasis on female submission and the subordination of women to men/wives to their husbands, the word "head" has nearly been robbed of its ties to the concepts of authority and leadership. But those concepts are key to an understanding of the biblical use of the word, as exemplified in the following verses;

+ "*Christ is the head* [source, supply, origin] *of the church*" (Ephesians 5:23).

+ "*The head* [source, supply, origin] *of every man is Christ*" (1 Corinthians 11:3). "*The head* [source, supply, origin] *of Christ is God*" (1 Corinthians 11:3).

+ "*The head* [source, supply, origin] *of the woman is the man*" (1 Corinthians 11:3).

+ "[Christ] *is the head* [source, supply, origin] *of all principality and power*" (Colossians 2:10).

Christ is indeed the Source, Supply, Origin, Support, Nourisher, and Builder of His body, the church. He is indeed the Source of life, energy, and care. But Christ is also the Head of the church. He is *the* authority in the church. The church, as His bride—His wife—submits to Him who is her Husband and Bridegroom. Christ does not submit to the church, though He indeed gave Himself for her. It is not consistent to strip the word "head" of its ties to the concepts of authority and leadership. In the natural family, the father and mother certainly have authority over the children. Although all the family members are of equal value in the sight of God, there must be order in the home. The children do not "head up" the household.

Christ is both (a) the Source, and (b) the Authority in the church, His body.

The man, the husband, is the "head" of the woman, the wife. (See 1 Corinthians 11:3; 1 Peter 3:7.) He is both (a) the source/supply, and (b) the authority in the home. Paul is not saying that every man is the head of any woman, but only the man who is a husband is head over the woman who is his wife. This is why Paul emphasizes that a husband is to love his *"own wife"* (1 Corinthians 7:2), and wives are to submit to their *"own husbands"* (Colossians 3:18; see also Ephesians 5:22, 24). Together, the husband and wife exercise "headship" over their children. To insert the term "source" or "supply" in place of "head" each of the fifty-plus times it appears in the New Testament is to rob the term of its full meaning. The word "head" cannot be stripped of the connotations "authority," "leadership," and so forth. The below diagram sharpens our focus on the matter.

The Order in the Godhead	The Order in the Home Life
1. The Father—God is the Head of Christ.	1. The man, the husband, the father is the head of the wife.
2. The Son—Christ is the Head of the man, and He is the Head of the church, His body, His bride.	2. The wife and mother is dependent on her husband, her source, her supply, and leadership authority.
3. The Holy Spirit flows from the Father through the Son to the church.	3. The children submit to the father and mother.
4. The church is subject to and also depends on her Source, Supply, and Authority in God.	4. The family is blessed as each follow divine order for the Christian home.

Because of such widespread misinterpretation, misuse, and abuse of the word *"head,"* we now endeavor to distinguish between biblical headship and the unbiblical perversion of it. If Christian men and women, husbands and wives, understood the true meaning of headship, as epitomized by the Godhead, there would be no need to fear any dictatorial exercise of headship. True biblical headship is evidenced in a loving, caring relationship.

Male headship does not *mean:*

+ Dictatorship by the man, the husband

+ Male superiority

+ Female inferiority

+ Man's exclusive right to make decisions without consulting his wife

+ Male authoritarianism

+ That the man is always right

+ Suppression of the wife masquerading as female submission

+ Infallibility of the husband

+ Inequality of the woman, the wife

Male headship does **mean:**

+ The husband loving his wife as he loves himself—Ephesians 5:2, 28–31

+ The husband loving his wife as Christ loves the church—Ephesians 5:25

+ The husband pleasing his wife—1 Corinthians 7:33

+ The husband protecting his wife from hurt and harm

+ The husband providing security—spiritual, emotional, material, and physical

+ The husband providing a covering mantle for his wife

+ The husband being a spiritual leader, a priest, in his home

+ The husband cherishing his wife

+ The husband honoring his wife—1 Peter 3:7

+ The husband recognizing that he and his wife are heirs together of the *"grace of life"*—1 Peter 3:7

+ The husband "rendering unto his wife true benevolence"—1 Corinthians 7:3

+ The husband praising his wife's godly qualities—Proverbs 31:28–31

Let us restate the divine order once more: God is the Head of Christ; Christ is the Head of the husband; the husband is the head of the wife; and the husband and wife together are to rule their house and children well. (See 1 Timothy 3.)

Christ—*the* Man, *the* Husband of the church, His wife—is under headship, and so He exercises loving headship over those who are under His authority. In the same way, a believing husband should be under Christ's headship and authority as he exercises loving headship and authority in his family. This should be part of the foundation of every marriage. Much of the trouble between husbands and wives, and between parents and their children, occurs because the man is trying to exercise headship over his family when he himself is not under the headship of Christ. According to true biblical headship, one must be "under" authority to exercise headship

234 *The Ministry of Women*

"over" his family. Though there is equality of persons, there is not necessarily equality of responsibility.

It is easier for the wife to acknowledge her husband as her "head" when he fulfills his divinely given role and responsibilities. Christ must be Lord of the husband's life. Headship has to do with loving relationship and divine order, as illustrated in the Godhead by the Father, Son, and Holy Spirit.

B. The Divine Order of Covering—1 Corinthians 11:4–7

The next key words in 1 Corinthians 11:1–16 are related: *"covered," "covering,"* and *"uncovered."* They are used some eight times, either literally or symbolically.

- *"Every man praying or prophesying, having his head **covered**, dishonoreth his head"* (verse 4).
- *"Every woman that prayeth or prophesieth with her head **uncovered** dishonoureth her head"* (verse 5).
- *"For if the woman be not **covered**, let her also be shorn: but if it be a shame for a woman to be shorn or shaven, let her be **covered**"* (verse 6).
- *"For a man indeed ought not to **cover** his head…"* (verse 7).
- *"Therefore she should [be subject to his authority and should] have a covering on her head…"* (verse 10 AMPC).
- *"Is it proper for a woman to pray to God with her head **uncovered**?"* (verse 13).
- *"But if a woman has long hair, it is a glory to her; for her hair is given to her for a **covering**"* (verse 15).

What is meant by the words *"covering," "covered,"* and *"uncovered,"* as used here? Is Paul saying that the woman must wear a literal "covering veil" on her head, while the man is free from such an obligation?

There are several particular Greek words used by Paul in this passage needing some comment.

Strong's Concordance

Katakalupto (STRONG 2619), from strong 2596 (*kata* = down) and strong 2572 (*kalupto* = to cover, meaning to cover wholly; i.e., a veil:—cover, hide).

"If the woman be not covered,…let her be covered…. For a man indeed ought not to cover his head…" (1 Corinthians 11:6–7).

Peribolaion (STRONG 4018), meaning "something thrown around one, i.e., a mantle, a veil:—covering, vesture."

"Her hair is given her for a covering [literally, a veil]" (1 Corinthians 11:15).

Akatakaluptos (STRONG 177), meaning *"uncovered or unveiled,"* so used in 1 Corinthians 11:5, 13.

In these verses, there are two aspects of "covering" referred to by Paul:

+ The covering veil—a fabric shawl or head scarf worn by women in that era, and still worn by many women in the Arab and Muslim worlds today

+ The covering hair—a woman's long hair

First of all, it is worth noting that in all the Bible, there is absolutely no commandment from God that a woman or a man must wear a covering veil.

Smith's Bible Dictionary has this to say:

With regard to the use of the veil, it is important to observe that it was by no means so general in ancient as in modern times. Much of the scrupulousness in respect of the use of the veil dates from the promulgation of the Koran, which forbade women appearing unveiled except in the presence of their nearest relatives. In ancient times the veil was adopted only in exceptional cases, either as an article of ornamental dress, (Song of Solomon 4:1, 3; 6:7) or by betrothed maidens in the presence of their future husbands, especially at the time of the wedding, (Genesis 24:65) or lastly, by women of loose character for purposes of concealment. (Genesis 38:14) Among the Jews of the New Testament age it appears to have been customary for the women to cover their heads (not necessarily their faces) when engaged in public worship.[38]

---

38. Dr. William Smith, "Entry for Veil," *Smith's Bible Dictionary* (1901), online. http://www.biblestudytools.com/dictionary/veil/.

- Abraham's wife, Sarah, must have been unveiled in order for Abimelech to have been attracted to her. (See Genesis 20.)

- Rebekah was veiled when she met Isaac, her husband to be, but she was not fully veiled when Isaac's servant met her at the well, for he could see how beautiful she was. (See Genesis 24:16, 65.)

- Tamar covered herself with a veil in order to deceive Judah. (See Genesis 38:14–15.)

- Hannah was unveiled enough for her husband, Eli, to see her face and lips moving in prayer and to think she was in a drunken state. (See 1 Samuel 1:13.)

- Moses veiled his face in the presence of the people as he came down from Mount Sinai. (See Exodus 34:33–35; 2 Corinthians 3: 13, 14.) But in the presence of God, his face had been unveiled. Thus, believers do not need to wear a covering veil in the presence of God. Under the new covenant, they may behold Him "face-to-face." Israel still has a "veil on the heart," but this is a "veil of unbelief." When the heart turns to the Lord, the veil that was torn at Calvary (see Matthew 27:51) is taken away, that men and women may behold the glory of the Lord directly.

Over the centuries, however, the wearing of the veil became a custom, possibly imposed on the wife by the husband as fulfilling Genesis 3:16, a symbol of the man's rule over the woman. It was never God's command. Jewish practice expected the woman to wear the *talith* in worship as a sign of her guilt and condemnation before the Law of the Lord because of the sin of Eve.

Paul is dealing with the social customs and culture of his era. He encourages the Christian women to follow the custom of the day by wearing the covering veil as a sign of proper relationship to their husbands.

According to *Halley's Bible Handbook*:

It was customary in Greek and Near Eastern cities for women to cover their heads in public—except women of immoral character. Within recent memory, Corinth had been full of temple prostitutes. Some of the Christian women, taking advantage of their newfound liberty in Christ, decided to lay aside their head covering in church meetings, which horrified the more modest types. Paul tells these women not to defy public opinion as to what is considered proper in society at large.[39]

For a woman to be *"shorn or shaven"* (verse 6) meant "to have the hair cut close, or to be entirely shaved as with a razor."[40] Paul was concerned about the testimony of the church woman. If, in her new liberty in Christ, the woman would *"cast off the veil"* (CONYBEARE), it would have the same effect on her acceptability as if she adopted the socially repugnant sign of the courtesan—having close-cropped hair or a shaven head. Priestesses in the temple at Corinth unveiled their heads in disgrace, and Paul does not want society to look on the Christian church as just another temple of prostitution!

"In a woman, this was at that time, a sign of disgrace, indicating that she was an adulteress."[41] In that day, a shaven head indicated that a woman was either a prostitute or an adulteress. Thus, for such women who had recently converted to Christianity, a head covering would have provided protection while their hair grew back. In addition, the use of a head covering by all the women at church gatherings would have effected a uniform look, so that no one appeared "above" the others.

Dr. Edersheim's *Sketches of Jewish Social Life* offers the following insight:

It was the custom in the case of a woman accused of adultery to have her hair "shorn or shaven," at the same time using this formula: "Because thou hast departed from the manner of the daughters of Israel, who go with their head covered;…therefore that has befallen thee which thou hast chosen."[42]

Thus, an unveiled Jewish wife might have been tried for adultery and, when found guilty, been shorn or shaven. Paul cites this obstruction to commanding women to unveil, but he permits it. (See 1 Corinthians 16:10.)

39. Halley, *Halley's Bible Handbook*, np.
40. Vincent, *Word Studies in the New Testament*, Vol. III, 247.
41. Stibbs, Kevan, and Davidson, *New Bible Commentary*, 983.
42. Rev. Dr. Edersheim, *Sketches of Jewish Social Life in the Days of Christ* (London: The Religious Tract Society, 1876), 154.

A Jewish man whose wife was seen abroad with her hair "not done up," i.e., with her head uncovered, could encounter problems. We learn from Dr. Edersheim's work that a Jewish man, even if favorably disposed toward his wife's profession of Christianity and toward the practice of unveiling her head in worship services, might have been compelled by his relatives or the synagogue authorities to divorce his wife if she chose to unveil.

And again, "In those days, custom dictated that men and women be separated in public services. This was true in the Jewish synagogues and Greek gatherings as well. Women were usually confined to a side room or a screened-off balcony, where they could barely hear what was being said. Consequently, attention would soon lag and they were on their way talking and chattering. In some buildings, the men and women were separated by an aisle."[43]

As already noted in our earlier discussion of 1 Corinthians 14:34–35, in some synagogues, the women whispering or talking upstairs could be overheard downstairs, where the men read from the sacred scrolls—with intermittent pauses for questions to be asked and answers to be provided—and spoke in the congregation. The women would call out to their husbands with questions and requests for clarification, thereby disrupting the service. This was the problem. Christian women were anxious to learn spiritual truths, and were frustrated at being unable to read or even hear the teaching clearly. Hence Paul's word to the women to be quiet, and to ask their questions of their husbands at home. Paul is dealing with the local situation at that time, not imposing timeless laws on all women everywhere.

The same principle applies to the use of covering veils. Paul is dealing with a local situation—his contemporary culture and its social customs. The practice of women covering their head in church gatherings grew out of a Jewish social custom, one that was too deeply ingrained in the social life of Christians in Palestine and Syria to be dismissed lightly by the Christian women of Asia Minor and Greece. Even as it was, Paul's declaration that the men were to go "uncovered" (bareheaded) in religious gatherings was a challenge to the Judaizers.

---

43. Beall, *Female of the Species*, 88.

Lamsa's *New Testament Commentary* says: "...in the East it would be difficult for men to worship at places where women were unveiled during preaching or prayers. The men would be looking at the women instead of worshipping. This is because men do not see women's faces on other occasions. Thus to see the face or arms of a woman is unusual."[44]

Paul does break with the custom of men wearing a head covering. He states that the man does not need to cover his head—and that, in fact, if he covers his head, he dishonors his "head"—that is, Christ. (See 1 Corinthians 16:4, 7.) Man is under the headship of Christ, who is the "head covering" of the man. Paul says that this is so because man is *"the image and glory of God"* (1 Corinthians 16:7; see also Genesis 1:26–28). As such, man represents God's headship and authority. Woman is the glory of the man, as well as the glory of the Lord. Man and woman, together, are the image and glory of God.

Today, Orthodox Jews are still required to keep their heads covered in the synagogue. And in some Christian circles, it is believed that men should wear a hat or other type of headgear that they remove when entering the church, that they may fulfill what they believe to be a scriptural command that men are to uncover their heads as they go in to worship the Lord. However, this custom is not based on an actual command of God. Christ is the man's "Covering," and man is under the headship of Christ. In Western culture, it is not considered proper for men to wear hats or other headgear in church services.

In Muslim mosques, the custom is to take off one's shoes and leave them at the door. In Muslim countries, the worshippers remove their shoes, not their hats or other headgear. The Lord told Moses, *"Put off thy shoes from thy feet, for the place whereon thou standest is holy ground"* (Exodus 3:5). Nothing was said about removing his headgear.

The Amplified Bible translates 1 Corinthians 11:4–7 this way:

Any man who prays or prophesies (teaches, refutes, reproves, admonishes, and comforts) with his head covered dishonors his Head (Christ). And any woman who [publicly] prays or prophesies (teaches, refutes, reproves, admonishes, or comforts) when she is bareheaded dishonors

---

44. Lamsa, *New Testament Commentary*, 272.

her head (her husband); it is the same as [if her head were] shaved. For if a woman will not wear [a head] covering, then she should cut off her hair too; but if it is disgraceful for a woman to have her head shorn or shaven, let her cover [her head]. For a man ought not to wear anything on his head [in church], for he is the image and [reflected] glory of God [his function of government reflects the majesty of the divine Rule]; but the woman is [the expression of] man's glory (majesty, preeminence).

(1 Corinthians 11:4–7)

Paul is dealing with the social customs of his time, attempting to instruct the new Christian churches in reasonable behavior that would convey the message of Christ to their generation and society.

"The social customs which provide the background for his thought are, of course, different from ours; but the factors involved are the same, namely, modesty, propriety and orderliness."[45] (See also 1 Timothy 2:9; 1 Peter 3:3.) In church life, it is appropriate for women, as well as for men, to be attired rightly, and more so if an individual is being used of the Lord in prayer and prophecy.

Katharine C. Bushnell sums it up as follows.

Paul...(1) forbids men to veil (since "There is now no condemnation to them which are in Christ Jesus" [see Romans 8:1–2]); (2) permits women to veil; (3) but guards against this permission being construed as a command to veil, by showing that ideally the woman should unveil, before God, man, and angels; (4) shows that there is special propriety in women unveiling when addressing God in prayer; (5) declares that (contrary to the teaching of the Jews) there is nothing for a woman to be ashamed of in showing her hair, for it is a "glory" to her; (6) and disavows veiling as a church custom.[46]

As mentioned previously, when Jesus died on the cross, the veil of the temple was torn from top to bottom. In Christ, the veil is done away with; and all believers, whether male or female, may behold the glory of God in

---

45. Stibbs, Kevan, and Davidson, *New Bible Commentary*, 983.
46. Bushnell, *God's Word to Women*, 98.

the face of Jesus Christ *"with unveiled face"* (2 Corinthians 3:18 NKJV). This truth has both covenantal and symbolic significance, indeed.

> Verse 16…is the conclusion of the passage, and it should be read in the light of all that has preceded it. In effect Paul says: if the women under specially difficult circumstances wish to veil, they are to have "authority over their head" to do so or not, as they please. But "if any man seemeth to be contentious" about it, let him know that as Christians and as a church we "have no such custom" of veiling.[47]

Historical evidence shows that women "sat unveiled in the assemblies in a separate place by the presbyters…[and] received a special ordination by laying on of hands,"[48] until the eleventh canon of the church of Laodicea forbade it, in ad 363.

C. The Divine Order in the Creation of Men and Women—1 Corinthians 11:8–12

Once again, the reader is referred to chapter 3 as a reminder of what Paul does here and in other places to confirm the divine order in the creation of men and women.

In these verses, we see a delicate balance in Paul's reasoning concerning the order of men and women in the original creation (see verses 3–12); as well as the present state of male and female. He alludes back to the creation order, and his thoughts are so very logical yet balanced so that neither man nor woman is exalted above the other. Neither is superior or inferior. Both are shown to be in need of each other.

+ Man was created first, and dominion was given to him in the divine order of creation.

+ Woman was made after man, taken from man, built for man, and presented to man. She was bone of his bone and flesh of his flesh.

---

47. Jessie Penn-Lewis, *The Magna Charta of Woman*, 1919 (online), https://web.archive.org/web/20071112131009/http://www.godswordtowomen.org/studies/resources/onlinebooks/magna.htm.

48. Charles J. Ellicott, *Ellicott's Commentary on the Whole Bible, Volume VIII: Ephesians – Revelation* (Eugene, OR: Wipf and Stock Publishers, 2015), 203.

In all her comeliness, loveliness, purity, and beauty, woman is an expression of man's honor and dignity, seeing as she owes her origin to him.

+ The original man is not of the woman, nor was he formed from a woman.

+ The woman is of the man, taken from his side, made for his comfort, happiness, and completion. (See Genesis 2:18–23.) The woman is the man's helpmeet, his friend.

+ However, lest the man become conceited and believe that the woman is meant exclusively for his use, Paul shows that all men, since Adam, owe their existence to a woman who carried them in her womb. All men, since Adam, have been born of a woman, their mother. Men today could not exist without the woman and the man, without the father and the mother. Each needs the other to exist. Neither is independent. Male and female depend on each other by an indispensable and indissoluble union.

We now set out, by way of comparison and contrast, Paul's wonderfully delicate balance of the man and the woman, redemptively equal in God's eyes, yet functionally different.

GOD

CHRIST

CREATION

ALL THINGS OF GOD

Man	Woman
1. The head of the man is Christ.	1. The head of the woman is the man.
2. Man is the image and glory of God.	2. Woman is the glory of the man.
3. Man is not of the woman.	3. The original woman, Eve, came from man.
4. Man was not created for the woman.	4. Woman was created for the man.

Man	Woman
5. Man has not been independent of woman since the original man, Adam.	5. Woman has not been independent of man since the original woman.
6. All men are born of woman.	6. Woman was made of man (conception).
7. Men may pray and prophesy.	7. Women may pray and prophesy.
8. Men need not cover their head, as that dishonors their Head (Christ).	8. Women need to cover their head, or else they dishonor their head (their husband).
9. It is shameful, humiliating, and degrading for a man to have long hair.	9. Long hair on a woman is natural, a glory and ornament.
10. Man is of God.	10. Woman is of God, of the man.

In 1 Corinthians 11:10, Paul writes, *"For this cause ought the woman to have power on her head because of the angels."* The American Standard Version, marginal reference, reads, *"a covering, in sign that she is under the power of her husband."*

In Jewish synagogues and early Christian churches, the worshippers recognized the presence of angels when they gathered for worship. (See Hebrews 12:22–24.)

As Albert Barnes puts it, "A woman in the public assemblies and in speaking in the presence of men, should wear a veil, the usual symbol of modesty and subordination; because the angels of God are witnesses of your public worship, (see Hebrews 1:14), and because they know and appreciate the propriety of subordination and order in public assemblies."[49]

+ Satan, the fallen angel, was the one who deceived the woman, Eve, in Eden. (See Genesis 3:1–7; 1 Timothy 2:11–15.)

+ Fallen angels may have been involved in the days of Noah and the corruption of the daughters of men. (See Genesis 6; Jude 6; 2 Peter 2:4.)

---

49. Albert Barnes, *Notes, Explanatory and Practical, on the Acts of the Apostles* (London: Thomas Ward and Co., 1840), 145.

+ An angel appeared to Manoah's wife and announced the birth of Samson. (See Judges 13.)

+ An angel appeared to Hagar and gave her a forecast of the life of her son, Ishmael. (See Genesis 21:14–18.)

+ The angel Gabriel appeared to the Virgin Mary and announced the birth of Christ-Child. (See Luke 1:26–35.)

Angels have ministered to women, as well as to men, but each of these women was under divine order in relation to her husband—with the exception of Eve, who came out from under the "covering" of her husband, Adam, and moved under the deception of a fallen angel, Satan, by taking of the fruit of the tree of knowledge of good and evil. This is the scene that Paul lays out for the Corinthian believers—men and women—to illustrate the necessity for staying under divine "covering" and in divine order!

D. The Divine Order of Grooming for Men and Women—1 Corinthians 11:13–15

The key word is *"hair,"* pertaining to men and women alike.

Verse 14 reads, *"If a man have long hair, it is a shame unto him."* The *Amplified Bible* renders it this way: *"For a man to wear long hair is a dishonor [humiliating and degrading] to him."*

But the opposite is true for a woman. Verse 15 reads, *"If a woman have long hair, it is a glory to her: for her hair is given her for a covering* [a veil]." Her hair is an ornament for her.

Paul notes that it is a shame and a dishonor, something humiliating and degrading, for men to have long hair, because it gives them an effeminate appearance. In Old Testament times, the only men who wore their hair long were Nazarites, who did so as a sign of consecration to the Lord. This lasted only for the duration of their vow, at the conclusion of which they cut their hair. (See, for example, Numbers 6:1–5; Judges 13:5; 1 Samuel 1:11.) But for men who were not Nazarites, it was considered improper and disgraceful to wear their hair long, since that look "belonged to" the opposite sex. In the present generation, long hair on men is often seen as a sign of rebellion, a casting off of restraint; of revolution; of indolence, drug abuse, and violence against authority and/or society in general. Any physical characteristic that causes a Christian to blend in with the culture of the world rather than the culture of the kingdom of God becomes evil. (That is not to say that a Christian man cannot have long hair, only that the appearance is likely to make a wrong impression on certain people—and this ought to be avoided.)

For the woman, long hair is her glory, an ornament given by God. A woman's long hair is a natural, God-given covering and veil, as opposed to the synthetic kind of "coverings" furnished by society. The issue Paul was dealing with is, men should be men, and women should be women. Society today is not altogether unlike the Corinthian culture of Paul's day, with the men becoming more effeminate and women becoming more masculine. "Womanly" men and "manly" women should not be the way of Christian culture. This is what Paul is dealing with, and the principle is applicable to Christian culture in every age and generation.

Paul wraps up his argument in verse 16, saying, "*Now if anyone is disposed to be argumentative and contentious about this, we hold to and recognize no other custom [in worship] than this, nor do the churches of God generally*" (AMPC). Again, Paul is not talking about the custom of having long hair but rather the custom of wearing veils in worship services. He is saying the following:

+ If a woman whose head is shorn or shaven as a penalty for immoral behavior life should come to Christ, then she needs to wear an actual head covering until her hair grows back.

+ If the custom and culture of the city dictate that Christian women ought to wear a covering veil, then the women should follow the custom, so as not to offend anyone.

+ Men do not need to wear a head covering.

+ If anyone is contentious over the wearing of covering veils by Christian women, then it is not necessary to enforce the custom on all churches everywhere.

Paul handles the issue of women wearing a head covering in the meetings of the Corinthian believers in the same way he handles the issue of women speaking in the church. His overarching aim is to prevent the testimony of Christ from being adversely affected by the improper behavior of Christian men or women.

To Summarize 1 Corinthians 11:1–16:

1. There is a divine order of headship in the Godhead: Father, Son, and Holy Spirit.

2. There is a divine order of headship in human relationships—the man and the woman/the husband and the wife.

3. Both men and women may pray and prophesy in the church gatherings.

4. The men do not need to wear a fabric covering on their heads, since the Head of the believing husband is Christ.

5. The women do not necessarily need to wear a covering veil on their heads, since their long hair is a God-given covering veil.

6. If a woman has her head shaven or shorn due to sins committed in her past life, then she needs to wear a head covering until her natural covering—her hair—has grown back.

7. The woman may wear a covering veil if the social custom and culture of her time require it. This is a cultural principle, not a universal commandment of God.

8. It is not the case that any man is the head of every woman, but the head of any Christian wife is her husband, who should be under the headship of Christ.

9. The wife is under the care and covering of her husband, and this is for her safety and protection before the angels, whether they be good or evil angels.

10. Christlike headship entails the essential elements of care, authority, and leadership. Christ is the Head of the church, just as the husband is the head of the home.

11. Creation shows that men and women are equal as persons before God, though they are functionally different. Sin marred the divine order.

12. Redemption restores men and women back to the creation order "in Christ," in the Christian home and in the Christian church alike.

19

CHRISTIAN MEN AND WOMEN IN THE BOOK OF ACTS

In the Gospels, Jesus foretold two major events that actually began to find their fulfillment in the book of Acts. These two major events were:

1. The outpouring of the Holy Spirit—Luke 24:47–49; John 15:26; 16:7–13

2. The birth and building of the New Testament church—Matthew 16:15–20; 18:15–20

The Holy Spirit would bring to birth the New Testament church, God's new community. The church would be built *"not by might, nor by power, but by my spirit, saith the LORD of hosts"* (Zechariah 4:6).

Before commenting on some of the notable experiences and ministries of men and women recorded in the book of Acts, we again acknowledge an Old Testament prophecy and then its fulfillment in the New Testament.

> And it shall come to pass **afterward**, that I will pour out my spirit upon all flesh; and your sons and daughters shall prophesy, your old men shall dream dreams, and your young men shall see visions: and also upon the servants and upon the handmaids in those days will I pour out my spirit. (Joel 2:28–29)

> [Peter said,] *But [instead] this is [the beginning of] what was spoken through the prophet Joel: And it shall come to pass in the last days, God declares, that I will pour out of My Spirit upon all mankind, and your sons and your daughters shall prophesy [telling forth the divine counsels] and your young men shall see visions (divinely granted appearances), and your old men shall dream [divinely suggested] dreams. Yes, and on My menservants also and on My maidservants in those days I will pour out of My Spirit, and they shall prophesy [telling forth the divine counsels and predicting future events pertaining especially to God's kingdom].* (Acts 2:16–18 AMP)

It should be noted that the "afterward" from Joel becomes "in the last days" mentioned by Peter.

Acts 2 records the original outpouring of the Holy Spirit—the "birthday" of the New Testament church, in fulfillment of Christ's prophetic words in the Gospels. Peter explains in his sermon that God's intention was that, in the last phase of human history, He would pour out His Spirit on "all flesh"—all mankind, all believers. The outpoured Spirit would be upon "sons and daughters" and on "servants and handmaidens." That is, God would pour out His Spirit on all people, regardless of their gender.

Under the old covenant, the Spirit was available to only a select few. But under the new covenant, the Spirit became available to all mankind. Ever since Pentecost, it has been that all believers may receive, and minister in, the power of the Holy Spirit. Men and women are together priests unto God. (See Revelation 1:6; 5:10.) No longer is it the case that only one person (the high priest) of a specific gender (man), age (25 to 50 years), nation (Israel), and tribe (Levi) may enter God's immediate presence, and that on only one day a year (the Day of Atonement), as under the old covenant. All new covenant believers are a new creation, a new community, a new covenant priesthood.

Such barriers as gender, age, and social status are set aside, for all believers, male and female, are now *"one in Christ Jesus"* (Galatians 3:28). The Holy Spirit is available to sons and daughters (legal heirs), as well as to servants and handmaidens (social servants).

A study of the references to Christian men and women in Acts—the book of the early church—shows that the Lord Jesus, by His Spirit, blessed both genders in the areas of ministry and experience. There is no way that the Christian women kept "silent" in the presence of men, but men and women alike ministered as the Holy Spirit enabled and anointed them. The following summary of this portion of Acts confirms these truths.

1. On the day of Pentecost, men and women were found in the Upper Room praying together. That's right—women were among the 120 disciples who prayed and made supplications *"with one accord"* (Acts 2:2).

    Those who were present in the Upper Room are identified as follows:

    > *Peter, and James, and John, and Andrew, Philip, and Thomas, Bartholomew, and Matthew, James the son of Alphaeus, and Simon Zelotes, and Judas the brother of James…all continued with one accord in prayer and supplication, with the women, and Mary the mother of Jesus, and with his brethren.*
    >
    > (Acts 1:13–14)

    The men and the women continued in prayer *together* over a period of ten days. Thus, the eleven apostles did not impose total silence on the women. As we have seen, Paul confirms the legitimacy of men *and* women praying. (See 1 Corinthians 11:4–5; 1 Timothy 2:8–10; Acts 1:12–14.)

2. On the day of Pentecost, the Holy Spirit came as a rushing wind and tongues of fire. He sat, as tongues of fire, on the head of each of the 120 disciples—the men and the women alike. All were filled with the Holy Spirit, and spoke with other tongues (languages) as the Spirit gave them the words to speak. (See Acts 2:1–4.) The Holy Spirit made no gender distinctions. Both men and women spoke in new languages under the baptism and filling of the Holy Spirit.

3. Comment has already been made on Peter's quotation of Joel's prophecy regarding the outpouring of the Spirit *"in the last days."* Acts 2 details the beginning of that fulfillment. Sons and daughters, servants and handmaids, are speaking in tongues, gender distinctions no longer being barriers to one's being filled with the Holy Spirit. (See Acts 2:17–18.) Peter could not deny this fact when he saw men and women alike being baptized in the Spirit.

4. In Acts 5:1–11, both the husband, Ananias, and his wife, Sapphira, are individually and independently held responsible by God for lying to the Holy Spirit. Both paid the penalty of divine judgment and were put to death for their sin.

5. In spite of the divine discipline meted out to the disciples Ananias and Sapphira, *"believers were the more added to the Lord, multitudes **both of men and women**"* (Acts 5:14).

6. The early church took care of the Grecian widows, whether Jew or Gentile, by appointing seven men to ensure the widows received their due in the daily distribution. (See Acts 6:1–6.) God cares for widows.

7. Before he became the apostle Paul, Saul the Pharisee wreaked havoc on the church as he entered home after home—probably the sites of various house churches—arrested men and women, and committed them to prison. Men and women were witnesses of the risen Christ, and so both genders were judged "guilty" by Saul. (See Acts 8:3; 9:2; 22:4–5.)

8. Thanks to the ministry of the evangelist Philip, men and women alike accepted Christ and were baptized into the death, burial, and resurrection of the Lord Jesus Christ. (See Acts 8:12.)

9. After the death of a woman by the name of Dorcas, who had been given to a ministry of good words and gifts for the poor, Peter raised her from the dead, making her the first individual in Acts to be raised to resurrection life. As a result of this miracle, many people believed in the Lord. (See Acts 9:36–42.)

10. Mary, the mother of John Mark, opened her house for prayer on behalf of Peter and James when they were in prison. James was beheaded, but Peter was delivered from prison. After his release, Peter came to the prayer meeting in Mary's house. A girl by the name of Rhoda could hardly believe it was really Peter at the door. (See Acts 12:1–19.)

11. In the city of Antioch of Pidisia, unbelieving Jews stirred up the devout and honorable women, as well as the chief men, against Paul and Barnabas. The opposition caused Paul and Barnabas to be expelled from the city for preaching the gospel. Thus, Jewish men and women rose up against the gospel message. (See Acts 13:50–52.)

12. Timothy's mother and grandmother, Eunice and Lois, were believers—godly women who had taught Timothy the Scriptures from his childhood. (See Acts 16:1–3; 2 Timothy 1:5; 3:14–17.) Timothy, along with Paul, thanked God for these women and the foundation of the Word of God that they had set in his life early on.

13. When a group of female disciples met on the Sabbath for prayer down at the riverside in Philippi, Paul, Silas, and Timothy sat down on the riverbank and spoke to the women about the Christ of God. (See Acts 16:9–13.)

14. A woman by the name of Lydia (of Europe), from the city of Thyatira, had her heart opened by the Lord to the gospel. She invited and constrained the apostolic band to come into her home for hospitality. She was probably the first convert to the gospel from Thyatira. (See Acts 16:14–15.)

15. A woman who had a fortune-telling spirit (also called the spirit of Python) was miraculously delivered under Paul's ministry as he was on his way to prayer. (See Acts 16:16–18.)

16. In Thessalonica, a great multitude of Greeks, as well as a number of chief women, received the gospel as Paul reasoned with them out of the Scriptures concerning the Christ of God. (See Acts 17:1–4.)

17. In Berea, many honorable Greek women and men received the Word with an open mind. (See Acts 17:10–12.)

18. In Athens, certain men accepted the gospel preached by Paul, and a woman by the name of Damaris also responded. (See Acts 17:34.)

19. In Corinth, Paul found a man named Aquila and his wife, Priscilla. All three were of the same trade, as tentmakers. (See Acts 18:1–3.) In time, they traveled together, spreading the gospel, and came to Ephesus. (See Acts 18:18–19.)

20. In Ephesus, Aquila and Priscilla heard Apollos speaking in the Jewish synagogue. He was *"an eloquent man, and mighty in the scriptures"* (Acts 18:24). They instructed him in the gospel more fully, as he had previously known only of John's baptism. (See Acts 18:25–26.) Both the husband and the wife taught the mighty Apollos the Scriptures in a fuller way than he had known. They worked as a team. And Apollos was humble enough to receive further enlightenment from this couple.

    Paul speaks highly of Aquila and Priscilla as co-laborers in the gospels, as will be seen in later comments.

21. Ephesus was dominated by the worship of the goddess Diana. (See Acts 19:34–35.) We dealt with this subject in great depth in our discussion of 1 Timothy 2:11–15.

22. Philip the evangelist had four virgin daughters who were gifted with prophecy and prophesied at times. The prophet Agabus spoke a prophetic word to Paul regarding what would happen at Jerusalem. (See Acts 21:8–11.) Paul did not "silence" these prophetic daughters of Philip. Here, we have Philip the evangelist, Agabus the prophet, the apostle Paul, and the four daughters who prophesied. What a time of fellowship these ministers must have had in Philip's household!

23. Although we do not know the final response of Felix and his wife, Drusilla (a Jewess), we know that Paul was able to preach the gospel to them. (See Acts 24:24–25.)

24. King Agrippa and Bernice also heard the gospel from Paul, along with his testimony of his conversion to Christ. (See Acts 25:13, 23, 26.)

So, we see that in the book of Acts:

+ Men and women prayed together. (See Acts 1:14; 12:12; 16:13; 21:5.)

+ Men and women prophesied. (See Acts 2:17–18; 21:8–9.)

+ Men and women spoke in tongues at Pentecost. (See Acts 2:1–4.)

+ Men and women were baptized in water in the name of the Lord Jesus Christ. (See Acts 8:12; 16:15.)

+ Men and women were imprisoned for the gospel. (See Acts 9:1–3.)

+ Women were called disciples. (See Acts 9:36.)

+ A woman named Dorcas was miraculously raised from the dead by Peter. (See Acts 9:36–41.)

+ Men and women believed in and received the gospel. (See Acts 17:34.)

+ A team of husband and wife taught the Word of the Lord more fully to the mighty Apollos. (See Acts 18:24–26.)

A study of the book of Acts reveals that neither the apostle Peter, nor the evangelist Philip, nor the apostle Paul ever took issue with women praying, prophesying, witnessing, and teaching along with men.

In the early church, we see "sons and daughters" and "servants and handmaidens" coming to salvation, getting baptized in water, being filled with the Spirit, speaking in tongues, praying, prophesying, and teaching, as the Spirit anointed them. There is no command for women to be "silent," nor is there a prohibition of women speaking or wielding authority when men are present.

The book of Acts confirms what we have already seen—that Paul is dealing with *local situations* in Corinth and Ephesus. He is not laying down *universal* and *timeless* commandments for all churches.

20

CHRISTIAN MEN AND WOMEN IN THE PAULINE EPISTLES

The apostle Paul has been counted as a rabbinical Pharisee of the most legalistic tradition. He is often painted as a male chauvinist, a woman-hater, and a suppressor of women, especially when it comes to women speaking in public. His writings are interpreted by many to mean that woman ought to be silent and forever banned from public ministry, as a sign of "submission" to men.

Paul is the most maligned, misunderstood, and misinterpreted of all the New Testament apostles. A serious study of Paul's life in Christ, and his treatment of the Christian women in his life, will set the record straight. And that is the purpose of this chapter.

A. Paul and Christian Women in the Book of Acts

In the previous chapter, we noted some of Paul's interactions with women in the book of Acts. The following is a brief summary.

1. Lydia was Paul's first convert in Philippi; she was soon leading the women in prayer and hosting gatherings of believers in her house. It was there that Paul met with his followers after his release from prison. (See Acts 16:13–15, 40.)

2. Prominent women in Thessalonica responded to Paul's preaching. (See Acts 17:1–4.)

3. Women in Berea also responded to Paul's message. (See Acts 17:10–12.)

4. Damaris in Athens responded to Paul's preaching of the gospel. (See Acts 17:34.)

5. In Corinth, Paul met Aquila and Priscilla, who became his companions in spreading the gospel. This couple explained the way of God more fully to the mighty Apollos. (See Acts 18:24–26.)

6. Paul was at the home of Philip with the prophet Agabus while Philip's four virgin daughters prophesied. (See Acts 21:8–9.)

Thus, in the book of Acts, Paul sees both men and women come to Christ, and he recognizes some members of both genders who are gifted in the gifts of the Spirit and the ministry of the Word.

B. Paul and Christian Men and Women in the Epistles

Paul shows no preference as he credits the men and women who labored with him in spreading the gospel. This fact suggests, once more, that Paul was no silencer or suppressor of women who were gifted in ministry. Most of these women, he merely mentions by name, but some are given more prominence.

Romans

Perhaps one of the most remarkable chapters in Paul's epistles is Romans 16. A study of the names mentioned in this chapter points to people of three distinct races: Roman, Greek, and Jewish—all of whom Paul considers "one in Christ."

In his closing greetings to the saints at Rome (at a church not founded by Paul), Paul names some twenty-seven people, at least seven of whom were women. While certain of these individuals are treated more prominently than others, each one is greeted in a spirit of Christian love and courtesy by Paul. None of them is silenced or suppressed by any "Pharisaic Paul," but all are commended by God's grace. Paul expresses his concern for specific individuals and the entire group at large, and acknowledges the commendable qualities of his brothers and sisters in the Lord.

We will now explore the people he mentions.

1. *Phoebe*

I commend to you Phoebe our sister, who is a servant ["minister" DAR-BY; "deaconess" AMP] of the church in Cenchrea, that you may receive her in the Lord in a manner worthy of the saints, and assist her in whatever business she has need of you; for indeed she has been a helper ["succourer" KJV] of many and of myself also.

(Romans 16:1–2 NKJV)

There are about fifty words used by Paul in his commendation of Phoebe to the saints at Rome. In the list of greetings here, Paul's first is that of a wonderful Christian woman. There is certainly no taint of male chauvinism here.

The name *Phoebe* means "bright, radiant."

+ *"I commend to you"*—Paul, by way of introduction and presentation, commends Phoebe to the saints at Rome. He does not seek to impose her on the saints but commends her. Early church writings show that some received "letters of commendation" to the various churches. (See, for example, 2 Corinthians 3:1–2.) These letters helped to protect the churches from any false or questionable ministries moving around and exploiting the hospitality of the saints. (See Philippians 2:25–30; 3 John 5–8.)

+ *"Phoebe our sister"*—Paul affectionately speaks of Phoebe as *"our sister."* It is recognition of the family of God, and that all who do the will of God are indeed "brothers and sisters."

+ *"A servant"*—in Acts 18:18, the Greek word for *"servant"* is *diakonos* (STRONG 1249). It means "an attendant," and originally spoke of one who "runs…errands" or "one who executes the commands of another." In some uses, it means "the servant of a king." Other definitions include "a table waiter," or "one serving food and drink." (See Acts 6:1–6.)

Elsewhere, this Greek word is also translated as…

+ *"Minister"* (20 times)

+ *"Servant"* (8 times)

+ *"Deacon"* (3 times)

The word is used of:

+ Christ, who was *the* Minister, Servant, and Deacon—Romans 15:8

+ Paul himself—Ephesians 3:7

+ Paul and Apollos—1 Corinthians 3:5

+ Tychicus—Ephesians 6:21; Colossians 4:7

+ Timothy—1 Timothy 4:6

In time, the title "deacon" was assigned to one who, by virtue of the office, served the church. Kenneth Wuest says that widows, and sometimes virgins, had the following duties to perform: "to take care of the sick and the poor, to minister to martyrs and confessors in prison, to instruct catechumens, to assist at the baptism of women, and to exercise a general supervision over female church-members."[50]

In the Gospels, during the ministry of Christ and the apostles, there were a number of women who ministered to Him and the twelve, of their substance, and served as "deaconesses."

Phoebe, then, was a servant, a minister, a "deaconess" of the church at Cenchrea, near Corinth.

The word *diakonos*, in the masculine, was used of both male and female deacons. In time, an order of female deacons was established, which gave rise to the feminine term "deaconess."

+ *"Of the church at Cenchrea"*—note the use of the word *"church"* in this chapter, for Paul cares for the individual as well as the churches. Paul always evidenced his love and passion for both the saints (individually) and the church (corporately).

  "The church in Cenchrea" (Romans 16:1 NKJV).

---

50. Kenneth Samuel Wuest, *Wuest's Word Studies from the Greek New Testament for the English Reader* (Grand Rapids, MI: Wm. B. Eerdmans Publishing Company, 1973), 257.

"All the churches of the Gentiles" (verse 4).

"The church that is in their house [the house of Priscilla and Aquila]" (verse 5).

"The churches of Christ" (verse 16).

✦ *"That you may receive her"*—the opposite would have been to reject Phoebe, or not to accept her, either because she was a woman or because she came from another city or race. Yet Paul commends Phoebe and acknowledges her as a sister and a deacon in the church at Cenchrea, then asks the church to receive—to accept her.

✦ *"In the Lord"*—the basis for receiving Phoebe is to be "in the Lord," the basis of redemption and fellowship. It is the equivalent of the statement that there is neither "male nor female" in Christ. (See Galatians 3:28.) Note the constant expression of "in Christ" in this chapter. The phrase is used at least ten times, in various forms:

1. *"In the Lord"* (Romans 16:2 NKJV)—referring to Phoebe

2. *"In Christ Jesus"* (verse 3)—referring to Priscilla and Aquila

3. *"In Christ"* (verse 7)—referring to Andronicus and Junia

4. *"In the Lord"* (verse 8)—referring to Amphias

5. *"In Christ"* (verse 9)—referring to Urbane/Urbanas

6. *"In Christ"* (verse 10)—referring to Apelles

7. *"In the Lord"* (verse 11)—referring to those of the household of Narcissus

8. *"In the Lord"* (verse 12)—referring to Tryphena and Tryphosa

9. *"In the Lord"* (verse 12)—referring to Persis

10. *"In the Lord"* (verse 13)—referring to Rufus, his mother, and Paul's mother

The key to receiving brothers and sisters is in seeing one another as new creatures *"in Christ"* (2 Corinthians 5:17). Believers are not "in Adam," or under the old-creation order, but "in Christ"—the new creation. (See 1 Corinthians 15:22.) This point of view is made possible only by the redemption Christ purchased at Calvary for believers.

+ *"In a manner worthy of the saints"*—the second reason for receiving Phoebe in the Lord is from the human side. Believers are called to be saints, "holy, separated ones." On the divine side, we receive each other because we are "in the Lord." On the human side, we receive each other because we are "saints." Believers are Christians: citizens of heaven first, then citizens of Rome or other places.

+ *"Assist her"*—that is, stand by her, help her.

+ *"In whatever business she has need of you"*—Paul encourages the Roman saints to help Phoebe with whatever business, anything or any matter or work, in which she needs help. She is about the Lord's business, just as Jesus said He was: *"I must be about my Father's business"* (Luke 2:49).

+ *"A helper* ["succourer" KJV] *of many and of myself also"*—the word *"succourer"* means *"helper"* (ASV, NKJV). The Greek word *prostatis* (STRONG 4368) is the feminine form, meaning "a female guardian, protectress, patroness, caring for the affairs of others, and aiding them with her resources. It actually speaks of an official position. Thus, Phoebe serves the ministry; and many people, including Paul himself, have been helped by this great woman of God. It is the feminine form of a derivative of STRONG 4291, *proistemi*, meaning "to stand before, i.e., (in rank), to preside, or (by implication), to practice. It is translated "maintain, be over, rule."

It is this woman whom Paul is sending to Rome, to deliver this valuable epistle to the Romans. Paul entrusts this letter to her, an act that shows his official and apostolic endorsement and recommendation of her ministry. What a great honor! What a wonderful recommendation by the apostle Paul himself. If Paul is against women's involvement in ministry, there is absolutely no sign of it here!

2. *Priscilla and Aquila*

Greet Priscilla and Aquila, my fellow workers ["helpers" KJV] *in Christ Jesus, who risked their own necks for my life, to whom not only I give*

> *thanks, but all the churches of the Gentiles. Likewise greet the church*
> *that is in their house.*   (Romans 16:3–5 NKJV)

After commending Phoebe to the saints at Rome, Paul sends greetings to Priscilla and Aquila, a married couple involved in ministry together. Priscilla is also known as Prisca.

The first mention of this couple is in Acts 18:1–2. They had been at Rome, but after the emperor Claudius banished all Jews from the city, in AD 52, they came to Corinth. They were tentmakers by trade, just as Paul was. After they came to Corinth, they teamed up with Paul in ministry. In due time, the threesome left Corinth and went to Ephesus, where Priscilla and Aquila settled for a time, while Paul went on to strengthen the other churches he had planted elsewhere. (See Acts 18:3–23.)

Apollos of Alexandria came to Ephesus and stayed with Priscilla and Aquila. He knew only the baptism of John, until Priscilla and Aquila explained to him the way of God more perfectly. (See Acts 18:24–28.) Though he was a great scholar and orator, the mighty Apollos was humble enough to receive teaching from this Christian couple. Both husband and wife were teachers of the Word, though it appears that Priscilla, the wife, was more gifted in instruction than her husband, since her name is mentioned before his on several occasions.

When Paul wrote his first letter to the Corinthian church from Ephesus, he sent greetings from Priscilla and Aquila and from the church in their house. (See 1 Corinthians 16:19.) Then, in Romans 16, they must have returned to Rome, for Paul sends greetings to the church in their house there. (See Romans 16:3–5.) Finally, when Paul writes to Timothy, Aquila and Priscilla are back in Ephesus, in the house of Onesiphorus. (See 2 Timothy 4:19.)

Thus, this couple's ministry took them from Rome to Corinth, to Ephesus, back to Rome, and then again to Ephesus. There are some significant details worth mentioning from the New Testament record of this couple.

+ Their names are always mentioned together.

+ On several occasions, Priscilla, the wife, is mentioned before her husband, Aquila. This order is unusual, as it would be in a letter written today.

  > *"Aquila…with his wife Priscilla"* (Acts 18:1–2)

  > *"Priscilla and Aquila"* (Acts 18:18)

  > *"Aquila and Priscilla"* (Acts 18:26)

  > *"Aquila and Priscilla"* (1 Corinthians 16:19)

  > *"Priscilla and Aquila"* (Romans 16:3–5)

  > *"Prisca and Aquila"* (2 Timothy 4:19)

+ Priscilla and Aquila are called Paul's *"fellow workers"* or *"helpers"* in Christ Jesus. The Greek word for *"helpers"* is *sunergos* (STRONG 4904), meaning "fellow-helper, fellowlaborer, fellow-worker, laborer together with, workfellow."

  This same Greek word is also translated as…

  > *"Helper"*—Romans 16:3, 9;2 Corinthians 1:24

  > *"Fellow-helper"*—2 Corinthians 8:23; 3 John 1:8

  > *"Fellow-worker"*—Colossians 4:11

  > *"Workfellow"*—Romans 16:21

  > *"Laborer together with"*—1 Corinthians 3:9

  > *"Companion in labor"*—Philippians 2:25

  > *"Fellow-laborer"*—Philippians 4:3; 1 Thessalonians 3:2; Philemon 1:1, 24

The term is used of some thirteen different people in the New Testament, men and women alike. Priscilla and Aquila were co-laborers in the gospel with Paul, as a husband-and-wife team.

+ Priscilla and Aquila risked their own necks for Paul. Only eternity will tell the stories of how they saved Paul's life from all the threats against him by Jews and Gentiles in the cities of Asia Minor.

+ Paul and the churches of the Gentiles gave thanks to this couple. The Gentile churches must have heard of the attempts on Paul's life, and how Priscilla and Aquila were willing to lay down their lives to protect him. How thankful these Gentile churches were, as was as Paul himself!

+ *"Likewise greet the church that is in their house"* (Romans 16:5 NKJV)—there were no special "church buildings" in these days, but many of the saints with larger homes or courts would open their houses to host church gatherings. "The church in the house of so and so" was a common phrase in those days.

> *"Aquila and Priscilla salute you much in the Lord, with the church that is in their house"* (1 Corinthians 16:19).

> *"Salute the brethren which are in Laodicea, and Nymphas, and the church which is in his house"* (Colossians 4:15).

> *"...to our beloved Apphia, and Archippus our fellowsoldier, and to the church in thy house"* (Philemon 1:2).

> *"The churches of Christ salute you"* (Romans 16:16)—possibly referring to the house churches that met in the homes of those individuals mentioned in verses 14–15.

> The *"elect lady"* to whom John wrote as an elder-apostle possibly had a church in her house. John warns her against allowing deceivers to be received into the house. (See 2 John 7–11.) Twice, he addresses a specific person rather than a congregation, which further suggests that the *"elect lady"* was the leader of a house church.

> Gaius possibly had a house church. (See 3 John 6, 9, 10.)

> Lydia hosted church gatherings in her home. (See Acts 16:14–15, 40.)

> Chloe possibly had a house church, and Paul received her household report of the problems in the church at Corinth. (See 1 Corinthians 1:10–11.)

What great commendation, praise, and gratefulness Paul expresses for Priscilla and Aquila and their help in advancing the gospel of Christ. There is no sign of Paul's being against a married couple teaching and preaching the glorious gospel of our Lord Jesus Christ, nor against working with them.

3. Epaenetus

> Greet my beloved Epaenetus, who is the firstfruits of Achaia to Christ.   (Romans 16:5 NKJV)

Epaenetus means "praised." This individual was a well-loved brother in the Lord to the apostle Paul, who calls him the *"firstfruits"* unto God. The Old Testament laws concerning the firstfruits show that these were very special offerings to God, representative of the whole harvest to come. (See, for example, Leviticus 23:17; Exodus 23:16–19; Numbers 15:17–21; James 1:18; Revelation 14:4.) So, this brother was very special to Paul, being the first convert, of many, to Christ in Achaia.

4. Mary

> Greet Mary, who labored much for us.   (Romans 16:6 NKJV)

There are at least six different women named Mary in the New Testament, and each one is counted as special in the gospel. The Mary mentioned in Romans 16:6 is another woman whom Paul greets, and whose labor— hard work—in ministry he acknowledges. Who is to say whether her ministry was hospitality, or the general work done in and around the house? Regardless, Mary was worthy of mention here among the saints at Rome.

5. Andronicus and Junia

> Greet Andronicus and Junia, my countrymen ["kinsmen" KJV] and my fellow prisoners, who are of note ["outstanding" NIV] among the apostles, who also were in Christ before me.   (Romans 16:7 NKJV)

Andronicus means "conqueror," while *Junia* means "youth."

The identity of these two, linked together as they are, is a question of great debate among expositors. We will note the terms and phrases Paul uses to describe them:

- Kinsmen, or kinsfolk; countrymen
- Fellow prisoners, having been imprisoned some time for the gospel, even as Paul himself had been imprisoned
- Of note among the apostles
- In Christ before Paul, having been converted to Christ before Paul's own conversion, thus prior to Acts 9

Andronicus and Junia have been designated by others as:

- Two men involved in ministry, in apostolic work
- A married couple, as were Priscilla and Aquila (see verses 3–5)
- A single or married man (Andronicus) and a single or married woman (Junia)

Of all the names mentioned in Romans 16, most occur on their own. But there are at least five names coupled together:

- Priscilla and Aquila, a married couple, a husband/wife team ministry—verses 3–5
- Andronicus and Junia, a male and male or a male and female, the debatable issue—verse 7
- Tryphena and Tryphosa, possibly sisters in the Lord—verse 12
- Rufus and his mother, son and mother, either naturally or spiritually—verse 13
- Nereus and his sister, brother and sister, either naturally or spiritually—verse 15

By process of elimination, Andronicus and Junia, whether single or married to other people, traveling together would not have been appropriate in Paul's day—or today, for that matter.

Andronicus and Junia traveling together as fellow male apostles, however, would have been appropriate, as Jesus sent the twelve and the seventy out two by two into every city He Himself would visit. (See Mark 6:7; Luke 10:1.)

If Andronicus and Junia were a team of husband and wife, like Priscilla and Aquila, it would have been appropriate for Christian ministry. Paul had already written that a husband could *"take along a believing wife, as do also the other apostles"* (1 Corinthians 9:5 NKJV).

There is some debate about the gender of Junia/Junias. Some scholars contend that both forms of the name may be either feminine or masculine. Andronicus was certainly a common male name, but there is no definitive evidence that Junias was a name used for men.

We now quote extensively from Dr. Gary S. Greig on Romans 16:7 concerning Junia. In Romans 16:7, Paul mentions that Junia and Andronicus—most likely Junia's husband—are among the apostles. The underlined emphases are Greig's.

> Junia was a common Latin female name in the Roman Empire. Some scholars have claimed that the name in the Greek text of Rom. 16:7, Iounian (the accusative form), is a hypothetical Greek abbreviation, "Junias," of the Latin male name "Junianus." But there is absolutely no evidence at all that there ever was a masculine name "Junias" in the Roman Empire, according to Dr. Peter Lampe, Professor of New Testament, Union Theological Seminary, Richmond, Virginia:
>
> "Without exception, the Church Fathers in late antiquity identified Andronicus' partner in Rom. 16:7 as a woman, as did minuscule 33 in the 9th century which records iounia with an acute accent. Only later medieval copyists of Rom. 16:7 could not imagine a woman being an apostle and wrote the masculine name 'Junias.' This latter name did not exist in antiquity; it's explanation as a Greek abbreviation of the Latin name 'Junianus' is unlikely." (P. Lampe, "Junias," Anchor Bible Dictionary, vol. 3, p. 1127.)
>
> The Church Father, John Chrysostom (died 407 AD), who had a negative view of women in many cases, understood "Junia" in Rom. 16:7 as a woman and marveled that she could be called an apostle: "Oh how great is the devotion of this woman, (2) that she should be even counted worthy of the appellation of apostle!" (St. John Chrysostom, Homily 31 on Romans 16:5–16, The Nicene and Post-Nicene Fathers, Series 1, vol. 9, ["Chrysostom: Homilies on the Acts of the Apostles and the Epistle to the Romans"],

Grand Rapids: Eerdmans, 1971–1980). The first commentator to understand "Junia" as the hypothetical masculine name "Junias" was Aegidius of Rome in the 14th century AD. (D. Scholer, *Theology News and Notes*, Mar '95, p. 22.) That Junia was recognized among the apostles in the early church is understandable, if the early church had Deborah in mind as the senior judge and a "mother in Israel," Miriam as a prophetic leader under Moses, and Huldah as a prophetic leader under King Josiah.[51]

Andronicus and Junia are spoken of as being *"outstanding among the apostles"* (Romans 16:7 NIV). Does this mean that Junia was well-known *by* the apostles or well-known *as* an apostle? The natural meaning, according to early Greek scholars, is that these two, Andronicus and Junia, were outstanding *as* apostles. The term "apostle" was used in the early church, not just for the twelve but for anyone who was an authorized Christian missionary.

Paul names both Junia and Andronicus as outstanding apostles who were "in Christ" before he came to Christ. This detail places them prior to the account of Paul's conversion in Acts 9, in the time period of the church in Jerusalem. (See Acts 1–7.)

The weight of opinion from those nearest to the apostolic period is that Junia was a woman, given the feminine name. Andronicus and Junia may be seen as a married couple, not unlike Priscilla and Aquila, both involved in apostolic ministry.

(Note: For some schools, the question of Junia's gender will not be settled until Jesus comes. There is, however, no Scripture that says God cannot use a woman in apostolic ministry. God is God, and Christ is the Head of the church; He can give His ministry gifts to whomsoever He wills, whether male or female.)

In Romans 16, then, Paul acknowledges and honors such women as Phoebe, Priscilla, Mary, Tryphena, Tryphosa, Persis, the mother of Rufus,

---

51. Gary S. Greig, *Biblical Foundations for Women Alongside Men in Ministry Advancing God's Kingdom*, printed in the course syllabus for the Wagner Leadership Institute (Kingdom Training Network/The University Prayer Network, April 1999), 16. Accessed online. http://www.cwgministries.org/sites/default/files/files/books/WomenInMinistry.pdf.

Julia, the sister of Nereus, and Junia. All of this refutes the idea that Paul had a low view of women and that he wanted to silence them and suppress them from participating in public ministry!

6. Amplias

Greet Amplias, my beloved in the Lord. (Romans 16:8 NKJV)

Amplias means "large." No doubt this was another brother in the Lord whom Paul loved.

7. Urbane / Urbanus

Greet Urbanus ["Urbane" KJV], our fellow worker in Christ.
(Romans 16:9 NKJV)

Urbane means "of a city; polite."

8. Stachys

Greet...Stachys, my beloved. (Romans 16:9 NKJV)

Stachys means "ear of corn."

9. Apelles

Greet Apelles, approved in Christ. (Romans 16:10 NKJV)

Apelles means "called" or "approved."

10. Aristobulus

Greet those who are of the household of Aristobulus.
(Romans 16:10 NKJV)

The marginal reference says "friends." *Aristobulus* means "best counselor."

11. Herodion

> *Greet Herodion, my countryman ["kinsman" KJV].*
>
> (Romans 16:11 NKJV)

Herodion means "heroic."

12. Narcissus

> *Greet those who are of the household of Narcissus who are in the Lord.*
>
> (Romans 16:11 NKJV)

The marginal reference says "friends." *Narcissus* means "narcotic." Paul was probably referring to a house church in Rome.

13. Tryphena and Tryphosa

> *Greet Tryphena and Tryphosa, who have labored in the Lord.*
>
> (Romans 16:12 NKJV)

Tryphena means "to live luxuriously, shining," while *Tryphosa* means "shining." These two may have been sisters in the Lord.

Adam Clarke makes an interesting comment concerning these two women:

> Many have spent much useless labour in endeavouring to prove that these women did not preach. That there were some prophetesses, as well as prophets, in the Christian church, we learn; and that a woman might pray or prophesy, provided she had her head covered, we know; and that whoever prophesied, spoke unto others to edification, exhortation, and comfort, St. Paul declares, 1 Cor. xiv. 3. And that no preacher can do more, every person must acknowledge; because, to edify, exhort, and comfort, are the prime ends of the gospel ministry. If women thus prophesied, then women preached.[52]

---

52. Adam Clarke, *Dr. Adam Clarke's Commentary on the New Testament*, Vol. II (London: J. Butterworth & Son, 1817), 61.

These two sisters *"labored in the Lord"*; surely, their labors went beyond extending hospitality by washing, ironing clothes, and cooking meals for the saints!

14. Persis

> Greet the beloved Persis, who labored much in the Lord.
> (Romans 16:12 NKJV)

Persis means "Persian." The two sisters Tryphena and Tryphosa labored in the Lord, and so did this sister. The same word is spoken of a number of people in this chapter, and the whole context of the chapter has to do with laboring in the gospel of Christ.

15. Rufus...and his mother and mine

> Greet Rufus, chosen in the Lord, and his mother and mine.
> (Romans 16:13 NKJV)

Rufus means "red." When Paul writes of *"his mother and mine,"* he may be speaking of a natural mother or a spiritual mother in Israel. (See also 2 John 1; Judges 5:7.)

16. Asyncritus

> Greet Asyncritus....   (Romans 16:14 NKJV)

Asyncritus means "incomparable."

17. Phlegon

> Greet...Phlegon....   (Romans 16:14 NKJV)

Phlegon means "burning."

18. Hermas

> Greet...Hermas....   (Romans 16:14 NKJV)

Hennas means "mercury."

19. Patrobas

Greet...Patrobas....   (Romans 16:14 NKJV)

Patrobas means "paternal."

20. Hermes

Greet...Hermes....   (Romans 16:14 NKJV)

Hermes means "mercury."

21. Philologus

Greet Philologus....   (Romans 16:15 NKJV)

Philologus means "learned."

22. Julia

Greet...Julia....   (Romans 16:15 NKJV)

Julia means "soft-haired." It is the feminine form of the name Julius.

23. Nereus and his sister—Romans 16:15

Greet...Nereus and his sister....   (Romans 16:15)

Nereus means "lamp, brightness." Paul greets Nereus's sister, as well.

24.   Olympas

Greet...Olympas, and all the saints....   (Romans 16:15 NKJV)

Olympas means "heavenly." No doubt Paul was referring to another house church in Rome, or a household of faithful saints.

Paul concludes his salutations to the saints at Rome by saying, "*Greet one another with a holy kiss. The churches of Christ greet you*" (Romans 16:16 NKJV). He gives a similar instruction elsewhere in his epistles. (See 1 Corinthians 16:20; 2 Corinthians 13:12; 1 Thessalonians 5:26; 1 Peter

5:14.) This so-called *"holy kiss"* was not a "Judas kiss" of betrayal. (See 2 Samuel 20:9; Psalm 41:9; 55:13; Matthew 26:47–49; Luke 22:47–48.) In Western culture, the gesture of a kiss has taken on evil associations with lust or sex, but this was not the case in the culture of the early church.

One cannot help but notice the variety in terms of endearment Paul uses in the first sixteen verses of Romans 16 as he commends certain individuals for their work and service in the Lord, including *"sister," "fellow workers," "beloved," "firstfruits," "countrymen," "fellow prisoners," "approved in Christ,"* and *"chosen in the Lord."*

Surely, Paul's inclusion of women in his commendations goes beyond a show of gratitude for everyday hospitality to involve actual ministry in the church. Paul acknowledges with gratitude his brothers *and* sisters in Christ, for *"there is neither Jew nor Greek,…neither bond nor free,…neither male nor female:…all [are] one in Christ Jesus"* (Galatians 3:28).

1 Corinthians

In 1 Corinthians, Paul also acknowledges the household of Chloe and accepts her report of the problems in Corinth that need to be addressed. (See 1 Corinthians 1:10–11.) It would also seem that Stephanas, Fortunatus, and Achaicus, along with Timothy, had to do with the contents of this epistle from Paul. (See 1 Corinthians 16:15–18.)

Philippians

In the epistle to the Philippians, Paul warns of two female leaders, Euodias and Syntyche, who pose a threat to the unity of the church.

> I beseech Euodias, and beseech Syntyche, that they be of the same mind in the Lord. And I entreat thee also, true yokefellow, help those women which laboured with me in the gospel, with Clement also, and with other my fellowlabourers, whose names are in the book of life.
>
> (Philippians 4:2–3)

Euodias and Syntyche are two women who had labored with Paul in the gospel. He called them his fellow workers—an expression that, as has been seen, is also used of others who labored or ministered in the gospel.

(See, for example, 1 Thessalonians 3:2; Philemon 1:24; Philippians 2:25; Romans 16:3, 6, 9, 21; Acts 18:26.) "Laboring in the gospel" surely goes beyond extending Christian hospitality. These two women were leaders in the church at Philippi, and Paul exhorted them to be of a good attitude, as becomes Christian women in the Lord. The conflict between these two women was adversely affecting the church, hence Paul's strong entreaty for them to be of one mind—not over a matter of hospitality but over the gospel work.

1 and 2 Timothy

The references to women in 1 and 2 Timothy have already been considered, but they are noted again here in brief.

+ Paul refers to Timothy's grandmother Lois and his mother, Eunice; without doubt, they had taught him the Scriptures from his childhood. (See 2 Timothy 1:3–5; 3:14–17.)

+ In 2 Timothy 4:19, he speaks of Prisca (Priscilla) and Aquila.

+ In 2 Timothy 4:21, he communicates greetings from a woman, Claudia, and three men: Eubulus, Pudens, and Linus.

Philemon

In this short letter, Paul writes lovingly to Apphia and Philemon, along with Archippus, and the church in their house. (See Philemon 1:1–2.) Evidently, Apphia and Philemon were a couple—a husband-and-wife team who held church gatherings in their house. Paul appeals to Philemon to receive the runaway and repentant slave, Onesimus. This letter is a masterpiece on reconciliation.

In light of all these references to Christian men and women, Paul cannot be charged as a male chauvinist or a silencer and suppressor of women in public ministry. Such a view does not give an honest treatment to all Paul's writings concerning ministry, especially as concerns women believers.

On the contrary, Paul is second only to Christ as an emancipator of men and women in the body of Christ. His greatest redemptive verse is Galatians 3:28: in Christ, *"there is neither male nor female."* In the church, believers are to see one another not primarily through the lens of gender but from the perspective of their being "in Christ." In the home, there is the man and the woman/the husband and the wife, and the children. But in the body of Christ, gender barriers cease to exist! This truth should bring an end to prejudice based on gender distinctions. This is not an end or removal of gender differences or distinctions; however, those distinctions are no longer a legitimate basis for restricting the roles and relationships of men and women in the kingdom of God—the body of Christ, the church, which is God's new community. In this community, all distinctions based on ethnicity, social class, gender, and age are demolished. Racial, social, and gender prejudices are exposed and nullified by the cross of Jesus and the grace of God.

Women are included in many of the church ministries in the New Testament. Paul's ministry team included women, and Paul honored those women who labored with him in the gospel. He recognized that men and women "in Christ" were created for partnership in the kingdom of God, and thus he released both men and women to serve in the church. The Scriptures show the number of women who were involved with Paul in ministry as they fulfilled their various roles and functions in the church.

SUPPLEMENTAL

Bibliography of Paul's References to Womanhood

The writer is indebted to Don Williams's excellent and highly recommended book *The Apostle Paul and Women in the Church*, in which the author comments on every reference to women in the writings of Paul, whether the reference names an actual person or is used in a typical or allegorical sense. He does so by employing the most important hermeneutical principle—that of context.

It is fitting to conclude this chapter with a simple summary of the particular passages and verses Williams cites.[53]

Romans

1. Male and female sexual perversions (homosexuality, whether in men or women) will be judged by God—Romans 1:26–27

---

53. See Don Williams, *The Apostle Paul and Women in the Church* (Ventura, CA: Regal Books, 1978).

274 The Ministry of Women

2. The faith of Abraham and Sarah—Romans 4:16–21

3. The law of marriage in effect until dissolution by death (allegorical use of the law by Paul)—Romans 7:1–4

4. God's elective purposes seen in the choice of Sarah and Rebecca and their children—Romans 9:6–13

5. Typical application of Hosea's wife and children (male = "not My people"; female = "not beloved"—Romans 9:25; see also Hosea 1:6

6. Salutations to brothers and sisters in Christ and in His church, coworkers in the gospel of Christ—Romans 16

1 and 2 Corinthians

1. Paul's reception of the report of the house of Chloe, as well as some of the brothers from Corinth—1 Corinthians 1:10–11; 16:17–18; postscript

2. Paul's discipline of a case of incest in the Corinthian church—1 Corinthians 5:1

3. Admonition that believers not prostitute their bodies, for such are members of the body of Christ—1 Corinthians 6:15–16

4. Treatment of the state of the married and unmarried:

   > Husbands and wives—1 Corinthians 7:1–5

   > Unmarried and widows—1 Corinthians 7:8–9

   > Married—1 Corinthians 7:10–11; see also Matthew 19:3–9

   > Mixed marriages between believers and unbelievers—1 Corinthians 7:12–16

   > Unmarried and celibate—1 Corinthians 7:25–31

   > Everyone, regardless of marital status—1 Corinthians 7:32–35

   > Engaged couples—1 Corinthians 7:36–38

   > Widows "in the Lord"—1 Corinthians 7:39–40

5. Ministers of the gospel may *"lead about...a wife"*—1 Corinthians 9:3–5

6. Paul's discussion of covering veils—1 Corinthians 11:2–16

7. The legitimacy of both men and women praying and prophesying, provided they do so in proper order, without disturbing the church gatherings by asking questions and chattering—1 Corinthians 14:33–36

8. Paul's delivery of greetings from Aquila and Priscilla—1 Corinthians 16:19

9. Paul's concern that the Corinthian believers not be deceived, as was Eve by the serpent—2 Corinthians 11:1–3

Galatians

1. *"In Christ,"* all racial, social, ritual, and gender barriers cease to exist—Galatians 3:28

2. Jesus was born of a woman, who was under the law, to redeem mankind. Thus, deity and humanity united in God's Son—Galatians 4:4–5; see also Genesis 3:15

3. Paul's allegorical illustration of the old and new covenants by use of Abraham, Sarah, and Isaac versus Abraham, Hagar, and Ishmael—Galatians 4:21–31

Ephesians

1. Creation and redemption motifs interwoven in the relationships of husband/wife and Christ/His church—Ephesians 5:21–33; see also Genesis 2:24

2. Responsibility of fathers, mothers, and children "in the Lord"—Ephesians 6:1–3

Philippians

1. Paul's *"yokefellows"* Euodias and Syntyche entreated to be at peace with each other and to have Christlike attitudes—Philippians 4:2–3

2. Poor attitudes affect the church—Philippians 2

Colossians

1. Husband/wife relationship *"in the Lord"*—Colossians 3:18–19

2. Fathers/mothers/children—Colossians 3:20; see also Exodus 20:
    12; Ephesians 6:1–3

1 Thessalonians

1. Paul's care for the Thessalonians likened to a nurse, mother, or
    father caring for children—1 Thessalonians 2:7–8

2. Husband and wife to live in holiness to the Lord, as *"vessels of
    sanctification and honor"*—1 Thessalonians 4:3–8

3. The tribulation will be as "travail on a woman with
    child"—1 Thessalonians 5:2–3

1 and 2 Timothy

1. Men and women are to pray—1 Timothy 2:8–10

2. Women are to learn in silence and not seize authority over the
    husband, as Eve did when she usurped Adam's authority and
    ate of the forbidden fruit; Adam was not deceived but willfully
    sinned—1 Timothy 2:11–14

3. An elder (also referred to as a bishop) must be the husband of one
    wife–1 Timothy 3:1–2

4. Deaconesses (female deacons) must be qualified—1 Timothy
    3:11; see also Romans 16:1–2

5. Older men and women are to be treated as fathers and moth-
    ers–1 Timothy 5:1–2

6. Paul expresses concern about widows, both old and
    young–1 Timothy 5:3–16

7. Paul expresses concern that "silly" or spiritually weak women may
    endanger their households—2 Timothy 3:6–7

8. Greetings to Priscilla and Aquila–2 Timothy 4:19

9. Greetings from several men, and a woman named Claudia—2 Timothy 4:21

Titus

1. An elder is to be the husband of one wife–Titus 1:5–6

2. Older women are to teach the younger women–Titus 2:3–5

Philemon

1. Greetings and instruction to Philemon and Apphia, and the church in their house—Philemon 1–2

21

MEN AND WOMEN IN THE FUNCTIONING BODY OF CHRIST

We endeavor now to answer, as completely as is possible, the questions raised in the introduction of this book and in the pages that have followed. What are the proper roles of men and women in the church—the redemptive community of the people of God?

As already mentioned, this issue will not be finally settled until Jesus comes again. Until then, every denomination, and every congregation, needs to decide its own position on the matter, as each will be judged by the Lord Jesus at His coming.

The position of this writer has been summed up in chapter 12, relative to the Four Position Schools. But since it is said that repetition is the "best teacher," that proposition appears here once again.

A PROPOSITION

According to Colossians 3:11 and Galatians 3:28, "in Christ" there is neither male nor female, but all are one in Christ, and Christ is all and in all. That is to say, men and women, as persons, are redemptively equal. National, racial, social, cultural, ritual, and gender distinctions are not to be viewed as barriers to limit the role and function any individual may perform in the church, the body of Christ. Both men and women, as they are called, gifted, equipped, and anointed of God, may function in the body of Christ. Whether this be in the gifts of the Spirit or any of the grace-gifts Christ has placed in the church, men and women may function accordingly. Men and women, if so called and equipped of God, may function in the areas of leadership, eldership, deaconship, or the fivefold ascension-gift ministries Christ has placed in the church. Men and women may function according to the character qualities of Christ, the level of their spiritual maturity, the measure of grace-gifts given them, and the charisma of the Holy Spirit required to function in that particular ministry. Both men and women are called to function together in divine order, love, unity, and harmony, as members one of another, members of the body of Christ, under God's supreme headship.

What, then, does the Bible teach us about the proper place, role, and function of men and women in the church, God's redemptive community?

In this chapter, we will consider both the Old Testament and the New Testament as we endeavor to discern that which men and women are able to be or to do in the church, the body of Christ on the earth. The new covenant is the fulfillment of the Old Testament prophecies concerning the Spirit being "[poured] out...upon all flesh" (Joel 2:29)—that is, "sons and... daughters,...servants and...handmaidens" (Acts 2:17–18).

The new covenant exceeds the old covenant in every way. Whereas the qualifications for ministering in the body of Christ were very limited under the old covenant, and basically restricted to males in the nation of Israel, the new covenant has made it so that the Holy Spirit is available for all believers, regardless of gender. The Holy Spirit is also available for every kindred, tongue, tribe, and nation. Therefore, it is to be expected that there will be a worldwide increase of manifestations of the Spirit—His gifts, grace, and power—in our day.

The church is the body of Christ on the earth, composed of men and women as members. And it is meant to be a functioning body, carrying out the will of God in the earth. It is unthinkable that only males are called to function in spiritual gifting in that body. The members of that body are male and female, and all may function according to their gifts.

The ministry roles we are considering will fall into one of two categories: (1) those spiritual blessings and functions that are general for both men and women, and (2) those spiritual blessings and functions that are more restricted for men and women, as the above Proposition explains. The former will be covered in this present chapter, the latter in the chapter that follows.

Those denominations and schools that sanction female participation in public ministry to some degree should feel reasonably "safe" with the following list of blessings and ministries.

1. New Birth

Both men and women may be born again—born from above, born of the Holy Spirit—and thereby become new creatures in Christ Jesus. (See John 3:1–5; 1 Peter 1:23.) Gender distinctions are no barrier to the miracle of the new birth.

2. Water Baptism

Both men and women may be baptized in water by immersion after coming to repentance and faith in the gospel of Christ. (See Matthew 28:18–20; Mark 16:15–20.) Water baptism in the New Testament is the equivalent to the Old Testament rite of circumcision. Old Testament circumcision was for the male and was of the flesh; New Testament circumcision is for male and female and is of the heart and of the spirit. (See Colossians 2:10–13; Romans 2:28–29.) Gender distinctions are no barrier to being baptized in water.

3. Holy Spirit Baptism

Both men and women may receive the baptism and anointing of the Holy Spirit, in fulfillment of the Old Testament prophecies in which the Lord said He would pour out His Spirit on all flesh: sons and daughters, servants and handmaidens. (See Joel 2:28–32; Acts 2:16–21.) Gender distinctions are no barrier to receiving the baptism of the Holy Spirit.

4. Prayer

Both men and women may pray together, as they did in the Upper Room prior to the feast of Pentecost. (See Acts 1:12–14.) It was difficult for Jews to have a woman pray or prophesy and have communion with them. The women in the upper room had been touched by the Lord Jesus and waited for the outpouring of the Spirit along with the men. This occurrence was a major departure from Jewish custom, as the temple had separate courts for the women and the men. The men and women did not pray together. In Jerusalem today, men and women are separated at the Wailing Wall. But a new day has dawned. Men and women pray together, waiting for the Spirit. Paul also confirms that men and women can pray, lifting up holy hands to the Lord. (See 1 Corinthians 11:4–5; 1 Timothy 2:8–10.) Gender distinctions are no hindrance to prayer.

Prayer, as practiced by women, may include:

+ Prayer with their husbands—1 Peter 3:1–8

+ Prayer for the sick—Mark 16:15–20

+ Prayer in public meetings in the church—1 Corinthians 11:5; 1 Timothy 2:8–10; Acts 16:13; 1 Samuel 1, 12–18, 27

+ Prayer with other women—Acts 16:13

+ Prayer of mourning and grief—Jeremiah 9:17–21; Isaiah 32:9–15

+ Prayer with the men of the church—Acts 1:13–15

5. Speaking in Tongues

Both men and women spoke in other tongues on the day of Pentecost, as the Spirit gave them utterance. The Holy Spirit came in as a mighty rushing wind, and tongues of fire sat on the men and the women alike. Men and women waited together for Pentecost, at which point men and women were filled with the Holy Spirit and became living stones in the new covenant temple. Peter, filled with the Spirit, had no hesitation in saying that this was the fulfillment of Joel's prophecy concerning the outpouring of the Spirit on all flesh in the last days—that is, on sons and daughters, servants and handmaids; both male and female believers. (See Acts 2:1–4, 16–18; Joel 2:28–32.) Again, gender distinctions are no barrier to being equipped by the Holy Spirit to speak in tongues.

6. Membership in the Body of Christ

Both men and women are baptized by the Holy Spirit into one and the same body of Christ, which is the church. (See 1 Corinthians 12:13.)

Believers have to see one another, regardless of gender, as fellow members of that body. The church is called to be the functioning body of Christ in the earth. Male and female members alike are called to function in their set place in the body. In many Christian denominations, there are untold thousands of female members who are nonfunctioning members. This is not God's will. Gender distinctions cease to be barriers in the functioning body of Christ, as various members are granted certain giftings and graces.

7. *Identity as Priests unto God*

Under the new covenant, both men and women are called to be priests unto God and Christ. (See 1 Peter 2:5–9; Revelation 1:5–6; 5:9–10.) Priestly ministry, and all that it involves, is no longer an office reserved for one tribe in one nation—the Levites of Israel. It is no longer just for males, as it was under the old, Mosaic covenant. On that side of the cross of Christ, it was one nation, one tribe, and one gender that was called to the priesthood. There were no priestesses. Today, this side of the cross, priestly ministry is for all nations, all tribes, and all believers, whether male or female. Every believer, regardless of sex, is now a priest unto God. This is such a contrast to the old covenant order. The new covenant grants all believers, male and female, to be members of that priestly body. Gender distinctions are no barrier to believers performing priestly services.

To limit the priestly ministry to male participation only is to lapse back into an old covenant practice and to rob females of their new privilege in Christ. Again, all believers, male or female, are ordained to be priests to God and His Christ. Some denominations have robbed women of their ordination right because of a male-dominated hierarchy.

Christ Himself is *the* Great High Priest. When He died on Calvary, the veil was torn in two. There is now no need to sew up the veil again to keep women out and only allow a male to enter therein, as was the case under the old covenant. (See Matthew 27:50–52.)

8. *Witness of Christ*

Both men and women may witness for Christ, telling of His *"so great salvation"* and His soul-saving power. All believers are called to be His witnesses. (See Matthew 28:9–10; Mark 16:15–20; Luke 24:9–11, 24; John 20: 17–18; Acts 1:8.)

In 1 John 1:1–4, John spells out the qualifications of a true witness: (a) having heard with the ears, (b) having seen with the eyes, and then (c) testifying with the mouth. A true witness must have heard and also seen before he or she speaks with the mouth. Christ has called both men and women to be His witnesses; the only qualifications are having ears for hearing and eyes for seeing. Along the same lines, the Bible establishes the necessity of *"two or three witnesses"* to constitute a proper testimony. (See Deuteronomy 19:15; Matthew 18:16; John 8:17.)

Many of the witnesses of Christ's life on earth were women. And, as we discussed in chapter 11, some of the most significant events in the life of Christ were witnessed by women exclusively, and not by men, even though these events were recorded by men. We now pick up that discussion with a fuller exploration of the qualifications and requirements of true witnesses.

Women were among the key witnesses of:

- ### Christ's Incarnation

  Who was the original witness of the incarnation, the virgin birth? Only Mary could really testify of the incarnation of the Son of God by the power and the overshadowing of the Holy Spirit after the angel Gabriel had made the announcement to her. Mary's cousin Elizabeth and her husband, Zacharias, received a similar message from Gabriel; but the account of the virgin birth comes first and foremost from the virgin herself, Mary. No man could have known the reality of this event as intimately as she. The doctrine of the incarnation rests on Mary's words, her testimony, and her experience, as confirmed by her husband, Joseph. Although the gospel writers Matthew and Luke both recorded the details of this event, the true witness was the Virgin Mary.

- ### Christ's Earthly Ministry

  Although Christ called twelve men to be His disciples, many godly women were also involved in His ministry, without whose testimony the four gospel accounts would be incomplete.

Luke's gospel mentions "*women...which ministered unto* [Christ] *of their substance*" (Luke 8:2–3). These women included Mary called Magdalene, Joanna the wife of Chuza (Herod's steward), Susanna, and "*many others*" (Luke 8:3). These "*many others*" would have included Mary the mother of James and Joses, the mother of Zebedee's children, Salome, and Mary the mother of Jesus Himself, all of whom are frequently mentioned. (See Matthew 27:56; Mark 15:40.)

To recapitulate, we see the following women involved in Jesus' earthly ministry:

> Mary Magdalene, out of whom went seven devils—Mark 16:9; Luke 8:2

> Joanna, wife of the steward of Herod Antipas, tetrarch of Galilee, a woman of a high social caste—Luke 8:3

> Susanna, about whom only her name is known—Luke 8:3

> Mary, the Lord's own mother

> Mary, the wife of Cleophas (Alphaeus), the mother of James and Joses—Matthew 27:56; Mark 15:40

> Salome, wife of Zebedee, the mother of James and John and a sister of Jesus' mother—Mark 15:40; 16:1

> "Many others," or unnamed women who were involved in Christ's earthly ministry—Luke 8:3

Many different women were witnesses of Christ's three-and-a-half-year ministry. They witnessed many of His miracles, listened to His discourses, witnessed His sufferings, and knew He was the Christ of God. These women were indeed qualified to be His witnesses.

• **Christ's Crucifixion**

The primary testimony of Christ's crucifixion and death comes from women. The eleven disciples "*forsook him, and fled*" (Matthew 26:56). Only John remained, until he left to take Jesus' mother to his home. He tells only what he had seen up to this point. He witnessed the crucifixion, but many of the events recorded in the gospels of Matthew, Mark, and Luke are not found in John's gospel. Thus, much rests on the testimony of the women who followed Christ.

These women are named. There were Mary Magdalene, Mary, and Salome, who were *"beholding afar off"* (Matthew 27:55). Later on, Mary Magdalene, Mary, and Jesus' own mother drew near in the darkness and *"stood by"* the cross (John 19:25), where they heard the instructions Jesus spoke to John concerning His mother. These women were the last witnesses present at the cross, and the authors of the gospels must have received their testimony of Christ's final moments.

- **Christ's Seven Sayings from the Cross**

John records three of Christ's seven sayings from the cross; two women—the two women named Mary—must have heard the other four and then reported them to the authors of the gospels (Matthew, Mark, Luke, and John).

These four sayings are as follows:

> › Jesus' prayer: *"Father, forgive them…"* (Luke 23:34).

> › His promise: *"Today shalt thou be with me in paradise"* (Luke 23:43).

> › His cry: *"My God, my God, why hast thou forsaken me?"* (Matthew 27:46; Mark 15:34).

> › His committal: *"Father, into thy hands I commend my spirit"* (Luke 23:46).

John does not record about the reviling of the passersby, or the account of the repentant thief. He does record the vinegar being offered to Jesus, but this took place after John had taken Jesus' mother to his home. After Christ's death, Joseph of Arimathea returned to the cross to retrieve the body of Jesus, in order to arrange His burial in a tomb. (See Matthew 27:57–60.)

- **Christ's Burial**

Again, it was a group of women who came to Jesus' tomb and witnessed the actual burial of Christ. *"The women also, which came with him from Galilee, followed after, and beheld the sepulchre, and how his body was laid"* (Luke 23:55). The last service performed to the body of Jesus was probably done by Joseph and Nicodemus. They were not concerned about being defiled by a dead body, in spite of what the Law of Moses said. As the stone was placed over the entrance of the tomb, we are told, *"There was Mary Magdalene, and the other Mary, sitting over against the sepulchre"* (Matthew 27:61). This means that women were not only the last ones present at the cross but also the witnesses of His burial. They saw "where" and "how" Christ's body was laid in the tomb. (See Mark 15:47; Luke 23:55.) Thus, the two women named Mary were crucial witnesses.

- **Christ's Resurrection**

Matthew recounts the earliest events on the morning of the resurrection.

> *In the end of the Sabbath, as it began to dawn toward the first day of the week, came Mary Magdalene and the other Mary to see the sepulchre. And, behold, there was* [not "there had been"] *a great earthquake: for the angel of the Lord descended from heaven, and came and rolled back the stone from the door, and sat upon it.* (Matthew 28:1–2)

The women must have witnessed the earthquake and then the opening of the tomb by the angel. The stone was taken away not in order that Christ might come out of the tomb but to allow the disciples entrance to the tomb. So, Mary Magdalene and the other Mary saw where and how His body was laid; they saw the sealing up of the tomb; they saw the tomb being opened.

From Matthew, we learn of:

> › The earthquake
> › The angelic appearance

> The great stone being rolled away

> The guards being as "dead" because of fear—not asleep, but probably not able to see the angel of the Lord

> The announcement "He is risen" by the two men in the tomb

All this was reported by the two women named Mary, the witnesses at the tomb, probably to Matthew.

From Mark, we learn:

> The women saw a young man (an angel) sitting on the right side of the tomb where Jesus' body had been laid, clothed in white.

From Luke we learn of:

> Two men in the tomb in shining garments

> The women giving the testimony to Peter and to John

From John, we learn of:

> Mary Magdalene running and calling Peter and John. John outran Peter and saw the linen grave clothes. Peter saw them, but John believed. (See John 20:3–8.)

> The empty grave clothes after the women had told the men that the Lord had risen indeed. All spoke of the resurrected Christ the women had seen.

So, the women were last at the cross (Christ's crucifixion), last at the tomb (His burial), and first at the empty tomb (His resurrection). The key witnesses of these three events were not the eleven disciples—not even the beloved apostle, John!

How did the male disciples receive the women's testimony of Christ's resurrection? "*And they, when they had heard that he was alive, and had been seen of her* [Mary Magdalene], *believed not*" (Mark 16:11). "*Their words seemed to them as idle tales, and they believed them not*" (Luke 24:11). The eleven, along with the rest of the disciples who heard the testimony of the women, dismissed their report and did not believe them. After all, they were women;

how could a woman be a true witness? Such would have been the attitude of the male disciples.

In the face of a Jewish prejudice against the testimony of women, Jesus selected women as witnesses of the most important and theologically significant events of His life:

> His incarnation

> His crucifixion

> His burial

> His resurrection

The gospel authors, though they did not initially take stock in the witness of these women, eventually realized they were telling the truth once those authors had seen the risen Jesus for themselves and accepted His reproof of their unbelief.

Women, as well as men, are called to be witnesses of Christ. (See Acts 1:8.) If it were not for the testimony of women, the gospel accounts would be incomplete.

9. *Evangelism*

When Christ evangelized the city of Samaria, His first convert was the woman at the well. (See John 4.) The woman of Samaria became a great witness for Christ to the men of the city, and many came to Christ because of her testimony. Who knows whether the ministry of Philip the evangelist was further fruit of what took place in John 4?

Only eternity will tell just how many thousands have been won to Christ through evangelism, whether the work of men or of women. Church history shows that the Lord has used women mightily in evangelism—personal evangelism as well as public evangelism.

10. *Worship*

Both men and women are called to worship the true God and His Christ. (See, for example, Psalm 99:5.) Under the old covenant, the temple was divided into various courts: the court of the women, the court of the priests, the court of the Gentiles, the court of the Jews, and so forth.

None dared to cross into a restricted court on pain of death. But through His death on the cross, Jesus broke down all those walls of separation and made it possible for men and women to enter into the Holiest of All, through faith in His blood. Men and women can worship together freely in the presence of God. Gender distinctions are no longer a barrier to any part of the practice of worship.

In spite of that truth, some churches, denominations, and cultures continue to enforce a separation of the sexes in their worship services and houses of worship. They fail to realize that Jesus broke down the *"middle wall of partition"* (Ephesians 2:14). Jews and Gentiles, men and women, can come openly before the Lord and worship Him in spirit and in truth. It should be remembered that the greatest revelation on worship was given to the woman at the well—the woman of Samaria. (See John 4:20–24.)

11. Music Ministry

Both men and women can be involved in music ministry, whether they sing, play an instrument, or dance for the Lord. In the return from the Babylonian captivity, there were *"singing men and singing women"* (Nehemiah 7:67). Consider the songs of Moses and the dance of Miriam and the women. (See Exodus 15:1–21; Deuteronomy 32.) Consider the songs of Elizabeth and Mary (see Luke 1:39–55) and the singers and musicians in the tabernacle of David (see 1 Chronicles 15–16; 25:1–7). Think of the song of Hannah. (See 1 Samuel 2:1–10.)

Women...

+ were often part of public processions—Psalm 68:25–26
+ danced and sang at festival occasions—Judges 21:19–23
+ chanted victory songs—1 Samuel 18:6–7
+ sang in the temple choirs, with the men—2 Chronicles 35:25; Ezra 2:65

Gender distinctions do not exclude anyone from participating in the worship arts, whether musical or another type.

12. Intercession

Men and women alike may be called of the Lord to the ministry of intercession. All believers may pray, but some are distinctly gifted to go beyond generic prayer to actually intercede on behalf of others. Christ shares the ministry of intercession with His saints. (See Isaiah 53:12; Jeremiah 7:16; 27:18; Romans 8:26–27, 34; Hebrews 7:25.) Only eternity will reveal the results of the intercessory ministry that the Lord has given to both men and women.

13. Counseling

Jesus is called the *"Wonderful Counselor"* (Isaiah 9:6–9 NIV), and He calls various members of His body—men and women alike—to the ministry of counseling, whether general counseling or counseling of a more specialized nature. In many cases, women are better equipped to counsel other women and to address their particular needs than they are to counsel men.

- David accepted a word of counsel from a wise woman concerning his son Absalom—2 Samuel 14
- A wise woman, through a word of counsel, saved a city—2 Samuel 20
- The "Proverbs 31 woman" gives much good counsel—Proverbs 31:10–31
- Women are more appropriate counselors than men of other women in certain areas—Titus 2:3–5

There are occasions that call for a team of counselors—a man and a woman, or even a married couple. Wisdom suggests that women counsel women, and men counsel men.

14. Hospitality

Both men and women may be involved in hospitality. All believers should treat one another hospitably, but certain people are called to the ministry of hospitality in the church, to believers as well as to others outside the church.

In the early church, there was an evident ministry of widows who showed hospitality, performed good works, cared for children, washed the feet of saints, and relieved the afflicted. (See 1 Timothy 5:1–16; James 1:27; Proverbs 31:20.)

Elders and their wives, along with deacons and their wives, are to be "given to hospitality." (See 1 Timothy 3:2.) Those involved in house churches certainly evidenced such hospitality; excellent examples include Lydia and Priscilla and Aquila. (See Acts 16:15; 1 Corinthians 16:19.) The Shunammite woman ministered to Elisha (see 2 Kings 4), and the widow of Zarephath ministered to Elijah (see 1 Kings 17). Mary and Martha showed much hospitality to Jesus and the twelve. (See John 11; Luke 10.)

15. Spiritual Parenting

Whether or not they have biological children of their own, men and women may have "children" in the church, to whom they act as spiritual fathers and mothers—mentors, guides. Every person needs a father figure and a mother figure in his or her life if balanced development is to take place.

John wrote to those who were "*fathers.*" (See 1 John 2:13–14.) Paul also spoke of being a "father or mother in the Lord." (See 1 Corinthians 4:14–17; 1 Timothy 5:1–2.) Deborah the prophetess was counted as a "*mother in Israel*" (Judges 5:7). In this generation of broken homes and fatherless children, there are many people in the church who need the guidance and support of spiritual parents.

16. Ministry of Helps

Men and women alike may be involved in the ministry of helps—providing services to the people of God. (See 1 Corinthians 12:28.) There are many areas in the church that fall under the ministry of "helps," whether or not they are specifically designated in Scripture:

+ Writing—creating books, tracts, church bulletins, curriculum for Bible classes, biblically based stories, and so forth.

+ Music—lending one's musical abilities to the choir, orchestra, band, worship team; leading worship; singing solos during services; and so forth.

+ Office Services—working as a secretary, personal assistant, book-keeper, graphic designer/artist, receptionist, filer, computer technician, and so forth.

+ Wedding Coordination—making arrangements for receptions, creating floral arrangements, and handling other details of these blessed events.

+ Children's Ministry—providing childcare in the church nursery, coordinating baby showers and child dedications, designing Sunday school curriculum, and so forth.

+ Youth Ministry—counseling young adults and teens; coordinating camping trips, retreats, and other spiritual/recreational activities.

+ Facilities Management—caring for the church property as a janitor, landscaper, kitchen cook, decorator, and so forth.

+ Hospitality—seeing to the needs of church members and visitors by providing refreshments and information, serving as an usher or parking lot attendant, and so forth.

+ Visitation—going to see the sick and needy at home or in the hospital, showing mercy in time of need. In some cases, it is more appropriate for women to visit than men.

+ Distribution—passing out clothes, toiletries, and other necessities to those in need; sewing or mending clothes for those in need; giving to the poor.

+ Baptism—assisting with the sacrament in whatever ways are needed; women should assist other women, and men should assist other men.

+ Communion—preparing the elements and coordinating their distribution.

+ Media—operating the sound system, managing the audiovisual ministry, and so forth.

+ Volunteer Coordination—recruiting and managing the much-needed volunteer base.

The above are just some of the activities that are included in the ministry of "helps" in the body of Christ. Clearly, there is a wide variety of opportunities for men and women alike to serve the Lord and the members of His body.

17. House Church Leadership

Both men and women may be used by the Lord to lead house churches. In the early church, the people of God did not meet for worship in formal buildings, as they do today. Most believers met in small groups at various homes. We have already talked about some of the house church leaders mentioned in the Bible. These leaders included…

+ Priscilla and Aquila—Romans 16:3–5; 1 Corinthians 16:19

+ Nymphas—Colossians 4:15

+ Philemon, Apphia, and Archippus—Philemon 2; Colossians 4:17

+ Mary—Acts 12:12

+ Lydia—Acts 16:14–15

+ Chloe—1 Corinthians 1:11

+ Phoebe—Romans 16:1–2

18. Business and Social Acumen

Both men and women may be gifted in business and with social acumen. The so-called Proverbs 31 woman was both virtuous and industrious, worthy of praise from her husband and children alike. (See Proverbs 31:28.)

Dorcas was a woman of good works who experienced resurrection life thanks to the evangelistic efforts of the apostle Peter. (See Acts 9:36–42.) God saw fit to raise a woman from death whose ministry was to make garments for the poor and needy.

19. Heroes of Faith

The "faith hall of fame" in Hebrews 11 lists men and women whose faith the believer would do well to emulate. The men listed include Abel, Enoch, Noah, Abraham, Isaac, Jacob, Joseph, and Moses. The women listed include Sarah, Rahab, and *"women [who] received their dead raised to life again"* (Hebrews 11:35), such as the widow of Zarephath and the Shunammite woman. (See Hebrews 11:35–40; 2 Kings 4:18–27.)

294 *The Ministry of Women*

20. Gifts of the Holy Spirit

Both men and women may be used by the Lord, as He wills, as they function in the gifts of the Holy Spirit, which are listed in 1 Corinthians 12. Men and women alike compose the body of Christ. Who is to say that only the men can minister in the gifts of the Spirit, and that women are excluded from these gifts? It is the gift in the member that makes that member a functioning member. As members of the body of Christ, women are therefore open to receive the gifts of the Spirit.

We now note the various gifts of the Spirit and gifts of the ascended Lord as listed in the New Testament writings before further comment.

1 Corinthians 12	Ephesians 4	Romans 12
1. Word of wisdom	1. Apostles	1. Prophecy
2. Word of knowledge	2. Prophets	2. Ministry (serving)
3. Faith	3. Evangelists	3. Teaching
4. Gifts of healing	4. Pastors	4. Exhorting
5. Working miracles	5. Teachers	5. Giving
6. Prophecy		6. Ruling (leadership)
7. Discerning spirits		7. Showing mercy
8. Divers tongues		
9. Interpreting tongues		
1 Corinthians 12:28		
1. Apostles		
2. Prophets		
3. Teachers		
4. Miracles		
5. Gifts of healings		
6. Helps		
7. Governments		
8. Divers tongues		
9. Interpreting tongues		

It will be noticed that there is overlapping of giftings in these lists. None of the lists, evidently, is meant to be exhaustive; but each is an example of what the Lord has set in the body of Christ, enabling the members to function accordingly. Who can glance over these lists of gifts and say that they are strictly for the male of the species? The gifts of the Spirit are available to all members of the body of Christ, regardless of gender, and are to be used according to His will.

In the next chapter, we will deal with the gifts of Christ referred to as "the ascension-gift ministries." (See 1 Corinthians 12:28; Ephesians 4:10–12.) In this present chapter, we will discuss the other giftings in relation to both men and women, brothers and sisters in the body of Christ, in the order Paul lists them.

Both men and women may operate the gifts of the Spirit as God wills. These gifts include:

+ Words of wisdom—1 Samuel 25:14–44; 2 Samuel 20:16–27; Acts 18:26

+ Words of knowledge

+ Faith—Hebrews 11:35; 2 Kings 4

+ Healing, in its variety of giftings

+ Miracles

+ Prophecy—Acts 21:9; 1 Corinthians 11:4–5; Joel 2:28–29

+ Discerning of spirits

+ Tongues—Acts 2:1–4

+ Interpretation of tongues

+ Serving—Luke 8:1–3; John 11

+ Teaching—Acts 18:26; Titus 2:4–5

+ Exhortation

+ Administration—Proverbs 31

+ Giving—Luke 8:1–3; Mark 15:41

+ Mercy-showing—Acts 9:39–42

Probably the most public of these gifts is that of *prophecy*. Prophecy is for men and women alike, and is a gift used particularly in church gatherings. If women were able to prophesy, then they clearly were not silenced from public speaking, as some would claim.

+ Joel said that men and women would prophesy. (See Joel 2:28–32.)

+ Peter confirmed Joel's prophecy. (See Acts 2:16–18.)

+ Paul taught that men and women may prophesy. (See 1 Corinthians 11:5.)

+ Philip had four daughters who prophesied. (See Acts 21:8–11.) Eusebius, the ancient ecclesiastical historian, says that Philip's daughters lived to a good old age, always abounding in the work of the Lord. "For indeed in Asia great luminaries have fallen asleep, such as shall rise again on the day of the Lord's appearing, when He comes with glory from heaven to seek out all his saints: to wit, Philip, one of the twelve apostles, who has fallen asleep in Hierapolis, [as have] also his two daughters who grew old in virginity, and his other daughter who lived in the Holy Spirit and rests at Ephesus."[54]

+ Paul warned believers not to despise prophecy. (See 1 Thessalonians 5:20–21.)

+ Prophecy is for the purpose of edification, exhortation, and comfort, according to Paul. (See 1 Corinthians 14:3.)

  Edify: "to improve the morality, intellect, etc., of, especially by instruction." In other words, "to build up."

  Exhort: "to urge or persuade (someone) earnestly; advise strongly." In other words, "to stir up."

  Comfort: "to ease the pain of; soothe; cheer." In other words, "to bind up."

Women cannot keep silent and prophesy at the same time.

Is there any greater honor than to be a mouthpiece of the Lord by speaking forth a prophetic word? Both men and women in the current dispensation may prophesy. The Spirit is available to all, regardless of nation,

---

54. John E. L. Oulton, trans., *Eusebius: The Ecclesiastical History* (1927).

social status, gender, or other distinctions. It is a great gift to be a channel of God's word, inspired by the Holy Spirit. Many expositors equate the gift of prophecy with those of preaching and exhortation. If women can stand before God and speak to Him, who is to say they cannot stand before men and other women to speak for God?

Peter said it well:

> As each one has received a gift, minister it to one another, as good stewards of the manifold grace of God. If anyone speaks, let him speak as the oracles of God. If anyone ministers, let him do it as with the ability which God supplies, that in all things God may be glorified through Jesus Christ, to whom belong the glory and the dominion forever and ever. Amen. (1 Peter 4:10–11 NKJV)

22

MEN AND WOMEN
IN CHURCH LEADERSHIP

This chapter is without question the most controversial in this text. We will now consider the roles of men and women in church leadership. What does the Bible teach about the proper place of men and women—and especially women—in leadership roles and functions in the redemptive community? Can a woman operate in any and all of the fivefold ascension-gift ministries listed in Ephesians 4? Can a woman serve as a deacon or an elder? Can a woman participate in church leadership, in a ruling or governmental position? Or is church leadership restricted to male participation? The giftings listed in Ephesians 4 are more restricted types of ministries that are not necessarily given to every member of the body of Christ. Can a woman be gifted of God with these ministries?

Please note that for a fuller treatment of the ministries dealt with in this chapter, the reader is referred to the author's book *The Church in the New Testament*.

A. The Ascension-Gift Ministries

Wherefore he saith, When he ascended up on high, he led captivity captive, and gave gifts unto men. (Now that he ascended, what is it but

that he also descended first into the lower parts of the earth? He that de-
scended is the same also that ascended up far above all heavens, that he
might fill all things.) And he gave some, apostles; and some, prophets;
and some, evangelists; and some, pastors and teachers; for the perfect-
ing of the saints, for the work of the ministry, for the edifying of the body
of Christ: till we all come in the unity of the faith, and of the knowledge
of the Son of God, unto a perfect man, unto the measure of the stature
of the fulness of Christ: that we henceforth be no more children, tossed
to and fro, and carried about with every wind of doctrine, by the sleight
of men, and cunning craftiness, whereby they lie in wait to deceive; but
speaking the truth in love, may grow up into him in all things, which is
the head, even Christ: from whom the whole body fitly joined together
and compacted by that which every joint supplieth, according to the
effectual working in the measure of every part, maketh increase of the
body unto the edifying of itself in love.   (Ephesians 4:8–16)

In the above passage, Paul explains that when Christ ascended on
high, He gave gifts to mankind. These gifts are generally referred to as the
"fivefold ascension-gift ministries," the reason being that they were given
after Christ ascended to the Father in heaven. These ministries are:

+ Apostles

+ Prophets

+ Evangelists

+ Shepherds (Pastors)

+ Teachers

The first two ministries—apostles and prophets—have caused the
most controversy. The cessationist school teaches that these two ministries ceased with the death of the last apostle of the twelve, John, and with
the completion of the New Testament canon of Scripture. The other three
ascension-gift ministries—those of evangelist, pastor, and teacher—have
been widely accepted over the centuries of church history.

The Pentecostal and charismatic schools generally accept that the gifts
of apostle and prophet, along with the other three ministries, have been
given *"till we all come in the unity of the faith, and of the knowledge of the Son*

of God, unto a perfect man" (Ephesians 4:13). There are varying understandings of these giftings, and some people argue that these gifts are for men only, not for women, as they relate to leadership ministries in the church. It is my position that these gifts are for both men and women, according to the will of the Lord.

The Greek word Paul uses in this passage for "*man*" is *anthrópos* (STRONG 444), defined as "the countenance…man-faced, i.e. a human being." This term is used some 552 times in the New Testament, most often to refer to the human race, to human beings, or simply to mankind.

Merriam-Webster's Collegiate Dictionary shows us that the English word "man" is often a generic term, with such meanings as:

+ "an individual human…"

+ "the human race: humankind"

+ "the individual who can fulfill or who has been chosen to fulfill one's requirements"

The word "*man*" cannot be locked in as referring to the male only, unless the context of the verse or passage in Scripture shows otherwise. When Jesus said, "*And I, if I be lifted up from the earth, will draw **all men** unto me*" (John 12:32), He was referring to mankind—the human race, human beings; not only males but females, as well. Christ "*died for all*" (2 Corinthians 5:15), and He "*desires all men to be saved and to come to the knowledge of the truth*" (1 Timothy 2:4 NKJV). Christ's death was not for males only but for men and women, or all mankind, which is the meaning of "*all men*" in the verse from 1 Timothy.

So, when Christ ascended on high and "*gave gifts unto men*" (Ephesians 4:8), He gave these gifts to all mankind—to all people, to every human being, whether male or female.

The Greek word that refers specifically to an individual man is *aner* (STRONG 435 as an individual male). It means "a human being of the male sex, not a woman," and it is translated "man" or "husband" some 156 times in the Bible.

Christ gave gifts to men—that is, *anthrópos*, not *aner*. *The Concordant Literal New Testament and Keyword Concordance* comments: "*Anthropos*—a living being as distinct from animals, including all ages and both sexes: men, women and children. *Man* = the race, mankind, humanity, people."

The majority of translations, including the King James Bible, the *New King James Version*, and the *New International Version*, simply say, "[Christ] *gave gifts to men*." Others read as follows:

+ "*...gave gifts to people*" (NCV)
+ "*...gave gifts to his people*" (NLT, NIV)
+ "*...gives gifts to mankind*" (CLV)

Thayer's Greek-English Lexicon gives us the following entry for *anthrópos*:

...man. It is used (1) universally, with reference to the genus or nature, without distinction of sex, a human being, whether male or female: John 16:21. And in this sense a. with the article, generically, so as to include all human individuals: Matthew 4:4;...b. so that a man is distinguished from beings of a different race or order; from animals, plants, etc.: Luke 5:10; Matthew 4:19; Matthew 12:12; 2 Peter 2:16; Revelation 9:4, 7, 10, 15, 18; Revelation 11:13, etc. (beta). from God, from Christ as divine, and from angels: Matthew 10:32; Matthew 19:6; Mark 10:9; Luke 2:15....[55]

E. W. Vine confirms the same, saying, "Anthropos is used...generally, of 'a human being, male or female,' without reference to sex or nationality, e.g., Matt. 4:4; 12:35; John 2:25....[56]

These ministry gifts, therefore, may be given to men and women, if the Lord wills. When Christ ascended to the Father, He gave these "gifts" to His people—to mankind, the church, the redeemed community, which includes both men and women, male and female, as He wills. To say that Christ gave these gifts to men alone, and not to women, is to misunderstand the apostle Paul and to misinterpret his writings on the silence of women. If Paul had used the word *aner* rather than *anthropos*, then we could understand him to mean that these gifts were exclusively for men.

---

55. *Thayer's Greek Lexicon*, Electronic Database. Copyright © 2002, 2003, 2006, 2011 by Biblesoft, Inc. All rights reserved. Used by permission.
56. W. E. Vine, *W. E. Vine's New Testament Word Pictures: Romans to Revelation* (Nashville, TN: Thomas Nelson, 2015), 166.

But Paul used the word *anthropos*, meaning that the Lord gave these gifts to mankind, which includes both male and female. He gave these gifts to human beings.

Of course, there are some who accept the idea of women functioning in the ministries of evangelism, shepherding, or teaching, but not as apostles or prophets.

But we see that the Lord may give any of His ministry gifts to any male or female believers in the body of Christ. This is done for the equipping of the saints, to bring the saints into the work of their assigned ministry and for the building up of the body of Christ, *"till we all we all come in the unity of the faith, and of the knowledge of the Son of God, unto a perfect man"* (Ephesians 4:13).

B. Men and Women in the Ascension-Gift Ministries

We now turn our attention to a brief discussion of the involvement of men and women in the fivefold ascension-gift ministries: apostles, prophets, evangelists, shepherds, and teachers.[57]

1. Apostolic Ministry

If the Lord so pleases, He can give the ministry gift of apostle to either a man or a woman. New Testament revelation points to several distinctions within the ministry of an apostle. In classical Greek, the word *apostolos* was used to identify a ship ready for departure. Later on, it came to be used for an ambassador, a delegate, or a messenger—simply put, one who is sent on a mission for another. The term is used at least 80 times in the New Testament, referring to several different categories of persons:

a. The Lord Jesus Christ

> *Wherefore, holy brethren, partakers of the heavenly calling, consider the **Apostle** and High Priest of our profession, **Christ Jesus**.* (Hebrews 3:1)

---

57. For a fuller exploration of these ministries, the reader is referred to Kevin J. Conner, *The Church in the New Testament* (Victoria, Australia: Acacia Press, 1982).

Christ Himself is *the* Apostle and High Priest of our confession. He is the only infallible Apostle, and all others will be judged by Him accordingly. None can compare with Him. He gives His ministry gifts, with varying measures of grace, to those whom He calls to these offices.

b. **The Twelve Apostles**

> *And the wall of the city had twelve foundations,*
> *and in them the names of the **twelve apostles** of the*
> *Lamb.*   (Revelation 21:14)

There is no doubt about the calling of the twelve male apostles. Jesus chose the twelve after a night of prayer. These men are unique among all apostles, being distinctly called the "apostles of the Lamb." The twelve were chosen at the close of the old covenant dispensation and at the opening of the new covenant dispensation. They were with the Lamb in His earthly ministry, His earth-walk, after the flesh. (See John 1:14–18.) They were male, representing the twelve tribes of Israel. (See Matthew 19:28.) Their names had been given to the Son by His Father, chosen by the Father's will. (See Matthew 10:2–5; Mark 3:14; Luke 6:13; Acts 1:26; 1 Corinthians 9:5; 15:5–7.) No other apostle will ever find a place among the twelve. They laid the foundations on which the New Testament church is built, and by these men all other apostles will be tried and tested.

c. **Post-Ascension-Gift Apostles**

> *And he gave some, apostles; and some, prophets; and*
> *some, evangelists; and some, pastors and teachers; for*
> *the perfecting of the saints, for the work of the minis-*
> *try, for the edifying of the body of Christ.*
>   (Ephesians 4:11–12)

Contrary to the tenet of the cessationist school, and of many others who claim that apostles are "not for today," we read in

Scripture that following His ascension, Christ chose further apostles beyond the twelve, though those apostles are not to be compared with the twelve. These are called "post-ascension-gift apostles," as they were chosen after Christ's ascension and upon His entrance into heavenly ministry. There are at least fifteen "lesser" apostles mentioned in the New Testament, distinct from the original twelve.

The following is a list of some whose identity as "post-ascension-gift apostles" we can be reasonably confident about:

- o Matthias—Acts 1:26

- o James, the Lord's brother—1 Corinthians 15:7; Galatians 1:19–20

- o Barnabas—Acts 13:2; 14:1, 4, 14

- o Paul—Acts 14:14; 1 Corinthians 9:1–2; 2 Timothy 1:11

- o Apollos—1 Corinthians 4:6–9

- o Timothy—Acts 19:22; 1 Thessalonians 1:1; 2:6

- o Titus—2 Corinthians 8:23

- o Judas—Acts 15:22

- o Tychicus—2 Timothy 4:12

d. Messengers of the Church

There were others included in the apostolic companies that traveled around the churches, establishing them. (See Acts 16:9; 18:2–24.) These are spoken of as "messengers" of the church, but the same Greek word for "apostle" is used of them. (See Philippians 2:25; 2 Corinthians 8:23.)

The office of apostle is still valid in the church today, and will continue to be until Christ returns for His church. A true apostle is identified by such traits as Christian character, soundness in the faith once delivered to the saints, ability to minister in the power of the Holy Spirit, and measure of apostolic authority. A true apostle will be sealed by the Lord and recognized in the body of Christ; and false apostles will be just as obvious, for the Scriptures provide plenty of warnings in what to look for. (See 2 Corinthians 11:13; 12:11; Revelation 2:2.)

e. *Female Apostles*

There is a consensus of opinion generally among the Pentecostal church world that God raised up male apostles. The question is whether there were or could be female apostles. The cessationist school rejects all those who claim apostleship since the death of John, the Beloved.

The only specific verse that possibly speaks of a female apostle is Romans 16:7, with which we dealt briefly in chapter 20. The reader will now kindly bear with some repetition as we investigate this verse further.

In Romans 16:7, Paul writes, *"Salute Andronicus and Junia, my kinsmen, and my fellowprisoners, who are of note among the apostles, who also were in Christ Jesus before me."* The point of debate concerns the gender of Junia. Some expositors hold that Junia is a masculine name, while others contend that it is feminine. As we saw in chapter 20, Paul greets at least nine women and some nineteen men in his salutations. He mentions Priscilla and Aquila, a husband-and-wife ministry team who operated a house church.

Here, in verse 7, he mentions Andronicus and Junia as being *"of note among the apostles."* Both were "in Christ" (i.e., were Christians) before Paul, and both had been imprisoned for the gospel for some time.

As mentioned previously, Andronicus and Junia were one of the following:

o   Two men traveling together in ministry

o   Two brothers in ministry

o   A man and a woman traveling together, either married or unmarried (a possible scandal, then and now!)

o   A husband-and-wife team, as were Aquila and Priscilla

The debate, first and foremost, hinges on the gender of Junia/
Junias. Is the name feminine or masculine?

Although many writers evidently believe Junia to have been a
man, most acknowledge that the weight of opinion in the earliest centuries is that Junia was a feminine name. The difficulty
is seen in the presumption that the term "apostle" could not
have been used of a woman. A woman could not be an apostle;
therefore, the name Junia must become Junias, a masculine
name. Rejection of the possibility of female apostleship leads
to rejection of Junia as a female name.

David Jones of Moffatt College of the Bible provides much food
for thought on this matter. His final and honest conclusion is
this: "Andronicus and Junias were two prominent messengers that
served Paul and the early churches.... I tentatively affirm that the
second person was a man named Junias, although I cannot be certain about the matter."[58]

Jones spends a significant portion of his paper treating the issue
of whether the name was Junia (feminine) or Junias (masculine).
He makes the argument that it could have been masculine or
feminine. Translators and commentators have been divided on
the issue throughout church history. Jones's research has shown
that there are only two references from the first century AD to the
name Junia.

One is the ambiguous usage in Romans [16:7]. The other is a
clear reference to a woman named Junia, who was both the wife
of Cassius and the sister of Brutus (one of the men who murdered
Julius Caesar). Apart from these two, there is perhaps only one

---

58. David Jones, "A Female Apostle?: A Lexical-Syntactical Analysis of Romans 16:7" (June
26, 2007), The Council on Biblical Manhood & Womanhood. Online. http://cbmw.org/
uncategorized/a-female-apostle/.

other reference to a person named Junia or Junias in all extant first-century Greek literature. It is found in a partially defaced inscription, which reads: "[ ]ia Torquata." This inscription may refer to a woman whom Tacitus mentions (Annals, 3.69), Junia Torquata, a Vestal Virgin who lived during the reign of Tiberius (c. AD 20).

Thus, neither the male nor the female versions of this name were common in Greek literature. Of these three individuals, two are definitely women while the third, the person mentioned in Romans 16:7, is ambiguous. Significantly, there are no unambiguous references to a man named Junias in the Greek literature in the first three centuries of the Christian era....[59]

In Latin literature, however, "Junia appears as a fairly common woman's name while Junias, the man's name, is virtually nonexistent."[60]

He continues,

> Although the evidence is by no means unanimous, the strongest case for understanding Iounian [Junia] to be a woman is found in the comments made on Rom 16:7 by some of the early Church Fathers. Many patristic exegetes understood the second person mentioned in Rom 16:7 to be the wife of Andronicus, such as: Ambrosiaster (c. 339–97); Jerome (c. 342–420); John Chrysostom (c. 347–407); Theodoret of Cyrrhus (c. 393–458); Ps.-Primasuis (c. 6th cent.); John Damascene (c. 675–749); Haymo (d. 1244); Hatto (?); Oecumenius (c. 6th cent.); Lanfranc of Bec (c. 1005–89); Bruno the Carthusian (c. 1032–1101);Theophylact (c. 11th cent.);Peter Abelard (1079–1142); and Peter Lombard (1100–1160).
>
> Junia was taken to be a woman basically up to the twelfth century. To quote Jones again, "The

59. Ibid.
60. Ibid.

clear majority of Church Fathers adopt a feminine reading of Rom 16:7."[61]

Perhaps the most notable example is John Chrysostom (Bishop of Constantinople, fourth century). Though he was certainly against women serving as bishops, he nevertheless took Iounian to be a woman. Commenting on Romans 16:7, he said: "To be an apostle is something great. But to be outstanding among the apostles—just think what a wonderful song of praise that is! They were outstanding on the basis of their works and virtuous actions. Indeed, how great the wisdom of this woman must have been that she was even deemed worthy of the title of apostle."

Two of the fathers, Origen and Epiphanius (ad 315–403, Bishop of Salamis in Cyprus), understood Junia/Junias to be a man, not a woman.

David Jones states his conclusion as follows:

> Perhaps I could sum it up this way: if I were serving on the NIV revision committee, my recommendation to the committee would be to translate the name Junias, but to acknowledge with a footnote the possibility that the name could refer to a woman named Junia.[62]

Varying Translations

Translations of the name in question vary from version to version, whether due to uncertainty as to the name's being Junia or Junias, or to a translator's biased opinion that a woman cannot be an apostle. However, as has been seen, the masculine form of the name is not to be found anywhere in the literature of the GrecoRoman period. Junia, on the other hand, was a quite common name, used several hundreds of times in records from that period.

---

61. Jones, "A Female Apostle?"
62. Ibid.

The Latin Vulgate Bible supports either reading of the name. Modern translations that render the name "Junia," in the feminine form, include the King James Version, the *New King James Version*, the *New International Version*, the *New Living Translation*, the *New Revised Standard Version*, and the *Richard Francis Weymouth New Testament*. Meanwhile, the masculine form, "Junias," is found in such translations as the American Standard Version, *The Living Bible*, the Revised Standard Version, the *Contemporary English Version*, the *New American Standard Version*, *Phillips New Testament*, and *The Amplified Bible*.

It is the conviction of this writer that Andronicus and Junia were an apostolic team of husband and wife, just like Aquila and Priscilla.

The next issue, beyond whether Junia/Junias is a feminine or masculine name, is whether the phrase *"who are of note among the apostles"* (Romans 16:7) indicates that Andronicus and Junia actually were apostles. Various translations render that part of the verse as follows:

> *"…who are of note among the apostles"* (KJV, NKJV, ASV, DRA).

> *"They are men of note among the apostles"* (RSV).

> *"They are outstanding men among the messengers"* (PHILLIPS).

> *"They are highly respected by the apostles"* (CEV).

> *"They are outstanding among the apostles"* (NIV).

> *"They are noted men among the missionaries"* (GOODSPEED).

> *"They are prominent among the apostles"* (NRSV).

> *"They are men held in high esteem among the apostles"* (AMP).

> *"…who are outstanding among the apostles"* (NASB).

> *"They are respected by the apostles"* (TLB).

> *"They are very important apostles"* (NCV).

> *"They are well known among the apostles"* (GNT).

> *"They are well known to the apostles"* (NET).

> "...*who are eminent among the apostles*" (THOMAS HAWEIS NEW TESTAMENT).

> "*They are prominent among the apostles*" (NRSVACE).

> "*Who are notable in the ranks of the apostles*" (BARRETT).

Most translators view these two individuals as "apostles," prominent and notable. Meanwhile, expositors from those schools of thought that do not accept the possibility of Junia's being a female apostle make the phrase applicable to men: "*highly esteemed*," "*well known*," "*highly respected*," and so forth.

But Andronicus and Junia were *not* "outstanding among the apostles." Neither one of them was definitely an apostle, although both were messengers of the apostles.

The point is made that the names Andronicus and Junia are not mentioned again in the New Testament. But this is true also of the twelve. Peter is the chief apostle featured in Acts 1–12, while Paul is the chief apostle from Acts 13–28.

Silence is no point of refutation. What about the rest of the twelve, whose names are not mentioned in Acts after the earliest chapters?

Taking Andronicus and Junia to be a team of husband and wife, rather than a man and a woman who were not related, it certainly does not make sense to place them among the twelve original apostles of the Lamb. They could have been some of the post-ascension-gift apostles, outstanding messengers of the churches. Paul speaks about the fact that these two were "*in Christ*" before he was, and that Jesus was seen alive by "all the apostles" and even by some five hundred others before His ascension. (See 1 Corinthians 15:6–7.) If an apostle is to have "seen the Lord," who knows whether Andronicus and Junia may have been in such a group, seeing they had converted to Christianity prior to Paul? Of course, this is speculation.

The question is this: Is the bias against women's participation in public ministry so great that translators have made the name Junia to be the masculine, Junias? And is it because male prejudice could never accept a woman in apostolic ministry, even if the Lord Himself confirmed such to be so?

Taking Andronicus and Junia as a husband-and-wife team, they could therefore, belong to the post-ascension-gift ministry, and this is what gave them some prominence and notability "among the apostles," of which there were more than the original twelve.

The following are excerpts from some expositors who hold Junia to be a female apostle.

Catherine Booth—wife of William Booth, founder of the Salvation Army—has this to say:

> "Salute Andronicus and Junia, my kinsmen and my fellow-prisoners, who are of note among the apostles; who also were in Christ before me" (Rom. xvi. 7). By the word "kinsmen" one would take Junia to have been a man; but Chrysostom and Theophylact, who were both Greeks, and consequently knew their mother tongue better than our translators, say Junia was a woman. Kinsmen should therefore have been rendered kinsfolk; but with our translators it was out of all character to have a woman of note amongst the apostles, and a fellow-prisoner with Paul for the gospel: therefore let them be kinsmen![63]

And from Don Williams:

> "Greet Andronicus and Junias, my kinsmen and my fellow prisoners; they are men of note among the apostles, and they were in Christ before me." The unresolved issue is whether Junias in Greek is a masculine contraction of Junianus or the feminine Junia. The spelling in the original language is the same for either possibility. Furthermore, the phrase "they are men of note"

---

63. Booth, *Female Ministry*, 11.

literally reads "they are of note." "Men" is absent in the Greek, and is inserted by the translators. Thus Paul could be referring to a woman here, quite probably a husband-wife team.

This would mean that Junia is a "kinsman," that is, a Jew. She is also a "fellow prisoner," that is, she like Paul had suffered incarceration for her faith in Christ. Most surprising, Junia is also an apostle, an early convert even before Paul. This has led most commentators to render the proper name as the masculine Junias rather than Junia. While a final decision cannot be reached from the text, why must we suppose that no woman could be called an apostle by Paul? In the wider sense of the word, an apostle is one who is sent with a commission. Second Corinthians 8:23 speaks of those who are bringing a gift of money to the Jerusalem church as "messengers (Greek—'apostles') of the churches."

Since, however, no special task is mentioned for Andronicus and Junias (or Junia), their apostleship would be from Christ, sealed in being eyewitnesses to the resurrection of the Lord (see Acts 1:21–26; 1 Corinthians 9:1; 15:3–8). This is also substantiated by the time of their conversion (before Paul's) which would make them among the first believers after the resurrection of Christ.

In Romans 16 Paul has already mentioned one married couple and two single women, thus the naming of another woman would not be unexpected in the context. Furthermore, it would be improbable that two of the earliest male converts would still be together about 25 years later so as to be mentioned in one greeting. The double greeting is much more likely if they are a married couple who have been sharing their witness to Christ through all the intervening years. Only an extra-biblical assumption that a woman could not be an apostle keeps most commentators from reading

Junias as Junia. The church father Chrysostom had no such bias. He writes, "And indeed to be apostles at all is a great thing. But to be even amongst these of note, just consider what a great encomium this is! But they were of note owing to their works to their achievements. Oh! How great is the devotion of this woman that she should be even counted worthy of the appellation of apostle!"[64]

Dr. Gary S. Greig offers the following comments on Romans 16:7:

> In <u>Romans 16:7</u> Paul mentions that <u>Junia and Andronicus</u> (most likely Junia's husband) are <u>among the apostles</u>.
>
> a. <u>Junia</u> was a <u>common Latin female name</u> in the Roman Empire. Some scholars have claimed that the name in the Greek text of Rom. 16:7, Iounian (the accusative form), is a hypothetical Greek abbreviation, "Junias," of the Latin male name "Junianus." But there is absolutely no evidence at all that there ever was a masculine name "Junias" in the Roman Empire, according to Dr. Peter Lampe, Professor of New Testament, Union Theological Seminary, Richmond, Virginia:
>
> b. "Without exception the Church Fathers in late antiquity identified Andronicus' partner in Rom. 16:7 as a woman, as did minuscule 33 in the 9th century which records iounia with an acute accent. Only later medieval copyists of Rom. 16:7 could not imagine a woman being an apostle and wrote the masculine name 'Junias.' This latter name did not exist in antiquity; its explanation as a Greek abbreviation of the Latin name 'Junianus' is unlikely."

64. Williams, *Apostle Paul & Women in the Church*, 44–45.

314 *The Ministry of Women*

(P. Lampe, "Junias," Anchor Bible Dictionary, vol. 3, p. 1127).

c. The Church Father, <u>John Chrysostom</u> (died
407 AD), who had a negative view of women
in many cases, <u>understood "Junia"</u> in Rom.
16:7 as a <u>woman</u> and <u>marveled</u> that <u>she could
be called an apostle</u>: "Oh how great is the
devotion of this woman, (2) that she should
be even counted worthy of the appellation of
apostle!" (St. John Chrysostom, Homily 31
on Romans 16:5–16, The Nicene and Post-
Nicene Fathers, Series 1, vol. 9, ["Chrysostom: Homilies on the Acts of the Apostles and
the Epistle to the Romans"], Grand Rapids:
Eerdmans, 1971–1980). The first commentator to understand "Junia" as the hypothetical masculine name "Junias" was Aegidius of
Rome in the 14th century AD. (D. Scholer,
Theology News and Notes, March '95, p. 22)

d. That <u>Junia</u> was <u>recognized among these apos-
tles</u> in the <u>early church</u> is <u>understandable</u>, if
the early church had <u>Deborah</u> in mind as the
<u>senior judge</u> and a "<u>mother in Israel</u>," <u>Miriam</u>
as a <u>prophetic leader</u> under Moses, and <u>Hul-
dah</u> as a <u>prophetic leader</u> under King Josiah.

Is it not ironic that many denominations that reject the idea of
Junia as a female apostle send women from their congregations
to serve as ministries—a work that is often connected with the
apostolic work of church planting? If the Lord chooses to equip
a woman with an apostolic gifting, who are the men to say nay to
Him?

Another point that is often made against the possibility of a woman being an apostle is that when Jesus chose the twelve, He selected
male apostles only, and no females. Those who raise this argument

say that if He intended for women to function as ministers in any apostolic capacity, then He, as Head of the church, would have chosen or appointed some. But He did not.

This kind of argument does not prove anything. It may be that Jesus did not choose any women as one of the twelve, but nor did He choose any priests, scribes, Pharisees, Gentiles (or members of any other race). All twelve apostles were Jews. Does this mean that priests, scribes, Pharisees, and Gentiles are excluded from the office of apostle?

There are several points to keep in mind regarding Jesus' selection of the twelve apostles. First of all, Jesus chose the twelve according to the Father's will, after spending an entire night in prayer. Second, the twelve apostles signified the closing off of the old covenant and the ushering in of the new covenant. This would close off the natural Israel, after the flesh, and bring in the spiritual Israel, after the spirit. Therefore, naturally speaking, it was appropriate, given the Jewish culture of His time, for Jesus to choose Jews— members of the chosen race—as His original apostles. Jesus said, *"Salvation is of the Jews"* (John 4:22). Until salvation was extended to the Gentiles, no woman, regardless of race—and no Gentile man, for that matter—would have been accepted as an apostle. Had Jesus selected someone "unacceptable" to Jewry, it would have placed a stumbling-block in the way of Jews' acceptance of the Messiah. This much was proven when the twelve did not believe the testimony of the women about Christ's resurrection. But, in due time, the new covenant would usher in a change, so that "in Christ" there would be neither male nor female, relative to the redemptive history. (See Galatians 3:28.)

Much has been written on the controversial issue of female apostles. As we have noted several times, this issue will not be settled fully for many until Jesus comes. Each local church must decide its own position. And where opinions differ, Christian grace ought to abound! It is the opinion of this writer, shaped largely by the research of others, that Christ may give gifts to men or women, as He wills; who can challenge His pleasure?

Church history, as well as the contemporary church culture, has shown many mighty women of God evangelizing, pioneering and planting churches, and doing missionary work, all of which may be considered apostolic ministry. Eternity alone will evidence the full fruit of the labors of these women. To call them the exception and not the rule would mean that the same must be said of male apostles. The Lord does not call every member of the body of Christ, male or female, to be the fivefold ascension gift ministries. He does call some, which is His exception but not the general rule.

2. Prophetic Ministry

While the apostolic ministry is a highly controversial issue when it comes to the roles of men and women, there is, in general, a more widespread openness to the possibility of women being called into the prophetic ministry.

The cessationist school, however, contends that the office of prophet, along with that of apostle, ceased upon the death of the apostle John and the completion of the New Testament canon of Scripture. Pentecostal churches generally accept that the ministry of the prophets was given *"till we all come in the unity of the faith,…unto a perfect man, unto the measure of the stature of Christ"* (Ephesians 4:9–16). While the ministries of evangelists, pastors, and teachers have always had widespread acceptance by the church, the idea that the ministry of apostles and prophets is still valid and legitimate has been one of the most difficult ideas for the contemporary church to accept.

But, again, I believe that the Lord may assign His ministry gifts, in varying measures, to either men or women, as all ministries are necessary until He comes again. Christ is the Prophet; prophecy is one of His ministry gifts given as He wills to various members of the body of Christ.

For those who say that God intended for prophets and prophetesses to operate only under the old covenant, it may be asked: Is the new covenant a lesser, or lower, covenant than the old covenant? The answer is evident: No. Hebrews 8:6 calls the new covenant *"a better covenant...established upon better promises."* (See also Hebrews 12:24.) And, as we have discussed, the Old Testament prophet Joel foretold the day when God would pour out His Spirit on *"all flesh; and your sons and your daughters shall prophesy, your old men shall dream dreams, your young men shall see visions: and also upon the servants and upon the handmaids"* (Joel 2:28–29). In other words, there would not be a decrease but an increase of the prophetic Spirit on men and women in the last days, under the new covenant.

The Scriptures indicate varying degrees of the prophetic function. They are noted as:

- **The Spirit of Prophecy (Revelation 19:10)**
  - o The testimony of Jesus as the spirit of prophecy—Revelation 19:10
  - o Adam's prophecy of his bride and the God-ordained marriage state—Genesis 2:20–25
  - o Enoch's prophecy of Christ's second coming—Jude 1:14–15
  - o Noah a *"preacher of righteousness"* (2 Peter 2:5) and a prophet of coming judgment—Genesis 6–8; Hebrews 11:7
  - o Abraham a prophet—Genesis 20:7
  - o The spirit of prophecy upon Isaac and Jacob as they blessed their sons—Genesis 27; 48–49; Hebrews 11:20–21; Psalm 105:9–15
  - o Joseph's prophecy of the Israelites' exodus from Egypt—Genesis 50:24; Hebrews 11:22
  - o For additional examples of the spirit of prophecy falling on companies of people, see Numbers 11:24–30 and 1 Samuel 10:10; 19:20–24.

- ### *The Office of Prophet*

> [The Lord said,] *I have also spoken by the prophets,*
> *and I have multiplied visions, and used similitudes,*
> *by the ministry of the prophets.*   (Hosea 12:10)

> *God…at sundry times and in divers manners spake*
> *in time past unto the fathers by the prophets.*
> (Hebrews 1:1)

A prophet is a person who has been given the distinctive ministry of representing God before man, by moving under the "prophetic mantle" that came upon him or her. The prophet was God's mouthpiece, or spokesperson, through whom the messages of God flowed, whether in forth-telling (preaching) or foretelling (prediction). There were many men of God, and even some women of God, throughout the Scriptures who held this office.

- ### *The Gift of Prophecy*

Prophecy is mentioned in 1 Corinthians 12:10, Romans 12:6, and Acts 2:18 as one of the gifts of the Spirit. It may be defined as the God-given ability to speak forth supernaturally in a known language as the Spirit gives utterance. It is seen as being an operation of the Spirit in the New Testament church, and one that must be exercised according to divine guidelines. (See 1 Corinthians 14:3, 25, 31; 1 Thessalonians 5:20.) Philip's four daughters possessed this gift. (See Acts 21:8–14.) However, these women were not prophetesses; for Agabus the prophet spoke to Paul directly, not to the four daughters of Philip. The Scriptures teach that all may prophesy, but not all are prophets. (See 1 Corinthians 12:29.)

- ### *The Prophecy of Scripture*

In 2 Peter 1:19–21, the expression *"prophecy of scripture"* (verse 20) refers to the prophetical books of the Old Testament.

Because the Scriptures are the inspired Word of God (see 2 Timothy 3:16), the prophecy therein must be regarded as inspired and infallible revelation. This, then, is the highest degree of prophecy and requires the most careful and systematic interpretation. Each of the previous three must be judged by this fourth. The first three listed above are fallible; the fourth is infallible. The first three must be judged; the last is not for judgment, as it judges all others. This type of prophecy is no longer given today, however, since the 66 books of the Bible are completed; and nothing is to be added to or taken away from the completed Word of God. (See Revelation 22:18–19.)

In Old Testament times, the prophet held the highest position of ministry. It is not so in New Testament times, as the Spirit has become available to all believers; under the new covenant, everyone may be led of the Spirit. (See Romans 8:14.) Nevertheless, the risen Christ, when He ascended on high, *"gave some…[to be] apostles; and some…[to be] prophets"* (Ephesians 4:11–16). *"God hath set some in the church, first apostles, secondarily prophets"* (1 Corinthians 12:28).

There are a number of references to the New Testament post-ascension-gift prophets and their ministry:

o   Judas and Silas as prophets—Acts 15:32

o   Prophets at the church in Antioch—Acts 13:1–4

o   Prophets sent from Jerusalem to Antioch—Acts 11:27

o   Prophets (also called disciples) at Tyre—Acts 21:4

o   Agabus proven to be a prophet—Acts 11:28; 21:10–11

o   Prophets in the church at Corinth—1 Corinthians 12:28–29; 14:27–29

o   Prophets at Ephesus—Ephesians 4:9–11

- o Prophets (false prophets, in this case) moving around the various local churches—2 Peter 2:1–2; 1 John 4:1–3

- o A prophet at Crete—Titus 1:12

- o Prophets are to be tested by:

- o The Spirit of God—1 John 4:1–3

- o The Word of God—Deuteronomy 18:22; Isaiah 8:18–20

- o Their fruit—Matthew 7:15–23

- o The nature of their ministry to the people of God—Jeremiah 23:18–22; Hebrews 12:7–14

In chapter 8 of this text, "Ministry in Old Testament Times," one of the callings on men and women was to the prophetic office. For those who accept the involvement of women in public ministry, there is not as much controversy over the idea that a woman may be called to the prophetic office.

The Bible offers numerous examples of female prophets/ prophetesses, in the Old and New Testament alike:

- o Miriam, who served alongside her brothers Moses and Aaron, both of whom were prophets; all three were selected by God to be leaders of Israel—Exodus 15:20; Micah 6:4

- o Deborah, a prophetess, judge, and mother in Israel, accepted in her leadership role by the men of the nation, whom she honored—Judges 4–5

- o Huldah, a prophetess who ministered to the king as well as to the priests of the temple services, and whom the men accepted in that prophetic role and position—2 Kings 22:14; 2 Chronicles 34:22

- o The wife of the major prophet Isaiah a prophetess—Isaiah 8:3

o   Anna, a prophetess recognized and accepted by the priests and the elders of the temple services—Luke 2:36–38

o   True and false prophetesses, as well as true and false prophets, in both the Old and New Testament, one of whom was Jezebel—Nehemiah 6:14; Ezekiel 13; Revelation 2:20

Again, the Bible teaches that women may prophesy, even as men. (See Acts 2:17; Joel 2:28–32.)

Prophecy may include:

o   Preaching (the Old Testament definition of a female prophet was "female preacher" [Hebrew *nabiah*])

o   Exhortation—Acts 15:32; 1 Corinthians 14:31

o   Edification—1 Corinthians 14:3

o   Conviction—1 Corinthians 14:24

o   Instruction—1 Corinthians 14:19

o   Comfort—1 Corinthians 12:1–8; 11:5; 14:3

o   Confirmation of God's will—Acts 13:3–4; 16:6

o   Encouragement—Acts 15:32

o   Discernment—1 Corinthians 14:29–30; 1 Thessalonians 5:20–21

Once again, we know that Philip's four daughters prophesied. (See Acts 21:8–11.) Neither Paul nor Agabus "silenced" them. The difference between the office of prophet and the gift of prophecy has already been noted. Anyone may have the gift of prophecy, but not all who prophesy are necessarily prophets.

The highest office in Old Testament times was that of the prophet. In the New Testament, the highest office is that of the apostle. *"God hath set some in the church, first apostles, secondarily prophets…"* (1 Corinthians 12:28).

What a great honor to be the mouthpiece of the Lord, to speak forth the prophetic word. The Holy Spirit is available to all, regardless of gender. If the Lord employed prophets and prophetesses under the old covenant, then we should not expect to see new limits imposed on this ministry under the new covenant.

Invoking the church historian Eusebius, Ronald Pierce and Rebecca Merrill Groothuis write:

> Philip's daughters were not lone exceptions [as women who prophesied]. A woman named Ammia in the Philadelphian church is also said to have prophesied during New Testament times (Eusebius Ecclesiastical History 5.17.2–4). In fact, the second-century Montanists Priscilla and Maximilla used women like Ammia to justify their own prophetic office (Eusebius' *Ecclesiastical History* 5.17.4).[65]

Moses expressed his desire that all God's people could be prophets and share his gift. (See Numbers 11:24–29.) If the prophetic ministry in the church was legitimate under the law, then how much more so under grace.

Throughout church history, and in our times, there have been and still are many, many female preachers ministering under a prophetic anointing. Only male prejudice would silence these godly women. The prophetic ministry is still available to men and women alike, as the Lord wills, and may be seen in the functioning body of Christ by those who believe!

3. Evangelistic Ministry

The Lord may also give the ministry gift of evangelism to men or women, as He wills. For those who accept the participation of women in public ministry, the idea of female evangelists is

---

65. Ronald Pierce and Rebecca Merrill Groothuis, gen. eds., *Discovering Biblical Equality* (Downers Grove, IL: InterVarsity Press, 2005), 123.

less controversial than the idea of women serving as apostles and prophets.

Christ is *the* Evangelist (see Isaiah 41:27; 52:7; 40:9; 61:1–2; Luke 4:18–19), and men and women alike may be evangelists, as well. All believers are called to "evangelize" the unchurched, the unsaved. All believers are called to be witnesses of the gospel and of the grace of God in Christ. Believers in the book of Acts went everywhere scattering the seed of the gospel. But to certain men and women, the Lord gives the fivefold ascension-gift ministry of evangelism, as church history has proven. *"And he gave some… evangelists…"* (Ephesians 4:11). *"Do the work of an evangelist…"* (2 Timothy 4:5).

An evangelist is simply "one who announces good news or glad tidings" (*Ork. Euaggelizo* STRONG 2097). Other related Greek words speak of the "gospel or the good message," or else they refer to the "preacher or messenger of good news." The words refer to the ministry, the man, and the message of the evangelist.

Evangelists are part of the fivefold ascension-gift ministries given for the equipping of the saints, to bring the saints into the work of their ministry, and for the building up of the body of Christ. In other words, evangelists equip their fellow saints to evangelize.

The only person (apart from Christ Himself) who is specifically spoken of as an "evangelist" is the deacon Philip. (See Acts 6:1–6; 8; 21:8–10.) Acts 8 is undoubtedly the greatest chapter concerning Philip's ministry as an evangelist. He certainly sets a worthy example for those who have been equipped with this gifting, as well as to all believers in general. In Acts 8 we see two facets of evangelism:

> › Public evangelism—Acts 8:1–25

> › Personal evangelism—Acts 8:27–30

Philip preached the Word, and the Lord confirmed the Word with signs following. People heard, received, and believed the good news. They were baptized in water, and then, under Peter and

John, they received the baptism of the Holy Spirit, and thus the church in Samaria was established. Philip exemplified both public and personal evangelism, in the city (public) and to the Ethiopian eunuch (private). He depended on the Holy Spirit in his ministry.

There is no specific "chapter and verse" that speaks of other evangelists, whether male or female; but no one can deny the reality of evangelism in Acts and in the early church period, as well as the fact that this is a continuing ministry for all times.

Because the Lord promised to pour out His Spirit on all flesh— "sons and daughters, servants and handmaids" (see Joel 2:28– 29)—it is to be expected that men and women will be called to be evangelists, to evangelize.

Psalm 68 is a prophetic psalm that speaks of the *"gifts"* (verse 18) Christ gave to mankind in His ascension. These *"gifts"* Paul defines in Ephesians 4:11 as "apostles, prophets, evangelists, pastors, and teachers." These *"gifts"* were given to mankind, to human beings, regardless of sex. They were given to men and women as the Lord willed.

Psalm 68:11 refers to evangelism as a "publishing" of the good news. Several different translations of Psalm 68:11 render the verse in these ways:

> › *"The Lord gives the word [of power]; the **women** who bear and publish [the news] are a great host"* (AMP).

> › *"The Lord gives the command; the women who proclaim the good tidings are a great host"* (NASB).

> › *"You gave the command, and a chorus of women told what had happened"* (CEV).

The same prophetic psalm speaks of the singers and the players on instruments, *"among [whom] were the damsels playing with timbrels"* (Psalm 68:25) in worship to the Lord.

In John's gospel, the woman of Samaria who came to Christ at the well then told the men of the city, many of whom came to Christ. Surely, this constitutes an instance of evangelism.

Men and women may be used in public evangelism as well as personal evangelism. Untold thousands of people have come to Christ through male and female evangelists, whether at public events such as church services or through personal relationships. Eternity alone will evidence the number of souls saved through the ministries of evangelists. Are women restricted to conducting personal evangelism only, and that strictly to other women, not to men? The Bible, and church history, declares otherwise. How many souls might never have been won to Christ if not for the work of female evangelists! Christ gave this gift to mankind, to His people, regardless of gender.

The apostle Paul requests help on behalf of *"those women which labored with me in the gospel"* (Philippians 4:3). The gospel is for every creature, everywhere, wherever and whenever the opportunity to evangelize presents itself. There are numerous areas and methods of evangelism, too many to list here.

4.   Pastoral Ministry

"And He gave some...pastors" (Ephesians 4:11). Christ may also give *His* pastoral gift to either men or women in the body of Christ, as He wills. The ministry of the pastor is yet another of the fivefold ascension-gift ministries of Christ given to and for the body of Christ.

In contrast to the ministries of apostle and prophet, which have been widely rejected by the New Testament church, the pastoral ministry has been accepted over the centuries. However, there has been, and still is, a great misunderstanding of the pastoral ministry. Most of the textbooks dealing with the ministry of the pastor place upon one man a burden that is nearly impossible to bear, often due to a lack of recognition of the fivefold ministry and the importance of an eldership in the local church.

In many cases, the "pastor" is viewed as an all-around "one-man ministry" who is expected to relate to everyone on every level, and every leader in every department of the church. This feat may be possible in a smaller church, but in larger churches, it is not feasible. The result is that numerous pastors, under such pressure, break down, either mentally, emotionally, morally, or spiritually. God never intended for this to occur!

The general denominational concept of a "pastor" is this: someone held responsible for the total flock under his care. He may call in a teacher or an evangelist for a special occasion, as the need arises; but the burden of the church is on his shoulders. Yet God intended for the pastoral ministry to be one of the fivefold ministries, so that a pastor would have co-equal elders working together and sharing the burden with him.

One of the difficulties in the church, as a whole, is that we have created, as it were, a "pastoral system" that does not line up with the pattern put forth in the New Testament Scriptures. Consider, for example, the following:

> Of the some 48 churches mentioned in the New Testament, whether house churches or otherwise, there is no mention of a traditional "pastor" or any one man presiding over them.

> There is not one person in the New Testament, aside from the Lord Jesus Himself, who is ever called "pastor" or addressed by that title in any church. No one was ever called "pastor," whether male or female.

> Nowhere can it be shown from the New Testament that a pastor must be the head of the local church.

The Greek word for "pastor" is *poimeen* (STRONG 4166), and in the King James Bible, it is translated this way only once in the New Testament. In most cases, it is translated "shepherd." (See Matthew 9:36; 25:32; Luke 2:8, 15, 18, 20; John 10:2,11–16; Hebrews 13:20; 1 Peter 2:25.) It would have been helpful if the translators had been consistent in their use of this word. If this had been so, then Ephesians 4:11 would read, in essence, "When Jesus ascended on high, He gave gifts to mankind; He gave some to be apostles, some to be prophets, some to be evangelists, some to be shepherds, and some to be teachers."

Today, the pastor is seen as the dominant leader of the local church; the other ascension-gift ministries of apostle, prophet, evangelist, and teacher have to fit their role, somehow or somewhere, around that of the pastor. There are many individuals called to be apostles, prophets, evangelists, or teachers who have been pressured into being the pastor of a local church instead of fulfilling their true calling.

Many denominations do not recognize the offices of apostle or prophet but hold that the pastor heads up the church. Evangelists may hold evangelistic crusades, and teachers may conduct teaching seminars, but the pastor is seen to be at the top of the ascension-gift ministers. Yet this order is not to be found in the New Testament.

For many people, the title of "apostle" or "prophet" seems presumptuous; calling oneself an "evangelist" or "teacher" is more acceptable. But "pastor" is the dominant title held by untold thousands of ministers. This is an inconsistency indeed, especially when weighed in the light of the New Testament. Why take this one title from the list in Ephesians 4:11 and neglect the others, all of which are, technically speaking, job descriptions (what a person does) more than titles (what a person is)? In Bible times, no one troubled with having a title; they did the work according to their title. They did not pay attention to titular authority.

Both Paul and Peter speak of the "elders" who are called to "shepherd" (feed, pasture) the flock of God. (See Acts 20:28–29; 1 Peter 5:1–3.)

However, in spite of these challenges, the Lord has set in the church "shepherds." When Christ ascended on high, He gave gifts to His people—to mankind—and He gave some to be apostles, some to be prophets, some to be evangelists, some to be shepherds, and some to be teachers.

The word concerning the shepherding role is a very common expression in both the Old and the New Testaments. The concept is as old as the Bible itself, and the words pertaining to the shepherding role are used in various ways. The verb "shepherd" simply means "to feed, to pasture." It is truly "feeding the flock of God." (See Acts 20:28–29.)

The Lord Jesus is *the* Shepherd—*the* Pastor—of the flock of God. (See Psalm 23:1.) He is spoken of as the...

> "*good shepherd*" (John 10:10, 14)

> "*great shepherd*" (Hebrews 13:20)

> "*chief Shepherd*" (1 Peter 5:4)

Jesus Christ is the pattern Shepherd by which all will be judged. In the great "shepherding chapters" of the Bible—Jeremiah 23, Ezekiel 34, John 10, Acts 20, and 1 Peter 5—the Lord lays great responsibility and accountability on both shepherds and sheep. The ministry of shepherding, feeding, ruling, or pasturing is woven into the tapestry of biblical revelation in the Old and New Testaments alike.

The apostle Peter was called to "shepherd, feed, pasture" the Lord's sheep and lambs. (See John 21:15–17.)

The apostle Paul authored the "pastoral epistles," 1 and 2 Timothy and Titus. Though they were called "apostles," the men for whom these epistles are named had a shepherd's heart, as should anyone who ministers in the body of Christ. Christ was *the* Apostle, *the* Prophet, *the* Evangelist, *the* Teacher; yet He had the heart of a Shepherd!

In Old Testament times, there was a custom of shepherds having large establishments with a chief shepherd over the total flock, and under him many "under-shepherds." These under-shepherds would be given as many sheep as they could handle, or pasture. They would be responsible for these sheep and accountable to the chief shepherd for their care.

As it is in the natural, so it is in the spiritual. The Lord Jesus Christ is the Chief Shepherd, and He has called many to be His under-shepherds. They are given as many sheep as they can handle, and all are accountable to Him.

In the Bible, there were men and women who shepherded literal flocks of sheep. Abel, Abraham, Isaac, Jacob, Moses, and David were shepherds in the natural sense of the word, caring for literal sheep. (See, for example, Exodus 3:1.) Rachel, Zipporah, the seven daughters of Midian, and the Shulamite are spoken of as shepherdesses. (See Genesis 29:1–9; Exodus 2:16; Song of Solomon 1:7–8.) There were leaders referred to as "shepherds" in the governmental, political, and spiritual realms, as well. Moses, Joshua, David, Cyrus, and Jeremiah were shepherds over God's nation, Israel, His flock. (See Numbers 27:15–25; Isaiah 44:28; 45:1; Jeremiah 17:16.) Kings, princes, priests, prophets, and elders in Israel were also called shepherds. The word "shepherd" became quite an all-inclusive term in Israel for those in national leadership. (See Ezekiel 34:1–10; 22:23–31; Zechariah 11:3, 4, 8, 15–17; Nahum 3:18.)

As is sometimes the case in all ministries, there were true shepherds and false shepherds. (See Ezekiel 34; Jeremiah 23:15.) The Lord has promised to judge both shepherds and sheep at the appointed time.

Without doubt, the analogy follows through to the church, the flock of God. (See 1 Peter 5:1–5; Acts 20:17–28.) God raises up men and women to be shepherds of His people—to feed, rule, and pasture them.

Most people accept that certain men are called to shepherd the flock of God. But what about women? May they serve as pastors? The answer generally depends upon one's concept and understanding of the role of pastor in today's system of church government. As noted in this chapter, most people view the pastor as the ultimate leader or authority over a church, and many associate the realm of leadership with males, therefore rejecting the possibility of a woman being a pastor or any other type of church leader.

It may be asked: What, then, of the untold thousands of women who are "shepherding the flock of God" throughout the world, in many nations and cultures, according to the measure of their grace-gift? There are women (as well as men) who shepherd in many areas, including:

> Children's ministry
> Youth ministry
> Women's groups
> Men's groups
> Senior groups
> Home churches
> Cell groups
> Counseling

If the women are removed from these and other areas of the church, many congregations would become paralyzed or even cease to exist.

Think of Dr. David Yonggi Cho in South Korea, and the thousands of women who are caring for people in the cell groups affiliated with his church. Think of similar cell churches in Colombia and other South American nations. Consider organizations such as the Salvation Army, and the numerous women who are officers over Salvation Army Corps; they may not be called "pastor," per se, but "captain" or lieutenant." Think of the many women shepherding people in other Christian denominations. If women ceased to function in all these areas of ministry, whether spiritual or social, what a sad condition the church would find itself in.

Some expositors hold the view that when the apostle John wrote *"unto the elect* [chosen] *lady and her children, whom I love in truth"* (1 John 1:1), he was addressing the leader of a house group, or a house church, and those under her leadership. He exhorts her, *"receive...not into your house"* (1 John 1:10) those deceivers not holding to the doctrine of the Father and the Son.

This *"elect lady"* was thus responsible for distinguishing between true and false teachings. She was responsible for what went on in her home, probably the meeting place of a house church under her leadership. The word used for *"children"* in 1 John 1:1 is often used in the epistles to refer to believers in various stages of spiritual development. (See 1 John 2:1, 12, 13, 18, 28; 3:7, 18; 4:4; 5:21; 3 John 4; 1 Corinthians 4:14; Galatians 4:19; 1 Thessalonians 2:7.)

John did not address the elders or deacons here, but *"the elect lady,"* as she was the leader of this home church. We have pointed out previously those women who were over house churches, but we will list them here again, to review.

> Lydia—Acts 16:14–15

> Chloe—1 Corinthians 1:11

> Nympha—Colossians 4:15 (NKJV)

> Apphia, along with her husband, Philemon—Philemon 2

> Priscilla, along with her husband, Aquila—Romans 16:3–5

Some people interpret *"the elect lady and her children"* as a symbol of the bride of Christ—the church—or as the lady of a house with her own biological children, but their belief really belies the content of the letter and John's warning about whom the elect lady receives into her house.

While no "chapter and verse" may be found in the New Testament that shows a woman in the role of senior pastor, neither can any "chapter and verse" be found featuring any one man in that role. But, in principle, Scripture shows us that men and women may "shepherd" the people of God. Some may be called to be the senior leader of a congregation, or a leader over the youth ministry, the children's ministry, or another area of church life.

While not all members of the body of Christ are gifted as apostles, prophets, evangelists, or teachers, many people have some grace for the shepherding and care of God's sheep and lambs. This is the "pastoral" ministry evident in the body of Christ. And one's ability to function as a pastor depends in large part on the measure of the gift of grace that the Lord has given to that member of His body, whether male or female, for the part of His body they are meant to shepherd.

5. Teaching Ministry

"And he gave some...teachers" (Ephesians 4:11). *"God hath set some in the church...thirdly teachers"* (1 Corinthians 12:28–29). *"[Jesus said,] Wherefore, behold, I send unto you prophets, and wise men, and scribes"* (Matthew 23:34).

Christ, when He ascended on high, also gave teachers to the church, for the equipping of the saints, to bring the saints into the work of their ministry and for the building up of the body of Christ.

There is certainly not the same level of controversy over the ministry of teacher in the church as there is over the ministries of apostle and prophet. Teachers, along with evangelists and pastors, have been widely accepted by the church over the centuries.

Some expositors see only four ministries listed in Ephesians 4:11; they group "pastor" and "teacher" together, as one and the same person. Yet, while many church leaders fulfill a ministry in which shepherding and teaching overlap, history and experience have proven that there are those with a unique and distinctive gift of teaching, who are not necessarily pastoral. The teacher handles the Word in a manner unique to teachers. (See Isaiah 30:20.)

The Lord Jesus Christ Himself is the Teacher—the Master Teacher, the Teacher of teachers. (See John 3:2; 13:13.) Jesus spent much of His earthly ministry both *"teaching...and preaching"* (Matthew 9:35; see also Luke 13:10; 20:21).

Jesus taught...

> the multitudes—Matthew 5:1–2; Mark 14:49

> His disciples, both men and women

> the twelve—John 13–16

> under the anointing of the Holy Spirit—Luke 4:18–19

> as One having authority, not like the Pharisees or scribes—Matthew 7:28–29

Matthew's gospel has been called "the didactic gospel" because of the systematic manner of Christ's teachings it sets forth. The

Great Commission involves making disciples of all nations, *"teaching them to observe all things"* (Matthew 28:18–20) that Jesus commanded. Meanwhile, the gospel of Mark is often referred to as "the preaching gospel" because of its contents.

The Old Testament Scriptures evidence an emphasis on teaching, especially in Israel, the nation of the covenant. They believed the truth that teaching founded on the Word of God develops character, builds good and godly homes, and, if obeyed, determines a person's destiny, for time and eternity.

> › The patriarchs taught their families the principles of divine revelation. (See Genesis 18:18–19; Hebrews 11:10–16.) They were men of faith who acted as priests in their homes.

> › Jewish parents—fathers and mothers in Israel—were faithful to teach their children the ways of the Lord, in fulfillment of their responsibility to their children and their accountability to God. They were to talk of God's Word at all times. (See Deuteronomy 6:7.) The books of Proverbs and Ecclesiastes contain the instructions of a father and mother to their son, and these teachings are applicable to all sons and daughters, in any family.

> › The Levitical tribe was chosen as the priestly tribe, and part of their responsibility was to teach the twelve tribes, the fathers and the mothers, the Word of the Lord. (See Malachi 1:1–10; 2 Chronicles 35:1–6; Deuteronomy 24:8; Romans 2:20.) There was a time when Israel had gone *"without a teaching priest, and without law"* (2 Chronicles 15:3). The evidence in the nation was tragic decline into idolatry and apostasy from the Lord God.

The elders and the scribes—the theologians and hermeneuticians of the Scriptures in Christ's day—generally taught the Scriptures in the local synagogues. But, sad to say, they took away "the key of knowledge" from the people, failing to enter the kingdom of

God themselves, and also hindering others who wanted to enter it. Jesus admonished them for this practice in Luke 11:46–49.

In the New Testament, the ministry of the teacher continued, with various methods of communicating the Word of God.

> While all fivefold ministries involve "preaching" or "teaching" the Word of God in some way, God distinctly calls some with a special gift of teaching. (See Ephesians 4:11.)

> Elders are to be able to teach the Word of God. (See 1 Timothy 3:2; 1 Peter 5:2.)

> Parents are responsible to teach and apply the Word of God to their children. (See, for example, Ephesians 6:1–4; Colossians 3:21.) Solomon advises his son, *"My son, keep thy father's commandment, and forsake not the law of thy mother"* (Proverbs 6:20).

> The saints are to teach one another with psalms, hymns, and spiritual songs. (See Colossians 3:16; Ephesians 5:19.)

> Older women are to teach the younger women to be sober, to love their husbands and children, and to be discreet, pure, skilled homemakers who obey their husbands. (See Titus 2:3–5.)

> The body of Christ requires the work of those who instruct children, young people, young adults, and seniors—the whole range of ages and levels of spiritual maturity. (See Hebrews 5:12–14; 6:1–2.)

> Timothy's mother and grandmother evidently taught him the Scriptures from his childhood. (See 2 Timothy 1:5; 3:14–17.)

God calls both men and women to be teachers. Priscilla and Aquila were a husband-and-wife teaching team, as seen in our earlier comments on the book of Acts. (See Acts 18:18, 24–28.) Together, Priscilla and Aquila operated a house church and occupied leadership roles. (See Romans 16:3.)

Similar to the other ministries, there are true teachers and false teachers. All teachers must be judged by the Word of God and the Spirit of God, and their degree of responsibility and accountability to God is high. (See James 3:1–2.)

There are those who permit women to teach children or other women only but forbid them to teach men, women, and children in a congregational meeting, based on their interpretation of the apostle Paul's writings. There is no need to repeat here our discussion of the propriety of women teaching in public ministry. We have found that it is not an honest exegesis to take Paul's word in 1 Timothy 2:12, *"I suffer not a woman to teach, nor to usurp authority over the man,"* as an intent to silence women. Women may teach in numerous areas, as well as men, as long as they do so in harmony with "the apostles' doctrine" as laid down in the Word of God. Women may teach, as well as men, as long as they do so without seizing authority over the church. Men and women who are gifted as teachers may exercise authority as long as they are under authority. This is divine order, which we have already discussed in detail.

As with all ministries in the church, there is, as it were, *"the cluster"* (Isaiah 65:8), or a variety of the gift of teaching. The Lord gives various measures of the grace-gift of teaching to men and women who instruct the various members of the body of Christ, whether via public ministry (such as a church service), a youth meeting, a children's Sunday school class, or another setting.

6. Deacon (Serving) Ministry

The next area of ministry is that of the *diakonate*, or the deacons. Once again, there is no question whether men may serve in this role. The issue is whether a woman may be a deacon. Varying opinions have arisen out of different understandings of what a deacon is.

It is the position of this text that men and women may serve as deacons in the church, according to the measure of the grace-gift Christ has given them. Christ is also *the* Deacon. He is among us as One who serves.

Paul opens the book of Philippians by addressing *"all the saints in Christ Jesus which are at Philippi, with the bishops and deacons"* (Philippians 1:1). This is the New Testament church order: the saints, the bishops (elders), and then the deacons. Paul also writes of those who *"have used the office of a deacon..."* (1 Timothy 3:13).

There is much confusion about this office, specifically regarding its qualifications and responsibilities. Some schools view deacons as ministers of the gospel, while others appoint arch-deacons; some denominations appoint a board of deacons over the almsgiving. The office of deacon has been taken to both extremes—underrated as well as overexalted—as church history has proven.

The Roman Catholic Church looks upon deacons as an inferior ecclesiastic, second in the sacred order; with the permission of the bishop, they may preach and even baptize.

The English Church looks upon deacons as clergymen of the lowest grade; they may perform all the duties of priests except for consecrating the sacred elements and pronouncing absolution.

German Protestant churches have an assistant minister called a deacon; if there are two such individuals, then the first is referred to as the arch-deacon.

In the Presbyterian Church, the office of deacon is commonly merged with the ruling elder; thus, deaconship is mostly disused.

In the Methodist and Episcopal churches (USA), the role of a deacon is basically the same as it is in the English Church.

In the Baptist Church, the deacons serve as the board of directors and control the administrative affairs of the church, primarily the "hiring and firing" of pastors.

Various other denominations do appoint deacons and deaconesses as appropriate to the needs of the congregation.

The above provides some idea of the confusion over the role and function of deacons in the church. This is far removed from the original intention of the Scriptures!

There are several interrelated Greek words that shed light on the meaning of the word "deacon." The most common word is *diakonos* (STRONG 1247–1249), which is translated in Matthew 20:26, Mark 10:43, Romans 13:4, Romans 15:8, and Colossians 1:27 as:

> "deacon" (five times)

> "servant" (seven times)

> "minister" (twenty times)—see Matthew 20:26; Mark 10:43; Romans 13:4; 15:8; Colossians 1:27. The word means "a servant of the people; a waiter, attendant, servant or minister." The related Greek words involve the same thought. The deacon is one who serves or ministers to the people, to the Lord, or to His ministers.

The word is also used in an unofficial sense to refer to household servants, and to the many different ways that people minister to and serve one another. And it is used in an official sense of those appointed specifically to *"the* [church] *office of a deacon"* (Philippians 1:1; 1 Timothy 3:10, 13).

Deacons in the Bible

> Christ Himself as *the* Servant of servants, the ultimate Deacon, who humbled Himself and took upon Himself the form of a servant—Philippians 2:1–8; Luke 22:26–27; Romans 15:8

> Angels and magistrates spoken of as ministers or servants—Matthew 4:11; Mark 1:13; Romans 13:3–4

> Satanic messengers spoken of as servants of Satan—2 Corinthians 11:15

> The apostle Paul as a servant, with Apollos—1 Corinthians 3:5

> John Mark's ministry to Paul and Barnabas—Acts 13:5

> Tychicus a faithful minister to the church at Ephesus—Ephesians 6:21; Colossians 4:7

> Timothy's service to the church—1 Thessalonians 3:2

> Epaphros a faithful servant of Christ—Colossians 1:7

> Timothy and Erastus minister to Paul—Acts 19:22

> Onesiphorus's ministry to Paul as a deacon—2 Timothy 1:16–18

> The household of Stephanas devoted to the service of the saints—1 Corinthians 16:15

There are many who serve the Lord and the ministry, as well as the churches, in the role of deacon.

Deaconesses in the Bible

It is evident from church history that there were also certain women chosen to serve the church as deaconesses. Some expositors believe that the qualifications for a deacon's wife set forth in 1 Timothy 3:11 could have been meant for an order of deaconesses in the church. In the King James Version, the verse reads, *"Even so must their wives be grave, not slanderers, sober, faithful in all things."* But other translations offer a different interpretation.

> *"Deaconesses likewise must be grave..."* (CTNT).

> *"The deaconesses too must be serious..."* (WILLIAMS).

> *"Deaconesses, in the same way, must be sober-minded women..."* (WEYMOUTH).

> *"[The] women likewise must be worthy of respect..."* (AMP); a footnote says, "Either their wives or the deaconesses, or both."

Clement of Alexandria (2nd–3rd century) understood the verse to be speaking of female deacons, as did John Chrysostom (4th century). Either way, the truth is consistent with Scripture, in which we see the following examples of female deacons:

> The Shunammite woman who ministered to Elisha—2 Kings 4

> Martha and her service (Greek *diakonea*) to the Lord and His disciples—Luke 10:38–42; John 12:2

> Peter's wife's mother, who ministered to Jesus following her being healed by Him—Matthew 8:14–15; Mark 1:31

> Mary Magdalene, Mary the mother of James and Joses, the mother of Zebedee's children, Joanna, and Susanna, all who ministered to Jesus—Matthew 27:55–56; Luke 8:1–3

> Dorcas, who ministered to the necessity of the poor—Acts 9:36–40

> Phoebe as a deaconess, a servant of the church at Cenchrea—Romans 16:1–2

Of Phoebe and Priscilla, Chrysostom said, "These were noble women, hindered in no way by their sex in the course of virtue…. *For in Christ Jesus there is neither male nor female.*"[66]

Catherine Booth quotes Theodoret, saying, "'The fame of Phebe was spoken of throughout the world. She was known not only to the Greeks and Romans, but also to the Barbarians,' which implies that she had travelled much, and propagated the gospel in foreign countries."[67]

R. B. C. Howell comments thusly on the historical evidences of deaconesses:

> Female assistants to the deacons, usually called deaconesses, existed in the primitive churches. They were ladies of approved character and piety; and their duty required them to minister to females, under circumstances in which it would have been manifestly improper that the other sex should have been employed. Their services were regarded as of very great importance, if not entirely indispensable. Ecclesiastical historians, the early fathers, and other writers, refer to them frequently and familiarly.

66. John Chrysostom, *The Homilies of S. John Chrysostom, Archbishop of Constantinople, on the Epistle of St. Paul the Apostle to the Romans* (Oxford, England: John Henry Parker, 1841), 479.
67. Booth, *Female Ministry*, 11.

Mosheim, for example, in his History of the First Century, introduces them thus:—"The eastern churches elected deaconesses, and chose for that purpose, matrons, or widows, of eminent sanctity, who also ministered to the necessities of the poor, and performed several other offices, that tended to order and decency in the church."[68]

Multiple early church fathers confirm the fact that deacons played a certain role in the church in the first few centuries.

> Ignatius, a contemporary of the apostle John, speaks of deacons being more than just servers of meat and drink.

> Pliny the Younger, Roman governor of Bithynia in Asia Minor (AD 110–112), mentioned two female slaves who were tortured for their faith in Christ. They are described in Latin as "ministers," the common Latin translation of the Greek word *diakonos* (BAGD, pages 184, 2b).

> Irenaeus perceived a pattern in Acts 6 and believed that the church should be under the direction of not more than seven men. In AD 315, the Council of Neo-Caesarea set seven as the number of men to administer in the affairs of the church.

> Clement of Alexandria (2nd century) confirms the same, using Paul as an authority on the matter.

> Jerome (4th century) also speaks of deaconesses.

Documents of the Early Church (page 5) speaks of two maidservants who were tortured, who were called deaconesses. In the SYRIA Didascalia, from the late third century, we are told that:

> Deaconesses were to assist women in baptism.

> Deaconesses were especially used in the "art of anointing and to go into the houses of the heathen where there are believing women, and to visit those who are sick and to

---

68. R. B. C. Howell, *The Deaconship* (Philadelphia, PA: American Baptist Publication Society, 1851), 124–125.

minister to them in that of which they need, and to bathe those who have begun to recover from sickness."

The Didache (the Teaching of the Twelve Apostles) mentions both elders/bishops and deacons who served as prophets and teachers. "Appoint for yourselves therefore bishops and deacons worthy of the Lord...for unto you they also perform the service of the prophets and teachers..." (*Documents of the Christian Church*, page 64).

In the first four centuries of church history, women were included with men in the office of *diakonos* (minister). The Greek masculine title *diakonos* referred to both men and women until a separate order of women, called deaconesses, first appeared in the Syrian church (ca. AD 380). (Refer to 16401 *Theological Dictionary of the New Testament* vol. 2, page 93.)

The "Excursus on the Deaconess of the Early Church" tells of the demise of female deacons in the early church:

> The principal work of the deaconess was to assist the female candidates for holy baptism. At that time the sacrament of baptism was always administered by immersion (except to those in extreme illness) and hence there was much that such an order of women could be useful in. Moreover they sometimes gave to the female catechumens preliminary instruction, but their work was wholly limited to women, and for a deaconess of the Early Church to teach a man or to nurse him in sickness would have been an impossibility. The duties of the deaconess are set forth in many ancient writings...[such as] what is commonly known as the XII Canon of the Fourth Council of Carthage, which met in the year 398....
>
> The deaconesses existed but a short while. The council of Laodicea as early as AD 343–381, forbade the appointment of any who were called presbutides (Vide Canon xi); and the first council of

> Orange, AD 441, in its twenty-sixth canon forbids
> the appointment of deaconesses altogether....[69]

Paul honored women in church leadership, as seen in his great commendation of Phoebe, by whom he sent his epistle to the church at Rome. (See Romans 16:1–2.) The demise of female leadership began several hundred years later, after the apostolic age.

The ministry of the *diakonate* can cover numerous areas in the church, such as house church gatherings, ushering, children's ministry, care of widows, baptism of women, Communion services, hosting visiting ministries, hospitality, care of orphans, visitation of the sick at home or in the hospital, secretarial work, and wedding preparations.

All believers should have the Spirit of Christ—that is, the spirit of a servant. Paul urged believers, *"By love serve one another"* (Galatians 5:13).

Christ Himself is *the* Deacon; the Master who is also the Servant. He came not to be ministered unto, but to minister, and to give His life as a ransom for many. And Jesus exhorted the apostles to take the place of a servant. (See Matthew 20:25–28; Mark 10:42–45.)

In 1 Timothy 3:8–11, Paul lays out the qualifications of those who would fill the office of deacon, whether men or women. These qualities include spiritual, character, and domestic qualifications. A deacon's spouse and children must be in divine order. The same is true of a deacon's household: the home must be in order, for one cannot minister in the house of the Lord if his or her own house is out of order.

Many expositors cite Acts 6:1–6 as the first example of deacons being appointed in the early church. The apostles and the church co-jointly appointed "the Seven" to this ministration. A study of the Scriptures shows that:

---

69. "Excursus on the Deaconess of the Early Church," in Philip Schaff and Henry Wace, eds., *A Select Library of Nicene and Post-Nicene Fathers of the Christian Church*, Vol. XIV (New York, NY: Charles Scribner's Sons, 1900), 41, 42.

> The church at Jerusalem had deacons. Two outstanding deacons are seen in Stephen, who was the first martyr of the early church, and Philip, the first specified evangelist in Acts.

> The church at Philippi had deacons. (See Philippians 1:1.)

> The church at Ephesus had deacons also. (See 1 Timothy 3:8–13.)

The purpose of the ministry of the deacon is simply to allow Christ to live, and manifest His servant heart, through various members of the body of Christ. Those who are part of the *diakonate*, whether men or women, are to serve the Lord, the ministry, and their fellow members of the body of Christ in the same servant's spirit as that of their Lord and Master, Jesus Christ.

7. Eldership Ministry

The position of this text is that the Lord Jesus Christ may call men or women to the eldership ministry as He wills and at His pleasure, in the same way that He may call men and women to any of the ministries previously dealt with in this chapter.

There is no question or doubt about the office of eldership being fulfilled in men, the male of the species. But the notion of female elders is almost as controversial as that of female apostles.

In chapter 12, "Four Position Schools," we saw that there are denominations that do not permit women to...

> minister in any public manner in church life, because of the argument that Paul commands "silence."

> claim to have been called to be any of the ascension-gift ministries; they believe that women are not meant to be apostles, prophets, evangelists, shepherds, or teachers.

> minister as deacons or elders, or in any area of church leadership or government, since leadership roles are reserved for males.

Other schools of thought advance the following beliefs:

> › That God may call some women to the prophetic, evangelistic, pastoral, or teaching ministries but not to the apostolic ministry.

> › That women may teach other women or children, as long as men are not present, as this would constitute a case of "usurping authority over a man."

> › That God may call women to deaconship but not to eldership.

> › That God may call both men and women to be apostles, prophets, evangelists, shepherds, and teachers, as well as deacons or elders, if it be His will.

Of the above beliefs, the final statement represents the position of this text. A number of ministers and expositors have come to this very conclusion after thorough research, a summary of which will be noted in the course of this chapter.

Definition of Key Terms

There are several words used in Scripture that throw light on the meaning of the term *elder*, and, by extension, on what an elder's ministry involves.

1. Old Testament Hebrew

The Hebrew word *zagen* (STRONG 2205) means "old" and is translated "aged, ancient (man), elder (-est), old (man, men and... women), senator." (See, for example, Genesis 10:21; 25:23; Deuteronomy 5:23; 1 Samuel 4:3; 1 Chronicles 11:3.)

The basic meaning of the word in the Old Testament is an old or elderly person, whether male or female.

2. New Testament Greek

Collins Dictionary provides the following definition of "elder": "older, more advanced in age, senior; one that is appointed to office on account of his age or presumable experience and wisdom; presbyter; a layman associated with the minister in the government and discipline of the church."

The word *elder* is generally defined as "an older or elderly person, or a senior." Sometimes it simply speaks of age; in New Testament times, it usually referred to someone holding an office—a member of the Sanhedrin of Israel or an office in the Christian church. From the use of this word, we conclude that those appointed as elders in the early church were mature people, measured either by their chronological age or their evident spiritual maturity. It should be noted that maturity does not necessarily come with age but through personal growth and with the acceptance of responsibility.

Because the word *elder* has to do with older persons, it will be helpful to note the use of several Greek words for "old" in the New Testament. There are four primary Greek words for "old," three of which we will consider here in brief.

+ *Arkaios* (STRONG 744, from STRONG 746), meaning "original or primeval." The English word *archaic* is derived from this Greek word. *Arkaios* is translated "(them of) old (time)" and is found twelve times in the Bible:

  > "…*of old time*"—Matthew 5:21, 27, 33; Acts 15:21

  > "*the old prophets*"—Luke 9:8, 19

  > "*a good while ago* [in days of old]"—Acts 15:7

  > "*an old disciple*"—Acts 21:16

  > "*old things are passed away*"—2 Corinthians 5:17

  > "*spared not the old world*"—2 Peter 2:5

  > "*that old serpent*"—Revelation 12:9; 20:2

+ Graódés (STRONG 1126), from *graus*, meaning "an old woman" and translated "*old wives*" (1 Timothy 4:7). Used once only.

+ *Palaios* (STRONG 3820), from *palai* (STRONG 3819), meaning "antique, i.e. not recent, worn out." Translated "old" at least nineteen times, of which the following are representative:

  > "*old garment*"—Matthew 9:16; Mark 2:21

  > "*old bottles*"—Matthew 9:17; Mark 2:22; Luke 5:37

  > "*old man*"—Romans 6:6; Colossians 3:9

> *"old leaven"*—1 Corinthians 5:7–8

> *"the old testament"*—2 Corinthians 3:14

> *"old"*—Hebrews 8:13

> *"an old commandment"*—1 John 2:7

+ *Presbuterion/presbutera* (STRONG 4244–47), meaning "old, or older, elderly," referring to men or women, translated "elder/elders" generally.

There are two Greek words used in the New Testament relative to eldership. It should be remembered that the New Testament concept of eldership is basically a continuance of the Old Testament office, adapted here to the local church situation. These words are translated *"elder"* and "bishop," and a careful study of them shows that they refer to one and the same person. History shows us that with the decline of the church, some made these two into separate offices, and exalted the bishops above the elders (by appointing archbishops, etc.). This was not in harmony with the Scriptures. "Elder" was more the Hebrew thought, while "bishop" was the Greek thought. However, they referred to one and the same person.

Attention needs to be given to the use of the word "old" as it pertains to the term "elder," or "elders." *Strong's Exhaustive Concordance* has several interrelated words, all coming from the same Greek root. When it comes to elders, whether people of age or those occupying the position by that name in the church, one word is used more frequently than any other.

+ *Presbeia* (STRONG 4242, from *presbeuó*), meaning "seniority (eldership), i.e. (by implication) an embassy (concretely, ambassadors)—ambassage, message."

  > *"…he sendeth an **ambassage**"* (Luke 14:32).

  > *"His citizens…sent a **message** after him…"* (Luke 19:14).

+ *Presbeuó* (STRONG 4243), "from the base of presbuteros," meaning "to be a senior, i.e. (by implication) act as a representative (figuratively, preacher)—be an ambassador."

  > *"Now then we are **ambassadors** for Christ…"* (2 Corinthians 5:20).

> "...for which I am an **ambassador** in bonds..." (Ephesians 6:20).

* *Presbuterion* (STRONG 4244) meaning "presbytery, body of elders. Neuter of a presumed derivative of presbuteros; the order of elders, i.e. (specially), Israelite Sanhedrin or Christian 'presbytery'—(estate of) elder(s), presbytery."

    > "...the **elders** of the people...came together..." (Luke 22:66).

    > "...all the estate of the **elders**..." (Acts 22:5).

    > "...with the laying on of the hands of the **presbytery**" (1 Timothy 4:14)

This Greek word equates with *"elders"* in Psalm 107:32, *"Let them exalt him also in the congregation of the people, and praise him in the assembly of the elders."* It is applied to the council (or senate, or Jewish Sanhedrin) of the seventy elders, as seen in Luke 22:66 and Acts 22:5. It is also applied to the group of elders in the local church, and was translated *"presbytery,"* as in 1 Timothy 4:14.

The word simply refers to any group of elders gathered together in session. The Presbyterian Church derives its name from this form of church government. The word occurs three times in the New Testament, as seen above.

* *Sumpresbuteros* (STRONG 4850), meaning "fellow elder...a co-presbyter—presbyter, also an elder."

    > "The **elders** which are among you I exhort, who am also an **elder**..." (1 Peter 5:1).

* *Presbutés* (STRONG 4246), "from the same as presbuteros; an old man—aged (man), old man."

    > "For I am **an old man**..." (Luke 1:18).

    > "That the **aged men** be sober..." (Titus 2:2).

    > "...being such an one as Paul **the aged**..." (Philemon 9).

* *Presbutis* (STRONG 4247), "feminine of presbutes; an old woman—aged woman."

> "*The* **aged women** *likewise…*" (Titus 2:3).

- *Presbuteros* (STRONG 4245), "comparative of presbus (elderly); older; as noun, a senior; specially, an Israelite Sanhedrist (also figuratively, member of the celestial council) or Christian 'presbyter'—elder(-est), old."

This word is applied in several ways in Scripture:

> To an older person, whether a man or a woman, who is advanced in years; a senior. (See John 8:9; Luke 1:18; 15:25; Acts 2:17; 1 Timothy 5:2; Philemon 9; Titus 2:2–3.)

> To the Old Testament saints and patriarchs, and the Old Testament persons who formed the traditions that nullified the Word of God. (See Matthew 15:2; Mark 7:3–5; Hebrews 11:2.)

> To the official leaders of the Jewish people, whether of the local synagogues or to the official Jewish council, called the Sanhedrin. (See Matthew 5:22; 10:17; 16:21; 26:3, 47, 57, 59; 27:1; Luke 7:31; 22:66; Acts 4:5–8; 24:1; 25:15.) The rulers of the synagogues were also called elders. (See Mark 5:22, 35; Luke 4:20; John 16:2; Acts 18:8.)

> To the officially ordained leaders of the New Testament church or local churches. (See Acts 14:23; 20:17, 18; 1 Timothy 5:1, 2, 17–19; Titus 1:5; James 5:14; 1 Peter 5:1.) This word appears some sixty-six times in the New Testament, twelve of these appearances being in the book of Revelation.

The next Greek word needing our consideration is the term that is translated as "bishops" in the English. We note several Greek related words:

- *Episkopos* (STRONG 1985), meaning "bishop, overseer…a superintendent." In the Greek, the word is compounded of two other words: the preposition *epi* (STRONG 1909, "over"), and *skopos* (STRONG 4649, "to look or watch, to peer about, to oversee"). The word is used five times in the New Testament and speaks of a

"Christian officer in genitive case charge of a (or the) church (literally or figuratively)...."

> "...the flock, over which the Holy Ghost hath made you *overseers*" (Acts 20:28).

> "...with the *bishops* and deacons" (Philippians 1:1).

> "A *bishop* then must be blameless..." (1 Timothy 3:2).

> "A *bishop* must be blameless..." (Titus 1:7).

> "Ye...are now returned unto the Shepherd and *Bishop* of your souls" (1 Peter 2:25).

Thayer's Greek Lexicon translates the term as "an overseer, a man charged with the duty of seeing that things to be done by others are done rightly, any curator, guardian, or superintendent."

Vine says, "In the Christian churches those who, being raised up and qualified by the work of the Holy Spirit, were appointed to have the spiritual care of, and to exercise oversight over, the churches."[70]

Wuest comments that "the word came originally from secular life, referring to the foreman of a constructive gang, or the supervisor of building construction."[71]

The Episcopal Church emphasizes this form of church government, as evidenced by its name.

✦ *Episkopé* (STRONG 1984), the noun form of *episkopos*, meaning "inspection (for relief); by implication, superintendence; specially, the Christian 'episcopate'—the office of a 'bishop,' bishoprick, visitation." It has to do with inspection, visitation, investigation; the office of oversight.

> "...his *bishoprick* let another take" (Acts 1:20).

> "If a man desire the office of a *bishop*, he desireth a good work" (1 Timothy 3:1).

---

70. Vine, W. E. *Vine's New Testament Word Pictures*, 1020.
71. Kenneth S. Wuest, "The Pastoral Epistles in the Greek New Testament," in Wuest's *Word Studies from the Greek New Testament*, Vol. 2 (Grand Rapids, MI: Eerdmans, 1979), 52.

> "...*thou knewest not the time of thy* **visitation**" (Luke 19:44).

> "*Glorify God in the day of* **visitation**" (1 Peter 2:12).

✦ *Episkopeó* (STRONG 1983), the verb form of the above, meaning "to oversee; by implication, to beware—look diligently, take the oversight."

> "**Looking diligently...**" (Hebrews 12:15).

> "*Feed the flock of God...**taking the oversight** thereof*" (1 Peter 5:2).

As already noted, the words "*elder*" and "*bishop*" refer to one and the same role, the former having a Hebrew background, the latter a Greek background. There is no elevation of either office above the other implied in these terms, as confirmed by the following.

Paul called for the "*elders*" (Greek, *presbuteros*) of the church of Ephesus and said they were "*overseers*" (Greek, *episkopos*), and told them to "*feed*" (Greek, *poimeen*) the flock of God; that is, to shepherd, pasture. (See Acts 20:17, 28.)

> Paul told Titus to ordain "*elders*" (Greek, *presbuteros*) in every city, and laid out the qualifications for these "bishops" (Greek, *episkopos*). (See Titus 1:5, 7.)

> Peter, who was a "fellow elder" (Greek, *sumpresbuteros*), spoke to the "*elders*" (Greek, *presbuterion*), and told them to "feed" (Greek, *poimaino*, shepherd, pastor) the flock of God, "*taking the oversight*" (Greek, *episkopeo*) thereof. This was the bishopric. (See 1 Peter 5:2.)

In the light of the above references, we see that an elder is a bishop, and a bishop is an elder; the work of both is to shepherd the flock of God. The relationship of these positions has been clearly summarized in this way:

✦ The *elder* is the older person, not a novice (who he is).

✦ The *bishop* is the office, the position held (what his responsibility is.)

✦ The *shepherding* is the work—the feeding, caring, and pastoring (what he does).

Again, these terms refer to one and the same person. Thus, in the church, the elders were to inspect, watch over, and oversee as bishops who tended, cared for, nurtured, fed, and ruled, as shepherds, the flock of God—His sheep entrusted to them.

Male Elders

The elder—the role, place, and function—is really as old as Scripture itself. Some references are noted in brief here of male elders in both the Old and New Testaments.

Old Testament and the Gospels

+ Elders in the land of Egypt—Genesis 50:7

+ Elders in the land of Moab and Midian—Numbers 22:7

+ Elders in the nation of Israel—Exodus 3:16, 18; 1 Chronicles 11:3

+ Moses assisted by seventy elders—Exodus 24:1, 9, 14

+ The *"assembly of the elders"*—Psalm 107:32

+ The Jewish Sanhedrin, consisting of the high priest (presiding elder), twenty-four priests, twenty-four scribes, and twenty-two elders of the synagogues—Matthew 26:57, 59; Mark 15:1; Luke 22:66

New Testament

The concept of eldership in the New Testament follows on from the Old Testament but in a more developed kind of ministry in the local churches.

+ Elders ordained in every church—Acts 14:23; 20:17

+ Elders ordained in every city—Titus 1:5

+ The apostles as elders in Jerusalem—Acts 1:14; 2:42; 15:2–6, 22, 23; 21:18

+ Prophets and teachers at Antioch—Acts 11:19–27; 13:1–4

+ Elders at Ephesus—Acts 20:17; 1 Timothy 5:17

+ Elders at Crete—Titus 1:4–5

- Elders charged to be examples for the flock—1 Peter 5:1–5

- Elders exhorted to pray for the sick—James 5:14

- Elders to be qualified men, able to teach the Word—1 Timothy 3:1–7

- The Lamb and the twenty-four elders—Revelation 4:4

- Spiritual, character, and domestic qualifications of male elders and for deacons—1 Timothy 3; Titus 1:9; Acts 20:17–28

- Greetings from the apostles Paul and Timothy to the bishops and deacons of the church at Philippi, the ideal local church—Philippians 1:1

Timothy and Titus were in charge of the churches at Ephesus and Crete. It may be safely assumed that they were the elders in those churches, even though the Scriptures do not specifically refer to them as such. It may be asked: How could Titus have followed the exhortation to ordain elders in every city if he himself was not an elder? And why would Timothy have been expected to deal with and reprove elders in false doctrine if he himself was not an elder? Both these young men were within the bracket of thirty and forty years of age when they received their epistles from Paul.

Female Elders

There is no controversy over men serving as elders. But when it comes to female elders, most schools of thought totally reject such a possibility, insisting that eldership—and all forms of church leadership—is reserved for males. However, as we will see, there are several Scriptures that, according to some expositors, point to the reality of female elders in the Old Testament church.

It should be kept in mind that the early church existed in a period of transition, from a strongly male-dominated society under the old covenant, to the new covenant, by which all people, men and women, were to be seen primarily as being *"in Christ"* (Galatians 3:28).

Gordon D. Fee, in *Listening to the Spirit in the Text*, asks: "What about ministry?" in Pauline writings). He writes:

The Pauline texts show a rather consistent view with regard to "ministry," meaning serving the church and the world in a variety of ways. Everyone, man and woman alike, minister within the context of their own gifting by the Holy Spirit. At the crucial point of ministering by verbal gifting, Paul consistently says such things as "all may prophesy" (1 Cor 14:23), to which 1 Corinthians 11:2–16 bears corroborating evidence. Despite some voices to the contrary, Paul made **no distinction between men and women** in the use of any verbal gifting (prophecy, tongues, teaching, revelation, etc.). Gifting by the Holy Spirit was the only criterion, and the Holy Spirit was obviously **gender-blind**, since he gifted men and women at will.

When we move to the question of "offices" in the church, of course, we move into an arena where Paul supplies us with almost no evidence. The idea that there are some who serve as "priests," and that they should be males (thus keeping alive the strictures of the older covenant!), would be about as foreign to Paul as one could get. In any case, it seems clear that "function" preceded the concept of "position." That is, people functioned as prophets or teachers before they were called that; there were not preordained "offices" that they should step into.

Thus the ultimate question before us in the matter of "gender and ministry" is not whether women ministered—of course they did—but whether, given the cultural norm, they also stepped into **roles of leadership** (which in itself is a nebulous term in light of the Pauline evidence). That they did so in fact would be consistent with the radically counter-cultural sociology that found expression in the believing community, as outlined above.[72]

With reference to the subject of eldership, the writer has gone through the 67 to 70 Greek words in the New Testament related to "*elders*." They have been set out in the following columns in order to sharpen our focus on these Greek words that have already been considered earlier in this chapter.

---

72. Gordon D. Fee, *Listening to the Spirit in the Text* (Grand Rapids, MI: Wm. B. Eerdmans Publishing Company, 2000), 72–73.

The terms all relate to the Greek word *presbus*, meaning "elderly"—the root word from which the other related words are derived. (Taken and arranged from *The Word Study Concordance*.)

Presbuterion	Presbuteros/ Presbuteroi	Presbuteros/ Presbuteroi	Presbutera	Presbutes
STRONG 4244 Masculine	STRONG 4245 Masculine	STRONG 4245 Masculine	STRONG 4245 in the Feminine form	STRONG 4246 Masculine
Always speaks of elders (plural)	Always speaks of elder or elders	Used mostly of elders in the NT church	Used of elder women in the church	Used of aged men
Luke 22:66 Acts 22:5 1 Timothy 4:14 "Assembly of the elders," or the presbytery	Matthew 15:2; 16:21; 21:23; 26:3, 47, 57, 59; 27: 1, 3, 12, 20, 41; 28:12; Mark 7:3, 5; 8:31; 11:27; 14:43, 53; 15:1; Luke 7:3; 9:22; 20:1; 22:52; Acts 4:5, 8, 23; 6:12; 23:14; 24:1 Acts 25:15	Acts 11:30 Acts 14:30 Acts 15:2, 4, 6, 22, 23 Acts 16:4 Acts 20:17 Acts 21:18 1 Timothy 5:1, 17, 19 Titus 1:5 James 5:14 1 Peter 5:1, 5 2 John 1 3 John 1 The 24 elders Revelation 4:4, 10; 5:5, 6, 8, 11, 14; 7:11, 13; 11:16; 14:3; 19:4	1 Timothy 5:2 Elder women (female elders, in the plural) **Presbutis** STRONG 4247, the feminine form of STRONG 4246 Titus 2:3. Aged women; some scholars see possible reference to women elders again.	Luke 1:18— old man, Zacharias the priest Titus 2:2—aged men to be sober Philemon 9—Paul, the aged (who is an apostle and an elder)

Presbuterion	Presbuteros/ Presbuteroi	Presbuteros/ Presbuteroi	Presbutera	Presbutes
Greek word used 3 times	Greek word used 34 times, 31 times of the Sanhedrin, the others as here: Luke 15:25. Eldest son John 8:9. Eldest of Pharisees Acts 2:17. Old men —dreams	Greek word used 19 times of church elders, or the presbytery; 12 times of the 24 elders; once of the patriarchs (Hebrews 11:2)	These Greek words used one time respectively and both times in the feminine form -of women, in the plural	Greek word used 3 times, as above

Of particular interest is the Pauline use of the *presbus*-related words in his pastoral epistles. As seen, Paul uses *presbuteros* in both the masculine and the feminine—that is, he uses the same word to refer to male elders and female elders. For a sharper focus on this consistency in Paul's usage of the terms, note the several Greek words in these columns adapted from the Pastoral Epistles.

Masculine/Male Elders	Feminine/Female Elders
1. Laying on of hands of the presbytery elders (*presbuterion*, plural)—1 Timothy 4:14	
2. Rebuke not an elder but entreat as a father elder (*presbuteros*, singular)—1 Timothy 5:1	The elder women as mothers (presbutera). Elder—feminine—1 Tim 5:2
3. Let the elders (*presbuteroi*, plural) that rule, be counted worthy of double honor—1 Timothy 5:17	

Masculine/Male Elders	Feminine/Female Elders
4. Against an elder (*presbuteros*, singular) receive not an accusation. Them that sin rebukebefore all—1 Timothy 5:19–20	
5. Ordain elders (*presbuteroi*, plural) in every city—Titus 1:5	
6. The aged men to be sober (*presbutes*, plural)—Titus2:2	The aged women (*presbutis*, feminine of *presbutes*) to teach the younger women—Titus 2:3–4

Some would contend that not all of these references refer to church-elders but simply to "older men" or "older women." Some would say that 1 Timothy 5:1 speaks of male elders, while 1 Timothy 5:2 applies to older women. Yet Paul is using the masculine and feminine forms of the same Greek word. This consistency implies that both instances speak of either "old men"/"old women" or "male elders"/"female elders."

Those who hold this view contend that Paul was referring to age groupings, not offices in the church, when he wrote, "*Rebuke not an* **elder**, *but intreat him as a* father; *and the* **younger** *men as* **brethren**; *the* **elder** *women as* **mothers**" (1 Timothy 5:1–2). But it may be asked: Why did Paul use the feminine form and the masculine form the same Greek word? If 1 Timothy 5:1–2 is simply speaking of "older" or "elderly" men and women," then the same should be true of every other instance where the word is used. In the eight instances of these interrelated Greek words (as seen in the chart), is Paul referring sometimes to age, and other times to an office in the church? If so, then his usage is inconsistent. If so, then he was referring to male elders (*presbuteros/roi*) in 1 Timothy 4:14; 5:17, 19; and Titus 1:5; to older men (*presbuteros*) in 1 Timothy 5:1; and to older women (*presbutera*) in 1 Timothy 5:2. And if this is so, then Paul uses the same Greek word for two different purposes: one to express age, and one to signify an office in the church.

It is certain that Paul knew the proper word forms to use, including when gender distinctions were desired. He uses the masculine Greek word *presbuteros* for the male elders and the feminine Greek word *presbutera* for the female elders. If the use of the Greek word here does not refer to female elders, then how can we interpret the same Greek word as referring to male elders? Consistency is necessary for a proper exegesis of Scripture.

Can there be women elders, or presbyters? According to Paul, male and female presbyters are of equal validity. He instructs Timothy to deal with any elders, male or female, who are teaching false doctrine, and to entreat them as fathers and mothers in the Lord as he does so.

In the Old Testament, there was a prophet, a judge, and a mother in Israel by the name of Deborah. (See Judges 4:4; 5:7.) So, we have the same implication in Titus 2:2, as well as 1 Timothy 5:2, where both the "older men" and the "older women" are told how to behave. These women in Titus are told to *"teach the young women,"* which indicates that they are in a senior role—one that would have been appropriate for female elders, given their charge to teach and to serve as examples to the younger women.

One of the biggest objections to women serving as elders is 1 Timothy 3:1–7, where Paul emphasizes the maleness of elders or bishops by using male nouns and pronouns at least ten times:

> *This is a true saying, if a **man** desire the office of a bishop, **he** desireth a good work. A bishop then must be blameless, the **husband** of one wife, vigilant, sober, of good behavior, given to hospitality, apt to teach; not given to wine, no striker, not greedy of filthy lucre; but patient, not a brawler, not covetous; one that ruleth well **his** own house, having **his** children in subjection with all gravity; (for if a **man** know not how to rule **his** own house, how shall **he** take care of the church of God?) Not a novice, lest being lifted up with pride **he** fall into the condemnation of the devil. Moreover **he** must have a good report of them which are without; lest **he** fall into reproach and the snare of the devil.*
>
> (1 Timothy 3:1–7)

There are many who, based on this passage, insist that elders must be male, and women cannot be elders—end of discussion.

In this and other passages where the qualifications of elders are set out, there is, admittedly, an emphasis on the male gender:

- Elder/bishop must be the husband of one wife—1 Timothy 3:2; Titus 1:6

- Elder/bishop must be a father of obedient children—1 Timothy 3:4; Titus 1:6

- Elder/bishop must have his house in order—1 Timothy 3:4

- The wife must be in subjection to the husband—Ephesians 5:20–23; 1 Peter 3:1, 5–6

- The wife must not usurp authority over the man (her husband)—1 Timothy 2:12

Citing these passages, in conjunction with Paul's teachings in Ephesians, 1 Peter, and 1 Timothy on female submission, certain people make the argument that elders *must* be male, never female.

But if these passages are to be interpreted as meaning that an elders must be a man, then the implication is that an elder also must be a married man, and that he must have children. If Paul's words are taken in this way, then there in our churches many ministers and elders functioning outside of scriptural order, because they either are not married or do not have any children.

But how many expositors would make this argument? Very few, or so we would hope.

A better interpretation of these Scripture is as follows: *If* a man is an elder (or a bishop), then he must exhibit Christian character, some qualities of which are listed in 1 Timothy 3:1–7. *If* he is married, then his wife must exhibit Christian character; *if* he has children, then they should be well-behaved.

This interpretation allows the Scriptures to apply to female elders, as well. *If* a woman is an elder, then she must exhibit Christian character, as should all Christians. *If* she is married, then she must be subject to "one husband"; *if* she has children, then they should be well-behaved.

The Christian home should be in divine order, so that the church—God's house—may be in divine order. The church is a reflection of the home! Homes out of order mean churches out of order, as both are linked.

Whether God's house is governed by male or female elders, it should be in order. The church consists of homes that have come together before God.

Dr. Jack Hayford writes, "Are there women elders? According to 1 Timothy 5:2, unquestionably yes. The feminine form the noun *Presbuteros* (*presbutera*) is employed, and it is clear that the mere matter of age is not in view." So, *if* God calls, equips, anoints, and appoints certain persons to be elders, then He may appoint men or women, according to His will.

Historical Evidences from the Early Church

We conclude this chapter with some interesting data from church history that confirms some of the things we have noted.

Make no mistake: Our foundation of faith and practice is the inspired Scriptures rather than church history. But there is much wisdom to be gleaned from church history when we study that which was learned by the believers who have gone before us as they grappled with various church issues. History can confirm what is scriptural, or it can expose the decline from what is scriptural. We may learn from the negative as well as the positive.

For example, in the Pentecostal Church, the practice of speaking in tongues, along with the use of spiritual gifts, has been based on the scriptural accounts in the book of Acts and Paul's teaching in 1 Corinthians. (See Acts 2; 8; 10–11; 19; 1 Corinthians 12–14.) But church history also confirms the validity of speaking in tongues, as well as the operations of the other spiritual gifts, in the writings of such early historians as Eusebius, Justin Martyr, Irenaeus, Tertullian of Carthage, John Chrysostom, and Augustine of Hippo; and, later, in the ministries of John and Charles Wesley, for example, or the Azusa Street Revival in Los Angeles.

These things are not based on church history but are simply confirmed by it. The truth is built on the Scriptures, because the Scriptures *are* the truth.

The same principle is true concerning the issue of women in ministry—specifically, women serving as elders. While the Pauline writings include two Scriptures that may point to the existence of female elders, history confirms the fact that female presbyters were, in fact, recognized and accepted in the early church, as we will soon see. There is evidence from the first, second, and third centuries of women's involvement in the areas of ministry and leadership in the church, including the forms of preaching and teaching, according to their God-given gifts. It was not until the fourth century that women began to be excluded from church leadership.

The early churches were governed by eldership—a lead elder who served along with other elders. In time, the role of "bishop" rose above that of the "elders," even though the terms originally signified one and the same person. Gradually, the churches transitioned to being governed by a bishop, to whom the elders were subjected.

According to Earle E. Cairns:

Practical and theoretical necessities led to the exaltation of one bishop's [or one overseer's] position in each church until people came to think of him and to acknowledge him as superior to the other elders with whom his office had been associated in New Testament times. The need of leadership in meeting the problems of persecution and heresy was a practical need that dictated an expansion of the bishop's power. The development of the doctrine of apostolic succession…[was] an important factor in his rise to power.

And Justo L. Gonzalez:

It is clear that by the end of the second century the official leadership of the church was entirely masculine. But the matter is not quite as clear in earlier times. Particularly in the New Testament, there are indications that women also had positions of leadership. Philip had four daughters who "prophesied"—that is, who preached. Phoebe was a female deacon in Cenchreae, and Junia was counted among the apostles. What actually seems to have taken place is that during the second century, in its efforts to combat heresy, the church centralized its authority, and a by-product of that process was that women were excluded from positions of leadership.

The following are some additional historical evidences of women in church leadership positions.

1. Pliny, writing to the Emperor Trajan (AD 100), said the two ministers of the church in his city were young women.

2. Justin Martyr, who lived till about ad 150, says, in his dialogue with Trypho, the Jew, "that both men and women were seen among them who had the extraordinary gifts of the Spirit of God, according as the prophet Joel had foretold."

3. Dodwell, in his dissertations on Irenaeus says, "that the gift of the spirit of prophecy was given to others besides the apostles; and, that not only in the first and second, but in the third century—even to the time of Constantine—all sorts and ranks of men had these gifts; yea, and *women* too."

4. Eusebius speaks of Potomania Ammias, a prophetess, in Philadelphia, and others, "who were equally distinguished for their love and zeal in the cause of Christ."

5. Tertullian, one of the earliest of the Latin fathers, notes that women appear in every early reference to ecclesiastical orders. Four titles, he writes, "are applied to the women clergy, all of which occur in the New Testament, 'Widow,' 'Deaconess,' 'Presbyter,' 'Virgin.'" "The two former," he adds, "are Apostolic orders."

6. Marcella preached Christianity publicly in Rome, and Jerome (born about AD 340, and the translator of the Latin Vulgate Bible), writes of her: "all that I learn with great study…the blessed Marcella learnt also but with great facility." He also celebrates her immense influence for good in Rome.

7. In the Catacombs are found representations of women clergy, and they are shown presiding at the Lord's Supper….

8. Mabillon, a French writer on ecclesiastical biography and antiquities, records that the evangelisation of Europe was due in great part to the Nuns of St. Benedict, many of whom publicly preached the gospel.

9. Among the Montanists,...who were the evangelicals of the third
    century, Priscilla and Maximilla, ladies of rank, served as evan-
    gelists over a wide extent of country. Women were elected by the
    Montanists as Deacons, Pastors, President-Presbyters or Bishops.
    Opinions vary as to when the recognized order of women clergy
    died out. All agree that it lingered longer in the East than in the
    West.... "It seems," says the writer, "as if the decay of women's
    ministry took place with the decay of Christianity, the rise of
    the Roman Apostasy, and the proud pretensions of an exclusive
    priesthood."

Dr. Gary S. Greig made the following comments about women in eldership positions:

> G. <u>Were women among the elders of the early church?</u> If <u>Debo-
> rah</u> as a female judge was included with men under the <u>masculine
> plural Hebrew title "judges"</u> (Heb. masc. plural shofetim) in Ju.
> 2:16, and <u>Phoebe</u> and other women were included with men under
> the <u>masculine Greek title</u> diakonos in Rom. 16:1 and I Tim. 3:8
> and 11, and <u>Junia</u> was included with Andronicus and other men
> under the <u>plural Greek title</u> "apostles" (Grk. masc. pl. dative **apos-
> tolois**) in Rom. 16:7, then it is not inconceivable that <u>women were
> included with men</u> under the <u>masculine plural Greek title</u> "elders"
> in the early church.
>
> 1. In I Timothy 5:1–2 Paul mentions "female elders" (pres-
>   buterai) alongside "male elders" (presbuteroi). Translators
>   often assume that the passage is only referring to "older
>   men" and "older women," but Paul uses the same word in
>   the masculine form of the church office of "elder" later on
>   in the same chapter—I Tim. 5:17, 19. It is hard to imagine
>   the same word being used in the same chapter with two
>   unrelated meanings. The fact that the masculine form of
>   the word denotes the office of "elder" in I Tim. 5:17, 19
>   suggests that the same word in its masculine and feminine
>   forms also refers to, or at least includes reference to, the
>   office of elder in 5:1–2.

2. There is clear archaeological evidence that in the post-biblical early church there were women elders alongside the male elders (D. Irvin, "The Ministry of Women in the Early Church: The Archaeological Evidence," Duke Divinity School Review 2 [1980]:76–86):

   a. Egypt: A 2nd–3rd century inscription refers to a woman named "Paniskanes" as a presbutera "**female elder**."

   b. Egypt: 3rd century Bishop Diogenes set up a memorial to a woman named "Amonnian the **female elder** (presbutera)."

   c. Rome: The 4th century Basilica of Prudentiana and Praxedis contains a mosaic including a woman referred to as "**Bishop** Theodora" (episcopa Theodora).

In the light of all this, it is evident that women did hold the office of elder and fulfill the ministry of eldership in the early church.

If women are called and gifted by the Lord in any of the fivefold ascension-gift ministries, then they may be called to be presbyters—female elders, or older women who are mothers in the church, even as older men may serve as fathers in the Lord.

The Council of Laodicea (AD 363)

It is worth noting that it was in the Council of Laodicea that the role of women in ministry and leadership was eliminated. As Jessie Penn-Lewis writes, "'Women sat unveiled in the assemblies in a separate place, by the presbyters,' and were 'ordained by the laying on of hands' until the Church Council of Laodicea forbade it in AD 363, three hundred years after Paul had written the Epistle to the Corinthians."

More from Gary Greig:

In about 363 AD the Council of Laodicea (Nicene and Post-Nicene Fathers, Series II, Vol. XIV [Grand Rapids: Eerdmans, 1971–1980]) stopped the practice, which was common until then, of appointing **"elder women"** (presbutides) to positions of leadership in the Church. The words of the Council prohibition suggest these elder women taught both men and women: <u>Council of Laodicea, Canon XI</u> "In old days certain **elder women** (presbutides) sat in Catholic churches, and took care that the other women kept good and modest order. But from their habit of using improperly that which was proper, either through their arrogancy or through their base self-seeking, scandal arose. Therefore the Fathers prohibited the existence in the Church thereafter of any more such women as are called presbytides or presidents. And that no one may object that in the monasteries of women one woman must preside over the rest, it should be remembered that the renunciation which they make of themselves to God and the tonsure brings it to pass that they are thought of as one body though many; and all things which are theirs, relate only to the salvation of the soul. But for women to teach in a Catholic Church, where a multitude of men is gathered together, and women of different opinions, is, in the highest degree, indecorous and pernicious."

Regretfully, it seems that many translators of the Scriptures were—and are—influenced by their own "theology" (what they believe God and Paul said about women), or their own bias toward the opposite sex in ministry and leadership, as well as by Judaism, and corrupted or twisted translations of God's Word. All this has helped to create greater bias in men against women filling leadership roles in the church.

Yet this is a day of restoration in the church. Women's God-given roles, functions, and ministries in the church, especially in areas of leadership, are expanding throughout the earth. God said through His prophet Joel that He would pour out His Spirit on *"all flesh"* in these last days—and *"all flesh"* includes "sons and daughters," "young men and old men," and "servants and handmaidens." (See Joel 2:28.)

Both men and women, if ordained as elders, should have:

1. The Christian character qualities of eldership, and

2. The ministry of eldership

It is not only who an elder is, but what an elder does, that makes him or her an elder. The "who" has to do with character; the "what" has to do with ministry. Both character and ministry are required for effective functioning.

Paul's redemptive word is applicable in these things. *"There is neither male nor female: for ye are all one in Christ Jesus"* (Galatians 3:28). *"Christ is all, and in all"* (Colossians 3:11)—men *and* women! Creation and redemption are brought as one in Christ. In creation, God meant for the man and the woman to function and rule together over creation. Redemption's plan is to restore both men and women back to that from which they fell, but to a greater and more glorious state.

One final quotation of interest, relative to the Jewish synagogue in Smyrna, from the notable Professor Ramsay:

> The honours and influence which belonged to women in the cities of Asia Minor form one of the most remarkable features in the history of the country. In all periods the evidence runs on the same lines. On the border between fable and history we find the Amazons. The best authenticated cases of Mutterrect [the matriarchate] belong to Asia Minor. Under the Roman Empire [in Asia Minor] we find women magistrates, presidents at games, and loaded with honours. The custom of the country influenced even the Jews, who in at least one case appointed a woman at Smyrna to the position of archisynagogos [chief of the synagogue].

In Conclusion

This chapter has presented the possibility of both men and women being called to be apostles, prophets, evangelists, shepherds, teachers, deacons, and elders.

The cessationist school rejects this possibility. Various other schools reject female apostles, prophets, and elders. Some schools accept women as evangelists, shepherds, and teachers but not as elders, while others accept females to serve as deacons only. And some schools accept women serving in some area of leadership, as long as it is not one of the fivefold ascension-gift ministries or eldership.

The position presented here is that the Lord may use men and women in any of these ministries, as He wills, on the redemptive basis that "in Christ" there is neither male nor female in the functioning body of Christ. (See Galatians 3:28.)

The general view of the Pentecostal Church is that all fivefold ascension-gift ministers are qualified elders, by reason of their calling, but all elders are not fivefold ascension-gift ministers. Some people in the Pentecostal movement hold that the fivefold ascension-gift ministries are all instances of eldership, and that there are no elders apart from them.

Peter, John, the rest of the twelve, and Paul are all seen as "elders" in the New Testament. (See 1 Peter 5:1–5; 2 John 1; 3 John 1.) The twenty-four elders in Revelation—or, at the very least, twelve of them—are seen as apostle-elders.

If either of the views above is held as true, then any man or woman gifted with an ascension-gift ministry is also a potential elder within the local church, in the body of Christ.

Once again, the issue of women serving in public ministry will not reach complete resolution until Christ returns. Every leader has to settle in his or her own mind which view corresponds most closely with Scripture, and adopt a Christlike attitude toward those whose beliefs differ.

23

WHAT ABOUT ORDINATION?

Related to all that has been considered in chapter 22 is the matter of ordination. Is ordination, as performed in various denominations, a scriptural rite? Is it a scriptural necessity to be fulfilled prior to any man or woman called of God beginning to minister? And should women be ordained, or not? This is a burning issue in many places in our generation.

A study of this subject will show that the rite of ordination, as it is practiced today, differs vastly from New Testament times. The word has fallen into ecclesiastical terminology that is foreign to apostolic times. Unscriptural concepts and practices have become a stumbling block in the mind of many of God's people. Such questions as these are often asked: "Are you ordained?" "Who ordained you?" "Have you received a Certificate of Ordination yet?" In many places, a person cannot perform certain religious services and functions unless he or she is "ordained"—whatever that may mean.

The practice of ordination needs to be subjected to the "Jeremiah principle." False ideas and misconceptions that have developed over the years need to be "rooted out, pulled down, plucked up, and destroyed" before one can "build and plant" biblical truth. (See Jeremiah 1:10.)

A. Definition

It is important to establish a clear definition and understanding of words if we are to reach a sound exegesis of Scriptures relating to the matter of ordination.

1. **Collins Dictionary**

   Ordain: "to set in order or arrange; to degree, appoint, establish, institute; to set apart for an office."

   Ordained: "settled; established; instituted; invested with ministerial or pastoral functions."

2. **Webster's American Dictionary of the English Language**

   Ordain: "properly, to set; to establish in a particular office or order; hence, to invest with a ministerial function or sacerdotal power; to introduce and establish or settle in the pastoral office; as, to ordain a minister of the gospel. In America, men are ordained over a particular church and congregation, or as evangelists without the charge of a particular church, or as deacons in the Episcopal Church.

   Ordained: "appointed; instituted; established; invested with ministerial or pastoral functions; settled."

   For example, Jesus *"ordained twelve, that they should be with him"* (Mark 3:14).

3. **Greek Dictionary**

   The word *ordained* is used in a variety of ways. There are, however, only two or three Greek words that really are relative to what we are studying.

   > *Kathistémi* (STRONG 2525), meaning "to place down (permanently), i.e. (figuratively) to designate, constitute, convoy—appoint, be, conduct, make, ordain, set." And so, in Acts 6:3, the deacons were chosen by the people and appointed by the apostles, *"whom we may appoint over this business...."*

   > o Paul tells Titus to *"**ordain** [kathistémi] elders in every city"* (Titus 1:5).

o The Old Testament *"high priest* [was] *taken from among men* [and] *is* **ordained** [kathistémi] *for men in things pertaining to God..."* (Hebrews 5:1).

o The *"high priest is ordained* [kathistémi] *to offer gifts and sacrifices..."* (Hebrews 8:3).

› *Cheirotoneó* (STRONG 5500), meaning "to be a hand-reacher or voter (by raising the hand), i.e. (generally) to select or appoint—choose, ordain."

o *"They had* **ordained** [cheirotoneó]*...elders in every church"* (Acts 14:23).

o Timothy was *"***ordained** *the first bishop of Ephesus"* (Timothy Postscript).

o Titus was *"***ordained** *the first bishop of Crete"* (Titus Postscript).

› *Tithémi* (STRONG 5087), meaning "to place (in the widest application, literally and figuratively; properly, in a passive or horizontal posture....)"

o Paul was *"***ordained** [tithémi] *a preacher"* (1 Timothy 2:7).

o Paul was *"***appointed** [tithémi] *a preacher"* (2 Timothy 1:11).

In its simplest Greek definition, the word *"ordain"* means "to select, to appoint, to choose, to set in place," in some cases by the act of a hand being stretched out, reached out, or raised. Thus, deacons and elders were "ordained by the laying on of hands," sometimes accompanied by fasting. (See Acts 6:1–6; 14:23; Titus 1:5.)

Under the old covenant, priests in the tabernacle or temple were chosen, selected, and appointed to their priestly functions and ministrations by the laying on of hands of the tribes of Israel on the tribe of Levi. (See Numbers 8:9–22; Hebrews 5:1; 8:3.) The Levites were ordained to priestly services on behalf of the whole nation of Israel. It was a simple yet beautiful service without any of the religious trappings that are found in some of the major denominations of our day.

Over the centuries, however, the church declined and instituted ordination rites and ceremonies that were not part of God's design for the New Testament church, such as the elaborate ritualism, pomp, and ceremonialism involved in the ordination of bishops, archbishops, and cardinals in the Catholic Church.

Many Protestant and Pentecostal denominations enforce the position that no person may minister fully unless officially ordained by the laying on of hands of "superior" authorities in the church, which shows the institutionalization of the church that took place with the passing of the original apostles. This subtle form of "apostolic succession," marked by an official ceremony or rite of ordination, is contrary to New Testament teaching and language.

As Alexander Strauch points out:

The word ordination is another example of misleading terminology that needs reform. Just as there is no way to use the words clergy or bishop without misleading God's people, there is no proper way to use the word ordination without creating misconceptions. Although ordination is accepted ecclesiastical terminology, it needs to be questioned because it creates false concepts in the listeners' minds. Until such unscriptural terminology is removed, it will be difficult—if not impossible—to adopt genuine, apostolic Christianity.

Even well-known Bible scholars who support clerical ordination say the New Testament's vocabulary speaks only of general appointment—never of a special ordination rite. For example, Leon Morris says: "Considering the role played by the ministry throughout the history of the church, references to ordination are surprisingly few in the N.T. Indeed, the word 'ordination' does not occur, and the verb 'to ordain' in the technical sense does not occur either. A number of verbs are translated 'ordain' in AV. But these all have meanings like 'appoint.'"

In similar fashion, Alfred Plummer makes the following remarkable comments on the Greek word for *"ordain"* in Titus 1:5:

In the A.V. the phrase runs "ordain elders in every city."....There are several passages in which the Revisers have changed "ordain" into "appoint." [See Mark 3:14; John 15:16; 1 Timothy 2:7; Hebrews 5:1; 8:3.] In these passages three different Greek words [poieo, tithemi, kathistemi] are used in the original; but not one of them has the special ecclesiastical meaning which we so frequently associate with the word "ordain"; not one of them implies, as "ordain" in such context almost of necessity implies, a rite of ordination, a special ceremonial, such as the laying on of hands. When in English we say, "He ordained twelve," "I am ordained an apostle," "Every high priest is ordained," the mind almost inevitably thinks of ordination in the common sense of the word; and this is foisting upon the language of the New Testament a meaning which the words there used do not rightly bear. They all three of them refer to the appointment to the office, and not to rite or ceremony by which the person appointed is admitted to the office....The Greek words used in the passages quoted might equally well be used of the appointment of a magistrate or a steward. And as we should avoid speaking of ordaining a magistrate or a steward, we ought to avoid using "ordain" to translate words which would be thoroughly in place in such a connexion. The Greek words for "ordain" and "ordination," in the sense of imposition of hands in order to admit to an ecclesiastical office...do not occur in the New Testament at all.

It is what the term "ordination" has become in the minds of many Christians (let alone the minds of worldly people) over the centuries that raises questions as to who can be ordained. Is ordination for men only, or may women be ordained? The answer depends on one's concept and understanding of ordination.

And again, "ordination" has been seen as the only way to secure a position of rule and authority in the church. This and other false concepts of ordination are the cause of much debate as to whether women should be ordained.

Stripping "ordination" of the unscriptural mysticism, trappings, and ritualism that have been applied to it over the centuries, we do believe that "appointment" in the church is in harmony with God's Word. We do believe that "ordination" is in harmony with God's Word.

Ordination, then, is simply recognizing, accepting, and receiving those whom God has gifted—men and women—in the areas of ministry or leadership, whether in the ascension-gift ministries or as elders or deacons. It is the church leadership and the congregation who appoint those whom God anoints. On the divine side, true ordination, or appointment, is of the Lord Himself. On the human side, ordination or appointment is a recognition by men and women of this divine gift in their fellow believers.

In both the Old Testament and the New Testament, church leadership was chosen either by God (divine sovereignty) or by God acting through man (human responsibility).

Examples of Individuals Appointed to Leadership Through Divine Sovereignty

+ Abraham—Genesis 12:1–3; Acts 7:1–4

+ Moses—Exodus 3

+ Samuel—1 Samuel 3

+ David—1 Samuel 16:12

+ Elijah—1 Kings 17

+ Jeremiah—Jeremiah 1

+ Ezekiel—Ezekiel 1

+ John the Baptist—John 1:6, 35–51

+ The Twelve—Mark 3:14; Luke 6:12–16

+ Miriam—Exodus 15:20; Numbers 12:4–5

+ Deborah—Judges 4:4

+ Huldah—2 Kings 22:14

+ Anna—Luke 2:36

Examples of Individuals Appointed to Leadership Through Human Responsibility

+ Aaron and the Levitical tribe of priests, by Aaron—Exodus 28–29; Numbers 1–4; 8

+ Joshua, by Moses—Numbers 27:15–27

- David, by Samuel—1 Samuel 16
- Elisha, by Elijah—1 Kings 19:15–19
- Deacons, by the apostles—Acts 6:1–6
- Timothy, by Paul—Acts 16:1–3; 1 Timothy 4:14; 2 Timothy 1:6
- Elders of the churches, by Paul and Barnabas—Acts 14:23; 20:17
- Ordaining elders, by Titus—Titus 1:5

While Acts 6:1–6 accounts for male deacons only, it seems evident, based on 1 Timothy, that, over time, female deacons were appointed to service in the church. The same assumption could be made regarding elders. Male elders were chosen in Acts (see Acts 14:23; 20:17), but 1 Timothy 5:1–2 points to female elders also chosen in time. The same principle is seen in the testing of prophets. Though the qualifications of a true prophet set out in Deuteronomy 18:18–20 apply to male prophets, they are also applicable to female prophets. Often, in Hebrew and Greek, the same word was applicable to both male and female.

B. Amplification

Lanny Hubbard, in his article "The Ordination of Women," writes:

> Titus 1:5 "For this cause left I thee in Crete; that thou shouldest set in order the things that are wanting, and ordain elders in every city, as I had appointed thee" (KJV).
>
> Of all the terms used for the act of ordination, this one most closely associates with this official process. The Greek word is kathistimi and means to conduct or to lead. It describes the process of leading someone to a place or state. It is also translated to appoint, or to put in charge, to assign someone a position of authority over others, to give someone authority.
>
> Vine qualifies this by saying that it is not a formal ecclesiastical ordination being addressed but an appointment for the recognition of the church. These are already people raised up and qualified by the Spirit with the evidence of such demonstrated in their lives. The action of ordination did not give them the abilities, but simply

pointed out for the church those that already were functioning in those giftings.

This is the term Paul uses for setting elders into their positions of authority in the church. The same word was used to describe the setting in of the high priest in the Old Testament to officiate over the spiritual lives of the nation, Hebrews 5:1, 7:28, 8:3. That whole occasion was very public including sacrifices, placing on of designated clothing, and imparting prayers. This is good counterpart for the setting in of New Testament leadership.

A passage to note is Acts 6:3. Here the leaders of the early church set in deacons for the ministry to the widows. These men qualified by being of honest reputation, and full of the Holy Spirit with wisdom. They were set in or ordained into this specific function. The position was known as a deacon. An interesting point is that the same word used for the setting in of an elder was also used for a deacon. The text does not designate a difference between them. So what went into the placing of an elder into office was similar in the placing of a deacon. This is an important point. If deacons experienced a type of recognition or ceremony to be placed in their position, and if this was similar to the process of placing an elder in his position, then is it fair to say that deacons experience an ordination?

Romans 16:1 presents us with a specific deacon in the early church. Her name was Phoebe. The text reads, "I commend to you Phoebe our sister, who is a servant [diakonos] of the church in Cenchrea...." Here was a woman holding the office of deacon. It appears that she was single, because no husband's name is mentioned. Paul places his approval and commendation of her. He tells the church at Rome to receive her and assist her with any needs she might have. She was recognized as a patroness, a protectress and a helper. She had been a benefit to the church as a whole, and to Paul personally. If she was a deacon, if deacons were ordained to their specific functions, then can we assume that she, a woman, was ordained? That is, that she would be recognized by the church, as having been placed into a functioning position. Was she ordained?

Therefore, if a woman has been called, equipped, qualified, and anointed of God to a ministry, whether an ascension gift, leadership, deaconship, or eldership, there is no Scripture forbidding her appointment—her ordination—in and by the church, following the scriptural precedent. Those who are appointed are those whom God has anointed. Ordination is simply a public recognition of the gifting and anointing on a man or a woman whom God has already placed in position.

C. *Ordination*

Having hopefully cleared away most of the false concepts of ordination or appointment to service in the church, the body of Christ, we now present a template of a simple service of public appointment, based on a number of pertinent Scriptures. The order of service could run as follows:

1. An appropriate song of consecration (e.g., "All to Jesus, I Surrender")

2. A profile confirming God's call on the person's life, character, and ministry, as recognized by the congregation

3. Scripture reading(s); some suitable passages would be Numbers 27: 15–27; Acts 6:1–6; 1 Timothy 3:1–7; 2 Timothy 4:1–8; Titus 1:5–9

4. Devotional word to new leader(s)

5. Questions and vows concerning calling, responsibility, devotion, home life, doctrine, and accountability, such as the following:

    › Do you believe God has called you to the ministry? If so, please say, "I do." ("I do.")

    › Do you accept the sacred Scriptures as inspired, infallible, and the final authority for all matters of faith and practice? If so, please say, "I do." ("I do.")

    › Will you, by the grace of God, seek at all times to live a consistent Christian life, both privately and publicly, and conduct yourself as behooves a minister of the gospel of Jesus Christ? If so, please say, "I will." ("I will.")

> Will you accept the responsibilities, privileges, and charge of the Christian ministry before these elders and congregation? If so, please say, "I will." ("I will.")

6. Giving of the charge, in sobriety, as all stand

   A charge given by Paul to Timothy, based on Numbers 27:15–23 and 1 Timothy 5:21:

   > "Brother/Sister _____, I charge you, before God and the Lord Jesus Christ, before the elect angels, and before this eldership and congregation, that you receive the authority in the church to perform the duties of an elder; to preach and teach the Word of God; to be instant in season and out of season; to reprove, rebuke, and exhort, with all longsuffering and doctrine; to administer the ordinances which Christ has ordained; to guard carefully the souls committed to your care; to live a godly life in thought, word, and deed, so that the ministry be not blamed; and to make full proof of your ministry. This charge I give you in the name of the Lord Jesus Christ."

7. The laying on of hands of the presbytery, demonstrating divine confirmation and impartation, as seen in Numbers 8:10–26; Deuteronomy 34:9; Acts 6:6; 13:3; 14:23; 1 Timothy 4:14–16; 2 Timothy 1:6.

8. Prayer of dedication over candidate(s)

9. Reception of candidate by church oversight and congregation

Conclusion

Ordination or appointment to public ministry is a recognition and acceptance of God's hand on a leader, whether male or female. However, it is not mandatory, either legally or ecclesiastically, to have an "ordination service" for an individual before he or she can start ministering. History has proven this to be so, for many ministers of the gospel—men and women alike—have done their work under God's recognition before the church ever recognized the call of God on their lives. If they had waited for the church to confirm their calling, they might never have done the will of God in serving their generation. But a double blessing is received in and by the church that ordains those whom God has already ordained!

24

WHAT ABOUT SUBMISSION
AND OBEDIENCE?

We return in this chapter to the issue of authority in the home and the church. Some would ask, for example, "Doesn't the Bible teach that the man is to be in charge, and that women have to submit to men?" "What about the teaching in Scripture that the woman is subject to the man, and that the women have to be subordinated to men as long as time shall last?" "What about male headship? Don't the Scriptures teach that man is the head of the woman, and the woman is to obey her husband?" "Isn't it true that the fall of mankind brought about the rule and dominion of the man over the woman, as a penalty the woman must pay for having brought sin into the world? (See Genesis 3:1–15.)"

Our search is to know what the Bible really teaches about these things. And in order for our search to be effective, we must first establish a definition of these oft-misused and misunderstood words: *submission*, *subjection*, *subordination*, and *headship*.

A. Definition of Key Terms

1. Submission

"act of submitting; act of yielding to power or authority; obedience;—state of being submissive; acknowledgment of inferiority or dependence; meekness...."

(*Submissive* is defined as "inclined or ready to submit; obedient; compliant; yielding; humble; modest; passive."

2. Subjection

"act of bringing under the dominion of another;—state of being under the control or government of another."

(*Subject* is defined as "one who or that which is placed under influence, operation or dominion in general.")

"Subjection" and "submission" come from the same Greek word, *hupotassó* (STRONG 5293), meaning "to subordinate; reflexively, to obey—be under obedience (obedient), put under, subdue unto, (be, make) subject (to, unto), be (put) in subjection (to, under), submit self unto."

3. Subordination

This word is not specifically used in the King James Version of the Bible. It is related to the meaning of the word *subjection*.

"act of subordinating, placing in a lower order, or subjecting;—state of being subordinate; inferiority of rank or dignity; subjection;—place of rank among inferiors."

(*Subordinate* [adjective] is defined as "placed in a lower class or rank;—holding a lower position;—inferior in order, in nature, in dignity, in power, importance, or the like." As a noun, it is defined as "one who stands in order or rank below another.")

4. Headship

Chapter 18 offered an in-depth treatment of this subject, so we will add only a few more comments in this chapter.

In 1 Corinthians 11:3–14, Paul uses the word *"head"* in both a literal and a metaphorical sense. It is used to indicate the literal or actual head, as part of the human body, as well as figuratively, to depict the relationship between a husband and his wife—for example, *"The head of a woman is her husband"* (1 Corinthians 11:3 RSV).

Let me emphasize that this verse does not teach that every man is the head of every woman. Rather, headship has to do with the relationship of a husband and wife—a marriage. It is not applicable to men and women in general, or in the church. It specifically teaches that a wife must be in right relationship with her covering, her "head"—her husband.

The word "*head*" is also used of Christ, the spiritual Head of man (and of woman, too). Christ is the spiritual Head of all believing men and women. Paul says that Christ is the Head of the church, His bride; and this church is composed of both men and women. (See Ephesians 5:23–33.) Believing men and women, including husbands and wives, are under Christ's headship. This headship is a spiritual covering, a spiritual source, and a spiritual authority. Christ is the Source of supply to every member of His body. (See Colossians 1:19; 2:9.) He is also the Authority over every believer, including single men and women (brothers and sisters in Christ).

How does Christ, as Head of the church, treat His bride, His wife? He does so with love, patience, compassion, and forgiveness. His is a loving headship. And love is to characterize the headship of men over their wives. Husbands are instructed to love their wives as they love themselves, and as Christ loves the church. (See Ephesians 5:25–29.) This is the headship of which the Scriptures speak. Headship, as seen already, is not the same thing as lordship. (See 1 Peter 5:3.) It is not the man domineering the woman, whether in the home or in the church. Male rule over the female came as a result of the fall. It was not God's command; it was what God said would happen because of sin. But, through Christ, believers move from the fall in creation to restoration in redemption.

5. Obedience

The Greek word for "*obey*" is *hupakouó* (STRONG 5219, from *hupo* [5259] and *akouó* [191]), meaning "to hear under (as a subordinate), i.e. to listen attentively; by implication, to heed or conform to a command or authority—hearken, be obedient to, obey." It is used some twenty-one times.

The word for *"obedience,"* *hupakoé* (STRONG 5218), means "attentive hearkening, i.e. (by implication) compliance or submission—obedience, (make) obedient, obey(-ying)" and is used some sixteen times.

Adam "submitted to" and "obeyed" his wife, Eve, by taking of the forbidden fruit she offered him. In doing so, he disobeyed God; because of this sin, the woman was subjected to the man, required to obey him. All this was a result of the fall. It was never God's original, perfect will. (See Romans 5:12–21.)

In Summary

The meaning of the above three words may be summarized in the following manner:

> *Submission* and *subjection* come from the same Greek word, meaning "to subordinate, be in subjection, be under obedience, submit oneself to another."

> Headship has to do with source, supply and spiritual covering, especially in the marriage relationship of husband and wife, and Christ and His church.

> Obedience has to do with attentive listening, taking heed of a command, obeying authority. It also includes submission.

B. *The Scriptures*

What, then, do the Scriptures teach concerning these things? Because the theme of submission and obedience is woven together throughout Scripture, we now provide an outline of relevant Scripture references. It will be seen that both men and women are to be in submission and obedience to God and Christ and to the Word of God. Right from the start, it should be remembered that:

+ Submission does not mean suppression.

+ Headship does not mean lordship.

+ Obedience is not indicative of oppression.

+ Subordination, from the Bible's viewpoint, does not imply inferiority.

We consider seven major relationships and their proper demonstration of submission and obedience.

1. God the Father and God the Son

In His incarnation, the Son of God, the Lord Jesus Christ—though co-equal with the Father and the Holy Spirit—came to a place of voluntary subordination to the Father in the plan of redemption. Yet the subordination of the Son did not imply His inferiority.

Jesus, the perfect Man, became the supreme example of submission and subjection to His Father's will. In His humanity, He subordinated Himself to the Father's commands. He learned obedience by the things He suffered in His earthly life. His obedience was voluntary, born out of love. God is the Head of Christ, and Jesus, in His humanity, came under God's headship for the purpose of redemption. As Jesus explained to His disciples, He came not to do His own will but the will of the Father who sent Him. (See John 5:30; 6:38–39.)

Christ Jesus is the supreme example of biblical submission, subordination, and obedience. (See Luke 2:51; Hebrews 5:8; John 5:30; 6:38; 1 Corinthians 11:3; 15:27–29.) It is these qualities, as He demonstrated them, that the Father God desires to see believers emulate in the home and in the church.

2. The Lord Jesus and Angels

Since Christ Jesus has ascended and been glorified in heaven, He is seated at the Father's right hand, and the Father has made all angels, principalities, and powers subject to Him. (See 1 Peter 3:22.) The angels submit to and obey the Lord Jesus Christ. They do His will, His bidding. They are ministering spirits sent to the heirs of salvation at the will of the Father and Son, as is seen in the many references in the books of Acts, Hebrews, and Revelation to the angelic ministry. Angels are ministering spirits sent forth by the

Lord Jesus to those who are heirs of salvation. (See Hebrews 1:1–13; Luke 16:22.) Angels understand what it is to be subject to the Father and Son, and they delight in doing the Father's will. Satan, and the other angels who rebelled with him, refused to submit to the Father and Son, and history shows the tragic results of their insubordination and rebellion.

3. Husband and Wife

Paul deals heavily with the theme of submission and obedience as it relates to home life, specifically in the marriage relationship. He teaches, *"Wives, submit yourselves unto your own husbands"* (Ephesians 5:22; Colossians 3:18). He tells wives that they are to be *"obedient to their own husbands"* (Titus 2:5; see also 1 Corinthians 14:34) and that they must submit to their own husbands *"as it is fit in the Lord"* (Colossians 3:18). The wife is to be under the headship, covering, and loving protection of her husband. Again, in Christ, subordination is not inferiority but an expression of co-equality as persons before God. It involves voluntary, mutual submission born out of love.

Peter confirms the same in 1 Peter 3:1–7. Wives are to be obedient to their own husbands, just as Sarah obeyed Abraham, calling him "lord" (or "sir"). However, it should also be remembered that God told Abraham, on one occasion, to obey his wife. (See Genesis 21:12.) Thus, we see in their example a mutual respect and obedience under God.

In these Scriptures, both Paul and Peter are talking about the relationship between husband and wife. They are talking about married women, not unmarried, or celibates. It is a marriage order, not a church order. In other words, not all women are subject to all men at all times and in all places.

The wife is to reverence or respect her husband. The husband is to love his wife just as he loves himself, and as Christ loves the church. Some six times, Paul uses the word "love" in relation to the husband's responsibility to his wife. If the husband loves his wife in this way, then it is easy for the wife to submit and obey his commands as an expression of love and care, not a response to control or suppression. (See Ephesians 5:23–33.) For many, the idea of submission has come to mean the suppression of the wife. Headship has become lordship. But husband and wife are co-equal as persons, and there is to be mutual submission in the home.

Note that Paul qualifies biblical submission and obedience with the phrase *"in the Lord."* Absolute submission and subjection are first of all to the Lord, the Savior and Sanctifier. If a husband commands his wife to do anything that is morally wrong, the wife should not submit and obey his evil commands.

4. Parents and Children

> *Children, obey your parents in the Lord: for this is right. Honor thy father and mother; which is the first commandment with promise; that it may be well with thee, and thou mayest live long on the earth.* (Ephesians 6:1–3)

> *Children, obey your parents in all things: for this is well pleasing unto the Lord.* (Colossians 3:20)

As long as they are living beneath their parents' roof, children are under parental authority and must submit to and obey their parents—father and mother—*"in the Lord."* Yet if either parent asks the children to do anything that is contrary to biblical morality and Christian conduct, then the children are not obligated to submit and obey. They should submit to the highest authority and obey God, regardless of the consequences, as did the apostles when they said, *"We ought to obey God rather than men"* (Acts 5:29).

5. Employer and Employee

The theme of submission and obedience is seen also in the teachings of both Paul and Peter on slaves and their masters, with a modern-day application to employees and their employers.

Servants are to be *"obedient unto their own masters"* (Titus 2:9; see also 1 Peter 2:18; Colossians 3:22). Slaves are to be subject to their masters. (See Ephesians 6:5–6; 1 Timothy 6:1.) Paul exhorts all workers to do their jobs as unto the Lord, and he reminds Christian employers to remember that they also are under the same Master as their employees. (See Ephesians 6:7–9; Colossians 3:23.) Submission and obedience are required of employee and employer alike.

6. Citizen and State

All believers are actually citizens of two worlds: heaven and earth. As such, they are to submit to the state authorities, who are "ministers of God" (see Romans 13:4) and also to obey the laws of the land. If these laws conflict with the higher laws of God, then believers must submit to God and obey His laws—and suffer the human-enforced consequences, if necessary.

Peter says, "*Submit yourselves to every ordinance of man for the Lord's sake...*" (1 Peter 2:13). Paul says, "*Let every soul be subject unto the higher powers. For...the powers that be are ordained of God*" (Romans 13:1). We are to do this in order to have a clear conscience before God and man. (See Romans 13:5.) If the "powers that be" ask us to submit to laws that are contrary to God's higher laws, then "*we ought to obey God rather than men*" (Acts 5:29). Obeying God may require civil disobedience, whatever the end result may be.

7. The Church and Its Leaders

There is no question that God places leaders in the church. These leaders are to work together in love and mutual submission. Believers are required to be subject to the leadership—to submit themselves in obedience to their leaders "*in the Lord*" and in obedience to the Word of God.

The author of Hebrews puts it this way:

Remember them which have the rule over you [who are your guides], who have spoken unto you the word of God....Obey them that have the rule over you, and submit yourselves: for they watch for your souls, as they that must give account, that they may do it with joy, and not with grief: for that is

> *unprofitable for you....Salute* [greet] *all them that have the*
> *rule over you.*   (Hebrews 13:7, 17, 24)

In this passage, the leadership is referred to as *"them"*—not just one person but a plurality of leaders, or elders, along with a leading elder, who is the "first among equals."

In the church—God's spiritual house—the leaders are to work together in mutual submission, as are the believers under their leadership. All are subject to the Lord, yet Paul says, "[Submit] *yourselves one to another in the fear of the God"* (Ephesians 5:21; see also Philippians 2:3; Galatians 5:13; Romans 12:10). And Peter confirms the same. (See 1 Peter 5:5.)

It should be noticed that the theme of submission and obedience assumes a different tone in church life. Married women submit first of all to their own husbands. Unmarried women submit to their own parents, as do the children. But in what has been called "God's chain of command," husbands and wives together submit to the spiritual leaders in the church, as do their children, by implication of their submission to their parents. In the church, all are "brothers and sisters" in the family of God.

If a woman is gifted by the Lord in an area of ministry or leadership within the church, then there will be mutual submission between her and the leadership of that church body. God's general order is a leading elder (or a leading ministry) along with the team of leaders, who are in mutual submission one to another. But this type of submission should be evident in the body of Christ, in all its members. No one should seek to usurp authority over another, but all should work together as a team, or as fellow members of the body of Christ. All should act under authority as leaders, under the Lord and His Word. Christ is the Head of the church, and all must submit to Him and obey Him, as these sample Scriptures support:

> ›   "[Submit] *yourselves one to another..."* (Ephesians 5:21).
>
> ›   *"Ye younger, submit yourselves unto the elder* [presbuteros, plural]" (1 Peter 5:5).

> *"All of you be subject one to another..."* (1 Peter 5:5).

> *"The spirits of the prophets are subject to the prophets"* (1 Corinthians 14:32).

> *"The church is subject unto Christ"* (Ephesians 5:24).

The church is the bride of Christ, and she submits to and obeys her loving Husband, the Lord Jesus Christ. The church represents the subjective, the feminine, while Christ represents the objective truth, the masculine. This is true in creation and redemption.

Leaders are not to be *"lords over God's heritage"* (1 Peter 5:3). Paul told the Corinthian believers that he did not exercise lordship or *"dominion over your faith"* (2 Corinthians 1:24). Jesus warned His disciples very strongly about and against the spirit of the Gentile world that loves to have dominion and lordship, and to exercise authority, over the citizens under them. This spirit and attitude was not to be in the disciples of Jesus, nor was it to creep into the church. (See Mark 10:42–45.) Yet church history has revealed many instances of the dictatorial spirit seeping into its leaders. This is the spirit of *"Diotrephes, who loveth to have the preeminence"* (3 John 1:9–10) and to control everything and everybody

No human leader is the "head" of the church. Christ alone is Head of the church, and no leader should usurp His headship, or His place of authority. All should be submitted to the headship of Christ. (See 1 Corinthians 11:1–3; Ephesians 5:23–33.)

8. The Believer and God

All believers—men, women, and children—are ultimately under divine authority. All are to submit first of all to God, and obey Him. It is from God, through Christ, that the order of submission and obedience flows, down into our relationships and areas of life. Relationship is what life is all about.

"Submit yourselves therefore to God..." (James 4:7). Believers are to *"be in subjection unto the Father of spirits, and live"* (Hebrews 12:9), as the below diagram illustrates.

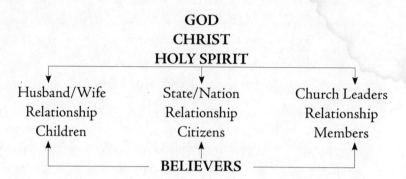

Conclusion

Christ came to earth to bring us back to the submission and obedience from which Adam and his bride fell. (See Romans 5:12–21.) He came to bring us to *"obedience and sprinkling of the blood of Jesus Christ"* (1 Peter 1:2).

Jesus came to restore, through redemption, the male/female joint relationship and joint rulership as originally intended in the garden of Eden. Sin has been a diversion and an interruption in the whole plan and purpose of God. Neither Jesus nor the apostles taught that women were subordinate or inferior to men. Nor did Jesus or the apostles ever teach that women could not serve the body of Christ in leadership or in ministry. In the home, the order is to be the husband and the wife engaged in loving submission and obedience. In the church, the order is to be all members mutually submitted to one another in loving submission and obedience under the church leadership and, ultimately, under Christ, the Head of the church. In redemption, no longer would it be that the man domineered and ruled over the woman, as he did because of the fall. Instead, together as believers, they would be partners sharing together, working together, in a loving relationship under God and His Christ.

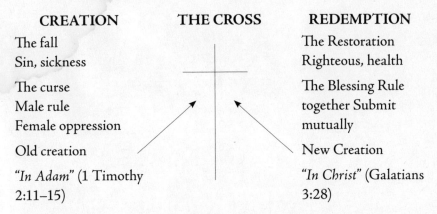

CREATION	THE CROSS	REDEMPTION
The fall		The Restoration
Sin, sickness		Righteous, health
The curse		The Blessing Rule
Male rule		together Submit
Female oppression		mutually
Old creation		New Creation
"In Adam" (1 Timothy 2:11–15)		*"In Christ"* (Galatians 3:28)

For those who invoke the concepts of submission and obedience to suppress women and to exclude them from participation in public ministry, and who misinterpret such Scriptures as 1 Corinthians 14:34–35, 1 Timothy 2:11–15, and Genesis 3:16 to demand the silence of women, we beseech another consideration of God's redemptive plan for both men and women; for *"there is neither male nor female...in Christ Jesus"* (Galatians 3:28).

25

WHAT ABOUT
CHURCH GOVERNMENT?

Undoubtedly, the greatest issue concerning the role and function of women in the church is that which pertains to females occupying governmental positions. The issues of ordination, submission, and obedience all relate to this question: Should a woman be in a governmental role in the church?

If God calls a woman to any of the fivefold ascension-gift ministries, or to be an elder, then her fulfillment of that calling will necessitate her occupying a position of rule and authority in the church. Is this valid, considering Paul's teaching on male elders in 1 Timothy 3?

Some denominations, breaking with the traditions of centuries, are ordaining female presbyters and ministers, publicly setting them in areas of church rule and governmental authority. But should just anyone—male or female—be able to exercise primary authority and rulership over a local church? Does not the idea of a woman exercising authority over men in the church run counter to Paul's warning about women usurping authority over men? (See 1 Timothy 2:11–15.) And so goes the debate over the role, function, and place of women in the church, as well as at home.

In this chapter, our approach will be to note the biblical forms of government that God has established in the earth. This will necessitate the establishment of a definition for several related words.

A. Definition of Key Terms

1. **Government:** "act of governing; exercise of authority; direction; regulation;—control; restraint;—system of polity in a state or community; mode in which legal authority is exercised;—territory over which rule is exercised; empire; kingdom; state; commonwealth;—administrative council or body; the executive power; the ministry."

   Govern: "to regulate by authority;—to influence; to direct; to manage; to keep in subjection; to restrain, as passion;—to steer, as a ship;...to exercise authority; to administer the laws; to have the control."

   Jesus is spoken of as *"Governor"* (Matthew 2:6), the Greek word for which is *hégeomai* (STRONG 2233), which means "to lead, i.e. command (with official authority)...judge, have the rule over." The same word is used of Joseph in Acts 7:10. The government is upon Jesus' shoulder. (See Isaiah 9:6–9; 22:21.) God has also set *"governments"* in the church. (See 1 Corinthians 12:28.) The word *"governments"* here refers to steering, piloting, and providing directorship. Without government in the earth, mankind would be in a state of lawlessness, anarchy, and resultant chaos.

2. **Lead:** "To show the way to; to conduct;—to guide by the hand, as a child or animal;—to direct, as a chief or commander;—to govern;...to exercise influence or authority."

   Leader: "A guide; a conductor;—a chief; a commander;—the chief of a party or faction."

   The Scriptures speak of the *"leader of the Aaronites"* (1 Chronicles 12:27). When David brought up the Ark of God, he consulted with the captains and *"every leader"* (1 Chronicles 13:1). David himself is spoken as being *"a witness to the people, a leader and commander to the people"* (Isaiah 55:4). The word *"leader"* means a commander, as occupying the front, civil, military or religious (STRONG 5057). God raises up people to be leaders in government. Jesus called the religious leaders of His day *"blind leaders of the blind"* (Matthew 15:14).

3. *Authority:* "Legal or rightful power to command or act; dominion;—influence of character, office, station;—mental or moral superiority, and the like; official declaration, opinion, or statement worthy to be taken as a precedent; a book that contains such...."

Authorize: "To clothe with authority, or legal power; to empower; —to legalize;—to establish by authority, usage, or public opinion."

Strong's Concordance defines the Greek word *exousia* (STRONG 1849) as "power, authority, weight, especially: moral authority, influence." Matthew 7:29 records that Jesus taught the people *"as one having authority."* (See also Luke 4:36.) And in Luke 9:1, it says that Jesus *"gave* [the twelve] *power and authority over all devils, and to cure diseases."* Government involves leadership; leadership implies vested authority.

B. Divine Forms of Government

An exhaustive study of biblical revelation on government shows that there are basically three forms of government God has established in the earth. We will give a brief consideration of each one as it relates to church government.

1. Government of Heaven—Supreme Authority

God is the supreme Governor of the universe. Divine authority is above all other authority, for all power belongs to God. He is the Supreme Being. There is none beside Him or before Him or above Him. All government is ultimately upon His shoulders, given by the Father to the Son. (See Isaiah 9:6–7; 22:21; Matthew 2:6.) All government belongs to God.

2. Government on Earth—Delegated Authority

Relative to creation and God's creatures, God has delegated authority on earth in three structures or forms: home government, civil government, and church government.

a. Government in the Home—Parental Authority

The first area where we see God's delegated authority is in the home. When God created Adam and Eve, He delegated authority to them, giving them dominion over all the earth—all creatures. They were commanded to be fruitful and multiply, filling the face of the earth with their offspring. As parents, they were to exercise authority in their home over their children. They were to lead and instruct their children in the ways of God, and their children were to honor and obey their parents. (See Deuteronomy 6:3–9; Exodus 20:12; Leviticus 19:3; Ephesians 6:2; Proverbs 6:20–23.) Together as husband and wife, father and mother, they would be partners, working together, sharing together, as a team together in the home. They would exercise authority under divine authority. There would be joint rulership by man and woman, husband and wife, father and mother. This was God's original intention, as seen in the book of Genesis.

In his epistles, Paul uses the natural house as a type of the spiritual house. In dealing with the qualifications of elders and deacons, he says that if a man does not know how to rule in his own house, he is unfit to rule in the house of God. (See 1 Timothy 3:5.) God's original intention was for man and woman to rule the household together, to govern the home together, to exercise authority together over their children.

Divine order places the man/husband/father as head of the home, with his wife submitting to his loving headship, even as the church (the bride of Christ) submits to His loving headship. The Head of the man is Christ, and the Head of Christ is God. The head of the woman is the man. It is simply a matter of divine order. Again, Adam and Eve were joint rulers together. Nothing alters the fact that God made the man first, and then the woman, but that, together, they had dominion over creation, and would rule and reign as king and queen. This is divine order, and this order was in place before the fall. Prior to the fall, man and woman were co-equal joint-rulers, having dominion over creation. There was, however, divine order of government in the home.

b. *Government in the Nation or State—Civil Authority*

Old Testament Israel is referred to as *"the church in the wilderness"* (Acts 7:38). Numerous features of the Old Testament church endure, in principle, in the New Testament church.

The prophet Isaiah lamented the failure of leadership and the breakdown of government, as God had established it, in the chosen nation of Israel. He decried the condition of the nation because of its leaders, and lamented the judgment of the Lord in the taking away of male leadership. The mighty man, the man of war, the judge, the prophet, the prudent, the ancient, the captain of fifty, the honorable man, the counselor, the cunning artificer, and the eloquent orator—all these were taken away because of divine judgment. (See Isaiah 3:2–3.) These were the men of the nation who were supposed to lead, guide, and govern the people of God, under God. In Isaiah 3:6–7, Isaiah refers to the men's refusal to accept their responsibility as rulers. What was the end result? God said, according to Isaiah, *"I will give children to be their princes, and babes shall rule over them....As for my people, children are their oppressors, and women rule over them"* (Isaiah 3:4, 12).

This was a great indictment against Israel, and certainly not a compliment from the Lord. The picture of children and *"babes"* in governmental positions spoke of immaturity and ignorance, and the idea of women ruling from positions of government because men had failed to fulfill their role and responsibility under God was equally distasteful. The prophet Ezekiel experienced a similar situation with false male and female prophets ministering to a deceived people. (See Ezekiel 13.)

But through it all, God always preserves for Himself faithful leaders, such as Isaiah and his wife, both prophets who served as a team. (See Isaiah 1:1–2; 8:1–3.) God preserved Jeremiah, Ezekiel, Daniel, and other leaders in the nation to speak the Word of the Lord.

God reminds the people through Micah, *"For I brought thee up out of the land of Egypt, and redeemed thee out of the house of servants* [bondage]; *and I sent before thee Moses, Aaron, and Miriam*" (Micah 6:4). The *New International Version* says, "*I sent Moses to **lead** you, also Aaron and Miriam.*" Moses was a leader, as a prophet. Aaron was a leader, as a prophet and a priest. Miriam was a leader, as a prophetess, a singer, and a worshipper.

God's government in Israel, over the centuries, was administered through priests, judges, kings, prophets, and elders of the nation. These were the spiritual leaders of the nation, and the nation rose and fell according to its leaders—those in authority. At times, God placed some prophetesses as leaders in the nation—women who spoke with the voice of God's authority—for example, Miriam and Huldah. God used men and women in roles of leadership and government in the nation of Israel.

As nations develop, in due time, there comes a need for some form of government. Nations develop, statehood arises, and delegated authority is vested in the rulers of these nations. Paul says of the Roman government, "*The powers that be are ordained of God*" (Romans 13:1). Jesus instructed His disciples to "*render therefore unto Caesar the things which are Caesar's*" (Matthew 22:21). The welfare of a nation depends largely on the form of government it is operating under, whether a democratic, dictatorial, or something else. But God has ordained that government is needed in every nation.

c. **Church Government—Eldership Authority**

The next area of delegated (and therefore limited) authority is the area of church government. God has set in the church "*governments*" (1 Corinthians 12:28). Again, the government is on the shoulders of Christ. (See Isaiah 9:6–9.) Christ is the Head of the church; He governs the church from the throne of His Father in heaven. He does this through ministers and elders, His appointed representatives.

God has set in the church apostles, prophets, evangelists, shepherds, and teachers, along with elders and deacons, to act as the governing body of leaders under Christ. (See Ephesians

4:10–16; 1 Corinthians 12:28.) He invests these leaders with degrees or measures of authority, according to their character, grace, gift, and anointing. It may be truly said that the measure of God-given ability is the measure of one's responsibility, which becomes the measure of authority, all of which becomes the measure of accountability.

Those who govern and lead the church are to do so as a team. Depending, of course, on the size of the congregation, the Lord has appointed team ministry. It is never to be the case that a single person governs the local church. The church is like the home, where father and mother are a plural authority, working together as a team. The Lord appoints elders, plural, to govern the church. This is why Paul speaks of *"them"* (Hebrews 13:7, 17, 24). We are to *"remember them," "obey them,"* and *"salute all them"* who have the rule over us, who are our spiritual guides.

Paul speaks of the elder who is, first of all, to be able to "rule over his own house" before he can "rule in the house of God." (See 1 Timothy 3:4, 5, 12; 5:17.) The word for "rule" in these verses is *proistemi* (STRONG 4291), meaning "to stand before, i.e. (in rank) to preside, or (by implication) to practice—maintain, be over, rule." It is leadership, rulership. Leadership is not lordship; it is not domineering the people of God. Christ is the Ruler and Leader of His church. He does not exercise domineering leadership in the governing of His church through the authorities He appoints.

Eldership is a team of elders working together. Church government/leadership is done by "the set man" (or the "first among equals") with the team of elders, as confirmed by the Old and New Testaments alike. (See Numbers 27:15–23.)

The Old Testament speaks of Moses and the elders, Joshua and the elders, David and the elders, and Ezekiel and the elders. The New Testament speaks of Peter and the eleven, James and the elders, Paul and the elders, Timothy and the elders, Titus and the elders, and, finally, the Lamb and the twenty-four elders. (See, for example, Acts 14:23; 16:4; 20:17;

1 Timothy 5:17–21; Titus 1:5; James 5:14; 1 Peter 5:1–5; Philippians 1:1.) It is never one person governing the church. The governing of the church is always found to be in the hands of the elders (plural), never with the one only (singular).

Men or women, according to their gifting by the Lord, may lead, guide, and govern the people of God according to the measure of divine grace given them. A number of women in Thessalonica are spoken of as *"chief women, not a few"* (Acts 17:4); the Revised Standard Version renders this phrase as *"not a few of the leading women."* The phrase is to be understood to mean "important, influential, prominent, or leading women." These were among the converts of Paul in that city.

As already discussed, Priscilla and Aquila were leaders over their house church. They were a team together, as husband and wife. (See Acts 18:18; Romans 16:3–5; 2 Timothy 4:19; 1 Corinthians 16:19.) It would appear that *"the elect lady"* to whom the apostle John wrote also led a house church. (See 2 John 1–13.) God uses both men and women to lead His church, as it pleases Him.

Below is a diagram showing the areas of divine government and earthly government.

```
                    ┌──────────────────────┐
                    │         GOD          │
                    │  Heaven's Government  │
                    │   Supreme Authority   │
                    └──────────────────────┘
```

HOME	NATIONAL	CHURCH
Government	Government	Government
Parental Authority	State Authority	Eldership Authority
Man/Woman	Legal	Ascension Gift
Husband/Wife	Social	Ministries
Father/Mother	National	Elders/Deacons
Children	Citizens	Congregation

The Issue of Governmental Authority

We have seen that God's government is supreme, over and above all. He is the supreme Authority. Then there is delegated authority, which God has set in the earth, among mankind. This authority is, therefore, limited authority. Unless each of the areas of delegated authority, as illustrated above, realizes the limited nature of its authority, there is the danger of usurped authority. Human history testifies abundantly to this problem, as the following examples illustrate.

+ Eve actually usurped (seized) authority over her own husband, Adam, when she took of the forbidden fruit and gave it to him. (See Genesis 3:1–16; 2 Corinthians 11:3; 1 Timothy 2:14–15.)

+ Jezebel usurped (seized) authority over her husband and king, Ahab, when she used his name and power to bring about the death of Naboth in order to possess his vineyard. (See 1 Kings 21.)

+ History exposes the nations where the state seized authority over the church, controlling and governing the church and its activities.

+ History also evidences where the church seized authority over the state, and the tragic results that ensued. Hence the "separation of church and state" in the United States.

+ History also shows where the church and/or the state seized authority over the home, usurping the authority of the parents over their children, and the devastating results that ensued.

+ Lucifer sought to usurp (seize) the authority of God in the realm of heaven, over the angels, and the damning results in the angelic realm were extensive. (See Isaiah 14:12–14; 2 Peter 2:4; Jude 6.)

+ Paul warns Timothy that a woman (let alone a man) is not to usurp (or seize) authority in the home or in the church over her husband, or over men in general. (See 1 Timothy 2:11–15.) The biblical principle applies to both areas.

National and ecclesiastical governments have been in conflict for centuries, and history has shown the damaging results of authority being seized in an unlawful manner. Such should not be done in the Christian home or in the Christian church.

Can a man exercise authority by governing in his home or in the church? Can a woman exercise authority by governing in the home or in the church? The answer is yes, on both counts, according to the measure of delegated/limited authority given a particular individual. Again, Paul's instructions to Timothy in 1 Timothy 2:11–15 do not forbid a woman to exercise authority. He is simply saying that a woman must not usurp, or seize, the authority over the man. And the same instructions apply to the men, as well. No man should usurp authority over another man any more than a woman should. Whether male or female, a minister or leader may exercise authority as long as he or she is under authority. Leaders are to act under authority, not seize authority. That is the real issue.

If a woman teaches other women or children, then she is exercising a measure of authority. If a mother disciplines her children while the father is away, then she is exercising authority in the home. After the father, the mother is next in line when it comes to an authority figure in the home. This is why the writer of Proverbs instructs children to honor their father and obey their mother. (See Proverbs 30:17.) Fathers and mothers together—not alone—exercise authority in the home over the children. Christian leaders, whether men or women, exercise a measure of authority in the church as they act under the authority of other church leaders, the elders in government, and, ultimately, God.

The order of governmental authority is, therefore, as follows:

1. Heavenly government—God, the supreme Authority in heaven and on earth (in the whole universe)

2. Delegated authority—given by God to men and women, according to His will and purpose

3. Home government—parental authority, father and mother ruling in the home together over the children

4. Civil government—national and state authority, enforced by governmental officials over the citizenship

5. Church government—ministry leaders, elders, and deacons, whether men or women, govern the church under Christ's ultimate headship and authority

6.   Rebel government—usurped authority, whether of fallen angels or lawless mankind

7.   Submitted government—under the government and authority of God and the Lord Jesus Christ

C. Government under God

Mankind has long been divided over the best form of government. From autocracy to bureaucracy to democracy, the various forms of human government have been ever in conflict. But what is God's will? God's will is theocracy. God raises up leaders, generally called elders, and sets them in order, that they might govern for Him. In any given group of elders, God generally places His mantle of leadership upon a leading elder, who serves with the rest of the team as "first among equals." For fuller treatment of this subject, please refer to my book *The Church in the New Testament*.

A Proposition

It is the position of this writer that both men and women may be involved in church government, leadership, and authority as they act under authority, according to the measure of grace-gifting and anointing that the Lord has given them. The ideal is a ministry team composed of men and women, led by a team leader. If a woman has been gifted with leadership, then her covering in the church is the elders in leadership; her covering at home is her husband. God's ideal is men and women serving His church together in unity and harmony.

The following are a number of examples from the Scriptures that set forth what we believe to be God's ideal for governmental authority, whether in the home or in the church. Men and women, in whatever area of leadership, should be under authority, submissive and obedient to those above them, and ultimately subjected to God.

+   In creation, the sun, the moon, and the stars are sometimes used as symbols of the components of the human family, with the sun representing the father, the moon representing the mother, and the stars representing the children. (See Genesis 1:14–16; Psalm 136:8–9.) The sun/father is to rule the day; the moon/mother is to rule the night as she reflects the light of the sun.

* The man who is an elder is to rule his house well, or else he cannot rule in the church, the house of God. (See 1 Timothy 3.) The same is true for deacons. (See 1 Timothy 3:4–5, 12, 15.) The natural points to the spiritual. Husbands and wives and children are to be in order in the home in order to be in order in the church, God's house.

* Christ, as the Husband and Bridegroom, rules over the church—His bride, His wife. He is the Ruler, and His bride is called to be a joint-ruler with Him. (See 1 Corinthians 11:3; Ephesians 5:23–33; Micah 5:2.)

* Male elders ruled in the Jewish synagogues, although there is a historic account of a female elder ruling in the synagogue at Smyrna. (See Luke 8:41, 49; 14:14; Acts 18:8.)

* The husband is the head of the house, the head of his wife. The wife is under the covering of male headship. (See 1 Corinthians 11:3.) The wife also exercises rule in the house over the children. It is a joint rule, with the husband leading the way. There is mutual love and submission in their leadership. (See 1 Peter 3:1–7.) This typifies the church, the wife of the Lamb, who is subject to the headship of Christ, her Husband. The church is under Christ's rule, yet she is called to also rule with Him. (See Ephesians 5:23–33.)

* The prophetess Miriam acted under the authority of her brothers Moses and Aaron. Together as a team, these three led the nation of Israel, but Moses was the senior leader and authority under God. Miriam was judged by the Lord for her critical spirit toward Moses. (See Numbers 12.)

* Deborah—a judge, prophetess, and mother in Israel—was a married woman, her husband's name being Lapidoth. (See Judges 4:4.) Deborah exercised influence and leadership in the nation of Israel, particularly in regard to Barak. The prophetic word she gave Barak was that he—as the man—should lead the battle against the enemy. Barak's faith was not enough, and he declined to go unless Deborah came with him. Even though Barak is mentioned among the heroes of faith in the eleventh chapter of Hebrews, it is evident

402 *The Ministry of Women*

that his faith was in the prophetic word of Deborah, a godly woman. As a man, Barak failed to rise to the occasion and take responsibility. So, Deborah reproved him, saying that the Lord would give the victory to a woman rather than to him, a man. Sure enough, God used a woman named Jael to smite the commander Sisera. Jael did not usurp authority; she was under the authority of God and of her husband, and it was under their authority that she led the way to victory when Barak would not do so. Deborah commended the governors of Israel who stood with her, even though she was a woman. (See Judges 4–5.)

+ Queen Esther, wife of King Ahasuerus, acted under authority of her cousin Mordecai's words and brought deliverance to the nation of Judah from the sword of death. (See the book of Esther.)

+ The prophetess Huldah was the wife of a man named Shallum, and she held a position of leadership, influence, and authority in the nation of Israel. Godly King Josiah, the high priest, and the princes of Israel were her council. These men recognized the mantle of the word of the Lord in her mouth, even though she was a woman. (See 2 Kings 22:11; 2 Chronicles 34.)

+ Isaiah's wife was called a prophetess, yet her husband was over her in the Lord. (See Isaiah 8:3.) Her covering and leadership was her husband, yet together, as husband and wife, they shared the ministry somehow.

+ The four women named in the genealogy of Christ in Matthew's gospel were all married, and their husbands are mentioned on the list, as well. These women were under the covering and headship of their husbands. (See Matthew 1.)

+ Philip's four daughters, gifted with prophecy, were under the covering and authority of their father, who was called the evangelist. (See Acts 21:9.)

+ Under the old covenant, any woman who made a vow needed to do so under the authority of her father or her husband; if either of those men deemed the vow unwise, he had the power to nullify it.

(See Numbers 30.) There was a covering, protection, and authority in the home for these situations.

+ Priscilla taught alongside her husband, Aquila, and was under his authority. They were a team together, as husband and wife. Most every reference to them lists Priscilla's name first, which intimates that she was the stronger teacher of the Word. (See, for example, Acts 18:18.)

+ Phoebe, the deaconess of the church of Cenchrea, acted under Paul's authority in her service to the church at Rome. She did not seize this authority, but she wielded authority as she also acted under it. (See Romans 16:1–2.)

+ Athaliah usurped authority over the throne of Judah and murdered all the royal seed in order to gain the throne. She recognized no male leadership as she usurped the authority in the nation, and the result was divine judgment. (See 2 Kings 11; 2 Chronicles 22.)

+ Wicked Queen Jezebel usurped authority over her husband, King Ahab, and brought about idolatry in the nation; she also ordered the death of Naboth to gain his vineyard for her husband's inheritance. Jezebel was a murderer who slaughtered the prophets of God while trying to kill the prophet Elijah. Ahab, her husband, was a weak, vacillating and wicked man. He came under divine judgment in due time, as did Jezebel. (See 1 Kings 21.)

+ The prophetess Anna was under the temple authorities. She lived a life of prayer and fasting in the temple chambers, the place where the priests of the Lord lived and served in their courses. She was recognized as a prophetic voice of her time, as evidenced in her words concerning the child Jesus. (See Luke 2:36–38.)

+ The woman Jezebel (some believe she was the wife of the "angelos" of the church at Thyatira) was a prophetess and teacher who usurped authority in the church. She taught idolatry and immorality, which was false teaching and absolutely contrary to the apostles' doctrine. (See Revelation 2:20.) If she was the wife of the senior leader, then she evidenced the characteristics of the wicked Queen Jezebel of the Old Testament. She controlled her husband just as Jezebel controlled Ahab, introducing great evil into the nation and, here, into the church at Thyatira.

+ The "elect lady" to whom the apostle John addressed his second epistle led a house church in her home, but she was evidently accountable to apostolic authority. (See 2 John 1:1–13.)

+ According to a word of wisdom from his father-in-law, Jethro, Moses selected men to be leaders and rulers of tens, hundreds, and thousands in the nation of Israel, the *"church in the wilderness"* (Acts 7:38; see also Exodus 15).

+ The virtuous woman of Proverbs 31 exhibited skills in business and leadership. Her husband spoke well of her, praising her gifts and abilities, and her children blessed her. (See Proverbs 31:10–31.)

+ The book of Proverbs gives many warnings against contentious or evil women, and praises those women who are wise and godly. (See, for example, Proverbs 9:13; 21:9, 19; 23:27; 25:24; 27:15; 30:21–23.) A woman, if married, is responsible to a man (her husband); a man, if married, is responsible for a woman (his wife). Single women are under the covering and protection of their father as long as they are in the home. This is for their safety.

In drawing this chapter to a close, it should be said that men and women may exercise authority in the church if they are under authority. If a married woman is gifted in ministry, then she is under the covering and protection of her husband at home; she acts under the authority of other elders on the leadership team at church. A woman gifted in such a way has a dual role, with responsibilities in the home and at church. The same is true of a man who is gifted in ministry. If he is married, he is responsible of keeping his home in order; in the church, he exercises authority as he acts under the authority of the leadership team, or an eldership.

Men or women who function in the church in any gift or leadership capacity should…

+ Have their home in divine order. (For how can anyone minister in the house of the Lord if his or her own house is out of order?)

+ Be scripturally qualified, according to the qualities listed in 1 Timothy 3.

+ Be scripturally gifted and anointed of the Lord.

+ Be under a covering and authority. For the married woman, this is her husband at home and the eldership or leadership team at church.

+ Be under authority as they exercise authority, and not usurp authority in either the home or the church.

+ Recognize and accept God's order, which is as follows:

    › Order in creation was the man, then the woman.

    › Order in the fall was the woman, then the man.

    › Order in divine judgment was the woman, then the man, then the earth.

    › Order in redemption is to restore the man and the woman back to God's original purpose.

    › Order in the Christian home is the man, as covering and protector; then the wife; and then the children.

    › Order in the church is male and female working together, according to the measure of grace and gifting God gives them.

    It is in this manner that male and female fulfill their roles together, under divine order, even as the church (the woman) is subject to Christ (the Man) and fulfills her role and ministry accordingly.

+ Men and women are to beware of humanistic and feministic philosophies that threaten to creep into church life and give way to male chauvinism or female feminism and resulting in a violation of God's established order.

+ Men and women are to be examples of godliness, in word, deed, and character, to all believers, as well as to a lost and dying world.

In creation, man and woman were to have joint dominion, to rule and reign together. In redemption, the Lord desires to restore believing men and women to that role as He calls, equips, and anoints certain ones for His service, according to His will. It is teamwork and team leadership, men and women working and leading in harmony together.

Men and women may occupy governmental roles and exercise authority in the church as long they are under authority. If God calls men or women to be apostles, prophets, evangelists, shepherds, teachers, elders, or deacons, then these individuals may exercise governmental authority as they are under Christ's governmental authority. Church government is subject to Christ's headship, exercised through men or women whom He appoints and anoints.

Redemption was intended to restore order in the home among husband, wife, and children, and to restore order in the church among men and women, brothers and sisters. There is equality as persons, yet there is God's order, as before the entrance of sin into the world. Christ, as *the* Man and Husband, is first, and then there is the church, His bride and wife. As it is in the spiritual, so it is in the natural. It is simply a matter of divine order.

+ God is the Head of Christ.

+ Christ is the Head of the man.

+ The man is the head of the woman.

+ The father and mother together share headship over and responsibility for the family, the children.

+ Christ is the Head of all ministers and leaders in the church, His body.

+ The church leaders are subject to Christ's headship, to their senior team leader, and to other leaders or elders.

+ The church congregation is submitted to the leaders under Christ.

This is the chain of command—the divine order of governmental authority as ordained by God. It is an order of loving care, covering, protection, provision, and responsibility. It is recognition without competition. Men and women, therefore, are redemptively equal but functionally different, according to the measure of God's gifting and grace, and they may minister and exercise authority as they act under authority.

26

FROM CREATION TO REDEMPTION

Our text has gone full circle, from creation to redemption. In creation, God fashioned the man and the woman—Adam and Eve—co-equal as persons but different in function. They were joint-rulers together over creation. They had dominion together. There was no male superiority or female inferiority, but man and woman were of equal value before the Lord, their Creator. Together, they would rule and reign as king and queen over all creation. They would complement each other, in time, as parents—Adam as father, and Eve as mother—again, creatively equal yet functionally different. They were partners together, workers together, fellow companions as husband and wife. Both were made in the image of God, reflecting His glory.

Creation showed that the man and the woman were of equal value before the Lord. Functionally speaking, man and woman differed in their roles as husband and wife, father and mother. In terms of order, the man and the woman understood God's intended order in the home, the family. The original man and woman understood their value, function, and order.

But sin undid this understanding. Sin marred the image and likeness of God in the man and the woman. Sin broke the relationship between God and mankind. Sin interrupted God's original purpose and intention. Sin caused mankind to feel devoid of value and to lose sight of their proper role and function. It disrupted God's order. The curse affected everything in creation, including the man and the woman. Eve, and all women after her, incurred suffering in childbirth. Male rule, which was not God's original will or command, came into effect. And men were affected by the curse on the earth in the labor, sweat, thorns, and thistles that their work would cost them.

The history of mankind has evidenced a struggle in the three areas of value, function, and order, as the following chart shows.[73]

VALUE, FUNCTION, AND ORDER		
Historical Society	**Biblical Balance**	**Militant Feminism**
Male Chauvinism	Divine Creation	Female Feminism
"Oppression"	Redemption	"Liberation"
Upholds *order* Reduces *value*	Holds that men and women are of equal *value*	Upholds *value* Destroys *order*
Patriarchal rule	Sovereign rule	Matriarchal rule
Domination by abusive male headship under the guise of submission. Male rule has become oppression. Men have taken advantage of the design and repress the *function* of women. (Talmudic Teachings)	Holds that all believers receive different grace-gifts so that they may *function* in the body of Christ accordingly in God's unique design. Appreciate the design and be released to *function*.	Teaches that women are more valuable than men and that women need liberation in order to function. Design of God ignored

73. Adapted from a paper by Ken and Glenda Malmin, City Bible Church, Portland, Oregon (1980). Used by permission.

VALUE, FUNCTION, AND ORDER		
Historical Society	**Biblical Balance**	**Militant Feminism**
Male Chauvinism	Divine Creation	Female Feminism
"Oppression"	Redemption	"Liberation"
This is the fruit of sin Extreme... Discord Disorder Division Chaos	This is fruit of redemption *Order* exists for the sake of effective harmony in the body of Christ Result: Divine balance Unity Harmony Blessing	This is the fruit of sin Extreme... Discord Disorder Division Chaos

Redemption is God's plan to restore men and women to their intended value, function, and order in and through the body of Christ.

It was in the midst of pronounced judgments in Eden that God promised a Redeemer who would be born of the woman, in spite of her initiative in bringing about the fall. Sin—the curse and death—would be dealt with on the cross of Calvary by the Redeemer. All the evil effects of disobedience would be judged, and redemption would be made possible for all mankind.

The Redeemer has come. Redemption made possible the restoration of man and woman to the image of God. All that was lost in the fall, and more, would be restored to mankind. In Christ, men and women find their value, discover their function, and come into divine order in the home life and the church.

It is, therefore, in the light of the whole-of-the-Bible-context that God intends men and women to be co-workers together, fellow-workers in the gospel of Christ. It is possible in the redemptive community, which is the church. The new covenant restores mankind back to a higher level than ever seen in the Edenic covenant.

Believers, whether male or female, have been taken from being "in Adam" to being "in Christ." Men and women "in Christ" are redemptively equal, though all may be functionally different, according to their place as members in the body of Christ. There is a togetherness "in Christ" that was forfeited in Adam. (See 1 Corinthians 15:22; Galatians 3:28.) Gender distinctions are no longer barriers to value, function and ministry.

Our conclusion is, then, that *if* it pleases the Lord to call, equip, and anoint either men or women for any function or area of church ministry, leadership, or oversight, then believers will rejoice together and accept the blessings of the Lord flowing through them. According to the measure of grace and gift given by the Lord, so will be their role and function in the body of Christ. This will be in divine order, from which man fell in Eden. Christians should not see one another from creation's point of view "in Adam" but from redemption's point of view "in Christ."

APPENDIX ONE: SCHOOL POSITIONS ON WOMEN IN MINISTRY

	Conscience Position	Pro	Con
1	Male domination Women not to be involved in any public ministry or areas of leadership	None	Male rule, women subjugated to male domination Women inferior, weak. suppressed, oppressed, and devalued
2	Women permitted in limited areas of ministry	Some measure of hope and expression for women	Limiting women's function limits the whole church Woman still inferior to man
3	Women accepted in ascension gift ministries if called and anointing evident in their life Not eldership	Much more freedom for gifted women if sealed by the Lord's anointing	Women still not equal in function as men are, even though their calling is evident

	Conscience Position	Pro	Con
4	Women accepted in ascension gifts, leadership and eldership role governmental role	Release of gifted women as the Lord calls, equips and anoints Measure of grace-gifts	Strong women might intimidate weak men from functioning in the body of Christ Potential problems in church life
5	Women take major roles of ministry gifts, eldership, and leadership, and suppress men Female domination	None	Women become mannish Men become weak The church of God lacks godly men and women as role models of godly men and women in the father/mother image of male/female for balance Dysfunctional churches Dysfunctional homes

APPENDIX TWO: COMPARISON OF THE LORD JESUS, JEWISH RABBIS, AND THE APOSTLE PAUL[74]

THE LORD JESUS	JEWISH RABBIS	THE APOSTLE PAUL
Associated with and taught women in all purity.	Believed that associating with women led to lust.	Did not segregate men and women in house churches. Held that men and women could minister according to their gifting.
Woman could divorce husband if it was justified.	Only a man could divorce his wife.	Permitted the same as Jesus.
Jesus touched "unclean women."	Rabbis were not to touch women.	The Bible does not mention any specific instances of Paul touching women, but many of his fellow-workers were women.

74. Adapted and arranged from Glen Miller, "Christian Think-Tank" (January 25, 1997).

THE LORD JESUS	JEWISH RABBIS	THE APOSTLE PAUL
Jesus spoke with women, healed women, allowed women to touch Him, and was served by women.	Rabbis not do so unless in a family situation.	Paul had many female helpers, fellow laborers in the gospel.
Jesus mentioned women in His parables.	Rabbis avoided mentioning women in their parables.	Paul spoke allegorically of himself as a "mother" and a "father."
Jesus spoke to women in public.	Jewish men shirked it.	Paul addressed women publicly and privately, in his epistles.
Jesus spoke to the woman of Samaria, a Gentile.	Rabbis did not speak to Gentiles.	Paul traveled in Gentile cities.
Jesus used women as witnesses of the major truths of His death, burial, and resurrection.	Rabbis generally discredited the testimony of women.	Paul had Phoebe, as deaconess, carry his letter to Rome. Women were among his co-workers, and he recognized them as legitimate leaders of various house churches.
Jesus allowed women to travel with Him and His disciples.	Rabbis did not permit women to travel with them.	Paul traveled with Priscilla and her husband, Aquila.

THE LORD JESUS	JEWISH RABBIS	THE APOSTLE PAUL
Jesus taught women freely.	The Talmudic Law forbade rabbis to teach women the Word of God.	Paul taught women freely.
Jesus never used women as negative examples.	Rabbis made many negative statements about women, especially in the Talmud.	Paul never used women as negative examples but entreated them to live in peace, as fellow-workers.
Jesus accepted and valued women. He Himself was born of a woman—the Virgin Mary.	Rabbi Judah prayed: "Blessed be thou for not having made me a Gentile, a woman, or an ignoramus."	Taught that "in Christ" there is neither male nor female, for men and women are one new creation.

APPENDIX THREE: DIVINE ORDER IN CREATION AND REDEMPTION

Order in Creation	Order in the Fall of Man	Order in Divine Judgment	Order in Redemption	Order in the Christian Home	Order in the Church
Genesis 1:26–28; 2:7, 8, 15–25; 5:1–2; 1 Corinthians 11:3–15; 1 Timothy 2:13	Genesis 3:1–13; 1 Timothy 2:14; 2 Corinthians 11: 1–3	Genesis 2:17; 3:14–24; Romans 5:12–21	Genesis 3:15; 1 Timothy 2:15 (AMP)	Ephesians 5:23–33; 1 Corinthians 7; 11:3–16; 1 Timothy 2:13–15	Ephesians 5:23–33
l. The man 2. The woman—Psalm 128:3; Proverbs 12:4; 14:1; 19:14; 31:10–31 • Co-equality • Plurality • Unity • Priority • Order • Function • Submission • Harmony • Perfect love • Co-Rulership	l. The serpent 2. The woman 3. The man	l. Judgment on the serpent—Genesis 3:14–15 2. Judgment on the woman—Genesis 3:16; 1 Timothy 2:12–14; Ephesians 5:22 3. Judgment on the man—Genesis 3:17 4. Judgment on the earth—Genesis 3:17–18	1. Virgin to bear a Son (prophecy and its fulfillment)—Isaiah 7:14; 9:6–9; Matthew 1:18–21; Luke 3:30–33; Galatians 4:4; 1 Timothy 2:15 (AMP) The *man* born of the virgin *woman* to redeem men and women back to God and to restore divine order. "In Christ" there is neither male nor female—Galatians 3:28; Colossians 3:11 Members of the body of Christ Redemptively equal as persons. but functionally different according to grace and gifts in Christ (Col.3:18-21)	Proverbs 18:22; 19:14 31:10–31 1. Bridegroom Husband/head The man Bride/body The woman The family order of the children in Home	l. Christ The Bridegroom Husband Head of the church The Man 2. Church The Bride/ Body The Woman
Kevin Conner					

416

APPENDIX FOUR: IN CHRIST THERE IS NEITHER MALE NOR FEMALE

(Gender Distinctions Not a Barrier to Participation in Church Life)

Ministry/Gifts/Service	Male	Female	Scripture
In the Body	What Men May Do	What Women May Do	References
Apostle	Yes	Junia *"of note"*	Romans 16:7
Prophet	Yes	Prophetesses Miriam, Deborah, Huldah, and Anna	Exodus 15:20; Judges 5; 2 Kings 22; Micah 6:4; Isaiah 8:1–3; Luke 2:36–38
Evangelist	Yes	Yes	Psalm 68:11; Isaiah 40:9–10; John 4; Acts 8
Pastor/ Shepherd	Yes	Shepherdess Zipporah, Rachel, etc.	The "elect lady" of 2 John; Song of Solomon
Teacher	Yes	Priscilla/Aquila	Acts 18:26; Romans 16:7 Older women— Titus 2

Ministry/Gifts/ Service	Male	Female	Scripture
Elder	Yes STRONG 4245 "Presbuteros" Elderly, a senior presbyter; elder, eldest, old	STRONG 4247 "Presbutera," feminine of SC4246: an old woman: aged woman	1 Timothy 5:1–2, 21; 1 Peter 5:1 Tertullian speaks of "widows," "deaconesses," "presbyters," and "virgins" among female believers
Deacon/ Deaconess	Yes	Yes, Phoebe	Romans 16:1–2; minister proba-bly—1 Timothy 3:11
Word of Wisdom	Yes	Yes, Abigail to David	1 Samuel 25:14–44; 2 Samuel 20:16–22
Word of Knowledge	Yes	Yes	
Discerning	Yes	Yes	
Faith	Yes	Yes	Hebrews 11:35; 2 Kings 4 Women received their dead raised to life
Healing	Yes	Yes	
Miracles	Yes	Yes	
Tongues	Yes	Yes	

Ministry/Gifts/Service	Male	Female	Scripture
Interpretation of Tongues	Yes	Yes	
Prophecy	Yes	Yes, Philip's four daughters	Acts 21:9; 1 Corinthians 11:5; Joel 2:8–32
Serving	Yes	Yes	John 11 Serve Jesus— Luke 8:1–2
Encouraging	Yes	Yes	
Giving	Yes	Yes, a woman ministered of her substance to Jesus.	The Gospels Luke 8:2
Leadership	Yes, Moses and Aaron	Yes, Miriam and Deborah	Micah 6:4; Acts 17:4, 2, 34
Showing Mercy	Yes	Yes	Dorcas—Acts 9:36
Celibacy	Yes, if it's God's will	Yes, if it's God's will	
Hospitality	Yes	Yes	1 Timothy 5:1–16; James 1:27
Missionary	Yes	Yes	Church history
Administration	Yes	Yes, the virtuous woman	Proverbs 31
Prayer	Yes	Yes	1 Corinthians 11:5; 1 Timothy 2:12 Acts 16:13

Ministry/Gifts/ Service	Male	Female	Scripture
Intercession	Yes	Yes, Hannah	1 Samuel 1–2
Judge/Leader	Yes	Yes, Deborah	Judges 4–5
In the Lord	Fathers in the Lord	Mothers in the Lord	Deborah— Judges 4–5
Preacher	Yes	Yes	Exodus 15:20; Numbers 12:1–10; Psalm 68:11, 25
Born Again/ Saved	Yes	Yes	John 3:5; Mark 16:15–20
Water Baptized	Yes	Yes	Mark 16:15–20; Matthew 28:18–20
Filled with the Spirit	Yes	Yes	Acts 1–2; Joel 2:28–32
Spiritual Gifts	Yes	Yes	Book of Acts
Witness for Christ	Yes	Yes, the Samaritan woman John 4	John 20:17–18; Luke 24:9–11, 24; Matthew 28:9–10
Worship/Praise	Yes	Yes, singing men and singing women	Nehemiah 7:67; Ezekiel 40:44; 1 Chronicles 25:5–6; Exodus 15; Luke 1–2; Song of Solomon
Industrious/ Business	Yes	Yes, the virtuous woman	Proverbs 31; Acts 9:36–43 Dorcas

Ministry/Gifts/ Service	Male	Female	Scripture
Helpers	Yes	Yes, Euodius and Syntyche (Philippians 4:2–3)	Romans 16—about ten women named by Paul
Fellow-workers Co-Labourers	Yes	Yes	As above
Minister Communion	Yes	Yes	Catacombs, history
Priest of the Lord	Yes	Yes, all new covenant believers are members of a royal priesthood	Revelation 1:6; 5:9–10; 1 Peter 2:1–10
Government Role	Yes	Huldah, Esther	Presbyters
House Church Leader	Yes	Yes	New Testament
Exhorter	Yes	Yes	1 Corinthians 12:1–8; 11:5; 14:5 Prophecy for exhortation, edification, and comfort
Counseling	Yes	Yes	Titus 2:4–5
Musicians	Yes	Yes	Tabernacle of David Restoration from Babylon I Chr.15–16; 25:5–6

Ministry/Gifts/ Service	Male	Female	Scripture
		Yes	Titus 2:4–5; 1 Timothy 5:2
		Yes	2 John
		Older women to teach the younger	Titus 2:4–5
		The elect lady and her children are to reject antichristal deceivers	
CHRIST IS ALL Ministries/Gifts Offices/Services THE HEAD OF CHRIST IS GOD Christ is under the authority of His Father God	GIFTS TO MEN As the Father wills THE HEAD OF THE MAN IS CHRIST Man is (should be) under the authority of Christ	GIFTS TO Women As the Father wills THE HEAD OF THE WOMAN IS THE MAN Men and women are (should be) under the authority of God and Christ	NEW TESTAMENT CHURCH, THE BODY OF CHRIST 1 Corinthians 11:1–16; 1 Timothy 2:11–12 Order in the Church Order in the Home Christ is Head of the Church, which is His wife, His bride, His body
	Kevin J. Conner		

BIBLIOGRAPHY

Anderson, John A. *Women's Warfare & Ministry*. Stonehaven, UK: David Waldie, 1933.

Barnes, Albert. *Notes, Explanatory and Practical, on the Acts of the Apostles*. London: Thomas Ward and Co., 1840.

Beall, James L. *The Female of the Species*. Detroit, MI: Bethesda Missionary Temple, 1977.

Booth, Catherine. *Female Ministry; or, Woman's Right to Preach the Gospel*. London: Morgan & Chase, 1870.

Bushnell, Katharine C. *God's Word to Women*. North Collins, NY: K. C. Bushnell, 1921.

Cairns, Earle E. *Christianity Through the Centuries: A History of the Christian Church* (Third Edition, Revised and Expanded). Grand Rapids, MI: Zondervan, 1996.

Chrysostom, John. *The Homilies of S. John Chrysostom, Archbishop of Constantinople, on the Epistle of St. Paul the Apostle to the Romans*. Oxford, England: John Henry Parker, 1841.

Clarke, Adam. *Dr. Adam Clarke's Commentary on the New Testament, Vol. II*. London: J. Butterworth & Son, 1817.

——. *The Holy Bible Containing the Old and New Testaments, Vol. 6.* New York, NY: A. Paul, 1832.

Conner, Kevin J. *The Church in the New Testament.* Victoria, Australia: Acacia Press, 1982.

——. *Headship, Covering (Hats) & Hair.* Victoria, Australia: Acacia Press, 1995.

Conner, Kevin, and Ken Malmin. *Interpreting the Scriptures.* Portland, OR: City Bible Publishing, 1983.

Edersheim, Rev. Dr. *Sketches of Jewish Social Life in the Days of Christ.* London: The Religious Tract Society, 1876.

Ellicott, Charles J. *Ellicott's Commentary on the Whole Bible, Volume VIII: Ephesians – Revelation.* Eugene, OR: Wipf and Stock Publishers, 2015.

Fee, Gordon D. *Listening to the Spirit in the Text.* Grand Rapids, MI: Wm. B. Eerdmans Publishing Company, 2000.

Gentile, Ernest. *What Does the Bible Teach about the Role of Women in Church Leadership?* San Jose, CA.

Giles, Kevin. *Created Woman.* Canberra, Australia: Acorn Press, 1985.

———. "A Critique of the 'Novel' Contemporary Interpretation of 1 Timothy 2:9-15 Given in the Book, *Women in the Church*. Part I." *The Evangelical Quarterly.*

Gonzalez, Justo L. *The Story of Christianity, Volume 1* (Revised and Updated). New York, NY: HarperCollins, 2010.

Greig, Gary S. *Biblical Foundations for Women Alongside Men in Ministry Advancing God's Kingdom.* Printed in the course syllabus for the Wagner Leadership Institute. Kingdom Training Network/The University Prayer Network, April 1999. Online. http://www.cwgministries.org/sites/default/files/files/books/WomenInMinistry.pdf.

Halley, Henry H. *Halley's Bible Handbook with the New International Version.* Grand Rapids, MI: Zondervan, 2000.

Hayford, Jack. "On the Question of a Woman's Place in Church Leadership." http://solidrockmb.com/wp-content/uploads/2015/02/The-Role-of-Women-in-the-Church.pdf.

Henry, Matthew. *An Exposition of the Old and New Testament, Vol. 3.* London: Joseph Ogle Robinson, 1828.

Howell, R. B. C. *The Deaconship.* Philadelphia, PA: American Baptist Publication Society, 1851.

Hubbard, Lanny. "The Ordination of Women." Elders Retreat. Portland, OR: City Bible Church, 2000.

Jacobs, Cindy. *Women of Destiny: Releasing You to Fulfill God's Call in Your Life and in the Church.* Ventura, CA: Regal Books, 1998.

Jones, David. "A Female Apostle?: A Lexical-Syntactical Analysis of Romans 16:7." June 26, 2007. The Council on Biblical Manhood & Womanhood. Online. http://cbmw.org/uncategorized/a-female-apostle/.

Kent, Homer A. *The Pastoral Epistles.* Chicago, IL: Moody Press, 1982.

Koch, George Byron. "Shall a Woman Keep Silent? Part 2." Tape #112 (June 2, 1996). Church of the Resurrection, Chicago, Illinois.

Kroeger, Richard Clark, and Catherine Clark Kroeger. *I Suffer Not a Woman: Rethinking 1 Timothy 2:11–15 in Light of Ancient Evidence.* Grand Rapids, MI: Baker Academic (a division of Baker Publishing Group), 1992.

Lampe, G. W. H. *A Patristic Greek Lexicon.* Oxford: Clarendon Press, 1961.

Lamsa, George M. *New Testament Commentary: Acts to Revelation.* Nashville, TN: Holman Bible Publishers, 2007.

Malmin, Glenda. *Woman, You Are Called and Anointed.* Portland, OR: City Christian Publishing, 2000.

Oulton, John E. L., trans. *Eusebius: The Ecclesiastical History.* 1927.

Penn-Lewis, Jessie. *The Magna Charta of Woman.* 1919 Online. https://web.archive.org/web/20071112131009/http://www.godswordtowomen.org/studies/resourres/onlinebooks/magna.htm.

Pierce, Ronald, and Rebecca Merrill Groothuis, gen. eds. *Discovering Biblical Equality.* Downers Grove, IL: InterVarsity Press, 2005.

Plummer, Alfred. *The Pastoral Epistles*. London: Hodder and Stoughton, 1891.

Ramsay, William Mitchell. *The Church in the Roman Empire Before* AD *170*. New York, NY: G. P. Putnam's Sons, 1893.

Rousu, Don. "The Truth about Women in Public Ministry." *Revival Magazine* (December 1, 1997). http://revivalmag.com/article/truth-about-women-public-ministry.

Schaff, Philip, and Henry Wace, eds. *A Select Library of Nicene and Post-Nicene Fathers of the Christian Church*, Vol. XIV. New York, NY: Charles Scribner's Sons, 1900.

Scroggie, W. Graham. *A Guide to the Gospels*. Grand Rapids, MI: Kregel Publications, 1995.

Stibbs, A. M.; E. F. Kevan; and F. Davidson, *The New Bible Commentary*. Grand Rapids, MI: Wm. B. Eerdmans Publishing Company, 1953.

Strauch, Alexander. *Biblical Eldership*. Colorado Springs, CO: Lewis & Roth Publishers, 1986.

Sunshine, Glenn S. *Why You Think the Way You Do: The Story of Western Worldviews from Rome to Home*. Grand Rapids, MI: Zondervan, 2009.

Thayer's Greek Lexicon, Electronic Database. Copyright © 2002, 2003, 2006, 2011 by Biblesoft, Inc.

Vincent, Marvin R. *Word Studies in the New Testament*, Vol. III. New York, NY: Charles Scribner's Sons, 1903.

Vine, W. E. *W. E. Vine's New Testament Word Pictures: Romans to Revelation*. Nashville, TN: Thomas Nelson, 2015.

Vine, W. E., and Merrill F. Unger. *Vine's Complete Expository Dictionary of Old and New Testament Words*. Nashville, TN: Thomas Nelson, 1996.

Williams, Don. *The Apostle Paul and Women in the Church*. Ventura, CA: Regal Books, 1978.

Wuest, Kenneth Samuel. *Word Studies from the Greek New Testament*, Vol. 2. Grand Rapids, MI: Eerdmans, 1979.

———. *Wuest's Word Studies from the Greek New Testament for the English Reader*. Grand Rapids, MI: Wm. B. Eerdmans Publishing Company, 1973.

WORKS CONSULTED

Beall, James Lee. *The Ministry of Women*. Detroit, MI: Bethesda Missionary Temple, 1977.

Beck, James, and Craig Blomberg. *Two Views on Women in Ministry*. Grand Rapids, MI: Zondervan, 2001.

Benjamin, Dick. *Women's Ministries in the New Testament Church*. Anchorage, AL: Abbott Loop Publications, 1983.

Bilezikian, Gilbert. *Beyond Sex Roles*. Grand Rapids, MI: Baker Book House, 1985.

Clark, Stephen B. *Man & Woman in Christ*. Ann Arbor, MI: Servant Book, 1980.

Finkelde, John. *Created for Partnership*. Perth, Australia: Finkelde Ministries, 1996.

Hayworth, Wayne. *Mates, Marriage & Ministry*. Portland, OR: Center Press, 1985.

Lockyer, Herbert. *All the Women of the Bible*. Grand Rapids, MI: Zondervan, 1967.

Maloney, Francis J. *Women First Among the Faithful*. Notre Dame, IN: Ave Maria Press, 1984.

Martin, Joan. *The Ladies Aren't for Silence*. London: Paternoster Press, 1991.

Payne, Sandra. *A Call to Women*. McClaren Way, South Australia: Living Way Publications, 1982.

Pawson, J. David. *Leadership Is Male*. Nashville, TN: Thomas Nelson, 1990.

Porter, Muriel. *Beyond the Twelve—Women Disciples in the Gospel*. Wisdom Press, 1989.

Tucker, Ruth, and Walter Liefield. *Daughters of the Church*. Grand Rapids, MI: Zondervan, 1987.

Truscott, Graham. *Women's Ministry*. Calgary, Alberta, BC: Gordon Donaldson Missionary Foundation, 1979.

Concordances/Commentaries/Dictionaries:

A Greek-English Lexicon of the New Testament

Collins English Dictionary of Words

Harper, The Analytical Greek Lexicon

New Englishman's Greek Concordance

Strong's Exhaustive Concordance

Vaughan, Curtis, ed. *The New Testament from 26 Translations*.

Webster, Noah, *Webster's American Dictionary of the English Language* (1828).

Papers:

Asplund, Larry. "Should City Bible Ordain Women Elders?." Portland, OR: 2000.

Conner, Mark A. "Women in Leadership." Victoria, Australia: Waverley Christian Fellowship, 2000.

Kinnaman, Gary. "Women in Ministry & Leadership." Phoenix, AZ, 1995.

ABOUT THE AUTHOR

Born in Melbourne, Australia, and saved at the age of fourteen, Kevin Conner served the Lord in the Salvation Army until the age of twenty-one before entering the pastoral ministry. Since then he has been involved in teaching ministry in Australia, New Zealand, and at City Bible Church in Portland, Oregon. After serving as senior minister of CityLife Church in Melbourne, he turned his responsibilities over to his son, Mark Conner, in 1995. Since that time, along with his wife, Rene, he has served the church locally as well as ministering at various conferences and writing many books, such as *The Tabernacle of Moses*, *The Foundations of Christian Doctrine*, and *The Church in the New Testament*.